THE
BIG THINK
BOOK

About the Author

PETER CAVE lectures in philosophy for The Open University and New York University (London). He is the author of eight books on philosophy, making it accessible to a wide audience, including the bestselling *Can a Robot be Human?: 33 Perplexing Philosophy Puzzles*.

Peter Cave

THE
BIG THINK
BOOK

Discover Philosophy Through 99 Perplexing Problems

ONEWORLD

A Oneworld book

Published in North America, Great Britain and
Australia by Oneworld Publications, 2015

ISBN 978-1-78074-742-2
eISBN 978-1-78074-743-9

Typeset by Tetragon, London
Printed and bound in Great Britain by Clay Ltd, St Ives plc

Oneworld Publications
10 Bloomsbury Street
London WC1B 3SR
England

Dedicated to:

all those who — forever — lack dedications

CONTENTS

PROLOGUE

Let's Do It

Many people would rather die than
think; and that is what they do.
Bertrand Russell

All of us think about things. That does not yet make us philosophers; but it nearly does.

If you puzzle about why, or whether, there are some things you ought or ought not to do – some things that are good; some things bad – then you are something of a philosopher. If you wonder how things really are – whether the mind is nothing but the brain; whether the world is divinely caused – you are philosophizing. And if you ask questions such as 'What does it all mean?' – well, there is yet more evidence of your living within the philosophers' realm.

Reflecting on the puzzles, paradoxes and perplexities in this book, from ethics to God to space and time, from politics to consciousness to logic, love and fiction, is to do philosophy. Well, it is to do philosophy, once trying to think systematically and clearly about quite what the problems are, the assumptions made and where they lead. The philosophy here is presented by way of a kaleidoscope of styles, varying from dialogues to monologues, from everyday experiences to bizarre thought experiments, from a discussion with God to arguments between Grasshopper and Ant – and from the light-hearted to the deeply serious. All, I hope, are polished with a lightness of touch.

The chapters are deliberately short, though designed to give rise to plenty of thought, further questions and debates, be they debates with yourself or with others, whether at work, at play, at romance or even when failing asleep.

The word 'philosophy', deriving from the Greek 'love of wisdom', suggests something grander and more insightful about life and the universe than that of other subjects. True, the purveyance of wisdom can seem far removed from the practices of today's philosophers; philosophers are usually lecturers, maintaining employment by forever publishing research, even trying to show economic impact. It was different in earlier times. Spinoza ground lenses; Leibniz was a librarian; John Stuart Mill worked for the East India Company, moonlighting as a journalist, and later became a Member of Parliament. Today there is a tendency for philosophy to be technical: take a look at some current volumes of academic philosophy. Technical studies have their place, but we should not be misled into thinking that, at heart, philosophy is open only to philosophical technocrats and professionals. Major philosophical thinking – from Plato to Hume to Wittgenstein – is open to us all. I hope that this collection shows that to be so.

'All things conspire'

These puzzles, tales and dialogues embrace the whole range of philosophical wonder, from formal paradoxes in logical reasoning to moral dilemmas. Although they are grouped into themes, to quote Hippocrates, 'all things conspire' – so, the sections overlap as do some puzzles, being different approaches to fundamental perplexities, such as the nature of the self and how we represent the world around us. A few puzzles might have more obviously appeared elsewhere. Newcomb's Paradox (Chapter 66), for example, more naturally would fit in Part V on Knowledge, but has an interesting link with religious belief. Let us celebrate the intermingling and weaving – and also the dipping into chapters that catch the eye and interest, rather than ploughing through sequentially. Note, too, the endnotes for further musings.

Simply by virtue of belonging to a community of speakers, we possess materials for philosophizing. There need be no special demands for mathematical ability, erudite historical knowledge or scientific investigations – just our everyday experiences. Philosophers rarely become directly involved in physical experiments, treks through muddy swamps or the hard work of archaeological digs. We prefer the armchair, pen and paper (well, keyboard), and even the occasional glass of wine – or two. Philosophers do, though, reflect on others' worldly investigations, be they physical, psychological or religious. Philosophizing itself displays the interconnection of things.

What's wrong with contradictions?

With the paradoxes, puzzles and perplexities, we often start with some comments, beliefs or principles, which appear obviously true. These can be seen as premises. We do some reasoning, expecting to reach acceptable conclusions. Perplexity arises when the reached conclusions hit us as manifestly false, unacceptable or, in some way, undesirable. They contradict or are in tension with our starting beliefs. Something must have gone wrong with the reasoning, or maybe our starting points are mistaken – or could the tensions be intrinsic features of the world? Philosophers try to locate any mistakes, seek to explain how the perplexities have arisen and aim to avoid contradictions.

Two contradictory thoughts cannot both be true. You come home and find two notes left by your partner. One says, 'Wait in for me,' and the other says, 'Don't wait in for me.' What do you do? They are contradictory instructions – so, you are baffled. Witness bafflement at this book's dedication. Hence, we need to avoid contradictions, to avoid being *contra* in speech or diction. That avoidance applies beyond instructions. Your friend tells you, 'It will rain today,' and then adds, 'It won't rain today.' You are bemused: what does she believe; what should you do umbrella-wise? Because we seek understanding, we may try to explain away contradictions: maybe the notes show a mind change; maybe the speaker of rain speaks of different locations.

Opening eyes, exercising the mind – and talking the sun down

Seneca of ancient Rome commented how things of daily occurrence, even when most worthy of amazement and admiration, pass us by unnoticed. We may be likened to sleepwalkers, successfully finding our way, yet unaware of what we are doing. Philosophy opens eyes.

Philosophy has value in itself, intrinsic value, but it is also a means of exercising the mind – exercising the mind about matters that matter. When difficulties in finding correct answers come to the fore, it may even generate some welcome humility. Further, philosophy is a means of sharing, of togetherness. Socrates of ancient Greece, often seen as the inspirer of Western philosophy, stressed the importance of dialogue. Discussing with others what counts as fair salaries, whether speech that offends should be permitted, how free we are really, may help to bring forth a common humanity, a genuine sense in which we are 'all in it together', trying to understand the universe and our place within. That contrasts with the mythical economic mantra of 'we're all in it together' which has been much loved in recent years by those in power in Britain.

Philosophical puzzles continue to perplex: that shows how they differ from puzzles that can be solved through scientific research or logical and mathematical reasoning.

Here is science. In 1616, a certain John Bullokar offered as paradox the affirmation that 'the earth doth mooue round, and the heauens stand still'. Today most people accept that the Earth both spins and orbits the Sun. The astronomical evidence is in.

Here is straight logic. Concerning only the three people mentioned, Osbert is in love just with Penelope, but Penelope is in love just with Quentin. Osbert is a philosopher. Quentin is not. Is a philosopher in love with a non-philosopher? Is the answer 'Yes', 'No' or 'Cannot tell'? Please see the endnotes for the answer, which, once explained, generates no controversy.

Here is probability. In the Monty Hall Show, there are three doors, A, B and C. One door has a desirable prize hidden behind, say, gold bars.

The other two doors each have a goat behind them. For this puzzle we assume that goats are neither desirable nor desired. You want the prize. Which door hides the prize has been decided randomly.

Consider a game. You choose a door: say A. Maybe a goat lurks behind that door; maybe the prize does. The show's presenter – she knows what is behind each door – opens one of the other doors, B or C, showing you one of the two goats. Let us say that she opens B. She then asks you if you want to change your choice from door A to B or C. Obviously, you do not want B (you see a goat there), but should you change to C? Is it rational to change your mind? Would you increase your chance of winning?

The solution, over which thoughtful philosophers and mathematicians are now agreed, appears in the endnotes.

Russell's tease and Nietzsche's greatest weight

In contrast to the puzzles just given – with scientific evidence or logical reasoning providing firm solutions – philosophical perplexities continue to haunt. Here are a couple, starting with a logical paradox.

Two of the most eminent philosophers of the early twentieth century are the Cambridge philosophers Bertrand Russell and G. E. Moore. Moore was perceived as a man of complete honesty and integrity. Russell was worldly wise, a lover of many women – and mischievous. One day, Russell naughtily asked Moore if he always spoke the truth. Moore, being suitably modest, replied, 'No.' Now, was Moore saying something true – or false?

Moore's answer amounted to: 'I do not always speak the truth.' Let us assume, though, that Moore was indeed being modest and everything else Moore ever said was true. Moore's answer amounts to: 'What I am saying now is not true.' That is baffling for, if what he is saying is not true, then, as that is what he is saying, it is after all true. Moreover, if what he is saying is true, then it is not true. That is an example of a famous paradox: the Liar. It can be traced back to antiquity; it and related paradoxes are examined in Chapter 25.

The tale illustrates how philosophers often have eyes for, and delight in, witty, humorous and quirky perspectives on everyday affairs. In fact, Wittgenstein – more on him below – proposed that some good philosophy could be written consisting entirely as a series of jokes. Jokes can both give rise to perplexity and yet, after some thought, be revealing. Mae West quipped, 'When I'm good, I'm very, very good; when I'm bad, I'm better.' That raises serious questions of morality and linguistic innuendo, yet initially generates merely a welcoming smile at the ambiguous perplexity.

Here is a different sort of perplexity, courtesy of Friedrich Nietzsche, the nineteenth-century thinker often deemed 'existentialist'. Nietzsche hypothesized the eternal recurrence – 'the greatest weight' – asking whether we could be so well disposed to our lives that we would welcome our lives being repeated eternally, exactly the same each time round. Of course, were the repetitions exactly the same, with the whole universe repeating itself in exactly the same way, then we should be unaware of the repetitions. We may even doubt the sense of there being repetitions of items exactly the same – a metaphysical puzzle. The eternal recurrence, this most dreadful and anguishing of thoughts, is probably intended, though, to concentrate our minds on how we ought to live, on what sort of life we value and on what we can bear in life – thoughts that can trouble all of us at times.

'He could teach me nothing'

Arguably the greatest twentieth-century philosopher is Ludwig Wittgenstein. Soon after he first arrived in Cambridge to see what Russell thought of him (yes, the same Russell as above), he was perceived as a genius, albeit tormented, strange and arrogant. Russell sent him to learn some logic from W. E. Johnson, the established and elderly logician. They survived only one session together. Afterwards, Wittgenstein reported to Russell, 'He could teach me nothing.' Johnson reported to friends, 'I could teach him nothing.'

Johnson and Wittgenstein, in one sense, were both saying the same thing about Johnson; yet they meant very different things. Johnson perceived the young Wittgenstein as conceited and unprepared to listen. Wittgenstein thought of Johnson as fuddy-duddy, out of date. Later they became friends, with Wittgenstein admiring Johnson's piano-playing – radically more so than ever he did Johnson's logic.

The story reminds us that we need to pay careful attention to meaning and to what is intended by what is said. That requires attention to context, motives and presuppositions. Suppose I comment that the Lord Chief Justice remained wide awake during the defence counsel's summing up today: my words alone do not logically imply that he usually nods off; but, given the context and presuppositions, his typically being half-asleep when in court may well be conveyed. It is the 'conversational implicature' of what I said.

Casimir Lewy, a philosopher who attended Moore's and Wittgenstein's lectures, was once asked his view of a colleague's recent book. 'It's printed on fine-quality paper' was his heavily Polish-accented response. Nothing more needed to be said.

Although most philosophers strongly reject the idea that philosophical perplexities end up being just linguistic matters, all would agree that linguistic care and clarity is much needed, if we are to gain a proper understanding of the world. Mind you, the demand for clarity is a challenge to certain 'postmodernists' who appear to value obscurity. I have in mind the excesses of Derrida, Irigaray and Kristeva; but perhaps the problem is mine, in my failing to comprehend.

Washing, evolution, even God

Søren Kierkegaard, a nineteenth-century Danish philosopher, now seen as a religious existentialist, saw a shop with the sign 'Bring your washing here'. Kierkegaard hurried back to his lodgings, collected his dirty washing and took it to the shop – only to discover that the shop was not a laundry, but a shop that sold shop-signs. The tale reminds us that we need to be careful in assessing what a sign is a sign of – in assessing how to interpret words and deeds. 'My actions have been open to misinterpretation' may be a truth – or an excuse.

Matters of interpretation come especially to the fore when we consider questions of how we ought to behave. Should letting someone die be seen as equivalent to killing? After all, the outcome is the same. Are human beings best understood as mere creatures of evolution or as 'created in the image of God'? If the former, what are the implications for morality? If the latter, what sort of divinity?

$$\gamma$$

I return to Wittgenstein. Wittgenstein had a feel for the enigmatic aphorism, as well as for some stunning thinking and profound metaphysical disquiet. He famously and controversially wrote:

> Philosophy is the battle against the bewitchment of our intelligence
> by means of language.

That should not identify him as 'just a linguistic philosopher'; he saw deep problems in grasping what we can and cannot say. He anguished and saw no easy or quick solutions or resolutions or dissolutions of the problems.

When two philosophers meet, wrote Wittgenstein, their greeting should be, 'Take your time.' The perplexities here are best dipped into – and out again – swirled with others for their thoughts, revisited when in the bath or on the train or even half-asleep. Throughout, though, I encourage resistance to quick answers. I encourage, 'Take your time.'

And so, whether or not birds, bees and educated fleas do it – presumably not – as philosophizing is the loving of wisdom, born in wonder and curiosity, let's do it; let's – right now – philosophize.

PART I: ETHICS

What ought we to do?

A man without ethics is a wild
beast loosed upon the world.
Albert Camus

We are often told what we ought – or, more usually, ought not – to do. We are in the realm of ethics, of morality, of duty. In this realm, perplexities are frequently those of dilemmas: witness forthcoming tales of the bear, a violinist who is plugged into you, and your opportunity for gainful employment as a hangman. The puzzles here also show how morality seeps into the law, political rights and even into the understanding of actions; after all, what makes an action *my* action and one that I intended? When, for that matter, did I come into existence and start performing actions?

Lurking behind this Part I's quandaries are questions of whether we ever do act morally, whether we ever ought to act morally, whether, in fact, there is any substance to morality at all. Should we be concerned about the plight of others – of the dispossessed, of our treatment of animals – or just about ourselves and a favoured few of our family and friends? Such questions also arise with later puzzles, when we try to handle God, religion and, working at a more earthly level, our relationship to the state, government and law.

Ethics – morality – is a distinctive human concern. No one should seriously think that pigs, peacocks and porcupines possess sense of what morally ought to be done as opposed to what they want to do. The human world embraces far more than does the non-human. Humans can handle mathematics, science and historical researches, in the pursuit of truth; the human world contains the arts, philosophical reflections and, yes, ethics.

Ethics is far wider than may be commonly assumed. It carries us beyond simple headline commandments against, for example, killing, enslaving and speaking falsely; in fact, they all merit thought and nuances. Ethics, as we shall see, gives rise to conflicts between, for example, maximizing welfare and respecting a person's right not to be used. Furthermore, ethical reflection draws our attention to how human flourishing has need of grace, refinements, compassion and empathy – and regard for our treatment of non-human creatures, such as the aforementioned pigs, peacocks and porcupines. In Ethics we try to get right about more things than the right.

Being human, we cannot easily close our eyes to others and how we affect them; being human, we ought not to close eyes, neither ours nor those of others.

1

ON THE RUN: ALL'S FAIR WITH BEARS?

Here are two explorers. Let them be Penelope Pessimist and Ophelia Optimist. They are exploring some mountainous regions, when they become suddenly aware of a bear in the distance, a bear big and hungry and intent upon feeding – feeding upon them. The bear heads in their direction, picking up speed, looking forward to a tasty explorer breakfast.

'We'd better run for it,' urges Ophelia Optimist.

'What's the point?' sighs Penelope Pessimist in despair at the bear. 'There's no way we can outrun a bear.'

'No need to do that,' smirks Ophelia Optimist. 'No need for *us* to outrun the bear – just for *me* to outrun *you*.' And with that, she's off.

〰

What are we morally allowed to do to save our lives? Assuming the bear needs to breakfast on only one, either could sacrifice herself. But does morality demand such self-sacrifice? And who should do the sacrificing? Before readers ask, let us assume that both women know that they cannot overpower the bear. Running is the only answer. In such circumstances, looking after oneself seems, at the very least, morally permissible.

Let us delete Ophelia's smirk. Both explorers recognize the tragedy of their plight. They recognize that it would be beyond the call of morality for Ophelia to have to sacrifice herself – or, indeed, for Penelope to do so. They both race away from the bear, not knowing who is faster or more skilled at twists and turns; they are letting fortune determine which one escapes – and which one dies.

The outcome, though, could be certain. They may know that Ophelia is the faster runner and will escape; so Penelope will provide the bear's

breakfast. If so, then Ophelia is letting the weaker, Penelope, go to the wall – more accurately, to the bear's digestion. Yet that is no good reason for Ophelia to sacrifice herself. After all, were she to make such a sacrifice, we could wonder why Penelope ought not to be sacrificing herself instead. And what value exists in their both yielding to the bear? They are not lovers who cannot live without each other.

Let us modify the tale: the only way one can be sure of escape is by tripping up the other. We probably think that doing that would be morally wrong. Maybe it would be unfair; it is unfair for one woman deliberately to interfere with the other. Yet how is it fair in the first place that one woman runs faster than the other?

Is it morally permissible for you to save your life, if an innocent individual's death results?

We swim in murky waters here. Let us focus. Consider only cases in which the life of solely one innocent person is lost through saving your own life. To avoid complexities of families, lifespan and so on, we assume that the individuals involved have similar responsibilities and potential for happiness and contributions to society.

Here are some different scenarios to test what we sense is permissible. Suppose that Ophelia and Penelope are in a queue, Ophelia at the front. A crazed individual is facing the queue, firing a revolver. Ophelia ducks to avoid being shot; as a result, the bullet kills Penelope. Ophelia, in defending herself, helps to bring about Penelope's death. Yet even if she *foresees* that Penelope will be shot – perhaps Ophelia lacks time to warn her – Ophelia does not *intend* Penelope's death. Her death is not the means whereby Ophelia saves herself. Had everyone in the queue ducked, maybe no one would have been killed. Penelope was an innocent and unlucky bystander.

Contrast the above with a different 'queue' example where Ophelia, to avoid being shot, pushes Penelope in front of her. Here, Ophelia is using Penelope as a shield – without informed consent. Surely, Ophelia is not morally permitted to do *that*. This suggests that an important, morally relevant feature is whether a person is being endangered through being used as a means of defence. Ophelia, if using Penelope as shield, shows no respect for her; she is using Penelope solely as means to an end. According to many, that is morally wrong – full stop. Respect for human beings involves treating them as rational agents, free to consent (or not) to how they are to be used. Respect for a person is central to the moral philosophy of Immanuel Kant, the highly influential, eighteenth-century Enlightenment philosopher. We see moral questions of respect arising when viewing another contrast:

A runaway tram hurtles towards you. You are trapped on the tracks, but you have a wireless points' control, so you are able to divert the tram onto a siding, thus saving yourself. Unfortunately, you know that there is a worker lying unconscious on the siding's tracks. By diverting, you save your life, yet bring about the worker's death. That may or may not be morally permissible, but it certainly is not as bad as what you do in the next scenario.

Once again, the runaway tram is hurtling towards you. The only means of saving your life is by firing a rubber bullet at a passer-by near the track. The passer-by, stunned, falls onto the track and is killed by the tram, bringing it to a halt. Thus, you are saved, saved by using the passer-by as a shield. The passer-by's death is the necessary *means* whereby you are saved, unlike the worker's death; you are certainly disrespecting the passer-by. A person surely has a right not to be used in that way. That 'right' amounts to its being a significant, fundamental moral wrong to deploy someone thus, without consent.

When we use someone as a shield, we are transferring our misfortune to someone else who is required to suffer. There are, then, two morally relevant factors.

One factor concerns the misfortune transferred and its significance for the recipient. If the only way to save my life is by causing an innocent person, 'as a shield', to have her nail varnish tarnished – well, that is morally acceptable; and if the shield protests, then she displays selfishness, lacking a sense of proportion. If I grab the fine silk scarf from a gentleman, the scarf needed to stem arterial blood flowing from my thigh, I have doubtless invaded his property; but saving a life at the cost of a silk scarf is a good deal, even if he complains about my violation of his property rights.

The second factor concerns the transference itself. In the shield examples it is deliberate and required. In the other examples, the life would be saved, even if no misfortunes were to occur to others. We may, though, question this distinction's relevance, if we know the misfortunes will in fact occur. You have a right to defend yourself from the tram by diverting it; but if you foresee that the worker's death will result, are you not behaving cruelly in passing that misfortune buck onto him? Of course, morally, things are different, if you know that he is conscious and could leap free to safety, with or without his nail varnish tarnished; but, in the case set out, you are surely not morally justified in passing the deadly tram onto him. The unconscious worker is, so to speak, an 'innocent threat' to you – a threat in that his presence, it seems, morally prevents you from doing what would otherwise be permissible to save your life, namely, diverting the tram.

♈

Returning to the bear, where does this leave the morality, or otherwise, of Ophelia taking to her heels, knowing that Penelope is likely to be eaten? After all, Penelope does need to be caught and feasted upon, to ensure that the bear does not continue to chase Ophelia. It may appear as if Ophelia is passing her misfortune to Penelope – minimally, that is as morally bad as your diverting the tram onto the unconscious worker. Yet we may feel that here 'every woman for herself' is morally acceptable.

Perhaps the relevant difference between the shield and bear examples concerns the tales' starting points. With the bear, the two explorers are in it together from the start; both are exposed to the bear's hungry eye. With the tram example, you alone are initially exposed to the danger. If you take no action, the worker is safe. If Ophelia takes no action regarding the bear, Penelope may still be exposed to the bear's dining desires. If the crazed gunman is out to shoot anyone, then again we may think that all in the queue are party to the misfortune. Suppose, though, that the gunman is specifically after Ophelia at the front of the queue. By diving down, avoiding the bullets, has she unfairly transferred a misfortune buck to others?

The worker on the track, Penelope standing behind Ophelia in the queue, Penelope being less adept at running – we may voice the mantra proclaiming the unfairness of all these conditions. Yet, of course, there is also the unfairness of Ophelia's happening to be at the queue's front, your being in the path of the runaway tram – and, spreading the net much wider, the unfairness of many being born into war, poverty and disease, when many are not.

When facing such unfairnesses and resultant dilemmas, we should, of course, try do what is 'for the best'. Sadly the best is often elusive, sometimes because there is nothing that is for the best; and even when there is, and we know what it is, it may yet be impossible to achieve.

As with many moral matters, over what to do, it seems – well, all we can do is muddle through.

2

JUST HELPING OURSELVES

Here are a few words, courtesy of John Aubrey, about Thomas Hobbes, a great seventeenth-century political philosopher. People often warm to Hobbes when they read them.

> He was very charitable (to the best of his ability) to those that were true objects of his bounty. One time, I remember, going in the Strand, a poor and infirmed old man craved his alms. He, beholding him with eyes of pity and compassion, put his hand in his pocket and gave him six pence. Said a divine (Dr Jaspar Mayne) that stood by: 'Would you have done this, if it had not been Christ's command?' 'Yea,' said he. 'Why?' quoth the other. 'Because,' said he, 'I was in pain to consider the miserable condition of the old man and now my alms, giving him some relief, doth also ease me.'

The moral often drawn from such tales is that we never act other than out of self-interest, that is, selfishly. It is true that sometimes we help others, but this is only to ease our distress at seeing them in distress – it is our distress that ultimately motivates us. Duty is never our true motivation.

The suggested story is that all our actions, despite contrary appearances, are really self-interested or selfish. The mother who runs into a burning house to save her child is motivated by fear, fear of how she would feel if she let her child die. Saints who sacrifice their lives, defending their Christian beliefs, are motivated by desire for an afterlife in heaven rather than hell. Atheists who, 'out of duty', volunteer to help the homeless really just want to feel good about themselves and perhaps impress their neighbours.

The ultimate consideration, to keep in mind in preparation for challenging the above, is its background assumption that when we perform any action, we must have some motivation – and that means that, in some sense, we want to do it and so we act to satisfy that want. But if we are doing something to satisfy our wants, then we are acting selfishly. That is the catch-all argument. What we want may not coincide with what is in our own interests – we often make mistakes about what is best for us – so the reasoning needs, more accurately, to speak of how we always act in accordance with what we want or what we believe to be our own self-interest.

Is it possible to do anything that is not, in some way, self-interested?

Various philosophical puzzles rely on views about what is 'really' the case. Curiously, students – and some philosophers – once in philosophy seminars, seem quickly to come to know or apprehend what is *really* so, even though this differs radically from what is reckoned to be really so outside the seminar room. It takes very little reflection to lead certain philosophers and students into believing that we never 'really' know anything much, can never 'really' be certain of much and are not 'really' free – even though it seems that, in our everyday lives, we frequently can tell whether someone knows something, is certain of something and did something freely.

What are we to make of the claim that 'really' we never act primarily out of concern for others? It may be an empirical claim, one that we assess on the evidence around us, yet if that is so, it looks to be false: people certainly seem, on occasions, to act purely out of concern for others. The self-interest claim, though, is often put forward in such a way that it *cannot* be refuted. Whatever examples we give of selfless actions, the response is, 'Ah, so if she did X, it must have been because really she wanted to do X – and so she was self-interested after all.' It looks as if altruism and acting solely for the benefit of others have been ruled out of existence – for just wanting to do these things is sufficient to show that the person doing them is not altruistic but selfish.

Some years ago, I saw Mrs Thatcher, then Prime Minister, being interviewed about a hospital crisis: nurses were going on strike. At one point, Mrs Thatcher said, 'But nurses do not strike.' The interviewer was flabbergasted. He pointed out that there, on screen, were pictures of nurses in Trafalgar Square, waving banners, announcing that they were striking. 'Ah,' replied Mrs Thatcher, 'they're not true nurses.' What had started off as a claim about the world which could be investigated, an empirical claim – the claim that nurses do not strike – became in Mrs Thatcher's worded worldly ways a claim that would be true come what may. No one would be allowed to count as being a nurse, if she or he went on strike.

The move – from an interesting empirical claim to one made true by linguistic fiat – is arguably at work when people tell us that all our actions are really self-interested. If it is an empirical claim, let us test it. Is it the case that mothers rush to save their children only through fear of their own future distress? Why believe that? Is it true that if anyone sacrifices his life for a cause, he is really doing it for his own benefit? Why believe that? If there is evidence that shows these things, let us see it; but let us not use the theory (plucked from where?) that all actions are self-interested to conclude that any seemingly altruistic action must really – even unconsciously – be selfish.

♈

Recently, there has been a tendency to move away from the level of people to that of genes, famously summed up by Richard Dawkins' book title *The Selfish Gene*. Of course, genes are not the kind of things that can be selfish and, if any metaphor is sought, 'vain' would be better, in so far as genes replicate themselves. Genetic considerations lead some to speak of altruism 'really' being a means for genes to increase their replication success; altruism is 'nothing but' gene survival or human self-interest in play. That is dangerous talk. Just because it is true that there are causal explanations (in terms of genes, replication and variation) for the existence of people with the range of features that they have, it does not follow that therefore no one is ever altruistically motivated. Just the reverse: the explanations are explanations of how it is that there is genuinely altruistic behaviour.

To load all human behaviour into the same selfish boat — maybe through tales of genetic explanations or unconscious motivations — blurs valuable distinctions between, for example, people who help you without any expectation of reward and those who help you only if there is a reward. Now, which sort would you prefer as your friends — or to meet, when you are stranded and lost, with car broken down?

Insist, if you must, in moving the linguistic goalposts and thinking of all humans as selfish; but then you need to distinguish between those who help you for a fee and those who help you for free.

3
IN THE BEGINNING

I am unfairly discriminated against.

Who am I? I am that person whom you failed to create some years ago, last year or maybe a few moments ago — that time when you avoided having sex or deployed contraception. There are billions and billions like me, all unfairly treated.

Those of you lucky enough to exist speak keenly about the value of human life. You make great efforts to keep people alive. You have legal systems, moral pressures, checks and balances designed to prevent people from being killed. You have hospitals, vaccinations and screening programmes; safety nets, health regulations, well woman and well man clinics, all to assist the living to carry on living. Virtually all of you are appalled by infanticide — at killing children, at killing babies. Most of you are repelled by very late abortions: what is the morally relevant difference, you say, between a new-born baby and a foetus in the womb a few hours before birth?

Some of you already treat abortion as morally equivalent to murder. If late abortions are akin to infanticide and hence are morally wrong, what of slightly earlier abortions — and earlier and earlier, as we count down the days? What is the morally relevant difference between a foetus of sixteen weeks and one that is a day younger — and what is the relevant difference between that foetus and one a little younger still? We may move on down the days in this way, going lower and lower, until we reach the moment of conception.

Conception! That's what marks the difference. Before conception, there is no individual entity that is likely to grow into a person; there is no potential person present at all. It is only once the egg is fertilized that we have something that is potentially a person, with feelings, intelligence, loves and desires.

I charge you with being space-ist and number-ist. I would even say 'materialist' but for the fact that philosophers understand the term peculiarly. Yes, the egg and sperm, pre-conception, have some distance between them – their structure or matter is greatly spaced – but why is that numerical and geographical fact morally relevant? That there are two elements does not show that the twosome is not a potential person. True, we cannot tell beforehand which sperm will fertilize the egg towards which the sperms are heading – the egg which will grow into embryo, foetus, baby, child and adult. Undoubtedly, though, before fertilization, there must have existed the particular sperm – let's call him 'Herm' – which would end up fertilizing the particular egg – Eggwina. Were that not so, that fertilized egg would not have come about. Not to have engaged in uncontracepted sex at that moment (whenever it was) would have prevented Herm and Eggwina from uniting; it would have prevented creation of the fertilized egg and hence the foetus, baby and adult life that people so greatly value.

If it is wrong to kill people, isn't it also wrong not to create people?

To get to the nub of the question, let us move to babies. After all, there are simple replies to the question above. One would be that people usually do not want to die, but people who are not yet created have no wants at all – well, not yet.

What is wrong with killing a baby? That is no outrageous question, but a request to work out what justifies the common belief that it is typically morally wrong. Philosophers, rightly, ask questions, even if unsettling – and sometimes they ask the questions because they are unsettling. Of course, there can be philosophical worries whether or not certain questions, in certain contexts, should even be raised; that leads into the value of free expression (reviewed in Chapter 9). Here our question is in a philosophical context: what is wrong with killing babies?

If the answer is simply in terms of the loss of its future life, a life which has value in itself, then abortion is also morally wrong. This is because had the abortion taken place, that future life (child, adult) would also have been lost. That future life would also have been lost had successful contraception been used, preventing the creation of the foetus which grew into the child who grew into the adult. Moving yet further back, sexual abstinence would have been wrong; it too would have prevented the existence of the child and later adult.

Being pregnant, of course, prevents the coming into existence of other foetuses. No one is arguing that it is possible to create all possible lives. Making more and more lives is also undesirable, if we are unable to support them. The puzzle is that if – *if* – what is wrong with infanticide and abortion is the loss of the future person who would otherwise come about, then contraception and, indeed, sexual abstinence, other things being equal, are similarly wrong. The chaste are as bad as the baby killers – at least with regard to the loss of the future lives that would otherwise exist. Yet most of us believe that to be a crazy conclusion. It is a conclusion that would paradoxically pop chaste monks and nuns, those committed to vows of chastity, next to murderers.

♈

Arguably, the mistake is to think that what makes killing a human being wrong is the loss of that being's future life. A more plausible account is that what makes it wrong is the loss that the individual suffers. Consider Esmeralda, just a usual person (even if unusually named): she has a sense of her 'self' continuing into the future. By killing her, we thwart her desires, her aims, her intentions. Fundamentally, Esmeralda wants to go on living. That is why it is wrong to kill her – and why it may well not be wrong to kill someone who really does want to die; why voluntary euthanasia and assisted dying should be permitted. Further, if we have a being that lacks any sense of itself continuing into the future and so lacks any desire for that self to continue, then killing that individual painlessly cannot harm it. Of course, there may be other reasons, good reasons, why it is wrong to kill such individuals; we may, for example, cause distress to others.

In this approach, sexual abstinence, contraception and abortion are not wrongs to the individual who fails to develop. That is because they involve no direct harm to a being that has a sense of self continuing into the future. No one seriously thinks the egg and the sperm have desires and intentions; no one seriously thinks the foetus does. For that matter, very young babies also lack such a sense of continuing self. Infanticide and some abortions, though, will still be wrong, in so far as they cause distress to others, notably and often the mother. Further, there could well be adverse knock-on effects, were we to allow rationality to diminish our natural discomfort or distress at very late abortions and infanticide. So, this chapter is no call for infanticide.

For a response to the approach, as above, that seeks to justify us in not worrying about those whom we do not create, consider the principle, a version of the Golden Rule, 'Do unto others as you would have them do unto you.' Most people are pleased to have been created (well, they tend to say that, though it could be self-deception). Were you to start creating children tonight, it is likely that the outcome would be people who are pleased that you did unto them what you are pleased was done unto you – namely, be created.

Does creating people count as doing something good for them? Those people do not exist, until the good is done; so, if you do nothing, surely there is no one there to have missed out on creation. Still, if you do believe that creating people is good for them, then you know your chat-up line for tonight – but beware, beware, the consequences.

4

THE VIOLINIST: SHOULD YOU UNPLUG?

You wake up one mundane Monday, only to discover that this Monday is far from mundane. A tube runs from your body to an unknown man a few feet away. A violinist, it transpires, is plugged into your lymphatic system.

Although bizarre, the tale possesses considerable relevance to the everyday. Before we bring the tale down to earth, let us fly this phantasy.

How did the violinist come to be plugged into you? Well, maybe you were in hospital for some minor tests. While you slept, the violinist, unconscious, was rushed into the ward. The doctors knew that the only way to save him was to plug his system into yours. Fortunately for the violinist, and unfortunately for you, your lymphatic system possesses a rare property, one essential for maintaining the violinist's life. The violinist's use of your system does not endanger your health; but, while plugged, your life is somewhat inconvenienced. The violinist will go everywhere with you – which could well give rise to embarrassments in your social, personal and romantic life.

Right now, the violinist is sitting by your bedside. He is fine, so long as he remains plugged. You flick the tubing connecting his body to yours. He is well aware that you could simply disconnect it. All would then be well with you; all not well with him. He would die, perhaps a horrible death. He needs you in order to live.

Understandably, the violinist begs you not to unplug him. It is life or death for him – of convenience or the opposite for you. Yet there are other factors. He has no right to use of your body – or does he? He surely has a right to life. By unplugging him, would you not be violating that right? You would certainly be causing him to die.

Are you within your rights
to unplug the violinist?

One line leads to the answer 'Yes'. You granted him no right to your body. No agreement was made. He is, so to speak, trespassing on your body; so, you are well within your rights to remove him. True, he would die as a result of the removal, but that is neither your intent nor your fault. It is an unfortunate consequence of you asserting your rights. If, miraculously, he were to survive, you should have no objection; presumably you would feel relieved. In unplugging him, your aim is not to kill him.

We may feel queasy with the above response. Are you not violating his right to life, by insisting on the higher priority of your right to be un-trespassed upon? Suppose he merely needs use of your body for one day, until some drugs arrive. Would you still be within your rights to insist on unplugging?

The thoughts above raise two fundamental questions. One question concerns what is involved in possessing a right. Another question concerns morality's extent.

On the first question, people speak readily of everyone having a right to life. People do not speak so readily of everyone having a right to whatever is required for life. The violinist has a right to life. He requires use of your body, but he does not have a right to that use. Millions of people suffer from malnutrition and disease that will kill them; they have a right to life. Do they therefore have a right to assistance from you – for example, by your giving to relevant charities? Someone needs a kidney transplant. Does he have a right to your kidney? After all, you only need one. We spend considerable money on luxuries: we assume a right to spend our money as we wish; we assume that our right outweighs the requirements of others, those with the right to life, for maintenance of their lives.

'Rights' talk is cheap: what is costly is providing means for people to exercise their rights. Possessing the right to life counts for little if it fails to carry any duty on others to enable that right to be fulfilled. 'Tis small comfort to the starving to know that they have a right to life, but no right to the excess food that we keep for ourselves.

Before offering more thoughts about rights, let us turn to the second question, namely, of morality's extent. Even if you would not be violating the violinist's rights by unplugging him – the result being his death – would you not still be doing something wrong, if you did unplug? Morality embraces not only rights, but also qualities such as honesty, loyalty, kindness, courage and forgiveness. In our violinist tale, it would surely be cruel to insist on your rights straight away. If the violinist needed use of your body for just a few hours or even weeks, would not granting him that use be the decent thing to do?

Of course, there are degrees and degrees. It would be extraordinarily kind of you, to accept the violinist attached for the rest of your life. Surely, morality does not demand such exceptional self-sacrifice. In that sort of case, maybe the violinist should recognize the unfair burden he would be putting on your life, and take the courageous path of sacrificing himself. Recall Captain Oates in Scott's disastrous South Pole venture of 1912. In order to avoid being a burden, Oates crawled out of the tent into the blizzards with the famous words, 'I am just going outside and may be some time.' No one had a right to demand that sacrifice, yet maybe Oates did the right thing – despite its ultimate futility.

The violinist, Captain Oates and many other examples remind us that moral dilemmas do not all reduce to conflicting 'rights'. Moral dilemmas can be fed from many quarters and the feeding makes morality something of a mess. You may, for example, think that a lot hangs on the value of the violinist – to himself, but also to society. Were the violinist a lousy player and a depressed drug addict, you may feel far less inclined to allow him use of your body than you would were he a famous violinist of impressive skills. Think how your attitude would change, depending whether the violinist was also a burglar and wife-beater, or a surgeon capable of saving many lives. Yet should the morality of which lives we save hang on the value of those lives to the community?

Rights range from the most trivial – I could give you rights over my laptop – to radically important ones concerning life and death. The United Nations seems to have uncovered a vast range of rights, taking us from the right to life to the right to maternity leave. This shows the danger of how, without care, 'rights' talk becomes devalued. Certain basic moral principles, it seems, justify talk of moral rights. We typically accept that it is fundamentally wrong to kill another human being; and it is that which immediately grounds the 'right to life'. In contrast, lots of reasoning would be needed to justify maternity leave as a significant 'right'.

Accepting that 'rights' talk highlights certain moral principles as fundamental – trump cards to be played, when in moral dilemmas – the question remains of the source of those principles (a puzzle raised by Frog and Scorpion, Chapter 63). Some philosophers have argued that there are 'natural' rights, rights built within nature, maybe courtesy of God, maybe of our human nature. Jeremy Bentham, an early nineteenth-century thinker, came up with the wonderful quip that such talk is 'nonsense on stilts'. Yet Bentham keenly embraced and promoted the utilitarian principle that we ought to seek the greatest happiness of the greatest number. Now, is that principle mysteriously built into nature? Is it standing on nature's stilts, though not God's, as nonsense?

Suppose keeping the violinist alive, plugged into you for years and years, would maximize overall happiness. We should surely still doubt whether morality could demand that you sacrifice yourself in that way – that you should be so saintly – however well the violinist played.

5
WALK ON BY...?

You know how it is: you saunter along, when you are suddenly aware of a beggar, sitting on the pavement a few yards ahead. Automatically, you quicken your step, trying to ensure that, as you draw near, others will be walking between you and that down-and-out 'other'. Or you cross the road: you really are too busy even to allow your eyes to meet with this other. He may be a charlatan, a con-man, off to wine and dine later that evening; well, there are stories and stories. Or maybe he engages in profitable transactions of a pharmaceutical kind. In any case, you reflect, the state provides. And so, you walk on by. As you walk, you feel some unease.

Or the above may not be so…

Instead, you feel for change, for small coins – must be neither too little nor too much – quite what is the right amount? Your eyes are averted – true, you are embarrassed – but you slip the coins into those dirty hands. What a relief! At least no contact – or maybe there was. So, out comes the antiseptic spray; of course out it comes only once you are at a distance suitably discreet. At least you did something; at least you were not touched by a meanness of nature. You feel, indeed, a touch pleased with yourself. And yet, did you give enough, or too much? Did you come over as superior? And so, as you walk on, you feel some unease.

〰️

Beggars make many of us feel uneasy. Maybe with both scenarios too much sensitivity is on show; but what ought people to do, when so confronted? There would be no dilemma if we lacked the recognition that suffering and extremes of wealth inequality are objectionable. Yet,

surely it is up to the state, through social structures and impersonal taxation, to rectify matters. We may even wonder whether the beggars have brought their sorry state upon themselves. Are they victims of bad luck, or have they wittingly made choices that led to their beggarly blight? If they are to blame, why should we care? Let us assume our beggar is genuine and unfortunate.

Is giving to beggars 'for good reasons' intrinsically wrong?

'Charity wounds him who receives.' People who beg, it is claimed, often conveniently so by the well-heeled, are humiliating themselves. The state, if anyone, should provide. If we succumb and give, we are party to the humiliation. Far better not to give. Better still: make begging illegal. But are those things far better?

In true charitable giving, we bestow goods upon recipients, without expectation of reciprocation. It is not simply that beggars *do not* reciprocate; typically, they cannot. In contrast, when you make gifts to friends, they may simply say 'thank you'; but they *could* reciprocate.

Reciprocation, here, does not demand sameness of monetary value, but some similarity of concern and care. Monetary value sometimes has relevance: exceptionally expensive gifts can cause embarrassment, even humiliation, to recipients who could not possibly reciprocate at that level. Well, genuine beggars are exposed to that embarrassment, intensely so.

To handle the reciprocation problem, some beggars offer items in return; but that raises the question of their value. If, on the one hand, they are worthless and unwanted, then it is hypocritical to pretend that the donation is really payment for the items: such pretence would manifest failure to respect the beggar. If, on the other hand, the items possess genuine value and are wanted, then we are no longer in the realm of charitable giving. We can buy or resist without qualms. Self-employed salespeople, living on commission, sometimes meet customers who buy out of sorrow for the sellers' plight. The salespeople may feel humiliated; or, if they have deliberately manipulated the customers' sorrow, then the customers have been humiliated, whether they know it or not.

For painful examples of humiliation, consider the following. A young man – 'Tutankhamen' – stands outside a museum. Totally covered in gold fabric, wearing an Egyptian mask, he is motionless, a bowl on the ground before him. Museum visitors drop money into the bowl. Each time this happens, he comes to life and bows. People – children – pop in further coins, to see him bow again and again. He may remind you of a dog, needing to beg for each morsel. He expresses his gratitude and servility – as a beggar.

With Tutankhamen, maybe the money is for his performance; so, let us look at a purer begging example. On the Paris Metro, a man gets down on his knees – and begs. On his knees, he shuffles along the carriage. The man is expressly humiliating himself, denigrating himself. One human being's relationship to another ought not to be like that. If, though, the man's behaviour is ironic, then the passengers are being humiliated. Witness your own discomfort, if you picture yourself as witness of the man, be he sincere or ironic.

The begging relationship, though, need not be seen as one of humiliation. Get Metro Man up, off his knees. He is then a fellow human being, down on his luck. True, he may be bowed by circumstances, but giver and receiver may recognize their common humanity. Fellow-feeling need not cause humiliation; rather, it engenders sympathy and generosity. Yes, the beggar is helpless. But a cry for help need not be humiliating; and a cry for help is radically better than starvation. As a rabbi has said, 'God stands with the poor person at the door.' Atheistic humanists substitute 'Our common humanity' for 'God'.

♈

None of the above promotes begging as therefore desirable. In view of the sheer chance regarding which beggars attract most attention, which ones are genuinely in need, which ones are most deserving, there are good reasons for authorities to aim at greater success in providing for the dispossessed. In view of the way in which many people treat beggars as disgusting and reprehensible – and many beggars are pitiful and abject, sometimes aggressive, sometimes mentally ill – the actuality of much begging is far removed from Metro Man being urged up off his knees into a shining shared humanity. Yet, with all that said, helping others in distress surely takes precedence over the alleged risk of causing humiliation.

Broadening the sources of humiliation, we may feel degraded by our human condition – by suffering the ills of ageing, unable to fend for ourselves, probably one day unable to perform many personal tasks. This is where, like beggars, we turn to others. And this is where, to avoid the risk of charitable help and humiliation, there is advocacy of human beings possessing a right to ____ – and fill in the gap with basic goods, from food and drink to education to nursing care to other welfare benefits. No magic wand wave exists, of course, that can conjure up resources to fulfil those rights; thus, sincere advocates need willingly to support the community, usually through taxation, to ensure provision of the required resources.

Humiliation, of course, is sometimes deliberately imposed upon unwilling victims. Those who suffered horrendously in concentration camps sought to preserve some dignity by dehumanizing their tormenters, viewing them as wild beasts. Suffering as a result of impersonal forces is not, it appears, as bad as from personal deliberation. The tormenters treated their victims *as if* animals or objects; but the victims needed, of course, to be human – for humiliation to occur. Arguably beasts of the field cannot be humiliated, and certainly you cannot humiliate a pebble, tree or robot.

The down-and-outs begging on street corners have a right to respect; they deserve, of course, to be treated as human beings. That is what they are. That, though, does not mean declining to help for fear of humiliating them. Declining to help can also humiliate. The beggars' humanity should block our temptation to walk on by – or, at least, to walk on by without concern, without serious reflection.

The beggars' humanity should also prevent us from seeing things, as we did above, in terms of black or white – of either the beggars are responsible for their plight or they are not; of either they are sellers with valuable goods and services offered for money received or they are just pretending to be so. Human beings have a mishmash of characteristics, motives and fortunes – good and bad. That mishmash leads to some people finding themselves begging. That mishmash should at least make us hesitate before dismissing a beggar. Indeed, that mishmash should stop us from outright dismissal of beggars – and arguably, in many cases, it should lead us not to walk on by.

6
THE INNOCENT MURDERER: A NOBODY DUNIT

Three singers trek across the desert. Being modestly inclined, they have their own separate tents, facilities and provisions. Let us give our singing trekkers names: Lena, Poppy and Barrington. Desert life is no happy life and while Lena and Poppy get on well, singing duets as sopranos, they take a dislike towards Barrington's baritone tones. Lena and Poppy are unaware of how much the other dislikes baritone Barrington; they do not discuss such matters. Relations with Barrington deteriorate so much that the women, independently and unbeknownst to each other, decide they must kill him. Well, it is hot in the desert – and his singing *is* pretty bad.

One night, while Barrington is asleep, Poppy steals into his tent and pours poison into his water container. Poppy, the poisoner, returns to her tent. A little later, Lena, knowing nothing about Poppy's jaunt, tiptoes over to Barrington, finds his water container and cracks the bottom, so that the water leaks out. Lena, the leaker, slips back to her tent. Early in the morning, before Barrington awakes, the women pack up their belongings and trek off, singing together, leaving Barrington alone. When Barrington awakes, he finds his water container empty; singing deeply and tragically, he dies of thirst. In due course, the desert police discover what has happened. The puzzle is: has either of the young ladies murdered Barrington?

Poppy argues: 'Yes, I wanted Barrington dead but I cannot be held guilty of murder. The poison didn't touch Barrington's lips. It had all drained away by the time he awoke. He didn't die of being poisoned.'

Lena argues: 'Yes, I too wanted Barrington dead and intended that he should die of thirst. In fact I drained away toxic water, so, if anything, I saved him from a horrible poisoning.'

Barrington is well and truly dead. It is difficult not to believe that Barrington has been murdered. Surely Poppy or Lena is a murderer? Yet are they not both innocent of murder? For Poppy to be a murderer, her actions should at least have caused Barrington's death, but she is right: she only poisoned the water and Barrington did not drink any poisoned water. For Lena to be a murderer, she should at least have caused Barrington's death, but Lena is right: she only drained out poisoned water, saving him from death by poisoning.

Can a murder be committed by the innocent?

Some will say that, as Barrington died of dehydration and Lena drained out the water, she is the murderer. But Lena drained out poisoned water and the poison could have been one that acted by causing dehydration, in which case it would perhaps not be quite so clear that Lena was the cause of death by dehydration – for Barrington would then have died that way in any case. Indeed, the poison might have made the water undrinkable or have solidified it, so Barrington would have died from dehydration, even without Lena's little leaking. Even were Lena clearly the cause of death, does that make her morally *the* murderer, given that, had she not acted, Barrington would have died courtesy of Poppy? Of course, it appears as if Lena did, unwittingly, prevent Poppy from murdering Barrington; she apparently did this by, unwittingly, making Poppy's poisoning ineffective. But appearances may be deceptive.

What is clearly missing in this *Desert Song* is a conspiracy. If the two women acted together as one, then maybe they could both be convicted of murder. Their actions, taken together, led to Barrington's death and that outcome was their intent. Acting separately, it seems that at best – or worst – they are each guilty of *attempted* murder but, arguably, innocent of murder.

An intention to do something wrong or against the law is rarely considered as bad as when the intention gets fulfilled. If we could be prosecuted solely for our intentions, however distant from success, we should almost all have criminal records. A comparison may be made with those religious doctrines which seem to collapse psychological states, including ones even more remote from actions than intentions, into the actions which would typically result. Following the New Testament, an American president, Jimmy Carter, accepted that lusting in one's heart for a woman other than one's wife is morally the same as the act of adultery. More recently, some extreme feminists have bizarrely claimed that watching the portrayal of rape is the same as raping.

Lest this *Desert Song* seems far-fetched, consider the following, based on a real court case:

Phillips wanted a member of his gang, Daniels, dead. Indeed, he beat up Daniels, took him for dead and bundled him into the back of his car. Phillips decided he must dispose of the body, so he drove the car to the edge of a cliff and pushed it over. The police later discovered that the beating Daniels had suffered failed to kill him; it merely knocked him unconscious. What killed Daniels was the downward journey from the cliff's edge to the rocks below. Was Phillips guilty of murder?

His defence counsel argued not. The argument went as follows. To murder people is intentionally to kill them. Phillips was guilty of attempted murder – witness the non-fatal beating that he gave Daniels, with the intention of killing him. What killed Daniels was, in fact, the fall over the cliff's edge. When Phillips pushed the car over the edge, he was not intending to kill Daniels but to dispose of the body. Phillips thought Daniels was already dead, so that action of his clearly could not have been intended to kill him.

The judge failed to fall for the defence counsel's silver tongue. The judge ruled that the actions by Phillips should be taken as one and, taken as one, they or it resulted from Phillips' intention to kill and in Daniels' death.

♈

These cases raise questions of the identity and individuation of actions. Actions are what we do; but quite what do we do? Last night, you woke the neighbours. Is that accurate? You turned up the music and the music woke the neighbours. Is that quite right? You twiddled a knob that caused the music level to rise that caused vibrations through the wall that woke the neighbours. Did you twiddle the knob – or did you, more accurately, move your fingers, causing the knob to turn? Where do we stop? Are there some 'basic' actions that we perform directly, that is, actions in which there are no further intermediate causal links? Look out for 'Man with Pulley' (Chapter 60).

As well as the question of the identity of actions, we must contend with the identity of agents or subjects. Phillips is a single agent. In the killing of Barrington, Poppy and Lena were not acting as one, though when Poppy and Lena duet together, they sing as one.

Counting tables and chairs in the room is easy but when counting actions and agents, things sometimes fall apart – and sometimes come together.

7
GIRL, CAGE, CHIMP

Picture, if you will, a four-year-old girl in a cage. She has been captured, screaming; she saw her parents beaten off by the kidnappers. She
rocks to and fro, showing obvious signs of fear and mental instability.
It is unclear quite what is being done to her, but some of the time she
undoubtedly suffers physical pain. Wires are attached to a shaven portion of her head and, although she is given food and water, it looks as if
some drugs are mixed within.

Perhaps I have asked you to picture a political torture camp. Maybe
she has been placed under these stressful conditions to frighten her
parents into confessing to political outrages. Perhaps I have asked you
to picture a daughter who has been kidnapped and is being held to
ransom. Or am I raising the question of whether picturing possesses
moral dimensions?

Not at all. For my purposes, you are picturing a child actress, playing
the part of a caged girl in *My Mate's A Primate*, a short advertisement made
by Animal Defenders International. Many people, if they encounter such
films, dismiss the scenes as phantasies dreamt up by crazy animal libera-
tionists. Some scientists, such as those engaged in testing on animals,
stress the unfair emotional appeal: they speak of how well animals are
cared for when undergoing experimentation – adding, in truth, that they
are thereby safe from their usual predators. Many people are shocked
by the images of caged and frightened animals undergoing all kinds of
testing. Some conclude that animal experimentation should be banned;
others argue that such experimentation is nasty, but also necessary for the
proper development of drugs to benefit mankind – and even animal kind.

Our puzzle rests not on challenging the facts but on the consistency of those who argue in favour of animal testing. Assume that the

favourers are right, that testing on live animals is needed for the development of safe drugs. Assume that the suffering caused by such testing is a necessary evil, far outweighed by the eventual benefits, for it would be irresponsible to distribute untested drugs to thousands of ill people. Note that such reasoning, in terms of overall consequences, is often deployed by people who are otherwise appalled at thinking about right and wrong in terms of consequences. Such people would usually speak of rights which should not be violated, however welcome the eventual consequences.

Based on the assumptions just given, here comes the puzzle. There are early stages of human lives in which the humans' emotional and intellectual awareness and their perspective on the world are less than those of (for example) adult chimps. Some claim that adult chimps possess the same mental and emotional development as four-year-old children – hence the particular film mentioned above. Whatever the exact age, whatever the animal, the question is:

Why is animal experimentation morally permissible if experimentation on children is not?

If the answer is simply that children are human, whereas chimps are not, the answerers are exposed to the charge of 'speciesism'. They are discriminating between creatures purely on the basis of species' membership; and that is akin to discriminating between people because of their race or sex. Such discrimination is unfair, unless some characteristics of that species, race or sex, can be shown to justify the difference in treatment.

We are not being sexist in providing prostate cancer screening for men but not for women. Obviously, a relevant male–female difference justifies the different treatment. Arguably, we are not speciesist when we kill sheep painlessly while rejecting the killing of humans. In killing sheep (in contrast to adult humans), we are not destroying individuals who possess a sense of continuing into the future, with plans, hopes and intentions. We are speciesist if we inflict suffering on chimps but not on children, when we have no reason to think the suffering would be less for the chimps – and when we know that no other differences are relevant.

Replies to this reasoning rely either on uncovering some morally relevant differences between the tested animals and humans or on justifying speciesism. The replies raise their own puzzles.

There are, of course, differences: children have the potential for considerably more enriched lives than chimps, monkeys and many other animals. That is no doubt true; but why should what is potentially the case carry such weight? Fertilized human eggs possess the potential to become people, yet we do not treat them as people and many, many people find abortions morally acceptable. We should also wonder whether it is really 'potential' that explains people's seemingly speciesist attitudes and, if it does explain them, whether their grounds are good. After all, the child could be one with such brain damage that she lacks any potential for further development.

Suppose a choice has to be made between saving a child and a non-human animal from temporary pain – pain which would cause no adverse long-term consequences for either. Most people would insist that protecting the child is the right thing to do. Yet, if the suffering is the same, what can justify that discrimination? And if we think that it is simply wrong to inflict suffering on a child, independently of overall beneficial consequences, why is that stance not also applied to non-human animals? Should not the relevant moral question be Jeremy Bentham's, when applying his utilitarian concern for overall happiness, namely, 'Can they suffer?' That is, of course, a relevant question; but is it the only one?

Let us take the rejection of sexism, racism and speciesism further. One such suggested 'ism' is family-ism. Is family-ism also morally wrong? Is the preference that mothers have for their own children over others justified? How about friend-ism? Is a greater affection for our friends than for unknown people morally wrong? How about blonde-ism, good-looks-ism, music-lover-ism, nation-ism? These weird examples should remind us that we have numerous preferences, based on how we feel, and without them we should probably cease to be human. These examples should also remind us that we need to assess when preferences are justified and when they are not, if we are to have flourishing lives. A woman's preference for bearded men in her personal life should – it almost goes without saying – not be condemned (the author declares no interest here); but using that preference to judge, for example, which man told the truth in court merits obvious rejection.

We are speciesist, and that in itself can paradoxically be used to show that we are not. Being speciesist, we feel far more distress at a child's suffering than a non-human animal's; so that itself generates a morally relevant difference in outcome – but one worthy of support?

♈

A four-year-old child, chimp or rabbit also suffers from not knowing what is going on. From this we may conclude that there can be more reason not to conduct painful experiments on children, chimps or rabbits than on fully grown rational people. If the experiments are intended to benefit mankind, then at least the adults can grasp the value of that aim. Furthermore, performing tests on the young will, in all likelihood, damage their future adulthood or radically cut short their lives. That suggests that maybe we should turn from children to the elderly. If testing is necessary, may there not be some people, nearing death, prepared to sacrifice themselves for others? At least their sufferings would be mitigated by the knowledge that the sufferings were all in a good cause.

In as far as we are repelled by such a suggestion (and, in view of my age and the topic, I do now declare some interest), perhaps we should cease to shut our eyes to the misuse of animals in experimentation. We should also cease to keep our eyes firmly closed to the many other harms visited upon many, many creatures, courtesy of various forms of horrendous farming methods. That ought not, of course, to lead us to reduce our concern for the sufferings, distress and sorrows of millions of human beings. There is much to be done to relieve pains and hardships. That we cannot do all the 'much' does not excuse doing nothing at all.

8
LUCKY FOR SOME

My apologies for another puzzling tale of violence. The puzzle occurs with all manner of actions which are open to moral blame or praise and which reap society's punishments or rewards. The excesses of violence can, paradoxically, bring puzzles to life. We start with Jack and Jill.

Jill took a liking to Jack's wealth and a disliking to Jack, so much so that she wanted to kill him, steal his money and escape to an isle of dreams. Jack was not keen on the idea and kept clear of Jill. Jill went hunting for her man. She found him at the top of a hill and tripped him up, knocking him unconscious, then drowned him in a bucket of water. It was horrendous behaviour. She was a deliberate killer. She was convicted of murder.

Had Jill failed to trip Jack or had the bucket been empty, then perhaps Jack would have survived. Jill would have been guilty of attempted murder, avoiding the longer sentence (or shorter, if a death sentence) associated with murder. Yet this difference in treatment resulted from events outside her control. She was as morally defective in both cases, though maybe practically more inept in the second. We may, though, ask – as we did with poor Barrington (Chapter 6) – why the law metes out different punishments when the moral wickedness is the same.

Whether people deserve moral praise or blame should not depend on accidents, luck or unluck, which are outside their control. The goodness (or otherwise) of our intentions is surely what matters morally. Suppose that when Jill met Jack at the hill's top, he happened to stumble, fell face down in the water and drowned – but Jill did nothing to save him. Is she not as morally culpable as in the first tale, when she drowned him? That raises a further puzzle of what morally relevant difference there is, if any, between killing and letting die, between the active and the passive – distinctions, it is claimed, that are relevant to the medical treatment of the terminally ill.

Here are two further examples of moral muddles, when we seek to evaluate responsibilities, praise and blame.

You are sometimes careless when you drive. You fiddle with your lipstick, mobile telephone or car radio. You might have taken the odd drink too many. Few people treat you as being significantly morally blameworthy; yet if children run into the road and your reactions are slow and they are killed, are you not seriously blameworthy? In all like-lihood, you would blame yourself for what you did. Yet the difference in extent of moral blame hangs solely on the children's running out, an event utterly outside your control.

Mr Miller is a family man, living in Britain, who has a limited choice of jobs available to him – security guard or gas fitter. He is easy to get on with, a man loved by his family and friends. Consider a similar family man with similar characteristics: Herr Müller. He lived in Nazi Germany and the only jobs available to him were working as camp guard or gas fitter in Auschwitz-Birkenau. Through his job, he ended up at that camp being involved in the killing of hundreds of thousands of innocent Poles, Russians and even more Jews. 'What a morally dispre-table person! How could anyone have anything at all to do with such horrendous evils!' Yet is it not circumstances – circumstances outside the control of both Miller and Müller – that determine which of these two is deemed morally nice and which morally nasty? Many of us are incredibly lucky not to have been placed in circumstances where, in all likelihood, we should find ourselves acting similarly to Herr Müller.

Should we be morally praised or blamed only for things within our control?

Immanuel Kant answered 'Yes'. Writing over two hundred years ago, he insisted that a good will should shine like a jewel, independently of what it accomplishes or fails to accomplish. A bad will, we may add, is like a black hole of evil, whether or not it draws in others. Even if Jill fails to kill Jack, her will or intent marks her as morally disreputable. Even if no child gets injured, we remain morally reprehensible if we drive carelessly. Although Miller has a peaceful gentle life, if his character is such that, in awful circumstances, he would allow himself to be involved in horrendous killings, then maybe he is as bad as Müller.

The puzzle is that, if we shield moral assessment from anything to do with what lies outside our control, we are in danger of losing morality completely. We spoke of Miller and Müller's characters. Did they have any control over what characters they would have – whether they would be courageous or weak-willed, principled or fickle, good at assessing moral responsibilities or not?

Consider Jasmin, a highly impressionable young woman who is swept along by what her family and close friends do. Consider how Jasmin's choices and actions depend, in part, on her surrounding culture. In a Western, liberally educated setting, in a family and surroundings of non-believers, she is pretty likely to be tolerant, easy-going, valuing individuality and the democratic vote. Bring her up, though, reciting the Qur'an every day, being told by certain teachers that she must sacrifice her life to further Muhammad's word and she may become highly intolerant, even turning to terrorism. Of course, we hasten to note, non-religious movements as well as Christian, Islamic and other faiths, have led to vast numbers of people being harmed or killed. The point here is not to engage in the debate of when, if ever, such killings are justified; it is not to try to assess whether the religious have done more harm than the non-religious. The point is that, if our moral worth must not depend on accidents outside our control, there seems to be nothing left of us that merits moral evaluation.

♈

In practice, we muddle through, sometimes allowing outside factors to excuse us for what we do and sometimes not. But should we? Some try to escape the muddle by examining what should be deemed to be within our control. Individuals are told to pull themselves together and be brave. If they fail, they reap the moral condemnation of being cowardly.

Whether they can pull themselves together, though, would seem to depend on characteristics over which, ultimately, they are powerless. It may also depend on the luck of having people around them, telling them to pull themselves together – or coaxing them, encouraging them.

In the legal world, we also muddle through. The sentences meted out to criminals can be reduced, or even quashed, if the defence lawyers manage successfully to argue that the criminal was mentally disturbed and that his actions were not really under his command, and so not really *his* actions at all. Yet being mentally *un*disturbed does not count as a mitigating factor.

A thief argued that he was terribly sorry but he could not help what he did, given his bad upbringing; hence, he should not be held responsible for his thievery. The judge replied that she too was terribly sorry but, given her own upbringing, she could not help but give him a long sentence.

9
VEILS OF WOE: BEATS AND PEEPING TOMS TOO

When Mandy strolls along the seashore and ruffians pepper her with pebbles, she is harmed. When Zahira crosses the park, veiled in Muslim garb, and hooligans mug her, she too is harmed. Many of us, devotees of John Stuart Mill, feel that people should be free to get on with their lives as they want, so long as they are not harming others, unless those others consent to their being harmed. This is Mill's Harm Principle, also known as the 'Liberty Principle'. The ruffians and hooligans are inflicting harms without justification and without consent; they simply ought not to be doing what they do. Now for puzzling cases.

Zahira is a modest woman, committed to Islam. Unbeknownst to her, when she undresses, a peeping Tom, Tom, peeps upon her. She never knows about Tom and his peeping predilections, but is she not harmed? She loves pottering in her garden, but, when summer suns shine, she stays indoors. Mandy, her neighbour, sunbathes topless. Zahira finds it offensive; yet is she harmed? Zahira knows that Mandy leads a sexually disreputable life, dismissive of religions, prophets and holy scriptures. Is Zahira harmed because of what she knows goes on next door, albeit veiled by curtains?

Mandy basks under the sun, on a public beach, topless, where others too are topless. Here, she is peppered by frequent glances from men who just happen to stroll nearby; they make her uncomfortable. Is she harmed? A few fundamentalist Muslims, including Zahira, and evangelical Christians, for once all united, parade along the beach. They wave placards denouncing atheists, public nudity and sexual immorality. More harms for Mandy? She is upset by some shouts of 'hellfire' for her friends, family and herself. 'How could they even think such things?'

Mandy gives up on the beach; Zahira gives up on the parade. They take the train back home, acknowledging each other awkwardly. In the carriage, they are peppered by the beats of leaking MP3 players, jingles from mobile phones and worse. At home, they cannot escape adjacent building works' drillings during the day. And, some nights, their very different thoughts and sleep are disrupted by car alarms and burglar alarms, all false alarms. Are they harmed?

On the next sunny afternoon, Mandy returns to her garden to sunbathe, but then feels uneasy at upsetting her Muslim neighbour. Her Muslim neighbour, now indoors, feels somewhat uneasy at her condemnation of Mandy.

Where do harms begin – and end?

Mill is often criticized for not defining 'harm', but a definition is unlikely to help. Were an accurate definition given, then it would feature the same fuzzy uncertainties that we already find in applying 'harm'. In the end, we need to consider cases: we need to consider them… case by case.

Zahira knows nothing of Tom's peeping. It is not necessary, though, to experience harms to be harmed. People are knocked unconscious and die; they are harmed, yet unaware. True, being peeped upon is not a harm like that. Some insist that it is a harm only if discovered; but that is unconvincing. Were Zahira to find out about the peeping, she would be distressed. Why? Because of what she found out about, namely being peeped upon: were that not harmful, why would she be distressed at finding out? Zahira's interests extend beyond what she experiences. It is in her interests, given her feelings about privacy, not to be peeped upon.

A compelling and similar example concerns betrayal. If you are betrayed, you are harmed – even if the betrayal remains undiscovered and has no effect on your life's progress. We are not, of course, remotely suggesting that non-experienced harms are typically as bad as experienced ones. To be peppered by gun shot is usually radically worse than being in receipt of some secretive peeping.

What of the distress that Zahira suffers simply in knowing of, to her mind, the unsavoury activities behind closed curtains next door? In the peeping case, although Zahira experiences no distress, she is being used by Tom for his peeping pleasure. Mandy's activities, though, do not make use of Zahira. Zahira's distress results because of her *belief* that such activities are immoral; and her belief is her responsibility. Perhaps we should, then, disregard, or at least treat lightly, harms, assuming that they should even be considered as harms, that rest solely on victims holding certain moral or religious beliefs. On this view, we should treat lightly Mandy's distress at the placards – as also certain religious believers' distress at some pop operas, cartoon caricatures and prophets' names assigned to teddy bears.

The reasoning just given may suggest that privacy violations should merit little concern, for the possible distress at being peeped upon, or learning that private intimate information has been publicly circulated, presumably needs victims to hold the belief that such exposure is wrong. We should remember, though, that privacy violations sport the morally disreputable feature of the victims being used by the violators for their own satisfactions, without the victims' consent. Earlier, in Chapter 1, we met Kant with his emphasis on the moral importance of respecting people, of not using them solely as means to our ends. In contrast to those who suffer privacy violations, it is not at all clear that those distressed by placards, cartoons, and teddy bears' names, are being used in some disreputable way by those who cause the distress – though, of course, sometimes that may be the intention.

As for disturbances by beat music and the like, we may be generous and agree that the racketeers – so named because of their disturbances – were not intent on deliberately irritating Mandy and Zahira. Had they been so intent, then Mandy and Zahira would have been being used, akin to Zahira being peeped upon for sexual pleasure. Maybe the racketeers are merely living their lives as they want, just as the two women are trying to live theirs. Should we simply accept and be tolerant?

Mandy's lifestyle offends Zahira, but only because of Zahira's religious beliefs. Do the racketeers affect Mandy and Zahira only because of the women's beliefs? Well, no. Loud noises and even quiet repetitive noises – think of dripping taps – cause discomfort, stress and 'on edge' feelings in many people; indeed, a higher incidence of cardiovascular disease seems to be associated with certain levels of noise pollution. Such harms do not appear to be dependent on belief. But the racketeers may also feel tense, if deprived of their beats and mobile burblings; perhaps they too could suffer some physical harms, if repressing what they want to do.

'Lifestyles clash.' Is that all we can say – or are there not some relevant differences here? Suppose our starting point is people sitting on the train, travelling from A to B. Let us add some activities. Mandy reads. That usually affects no one else. She falls asleep; that usually affects no one else. Non-racketeers could listen to music turned down; that would affect no one else. Harms and disputes arise because the racket is being inflicted on unwilling others – unnecessarily so.

Perhaps the morally relevant feature here is the physical *one-way* imposition of harms, an imposition that offends the Golden Rule, a version from Confucius being: do not do to others what you would not like yourself. We met a version earlier in Chapter 3. Even if this glittering rule is accepted, it does not follow that it should take highest priority in our moral thinking. Further, it says nothing about what counts as 'doing the same'. Those who enjoy loud noise or leering at others may not mind loud noise and leers in return. True, we may avoid that objection by arguing that at the very least those who harm others probably do not want to be harmed themselves; but that returns us to our puzzlement about the nature and extent of harms.

$$\Upsilon$$

Displayed above are some factors that are relevant to the question of which harms are morally significant. Two points should be added.

The first is: as Mill notes, even when some activities are harmful, they may rightly be permitted. Car driving leads to accidents; but travelling benefits are taken to outweigh those harms. The overall benefit of free expression may well outweigh the distress caused to Zahira and

Mandy. We should, though, be cautious when told that because certain benefits clearly outweigh certain harms it follows that therefore some specified harmful means to those benefits are justified. Other possible means need to be taken into account. Here is an example.

Burglary prevention is, no doubt, of overall benefit. But it follows neither that burglar prevention through inefficient noisy alarms is over-all beneficial nor that there may not be better means of prevention. After all, those benefits arguably could be achieved by the fun of neon lights announcing across the property 'Help, help, I'm being burgled' or, more seriously, direct alerts to the police. We may even question the necessity of much building works' noise that distresses many people, reducing their quality of life: research could probably lead to effective silencers or quiet laser equipment. Some may immediately respond that all this would be too expensive or impractical, forgetting how over the decades authorities had made similar claims about the expense or impractical-ity of national health services, lead-free petrol and banning cars from city centres – the list could go on. 'Where there's a will…' as they say.

The second point to note is: let us not forget courtesy, grace – fellow feeling and good will. Muslims, in non-Islamic countries, who demand the right to wear the niqab in public may lack sensitivity to those coun-tries' traditions and ways of living; in response it may be claimed that prohibitions on religious garb are disrespectful of the religious (please see Chapter 19). Perhaps deep and troubling divides exist when religion enters the fray; but not with other frays. To return to non-religious examples, for people to insist that they should be free to do whatever they want, by way of leaking beat music, dirty shoes on public trans-port seats – for bars and media organizations to promote excessive drinking and loutish culture – is to display basic discourtesies and ill will. Arguably, many individuals who do these things know no better, or – and for an additional sad reflection – have nothing better to do.

Are these last points a manifestation of grey beard and age – or of some minimal sensitivity that many people quietly endorse and many others would endorse once seriously reflecting on not harming others?

10

SOMEONE ELSE WILL…

Jobs are not easy to come by in Little Rock, out in mid-West America, so imagine how pleased Goodman was when offered employment by the local sheriff. His luck was on the up – or so he thought, until the sheriff said a little more.

'You see,' said the sheriff, 'what we really need is a professional hangman. You're ideal for the job, in view of your skill with ropes and knots and shortly, I hope, nooses.'

Goodman gulped. Yes, he wanted a job – he had a family to support – but unlike so many of Little Rock's citizens, the Little Rockeans, he was opposed to hanging. He was a man of principle, at least on this matter.

'No, I really can't take the job,' stammered Goodman. 'It's a pity, but I'm deeply opposed to the death penalty. It's as simple as that.'

'Look,' replied the sheriff, 'I respect your view – though it's not mine – but if you don't take the job, I'll have to offer the position to someone else. Someone else will do the hanging. So, what have you achieved by your refusal?'

'Steadfastness to principle,' replied Goodman, with a sad expression, wondering how to break the news to his family that he had rejected employment so well-paid.

'That's not much of a principle, if it makes you look so sad,' beamed the sheriff. 'Anyway, what of your other principles – your duties such as feeding and educating your children?'

'I know, I know. Principles clash; but there are some things I cannot bring myself to do. Before and after the hangings, I'd have nightmares. They'd show me how morally wrong it would be.'

'That's just a psychological problem of yours, Goodman; but your duty is to your family – and, to repeat, if you don't take the job,

someone else will get it. Nothing is gained by your standing high and mighty on principle. In fact, between you and me, I really want you for the job as I know that you'd treat those awaiting execution humanely, whereas the other contender for the job, Badman, would taunt the prisoners as well as eventually hanging them pretty painfully. That's another reason for you to accept. Come on – take the job!'

Should Goodman go against his principle and take the executioner's job?

'Someone else will, if I do not' is often an attempted excusing factor both for doing what we think that we ought not to do and for failing to do what we think we ought. For example: a woman has fainted on the railway platform; we are in a rush. 'Well, someone else will look after her,' we reflect, as we dash by.

What should we advise Goodman to do? Looking at the dilemma solely in terms of consequences – outcome – regarding overall benefits,

Goodman, it would seem, should accept the sheriff's offer. It would help his family; it would make things not quite so bad for those on death row. Those factors should outweigh his discomfort. He may even feel good about himself, something of a martyr, in overcoming his principle.

True, other factors could be cast into the calculation, factors pointing to the opposite conclusion: for example, Badman may have an even bigger family to support.

So far, our reasoning has been directed at likely consequences. Furthermore, if Goodman's declining the job would lead others to reconsider their support for the death penalty, aiding its eventual prohibition – and were the prohibition to lead to a more flourishing society – then, still on consequential grounds, Goodman would be right in his refusal. But let us assume that, on straightforward consequential grounds, it would be better for Goodman to accept the sheriff's offer. Could anything still be said in support of Goodman's refusal?

This is where we may focus on what sort of person Goodman wants to be, and how integral his principle is to his life. Could Goodman live with himself, live with his conscience, if he allowed himself – as he sees it – to dirty his hands by being executioner? Perhaps staying faithful to his principle, regardless of overall consequences, carries its own moral weight.

An immediate response is that Goodman, in declining the job, is being self-indulgent, putting his own sense of moral well-being above helping his family. Yet is that a fair riposte? Can morality demand that Goodman sacrifice his integrity? Goodman has to live with himself. Perhaps that factor, though – of what makes for Goodman's flourishing life – could simply be entered into a more nuanced consequentialist calculation, with Goodman's sense of integrity given extra weight.

〰

The above consequentialist approach to morality rests on a detached perspective, a perspective that stands outside Goodman's particular circumstances. It seeks objectivity, taking into account the effects of the proposed action on Goodman, on the prisoners, on Badman, and so forth. Now, Goodman may picture himself lacking certain attachments – he becomes un-swayed by his wife, blind to images of hanging victims – but his decision and resultant action needs, it seems, the motivational *oomph* of his actual feelings, worries and concerns. One question, then, is whether morality, understood as totally detached, could ever provide that oomph. That apart, morality, it may be argued, demands special regard for certain attachments that Goodman has – his loyalties, relationships and what matters to him.

Goodman, in making his choice over the job, is making himself. His motivation may arise from his seeing himself as a man of firm principle against the death penalty, or as a man devoted to his family such that he will sacrifice certain principles for that family. In taking the job, though, he could be accepting himself as a hypocrite or coward, unprepared to uphold his principle.

What moves Goodman, and what should move all of us, are our projects and what we see as giving moral sense to our lives. 'Someone else will, if I do not', in itself, should carry little weight when we consider how we ought to live our lives – well, usually so.

Similarly, 'Others do it, so I'll do the same' also ought to carry little weight. Consider how some parents lie about their religious faith or their home address in order to get their children into the better school: 'Well, everybody else does.' Insurance claimants over-claim with similar attempted justification. That others do is not sufficient to shield us from condemnation or praise, for we have still chosen to be that sort of person who does as others do.

♈

Where does this leave us over Goodman and the job offer? Well, we can discuss with Goodman; we can draw attention to factors unnoticed. In the end the decision is his. He has to live with what he decides. He ought not to expect a detached answer which he must follow as a puppet follows the pull of the strings, the puppet being no agent, no person, at all. Of course, he could choose to behave *as if* a puppet; but that also is then his personal choice.

When important dilemmas arise, such as our dilemma for Goodman, there is a lot to be said for D. H. Lawrence's injunction, 'Find your deepest impulse and follow it.' Mind you, reflecting on some people and their deepest impulses, there is also a lot to be said for not recommending such action.

It may appear 'all very well' to encourage people to realize themselves, to be authentic, true to their beliefs, desires and projects; but sometimes it is far from well. Indeed, it may not be well at all. Certain deepest desires and commitments ought not to be realized. Reflect on the many horrors – lives trampled upon or destroyed – horrors caused by certain powerful leaders with deep convictions, being true to themselves. Evaluation is needed of the content of the beliefs, projects, attachments – for only some are worthy of promotion. The puzzle is often: which ones?

PART II:
POLITICS AND SOCIETY
What's all this about
democracy and the law?

The best argument against democracy is a five-minute conversation with the average voter.
Winston Churchill

Our lives are constrained by the state, by government, by law. Disobey the law? Well, the results are fines, imprisonment, condemnation – at least, usually so. What, then, justifies the state's power?

Most states these days keenly parade their democratic credentials. Their powers, they say, derive from votes of the electorate, manifesting the 'will of the people'. The near-universal adoration of democracy is, though, a recent phenomenon: look out for Plato and squabbling sailors.

Democratic states juggle with questions of how to rig – sorry, 'best arrange' – voting procedures and how to protect certain rights. After all, democratic majority votes can lead to some horrendous outcomes, for example, the enslavement or expulsion of minorities. As well as puzzles over rights, liberty and free expression, there are problems with justice itself, of what counts as equal treatment and fair distributions, exemplified in this Part II when we muse upon the dangers of health.

The perplexities here are within political philosophy, essentially a division of ethics. The moral and legal, we should remember, are distinct. Breaking the law is sometimes the right thing to do. Witness law-breaking protests that eventually secured votes for women. Witness civil rights battles in the US only a few decades ago, as well as recent protests at certain police behaviour that smacks loudly of racism and injustice. Witness, indeed, how the law typically treats, as criminals, those who break the law, yet who break the law only because they are desperate, being asylum seekers from far-off lands or our own citizens, hungry for food and shelter.

Let us not forget governments that, even today, condone torture, genocides and oppression of those who dare to speak out. Let us also not forget governments of the West; they condemn such barbarities while supporting those who engage in them – through trade, defence agreements and welcoming hands for the oppressive regimes' leaders and families as they buy up property in London and elsewhere. Clean rhetoric does not thereby make for clean hands.

11
THUG: PAST CARING?

Allow me to make the introduction. Here is a thug, hereafter named 'Thug'. He is a complete and utter brute. Thug wallows in out-and-out violence, violence on defenceless others. He is about to be sentenced for raping, torturing and then leaving a couple of women for dead. They survived, but have permanent injuries, both physical and psychological. He has terrorized neighbourhoods, beaten up frightened pensioners — and always with great glee. Thug stands in the dock. There is no flicker of remorse, no words of regret, no sense of guilt. Thug offers just a jeering defiant expression at the judge, jury and victims left living.

Let us ignore practicalities of what prison sentences could or should be delivered. Let us not wonder about the best means of protecting society. Instead, let us wonder why we are, if we are, concerned about Thug, *for his sake*. After all, many would defend his human rights and be concerned for his welfare. In summary:

Why should we care about Thug?

Some immediately insist that we ought not to care; others stress our humanity, to justify our helping Thug, reforming Thug, making him see the error of his ways. We may approach the puzzle from two distinct starting points, namely, whether he is someone who cannot — or who can — help what he does; that is, whether he is not truly responsible for his actions and attitudes — or whether he is truly responsible.

First, suppose he is not responsible. He cannot help what he does; he cannot help his anti-social attitudes, his violence, his jeers. He is, in some way, a victim of forces outside his control. That is possible.

We recognize that brain damage, drugs and unknown factors can cause people to do and say all manner of things. Thug, instead of acting as a free agent, is more akin to a tree being buffeted by gales, a ship broken by storms or an insect driven by surrounding scents and colours. In this case, we may think of Thug as needing – and deserving – treatment rather than punishment, aid rather than pain.

If, indeed, he is not responsible, then he may also, though, be likened to a raging bull or a mad dog – so why not put him down? 'But that is inhumane,' it is said. 'Although he acts like an uncontrollable animal, he still possesses human rights. He has the potential to be a responsible agent, to be a person and not just a brutish animal.'

But suppose that there is no cure for Thug. Suppose there is no potential. What then? Perhaps we cling to the thought that we can never be sure. Or maybe the motivation to care is irrational and in a sense mercenary. Society has supported his growing up; so, we are disinclined to give up on our investment, even though we should. Perhaps we simply cannot help but feel sorry for him; at some level, we empathize, compassion to the fore, reflecting on how dreadful it would be to find ourselves in his position, with his character.

Turning to the second approach, we suppose he is responsible for his actions. He happily embraces what he did, shows no signs of mental illness, other than his performance of the horrendous deeds. He vaunts being Thug. Why ever should we care about him in these circumstances? Two thoughts come to mind. One starts from him; one from us.

Starting from him, many religious believers insist that there exists a spark of goodness, of God, within us all – or at least a spark of divine potential. If only we could get through to Thug's spark, then he could be improved. Even if we cannot get through, he was made in God's image; that is why we should care. This approach is not exclusive to the religious. Humanists may hold a similar view, not in terms of godly sparks, but in terms of sparks of humanity. There may be the belief that, deep down within, there must be some good, or potential for good. In view of what Thug has done, though, and his continuing attitude, we may well wonder: why believe that there is any good within him at all?

Confronting the Second World War's horrors of the murder of millions – the Shoah, the Holocaust – some religious believers ask, 'Where was God?' The non-religious may ask, 'Where was man?' Both questions display a startled despair – despair that some human beings lack all sparks of divinity, all sparks of humanity, when dealing with certain other individuals or groups. Their eyes are closed to the humanity of those who have the 'wrong' looks or beliefs or origins.

Sometimes concern for Thug is based on simple thoughts such as that every human being is unique and valuable. But what is the relevance of his being unique? Each pebble is unique, but it does not follow that each pebble merits valuing. Thus, focusing on Thug does not adequately show us why we care; so, next, as promised, we should point the spotlight in our direction.

Starting from us – to see why we perhaps care about Thug – we may possess a horrible feeling that we could have acted as he did. We may recognize that we possess potential for injuring others, for unkindness, even outright brutality, both calculated and spontaneous. Reflect on the sheer luck, the good fortune, of our upbringing and chances in life. Could anyone, in normal circumstances, truly want to be like Thug? That simply could not be a life-choice, save by people so damaged in their upbringing or so overwhelmed by circumstances. Might we not have been so desperate, so hopeless, or so misguided, that we would have acted in the ways of Thug? Think of how violent and brutal people can so quickly become, when whipped up. Think of neighbours burning neighbours, sparked by political crises in Kenya, Rwanda, the Middle East – and many places elsewhere, including Europe. Think of the mistreatment of prisoners in Guantanamo Bay, Iraq and Afghanistan by US authorities – and of the horrors inflicted on innocent journalists and so-called heretics by various factions in the name of Islam. Sadly, many, many more examples of deliberately inflicted suffering could be cited, from ancient Rome to the Crusades, from 1970s Chile to today's China.

Returning directly to how we feel about Thug, the vexed and compassionate religious speak of 'there but for the grace of God go I', and the non-religious of our sheer good fortune in not living within such fervour and ferment.

♈

We have deliberately ignored what needs to be done to protect society; so, let us not consider punishment as justified on the basis of deterring others. That is another matter. We remain intrigued about our concern for Thug for his sake. Paradoxically, sometimes concern for him, as a free agent, is the attempted justification for punishing him.

Punishment is required, it can be argued, because it respects Thug as a person, someone responsible for his actions. This is a retributive approach: a vital element is that he suffers for what he has done. If he deserves anything, it is certainly not, for example, a five star hotel, by golden sands and lapping ocean, waited on hand and foot. But how do we determine what he does rightly deserve? Use of the 'an eye for an eye' principle is of no help in many cases and would lead to punishments that are morally repugnant. Would any decent person really, on reflection, want to mete out to Thug what he did to others?

What we should like, I suspect, is for Thug to repent, to be genuinely sorry for what he did – and to make some amends. This is secular penance. We may even countenance the thought that his recognition and repentance could be so heartfelt that he himself ends his life. Those who baulk at inflicting pain on the guilty should note that, in wanting Thug sincerely to repent and undergo remorse, we want him to inflict pain on himself. Remorse is not enjoyable.

Suppose Thug will not repent. Imprison him, torture him, execute him – whatever we do, suppose we cannot get him to see his ways as evil. Then, we are impotent. Then, for always, Thug claims a mysterious power over us, a power that unsettles us, that shakes our humanity or our belief in humans as made in God's image. We want to nullify, cancel, neutralize that power. If only we could break down the barrier that protects him from all moral concern, from all sense of humanity. If only we could get him to be human, to say sorry and mean it. If only…

Is that why we care about Thug?

12

MERCY:
TEMPERING OR TAMPERING WITH JUSTICE?

In the days of duels, let us imagine that a Sir Percy challenged a Lord Walsingham. It was to be a duel to the death. They met at dawn, pistols ready. The handkerchief dropped – the agreed signal – and they advanced upon each other. The noble Lord, nervous, fired two shots rapidly – and too soon. He missed. Sir Percy's pistol glinted under the rising sun as he drew closer. His eyes met those of the man who had so painfully cuckolded him. Walsingham was at his mercy.

Supporters of Sir Percy praised his mercy, for, although he was a fine marksman, his firing merely grazed the noble Lord. Sir Percy had not blown Lord W to his Maker, yet honour was satisfied. Sir Percy's detractors, though, whispered that he was no merciful man at all; he had performed the 'merciful' act in the hope that the indebted Lord would aid his further advancement in society.

Merciful acts are those that are less harsh than they need be, under the rules or assumptions in question. To be properly merciful the actions are grounded in compassion for recipients of the mercy. 'It is a fault to punish a fault in full,' remarks Seneca.

When somebody who has been harmed displays mercy to the agents of that harm, he may also forgive those agents; this may quell his resentment, his anger. Despite that, forgiveness is independent of mercy. Some women may forgive their rapists, but they are rarely in a position to be merciful and, even with forgiveness at heart, they may oppose mercy in the sentencing. Even if Sir Percy manifested genuine mercy for the noble Lord, he may never forgive.

'Blessed are the merciful.' Whether believers or not, people typically view mercy as a virtue, as they do forgiveness. Mercy, though, cannot be demanded: for mercy, we beg. Mercy is a gift which those in authority may choose to bestow, be the authority legitimate lenders with the right to repayments or kidnappers possessing the power to take victims' lives illegally.

That justice should be tempered with mercy is a common thought. To temper justice, though, is to tamper with justice – and such tampering seems to undermine the justness of justice.

Is mercy always unjust?

The puzzle arises from two presuppositions. The first is that mercy, although perhaps to be encouraged, is not obligatory; it is something that we may freely choose to give. The second presupposition is: Justice is demanded and is what people deserve.

Consider two court cases concerning two seemingly similar offences and offenders. One judge, Judge Merciful, shows mercy, delivering a reduced sentence; the other judge, Judge Strict, does not. Merciful seems to offend what justice requires. The sentencing difference also seems unfair. To look more closely, perhaps we need to separate areas where justice should be dispensed from other areas.

Judges should judge on the basis of law, not their personal sense of compassion and inclinations to mercy. The law may permit leniency, if there are mitigating circumstances. The different sentences delivered by Merciful and Strict may in fact rest on some relevant differences. Perhaps Merciful's offender, in contrast to Strict's, was filled with remorse or acted under provocation. The difference in sentences resulted from a finer awareness of circumstances. If so, Merciful is wrongly described as merciful. She and Judge Strict are judging according to the law. The leniency showed by Merciful is not a gift, but a legal obligation.

On the view above, permitted pardons and reduced sentences should not be instances of mercy, but of justice based on close examination of circumstances. If the close examination does not yield justification for reduced sentences, then reductions ought not to be given. Mercy has no place where justice should be dispensed.

If mercy, properly understood, has no place in the judicial system, what role may it rightly play in other institutions and individual relationships? School teachers sometimes, with changes of heart, cancel detentions. Parents may relent and, instead of stopping proposed treats because of their children's misbehaviour, they feel sorry, letting the treats go ahead. Perhaps, though, these leniencies, as a result of pity or compassion, are too trivial to merit accolades of 'mercy'.

In case stakes need increasing, let lives be at stake, with pirates, hijackers and kidnappers seemingly exercising mercy: instead of killing their victims, they release them – and not because of special mitigating conditions. These serious cases are, though, of wicked acts being threatened and then dropped; so, there already existed moral obligations for the hijackers and others not to go ahead with the threats. Hence, they were not bestowing gifts: properly speaking, they were not being merciful.

It appears that we are left with the relatively trivial cases, such as those cited of teachers and parents; but appearances are mistaken.

Within the context of duelling – and assuming Sir Percy and Lord Walsingham both freely consented – we have a life-and-death matter, possessing the possibility of mercy. To take the well-known example from *The Merchant of Venice*, when Shylock, having lent money to Antonio, pursued his claim for payment by way of a pound of Antonio's flesh, he could have exercised mercy, as urged by Portia, waiving his contractual right. If I break my promise to repay £100,000, the lenders could take me to court, knowing that it would result in the break-up of my family and my refuge in whisky. They could, though, be moved by compassion: they could exercise mercy and not pursue the claim. In waiving their contractual rights, arguably, the lenders are not thereby being unjust or shirking duties.

The overall approach outlined above is that in formal judicial cases, where justice should prevail, mercy has no place. It has a place where questions of injustice do not arise. And that may seem right.

♈

Our mercy puzzle may appear to be resolved, but the resolution is too tidy, too easy. Let us return to Sir Percy and his mercy towards Lord Walsingham. We may praise that exercise, but, as noted, Sir Percy was not obliged to exercise thus.

Suppose Sir Percy found himself in another duel, with similar dishonour at stake and similar vulnerability of his opponent, but now facing someone else, say, Lord Willingham. Sir Percy, on this occasion, chooses no exercise of mercy. Has he not now acted unfairly? He showed mercy to Walsingham but not to Willingham. To be fair, he ought to have treated them in the same way. Further, if Sir Percy was right to exercise mercy with Walsingham, ought not others to exercise mercy in similar circumstances?

Once again, as with our discussion of Judges Merciful and Strict, mercy is losing its flavour of being a voluntary gift bestowed. If it is justified in one case, then fairness dictates that it should be applied in similar cases. Mercy would then be no gift to give, but a quality demanded of us; yet then, paradoxically, it is no longer mercy.

Humans that we are, on occasion we act with caprice: we value exceptions; we value showing greater kindness for some over others, despite offence to fairness. That is being merciful. It is unsurprising that we should have such muddles in our lives. After all, we are human – all too human.

13

SQUABBLING SAILORS: IF THIS BE DEMOCRACY...

When seriously ill, you are well advised to visit a doctor, consultant or nurse. If your shoes need to be repaired, sense suggests you should nip to cobblers versed in their trade. To learn the mandolin – well, being taught by mandolin players is best. The call is for experts. No one rational would seek submission to surgeons anatomically ignorant, or want their pianos tuned by those poor at tuning. With regard to how best to solve mathematical, medical and musical problems, we do not urge, 'Let us be democratic'; we do not seek decision by majority votes. Instead, we seek expertise. We do so because we know that majority votes are unreliable means for acquiring what is required where skills and knowledge are concerned. Why, then, turn to the democratic vote to be well governed? As Winston Churchill once quipped, five minutes with average voters should shatter any faith in democracy.

Democracy is pithily exemplified, in Abraham Lincoln's words, as government *of* the people, *by* the people, *for* the people; but nations possess different criteria for what counts as 'the people' and rule 'of', 'by' and 'for'. Rule 'by the people' means by adults, some informed, many misinformed, voting for representatives or in referendums. Many vote on the basis of self-interest, others on what they perceive to be best for the country overall. The rule may be by so-called majority votes derived from a rag-bag of differently sized constituencies on a 'first past the post' system or on a proportional basis. Whichever means are deployed, there is no good reason to believe that the resultant government and policies will be best or even much good, or even representative of a mysterious 'will of the people'.

Judging what is good for society requires assessments of economics, morality and sociology, involving the causes of crime, alienation and

YES MISS, YOU DID ORDER THE FILET MIGNON, BUT WE ALL VOTED YOU SHOULD HAVE BANGERS AND MASH

illness, and the socio-economic consequences of taxation levels, nuclear power and going green. No one sincerely believes that the majority of the electorate, or even a significant minority, have much understanding of those matters. True, where experts disagree, the expert majority may be followed; democracy, though, gives the vote, not to experts, but to virtually all; and the 'all' easily swamps those few with relevant expertise.

Why be democratic?

The above anti-democratic considerations derive from Plato's dialogue *Republic*, written two and a half thousand years ago. Plato reminds us that, when on a ship, we should prefer to be navigated by the expert navigator, not by squabbling sailors – and not by squabbling sailors even if we are the sailors, voting on likely weather conditions and the location of hazards.

Plato's squabbling sailors may be seen as the mob – rule by the mob being an ochlocracy, distinguished in the ancient world from democracy. 'Democracy', in Plato's times, applied to rule by citizens of a certain status: it could be a direct democracy, where relevant citizens would gather in the city's square, argue and then directly vote on proposals. Because of this ancient understanding, James Madison, a founding father of the US, described the States as a republic rather than a democracy.

Today's democracies are very different from the ancients'. Today's are usually orientated to professional politicians competing for votes to become the people's representatives. The voting mechanisms are likely to give power to representatives who are persuasive and charismatic, with commercial support. That is one reason why, in some ancient democracies, the leaders would be selected by lottery: it avoids the charismatic charmers having unfair advantage over the plain and bland.

What is wrong with Plato's argument? Plato's ship analogy may be used to attack his position. Plato's navigator is no regular navigator who merely sails his passengers to their chosen destination. Plato's navigator sees his professional duties as extending to choice of routes and destination. It is as if a waiter's role is not merely to take your order and serve dinner, but also to tell you what you must eat. Mind you, this happens in some restaurants.

The above criticism of Plato's analogy has its own defects. It suggests that there are significant areas of political decision-making that should be determined simply by what people happen to want. At the restaurant, I may fancy lamb today rather than salmon. Society, though, is far from that simple. Even in the restaurant, there could be discussion about which is better for me, given my heart condition or concern for animal welfare. Citizens may mistakenly think, for example, that their best interests and society's are served by tax reduction for those already relatively well-off.

The criticism of Plato's analogy may also give rise to the crude and mistaken idea that, with regard to values, one person's opinion and hence vote is as good as another's – as if 'anything goes' with regard to what is right and what is wrong. Plato reminds us, albeit with exaggeration, that we can make mistakes about routes and destinations – about what is worthy of desire and which values a society should prize. This may point to the ideal – very much an ideal – of a small direct democracy in which well-informed people debate and discuss, reaching a unanimous view about the best way to run their society. There is, though, no reason to think that, even with maximum good will – with all voters intelligently seeking the best for society – there would be agreement about the best means and ends. Reflection and a moral sense, for example, lead well-meaning people to value fair treatment; but disagreements still arise over what counts as fairness in, say, taxation, salary levels, university admissions and welfare benefits.

♈

Priorities conflict. Democratic voting is machinery for delivering decisions; and, whatever the decisions, voters have at least participated in the mechanism. That may increase the likelihood of consent to the resultant government and laws. You as voter take part; but, of course, if the electoral mechanism delivers a result opposed to your vote – if you are in a minority – then you may be alienated by the result, with your liberty infringed. You may have voted for voluntary euthanasia, legalized brothels and high levels of inheritance tax, yet the elected government legislates in a different direction. You cannot then identify with that society's values.

People remain part of the electoral process, even when their voting choices are severely limited and ineffectual. Participating thus is but an illusory advantage; yet politicians do, at least, have to battle for votes, so they seek to appeal to many of those likely to vote. The appeal, though, is typically in terms of voters' perceived short-term interests.

More fundamentally, perhaps, democracy is valuable because it promotes equality and liberty. With the exception of children, the insane and certain other groups, everyone has a right to vote. Hence the voters, it is said, are governing themselves: they are autonomous agents rather than recipients of diktats. That is, though, highly misleading – for, as mentioned, many voters of minority groups may well suffer laws opposed to their preferences; and the democratic machinery is such that even the majority of voters rarely have supported the party in power and the laws that result.

Maybe democracy is valuable because it emphasizes respect for people's rights (when it does). It is valuable not so much because of the right to vote, but because of the rights that impose vetoes on how others may behave. Vetoes protect individuals from tyrannies, be they of the majority, of custom, of a powerful state, of religious authorities – or, indeed, of minorities seeking to take control.

Plato's ship metaphor leads us well: democracies need navigators to navigate us away from tyrannies, whatever the votes may be. The perennial problem is that we do, of course, have conflicting and muddled aims. At least democracies allow the muddle to be voiced through freedom of expression. It is that muddled voice which gives us variety and criticism. Democratic institutions, though, do not provide the space only for a plurality of voices, but also for a plurality in ways of living, be those ways religious or secular, austere or fun-loving, horizontal or vertical. Democratic institutions, in the spirit of democracy, would permit neither majorities nor minorities to compel everyone to sing from one and the same hymn-sheet of life.

And so, as recommended by E. M. Forster many decades ago, despite its illusions, inefficiencies and dangers, democracy arguably does merit the 'two cheers'.

14
VOTE! VOTE! VOTE?

It's election day. You are a keen citizen of a democratic country, with a genuine choice between the parties and candidates. You know which party you want to win, so you are about to vote. But why bother?

'I want to come to the aid of my party and help it achieve success. By voting, I shall be doing my bit.'

That could be a good reason on some very exceptional occasions – but I bet this occasion is not one. I bet you live in a constituency in which you have no reason to think that the successful candidate will win by one or even just a few votes. Your vote, in such circumstances, will make no difference to the electoral outcome in your constituency. And even if it did, think how unlikely it is that whether your party gains power hangs on whether your preferred candidate is elected.

'Surely, my vote will make a teeny difference.'

Suppose you do vote. What difference would you have made? If your candidate wins, then she'll win by one more vote than she would otherwise have done. If your candidate loses, then she'll lose by one fewer vote than otherwise.

'Well, that is a difference.'

But that is no difference with regard to who wins and who loses. And the difference it does make with regard to the size of the win is negligible. No one seriously thinks that a candidate who receives 29,547 votes would be so sensitive that she would be even happier had she received 29,548. No one seriously thinks that other voters will be more impressed by that extra one vote of support for your chosen candidate. It would be better, instead of voting, to do the ironing, stroke the cat or visit your lonely neighbour.

'But what if everyone thought like this?'

I guess your ironing would be done ever so quickly, your cat may get scared and your neighbour would be overwhelmed.

'Don't be silly. I mean, what if everyone decided not to vote?'

If everyone followed my reasoning, then arguably there would be undesirable consequences. But not everyone is going to follow the reasoning and think in this recommended way. So the 'What if everyone…?' test is redundant.

Why vote?

Some things that we do make only a very small difference – maybe a difference that we do not even notice, yet none the less a difference. If we join others who are also making only a very small difference, we may contribute to an overall big difference. In times of water shortage, cutting down my water use will not be noticed, but it does contribute in a teeny way to the overall reduction. In a tug-of-war, perhaps my contribution to my team's tugging is puny and my team would still win without it, yet, by joining in, I am helping to secure the winning outcome; other members of the team need not tug quite so much.

Voting is different. Suppose that I do not vote. If my candidate loses by more than one vote, then had I cast my vote I should still not have helped her to win. If my candidate wins, then had I cast my vote I should not have made a difference to the fact that she won.

There are some reasons to vote that may stand up. You may feel it is your duty as a citizen. Mind you, it would be a curious duty, seeing that it is one without point. You may simply enjoy taking part or being seen to be casting your vote. In sceptical mode, we may endorse Mark Twain's observation, 'If voting made any difference they wouldn't let us do it.' Allow me to add: feel free to take part in pointless exercises if you want, but would it not be more valuable to be seeing that lonely neighbour or getting the ironing done?

♈

What if everyone thought that way? That refrain fascinates many people, including moral philosophers. The thought is that morality must generalize. We should not ask, 'What difference will it make if I do not vote – or if I walk on the grass or pick the flowers?' After all, no one will notice. The question to ask is, 'What difference would these actions make, were everyone to do the same?' It is a generalization test.

Let me give the generalization test a run for its money. Suppose that I really should take into account the consideration, 'What if everyone…?' What if what exactly? What if everyone who knew lots of other people were going to vote decided not to vote and do something more worthwhile? There is now a muddle over how to include or exclude knowledge that many people will in fact vote. Maybe I should ignore all facts about anybody else voting and act as if I am going to be the sole voter. Then my voting becomes highly, highly important, making the electoral outcome hang on my vote. Were that right, I should risk life and limb to vote. But that cannot be right – for I surely do not remotely rate my voting as *that* important.

We need to return to what is actually, in all likelihood, going to happen, rather than to the 'What if…?'s. What others do is sometimes affected by what I do. If I am the Prime Minister's partner, the latest pop group idol or a charismatic drug-crazed model, then, announcing that I cannot be bothered to vote may well influence others not to vote. Most of us lack such influence. So it looks like ironing, cat-stroking or neighbour-visiting should be our task at the next election.

Mind you, I strongly recommend that you do not spread this argument around.

15
MAN OR SHEEP?

Thomas Hobbes — we encountered him when thinking about self-interest — wrote that man's life was 'solitary, poor, nasty, brutish, and short'. The obvious reply is, 'It could have been worse, Thomas; it could have been solitary, poor, nasty, brutish — and long.'

Hobbes was describing life before the existence of a state, government and law. Humans are competitive. They lack reason to trust each other, unless there is a powerful authority that sets laws and punishes law-breakers. In a state of nature, individuals would be in constant conflict or, at least, always on their guard, insecure, and ready for battle. The state of nature, of life pre-government, is a state of war. With the state of nature so horrible, human beings would obviously want to escape into something better. According to Hobbes, they would come together and agree on a sovereign, an absolute authority, to represent and rule over them, giving them security and opportunity to lead reasonable lives.

There are many Hobbesian puzzles, not least why individuals in the state of nature would risk trusting each other to keep any agreement. Let us, though, not worry about how government arises. Here we are, living within a state. Let us assume we have a government democratically elected. Whatever the degree of democracy, laws are imposed that restrict what we may do. We may disapprove of some laws because of certain moral or religious principles; we may disapprove of other laws simply because they prevent us from getting what we want. The general concern becomes: by what authority does any government rightfully rule over us?

Why should we obey the state and its laws?

We may answer in practical terms. We obey the law because we are scared of the consequences of disobedience, not wanting to risk fines and imprisonment. The rational thing to do, given the aim of getting on with our lives as best we can, is to obey. When asked whether man or mouse, some of us tend to squeak and take the cheese. Even more so may most of us squeak, when the tentacles of the law and the long arm of the police take hold. We mice may, indeed, be more akin to sheep, sheepishly following each other in our general obedience. Our puzzle though is what, if anything, makes obeying the law the *right* thing to do – even if we could get away with disobeying.

Many of us benefit because of the state's existence: we are defended from others, receive state education, health services, in return for paying taxes. We are better off with law than without. So, we are obligated, in return, to obey the laws that confer those benefits. One immediate objection is that this justification for lawful obedience fails to work for those who overall do not benefit. A significant number do very badly, sleeping rough, being denied state benefits, and being avoided by those better off. Why should they obey? Also, some at society's top may argue that they contribute more than they receive – probably forgetting that they secured the more because of society's stability and protection of gross inequalities, often inherited.

Even when overall we do benefit from the state's existence, it does not follow that we are under any obligation to the benefactor. Did we ever sign up, agreeing that we would accept benefits in return for obeying the law? If someone buys us a drink, without our asking, are we under an obligation to buy one in return?

Reference to 'signing up' casts us along another line, a line orientated towards the 'social contract'. What justifies the state and our obedience is that we consented to the set-up. Some philosophers, John Locke, for example – probably the most influential political philosopher from the seventeenth century – believed that historically some individuals made contracts to be governed by an authority acting in their interests, leading to our societies. Of course, there is no reason to believe in such historical events; but, even if they occurred, what relevance do they have for us today? We were not around hundreds of years ago, engaging in any contractual deals.

The response to that last thought is to spot features of our current lives that may indicate consent. We make use of the state's services; in Britain, we travel freely on the King's highway, notes Locke – well, today the Queen's highway. This shows that we tacitly consent to the state – or does it? Just because we remain in this country, using its facilities, it does not follow that we consent: after all, what other options are available? Can most people afford to go elsewhere? Would other countries, with acceptable laws, permit entry? It is, notes David Hume, key eighteenth-century philosopher and historian, as if we find ourselves on a ship in the middle of the ocean, with the captain making the point that, if we disapprove of his orders, we are free to leave.

$$\gamma$$

Rationality is often wheeled out, to come to the rescue. True, we were not involved in any original social contract; true, our remaining within our society fails to establish consent. But suppose we were rational, not yet in a society, and needing to create society's basic principles. Suppose, too, we were ignorant of our sex, race, abilities and the position we probably would reach in society, be it through chance or talent. In such an original position, behind a 'veil of ignorance', where everything is fair between us, our thinking, even though we remain as individuals, would not be distorted by a distinctive self-interest differing from the self-interest of others. Rather, our common rationality and interests should lead us to see and accept what would constitute fair laws, benefits and rights for all. Behind the veil of ignorance, it would seem rational to consent to a society that permitted basic freedoms, did not discriminate between individuals on irrelevant grounds, and provided welfare benefits for when things go badly. After all, behind the veil of ignorance, we have no idea whether we may end up belonging to minority groups or hitting hard times. If our current society possesses the features it would be rational to consent to behind the veil, then our obedience today is justified by this hypothetical consent, by what is seen as a hypothetical contract.

The response, by way of jibe, is that hypothetical contracts are not worth the paper they are *not* written upon. Hypothetical consent is not consent. The jibe, though, misses the point. Justifications can rightly involve hypotheticals. Why did you battle with the man, yanking him from the cliff's path, despite his protests? 'Because, had he been sober, he would have consented to the yanking, to save him from risking a fatal fall.'

The resort to the veil of ignorance, to rationality and to consent, even if hypothetical, raises its own puzzles. Quite what does rationality involve behind such a veil? Is it rational, for example, to place liberty higher than greater welfare benefits requiring higher levels of taxation? Further, once in society, if now convinced that eternal life demands obedience to God, it would be rational to oppose liberal laws that were once appealing, when ignorant and behind the veil.

Whatever justifications are offered for general obedience to the state, sometimes we morally ought to disobey. Had only many, many consulted their humanity instead of the law, various atrocities, instituted by governments, could have been avoided. Had only many, many opened themselves to fellow feeling rather than going along with the mice and the sheep…

Mind you, that is so easy for me to say and you to read as, in all likelihood, we sit reasonably well off, looking at this book, not having to stand up and be counted – and also not scraping a living in desperate circumstances, on the point of starvation. Recall Chapter 8 and Mr Miller's fortunate circumstances compared to Herr Müller's. Many of us are fortunate – through good fortune. We form a minority. We are cocooned from millions of dispossessed in the world for whom life is certainly, to return to Hobbes, nasty, brutish and short.

16
'I SHOT THE SHERIFF'

Sheriff has been seriously wounded while trying to stop Bandit's raid on a remote ranch. He clings on to his faithful horse, which gallops him back to Little Rock (as faithful horses do); Bandit returns to the Bandit family in its mountain hideaway. Bandit boasts, 'I shot the sheriff,' shows off his ill-gotten gains and initiates sustained celebrations. Back in Little Rock, beloved Sheriff is tended by the Little Rock doc, while a lynch mob sets off in search of Bandit. Sheriff, man of the law, makes clear his opposition to any lynching – 'I'm only shot, not killed. Bring Bandit back alive!' – but he (rightly) fears the worse, both for Bandit and for respect towards the law.

Celebrations in the hideaway are so noisy and drunken that Mob, after a few days' riding, has little difficulty in finding the required bandit. Bandit is lynched. Mob returns to Little Rock, where the Little Rock doc still struggles to keep Sheriff alive. Doc does his best – but his best is not good enough (no doubt aided by Doc's propensity for gin). A few weeks later, Sheriff dies from his wounds, still displeased by the lynching. It is worth noting that we already have a puzzle: given his gin-soaked ineptness, should the doctor be held directly responsible for Sheriff's death rather than Bandit? Let us place that matter to one side by making Doc a highly competent teetotal doctor. Bandit undoubtedly killed Sheriff; he died of the wounds from Bandit's gunshots.

When Bandit killed him may be thought to be baffling. Did he kill him when he shot him? That is highly implausible: Sheriff remained alive for weeks after the shooting and so there is no way he could have been killed by the shooting, *at the time of the shooting*, while yet going on living afterwards. Did Bandit kill him at the point when he died? That too seems implausible, for when Sheriff died, Bandit had been dead for a few weeks, lynched by Mob. How could a dead man, in these circumstances, kill? It is not as if Bandit's corpse swung round in the noose and gave Sheriff a fatal blow.

Where the killing took place may also be thought baffling. The shooting occurred at the ranch but Sheriff was never dead at the ranch. He died in Little Rock, yet Bandit never went into Little Rock. When Sheriff eventually died there, Bandit was but a corpse in a remote mountain range.

When and where does a killing take place?

This is no mere academic question: the law needs to decide about such matters. Assuming Bandit acted intentionally (and that various other conditions were met), Sheriff's killing is a murder – but where and when did the murder take place? The location may be highly relevant because where a law is broken usually determines the punishment: in some places murderers receive short so-called 'life' sentences (maybe ten years), yet elsewhere they meet with the death penalty (an extremely shortened life sentence). The time a crime occurred can also be highly relevant, for which punishment is meted out hangs on the law at the time of the offence and the age of the offender.

The right way of looking at this may be simply to remember that the law needs to decide about such matters. For practical reasons, we do just need to make decisions. It would be a mistake to think that, by investigating the world, we can rightly conclude that the murder occurred at precisely this point or that point. Perhaps the underlying mistake is to think that there must be precision when there is none.

The facts may be, for example, that a murder occurred in Virginia and in 1892 – but Virginia, and indeed 1892, are pretty big. No doubt we can be more precise about the murder, but we should not assume that, in principle, we are always able to pinpoint a murder's time and location to a very high degree of specificity. A murder need not be space-time specific or have a precise location, akin to that of when and where a small alarm first went off.

Returning to Sheriff and Bandit, the correct description is as given in the tale. There was a shooting; it was fatal because some weeks later, in a different place, Sheriff died from his wounds. Legislators need to make decisions as to which laws should apply and, for the sake of justice, they need to ensure consistency. That is all that can be said.

$$\gamma$$

Or perhaps we can say more. There are many areas in life where the need to make decisions about which rules, regulations or laws should apply has not yet arisen. Imagine a football game in which a player kicks the ball a moment before being shot dead; a few seconds later, the ball ends up in the net. A dead player scored. Do the rules permit that? Not being a footballer, I do not know, but there is no difficulty in football games occurring without specific rules to cover that unusual eventuality. Or imagine a chess player makes a move, has a heart attack and immediately dies; his opponent studies the board, slowly realizes his position is impossible and resigns. The deceased player won – after his demise? Is that allowed?

We should not be surprised that what is true of people can start to apply after their death. Someone who has deliberately taken a poison, one which works slowly, only becomes a successful suicide when dead, not when she took the poison – but there is no clear answer, in such a case, as to when she committed suicide. Bandit became the murderer of Sheriff after his, Bandit's, death but that should no more strike us as curious than the fact that a woman in New York can become a widow because something happens in Shanghai – the death of her husband – and can become a grandmother because her daughter gives birth thousands of miles away in London. To think that, for there to be such truths, there must be changes in the New York woman over and above the changes in Shanghai and London is a mistake that (arguably) was made by Leibniz – Gottfried Wilhelm Leibniz – a German thinker of the seventeenth century. Leibniz's own life illustrates the point that changes in what is true about someone do not necessitate changes in that someone.

Leibniz sought fame and fortune, but died disenchanted. Only his secretary attended his funeral; he was buried in an unmarked grave. Subsequent researches into his vast quantity of writings (still not fully investigated) have led to significant reassessments: he is now a great and famous philosopher and mathematician, intellectually admired; yet nothing, of course, has changed in him, despite these new truths about him, resulting from the causal transmissions of his work over the centuries.

Usually what we do involves causal chains; and our focus is normally on quite what it is that we do, rather than the effects centuries later. Here is an illustration: Samantha poured the petrol and threw a lighted match, which ignited the petrol and set fire to the curtains, which caused the wood panelling to catch light which caused the roof to collapse, which caused the fire to spread, which caused people to scream… and so on. Small wonder that whether Samantha burnt the house down depends on what happened some time after the initial pouring and match throwing; but her 'doing' does not extend to years.

Developments in the preservation of frozen human sperm, eggs and embryos may well raise more questions – in this area, about when and where fathering and mothering take place. Oscar's sperm and Olivia's eggs were taken in 2007; fertilization occurred in 2011; the embryo was implanted in a womb in 2014 and the child was born in 2015. When did Oscar father, and Olivia mother, the child? Maybe they both died just before the sperm and eggs were collected; maybe they died in 2008 or 2012 and at different times. Some men have said, with a twinkle in their eyes, that they are not *knowingly* fathers. Give it time and both men and women may sometimes be able to say that – and be able, metaphorically, to say it even from the grave.

The grave may be a 'fine and silent place', but even there, where we are well and truly deceased – and perhaps long-timed deceased – we may yet become parents.

17
A BIT RICH

Without a doubt, we live in a grossly unequal society. Numerous people, through no fault of their own, scrape by on low wages or no wages at all – and, if the latter, are at the whimsical mercies of state benefits. The poor have pretty dreadful living conditions and unhealthy lives, with little scope to improve themselves. Their children typically find themselves following suit. Okay, some of these 'poor' are, I guess, scroungers and not really poor at all, but that does not mean we should ignore the many who are genuine. Society should be far more egalitarian; there should be far greater equality between people's standards of living and access to health and education – and far greater equality of opportunity. And then there's global poverty…

Polly – Polly Titian – is in full flow, interviewed in a pub near the Houses of Parliament. On her way out, she drops a pound coin into a beggar's hat and is then whisked off, in her chauffeur-driven Rolls, to her mansion in Hampstead; she needs to pick up her children, just returned from a well-known public school, before they all fly off to her yacht, moored near St Tropez. While on holiday, her children receive additional tuition; Polly wants them to do exceptionally well in their school examinations.

Polly – more accurately, Lady –Titian is an extreme case of wealth commenting on poverty, but she is no different in kind from many politicians who argue that private schools should be abolished, yet send their children to private schools; from religious leaders who preach sermons, wringing their hands over the world's dispossessed, yet their preaching takes place in fine churches bedecked with great works of art; and no different from world leaders, corporate, political, even celebrity, discussing global starvation at banquets with fine food and wine being served. She may, indeed, be no different from the many of us who agree that there are unjust inequalities and yet do little, so little.

We may explain Polly's position simply as hypocrisy. She knows what she ought to do – give away much, much more money – but she is selfish. Perhaps she is not weak-willed but ill-willed, even by her own lights. Let us not be satisfied with that response. Let us grant her some sincerity.

Can you sincerely want a more equal society while knowingly being wealthy?

'Champagne socialist' is the term that readily comes to mind but many non-socialist politicians are also committed to greater equality. It is plausible to believe that some – Polly, for instance – are sincere. She recognizes some obligation to help others: she makes small charitable donations and canvasses for electoral candidates who are for greater equality. She could, however, give much more, without dropping her standard of living at all. And she could give much, much, much more and still live comfortably, though without the chauffeur-driven Rolls, the yacht and private education for her children.

Excuses for her behaviour are available. She may confess to being unable to part with money, even though she knows that she should. Alternatively, we may see her as irrational, engaged in self-deception over what she truly believes; but we are interested in whether she can be justified in declining to help more, despite her attachment to greater equality. In view of the small help that she does provide, she clearly is not a person who insists, 'It's nothing to do with me.' Can her stance be justified?

Whatever she gave, she would make little overall difference; society would still be radically divided between rich and poor. That thought does not carry weight: she makes small charitable donations, so why not bigger? It is true that if she is solely concerned about the relative poverty of the poor compared to the rich, then her donations, however large, would make little difference; but it is not true that they would make no radical difference to the welfare of *some* poor people. Improving the lot of the poor is typically the reason for seeking greater equality and Polly could achieve this for some, were she to give much more.

Maybe she believes that she has no obligation to help to put right injustices, such as inequalities, that are no fault of her own; but it looks as if she feels she does have some sort of obligation in these matters. For example, she feels she ought to promote a more egalitarian society: witness her electoral work. It looks as if Polly is closing her eyes to what more she should be doing.

$$\gamma$$

How Polly views her wealthy position is relevant. We are assuming that she acquired her wealth legally but she may, none the less, agree that she is not entitled to so much wealth, given the many poor around her. Perhaps she was lucky on the stock market or inherited her wealth. It is curious that many people who praise equality of opportunity and the importance of reaping benefits solely on the basis of merit also strongly condemn the taxation of inheritances – as if what people inherit should be fenced off from all questions of desert, merit and equality of opportunity. Inheritances are typically as much 'something for nothing' as state benefits; mind you, if we think of parents and their children as a composite entity, rather than separate individuals, then taxing inheritances could be seen as akin to taxing a transfer of money from the left pocket to the right. There are, though, good reasons not to think of parents and children thus.

Perhaps Polly's wealth derived from her entrepreneurial skills and business ventures. Even so, no doubt, she could have helped her employees much more than she did and, indeed, her business success occurred within the existing unjust society from which, doubtless, her business benefited. She was also lucky in possessing her business skills.

There is a difference between thinking that a more egalitarian society should come about and thinking that you should help to bring it about personally. Were taxation increased and distribution of benefits changed, so that Polly's wealth was radically reduced, she may find that to be no problem at all. She would know that other wealthy people would be treated similarly. If, however, she were to reduce her wealth by her own charitable means, she would risk placing herself at a disadvantage compared to the wealthy who do not do likewise. She also would have the burden of deciding voluntarily to effect the reduction and, indeed, the burden of deciding which particular poor individuals to help – and can that be done without being unfair? Further, she may claim that, with her current wealth, she is able to influence government ministers and is, in fact, encouraging them to improve their policies on poverty. (She would, no doubt, hasten to add that her aristocratic title no way results from the influence of her riches.) The strength of these claims is moot. Whether they are sufficiently strong to justify her lack of significant donations to the impoverished and dispossessed is highly doubtful.

Polly may insist that charitable help makes the poor dependent on charity and it would be better to be in a society where people received decent wages. Surely, though, having an improved standard of living through charity is better than no charity and no improved standard of living.

Some deploy the mantra, 'wealth trickles down': vast inequalities ultimately benefit the poor. Evidence for that mantra is very weak; and let us remember, even if the mantra is true, it is no 'get-out' card, excusing the wealthy from helping the poor far more, be it through charitable donations, accepting higher taxation or, at the very least, not engaging in every trick possible to secure tax avoidance.

Can we square Lady Titian's wealth with her commitment to equality? Are not the attempted justifications for the concerned rich hanging on to their money all – dare we say? – a bit rich?

18
'WOMEN AND MEN ARE EQUAL' – REALLY?

Where is the equality? The female differs from the male, the average woman differs from the average man – and individual women differ from individual men. They differ biologically – at the genetic level and, of course, in reproductive features and likely lifespans. True, individual men and women have features in common simply because they are human. True, although the average woman and man vary in height, weight and shoe size – in tearful propensities, sexual preferences and shopping desires – in these respects some individual women and men are equal. In view of the biology, it should be no surprise that the average woman and man differ emotionally, intellectually and perceptually in many respects. Individual men differ from individual men, women from women, and women from men – in numerous ways.

Talk of sexual equality is typically shorthand, or short-talk, for saying that women and men *should* be treated equally – that equal treatment is justified. Yet equal treatment should no more be dished out to women and men than to the healthy and unhealthy. Individuals with broken legs rightly need treatment, but those with unbroken legs do not; if they demand it, they may need a different treatment – from psychiatrists. It would be crazy to screen men for cervical cancer or women for prostate cancer. These are but reminders that treating the sexes differently is often the right thing to do.

The puzzle is quite what constitutes sexual equality and what justifies the demand for it. Another way of raising the matter, with both a general and a particular question, is to ask:

Which differences between women and men should be retained?

Should men receive preferential treatment to equalize female/male average lifespans?

The call for sexual equality is probably for an equal concern for both males and females and their roles in society. That equal concern is often restricted to some sort of equality in opportunities rather than outcome, yet they are sometimes entangled.

Typically, there is no good reason to promote the lives of one sex over the other – though occasionally there is. In a declining population, encouraging women to bear children may be a high priority, suggesting more resources for females than males. If couples are reluctant to have children, then there may be good reason to provide incentives for childbearing. These are not thereby examples of equal concern for both women and men. They would justify inequalities in treatment on the basis of a value such as society's continuance or requiring sufficient people of working age to support others. Also, they would not necessarily benefit women: they may be pressurizing some women who would prefer childless lives. In some countries, we witness opposite pressures, with childbearing being restricted.

A simple point here is that sexual equality, quite whatever it is, does not always merit highest priority. Further, equal concern for lives faring well does not mean that lives should fare well equally, in the same way. Some men want children; some do not. Some women do; some do not. We still have not, then, discovered the heart of the 'sexual equality' demand, if intended to be more than a vaguely expressed equal concern for lives, regardless of gender.

Sometimes the equality demand is linked to proportions: things are wrong when the female–male ratio in the same occupation or college course radically differs from fifty–fifty. Many feminist-minded women rail at societies where more women than men typically stay at home, raising children, without paid careers. Yet why ever assume that numerical equality is how things should be? Perhaps there is something in the biology that accounts for such differences; and perhaps there is nothing wrong in that.

Perhaps there is nothing wrong, but there could be something wrong. The numerical differences may result, not from biology, but from unfairness or coercion.

Unfairness first. Whatever the exact biological differences, there is no obvious good reason why, for example, one sex should have the vote but not the other. Whether there should be numerical equality between the sexes in parliaments, congresses and senates is, though, a different matter. If representative bodies ought to reflect citizens represented, should we not ensure the 'right' parliamentary proportions of philosophers, homosexuals, ballet lovers, even criminals – and, indeed, regardless of people's votes? The call for equality between the sexes among representatives suggests that women and men, as groups, possess some significantly different concerns. Paradoxically, this particular call for sexual equality is probably justified by some important sexual inequalities, inequalities not needing eradication.

Returning to employment, if women are rejected for jobs simply 'because they are women', then that is usually unfair. By contrast, it is not unfair if, for example, the drama requires male actors. It is not unfair to men if beauty salons prefer employing women, conscious of clients preferring the female touch or, at least, its image. Of course, if women and men do the same work, then they deserve equal pay. If – if – society, though, has customs, even legislation, whereby it is far more likely that women, rather than men, will disrupt their employed careers for child-rearing, then it is not obviously unfair for employers to prefer equally good candidates lacking such future disruption dangers. Or is it?

Such discriminatory practices may be unfair if women are forced or customarily expected to have children; coercion is touched on below. The practices may be unfair if it is simply assumed that 'because they are women' the individuals concerned are bound therefore to want children and disrupt their careers. They may not; and perhaps this could be established. At least on the surface, though, many women and men, without coercion, simply want to have children. Further, as a matter of biology, women will, therefore, usually have more time away from work than men, which, but for special provision, is likely to affect the women's careers. So, it would seem, many are arguing that fairness in such cases requires that special allowances be made for women in such circumstances.

Once we enter the arena of justifying allowances – an arena we are bound to enter – it is pretty difficult to find firm groundings. Here is a silly example. Some people may really want to be fire-fighters, yet seriously lack the appropriate stamina. Presumably no one truly believes that such individuals should be specially catered for, perhaps by providing special fitness training, drugs and reduced duties. Some people are more prone to illnesses than others – but here, in contrast to our response to would-be fire-fighters, we often do make special allowances. The puzzle here concerns which special allowances can be justified.

'Coercion!' alerts us to another important factor concerning sexual equality – and one that can lead to special compensatory allowances. A rhetorical reference is to the 'tame housewife': she has been brain-washed, 'tamed', into preferring to look after the family. It is not what she truly desires. Maybe she is akin to the slave who, brought up in slavery, knows of nothing better. In some societies, women clearly are not free to realize themselves, being denied proper education, subjected to veils, and much worse. In liberal societies, pressures and customs can still inhibit various free choices. Another puzzle is then: which inhibitions matter? After all, should we be distressed by male bank employees being banned from wearing dresses? More on 'exemptions' occurs in the next chapter.

When freedoms are present, if different outcomes persist, why should that lead us to think that something has gone wrong? Some argue that numerical differences between the sexes – more males are company directors, mathematicians, members of parliament – do show that the freedoms clearly were lacking. Inappropriate nurturing or cul-tural pressures must be the explanation; and so, special arrangements should be made for those who have suffered. But how is it known that such pressures must be the explanation of the differences? Yes, on many occasions – in some countries, on a vast number of occasions – we can spot the coercions, the pressures; but it is an unjustified and curious leap to conclude that when none can be spotted, they must still be lurking somewhere, if numerical differences are present.

A curiosity is the seeming assumption that, were numerical differences to result from what is 'natural' and biological, then they would be acceptable. It is as if it is believed that nurturing and cultures do not ultimately result from nature; yet, from where else can they result? Further, why is the alleged nature–nurture distinction thought relevant in determining how things *should* be? We often rightly want to interfere with what is natural.

These comments should not blind us to those millions of women, throughout the world, who are treated badly just because they are women. That horrendous fact should not blind us to another, namely, the millions of both women and men who are treated badly because of wars, religious intolerance, corrupt governments and uncaring others.

$$\gamma$$

Living dangerously, here is Arthur Schopenhauer.

> Women are directly adapted to act as the nurses and educators of our early childhood, for the simple reason that they themselves are childish, foolish, and short-sighted – in a word, are big children all their lives… Consider how a young girl will toy day after day with a child, dance with it, and sing to it; and then consider what a man, with the very best intentions in the world, could do in her place.

Unsurprisingly, Schopenhauer gets it in the neck from women. Quite what is the evidence he wants us to assess? And what is his reasoning? Rejecting Schopenhauer, though, should not lead us to insist, against all evidence, that typically there are no female–male differences in outlooks and emotions. Genuine free choices of women and men *may* well generate very different lifestyles and variable ratios between men and women in a variety of occupations – and, in some cases, free choices, it seems, *do* beget just such different lifestyles and ratio variations.

Arguably, the ultimate ideal sought should be that of flourishing lives for all. The call for sexual equality has led to increased awareness of women's differing needs concerning flourishing lives. There is also increasing awareness more generally of the significance of parenthood for many. Parenthood is often promoted through maternity and paternity leave – and promoted in some countries not fearing, well, not obviously fearing, significant population decline. The question then arises whether the special provisions for parenting should take priority over, say, special provision for the childless, male or female. The childless, to flourish, may require careers undamaged by taking long breaks for travel, voluntary work, even champagne drinking.

There are different ways of flourishing and different groups, for various reasons, typically secure more opportunities and more flourishing than others. Societies muddle through, selecting some groups to promote over others, but which deserve that promotion? Which discriminations are fair? Which equalities are worth seeking? – be they sexual, educational or even by way of monetary income and outcome regarding quality of life.

Most people accept that at least a reasonable lifespan is a central element in flourishing. Over this, in many countries, men are worse off than women, as, for that matter, are the poor compared with the wealthy. Improving the male lifespan would typically benefit both sexes. So, should resources be diverted to promote sexual equality in that regard? Perhaps the answer is 'yes'. Perhaps, then, men need a lower retirement age than women or extra health care or leisure hours. Should that be a high priority? Should that be up for discussion?

The puzzling heart of sexual equality remains. Which sexual discriminations amount to sexism, to discriminating against one sex without good justification? Which sexual equalities should – and should not – be promoted? After all, there just is a greater demand for female beauticians than male. Does that need to be changed?

19
EXEMPTIONS:
DOCTORS, CONSCIENCE AND THE NIQAB

In some countries and at some times, men and women are conscripted into armed forces, to fight for country and king – for dictator or democracy – yet in some countries and at some times exemptions are permitted on grounds of deeply held belief. Conscientious objectors may sincerely insist that 'in all conscience' they cannot be engaged in the military.

Catholic doctors, nurses and surgeons – in Britain at least – are permitted to refuse direct involvement in abortion procedures. It is their deeply held belief that such procedures lead to the destruction of at least potential persons; so they are allowed to discriminate against women needing that medical intervention. Adoption agencies of a Catholic persuasion would ideally accept only married heterosexual couples as adopting parents. The Catholic deeply held belief is that same-sex relationships provide no proper family home. Such agencies in Britain, though, have received no exemption from accepting homosexual couples as adopting parents. Is there not a puzzling inconsistency?

Sikhs, because of their turban commitment, are exempt from crash-helmet regulations. Employers revise their dress codes so that the religious may wear the yarmulke, niqab, burqa or crucifix. Yet the founder of the International Church of Jediism was prohibited from wearing his hooded head-dress, despite claiming it essential to his newfound religion, and men would usually be prevented from wearing skirts – and women from wearing bikinis – at City meetings. Mind you, perhaps that is not so puzzling: one may doubt the authenticity of Jediistic belief; one may doubt the overwhelming importance to men of skirt wearing and to women of bikini wearing, when in most jobs, serving the public.

Paradoxically, to promote equality – in employment and lifestyle opportunities – unequal treatment is required. Exceptions and exemptions are made, either in law or in practice, usually to accommodate religious beliefs. Yet what moral guidelines are there for permitting some exemptions, but not others? If doctors are permitted exemption from abortion work, why are adoption agencies refused exemption from accepting same-sex couples onto their books? If Muslim women are free to wear the burqa or niqab at work, ought not satirical atheists be free to wear T-shirts displaying cartoons of Muhammad?

We are looking at justifying exemptions from legal requirements and duties of employment, requirements and duties from which normally we should expect no exemption. We seek moral justifications.

What justifies which exemptions for which believers?

A basic ethical intuition is that people should be free to express themselves, so long as not causing unwanted harm to others. The intuition presents an equality concerning respect – though it raises immediate problems. Why, for example, should not some bars, with smokers as employees, be exempt from anti-smoking laws, so that both smokers' and non-smokers' lifestyles are respected? Let us focus, though, on exemptions sought because of people's deep values.

A person's sense of identity may be tied to religious values and belief. 'Asking people to leave their belief in God at the door is akin to asking them to remove their skin colour.' Of course, atheists cannot shunt off atheistic beliefs as they enter employment; yet we may agree that the proposed atheist T-shirt above is discourteous, even inflammatory – and inessential to atheists' lack of belief.

The niqab, burqa and similar, for many (even some Muslims) are provocative and barriers to an integrated community, when worn within a secular society; thus, France has a ban on face coverings in public, yet no ban on displaying the Christian cross or wearing the Jewish yarmulke. That manifests unfair discrimination, argue Muslims who disregard the 'integration barrier' point; and when employers prohibit the niqab and similar, those Muslims insist that too is unfair – their religious views are being disrespected – with the resultant lack of employment opportunities that others enjoy. To secure those opportunities, these Islamic believers would need to leave their religious dress at the employment door; but that dress is essential to their lives.

Addressing the alleged unfairness, we may note that, according to many experts on the Qur'an, the niqab and so forth are not required by Islam; so we may challenge the religious significance of the dress demand. Muslim women who insist on wearing such dress could be seen as disqualifying themselves from public employments. A response is that some women wear the niqab (or similar) through family pressure rather than genuine belief: if exemptions are disallowed, then those women would be all the more trapped, having to remain at home. The debate has hence moved into factual matters of belief sincerity and benefits for the women.

Let us, then, focus on Muslims and other believers for whom their religious observances are justified as profoundly important – for, surely, any special exemptions from the norm minimally require 'deep belief' sincerity. Were exemptions permitted, based on mere whims, we could be opting out of numerous requirements, from dress codes to vaccination practices. In societies that value diversity, conformity still has a place – in certain places. Many City offices require high collars and ties on men, while allowing low-cut blouses on women; others insist on modesty in female dress. What is socially acceptable gradually changes, but, in the main, people acquiesce in numerous conventions – until in conflict with deep belief.

The oft-made assumption that a religious basis is required for depth of belief, though, needs challenge. True, religious commitment can afford some evidence of depth, but so too can significant non-religious movements, sometimes for the good – maybe ecological movements – sometimes for the bad, as with certain political creeds.

With deeply held beliefs, people may sincerely claim that they could not live with themselves if engaging in certain activities. They may appeal to conscience; yet who knows what conscience reports? Were conscience or depth of belief sufficient to justify exemptions, deeply committed racists could use it to avoid anti-racist laws, and misogynist employers to justify paying women less than men. We need something more. For a start, the deeply held beliefs, the conscience consultations, must not be morally obnoxious. They must also, even if false, be understandable, as possessing deep importance for the believers. And sometimes they are.

Even the most fervent admirer of just wars may respect people who judge war morally beyond the pale. Even the strongest defenders of women's rights may recognize that abortion poses genuine moral dilemmas. The grounds for exemptions related to war and abortion make recognizable moral appeals to how we should respect the lives of others. In such cases we should at least be receptive to the possibility of exemptions: the deeply held beliefs are clearly 'other-regarding', concerned for protecting others. Of course, this does not remotely solve the puzzle of which exemptions, whether other-regarding or merely concerning one's own personal salvation, should be permitted.

Circumstances, for example, may be so desperate – too few soldiers; too few doctors – that the relevant exemptions cannot be granted.

Practical considerations, though, sometimes boost granting the desired exemptions. Pacifists are unlikely to be good soldiers, but they may give excellent care to the war wounded. Inevitably, competing and practical factors have to be weighed. Of course, some believers, if not exempted, may still refuse to do whatever it is to which they object – they may resign their posts – but, as a matter of fact, practical disadvantages can often cause 'deeply held beliefs' to be less deep. People compromise, juggling principles with comforts.

When considering how people with different entrenched beliefs can live together, there are bound to be grey areas: people and authorities need to adapt and adjust. Let us return to the adoption agency.

The Catholic concern is genuinely other-regarding: they want what they perceive as best for the children; but homosexual couples may see only homophobia in the Catholic stance. How ought we to view the problem? Assuming a sufficient number of secular adoption agencies – and a society which allows children to be religiously nurtured and taught (highly controversially) that certain sexual practices are immoral – consistency would suggest that the required exemptions for Catholic agencies should be permitted.

In the end, exemptions rest on practical and muddling considerations. This may disappoint some readers, but it is often a mistake to think that there must be a principle that is both right and also determines what should be done on every occasion.

♈

A war criminal's defence is sometimes 'I was just doing my duty.' If the laws are so bad, exemption from duties is no longer the issue: what is wanted is civil disobedience, where we have to stand up and be counted or, in the days of the CND, be counted while sitting down. But let us remember that old texts, just because they possess the accolade of 'holy', are not thereby reliable sources for when we should stand up – or, indeed, sit down.

20
'IT'S ALL RELATIVE... ISN'T IT?'

An adulteress is stoned to death – a slow, painful and humiliating death – in a country ruled under a version of *Sharia* law. In Britain today, no legal sanction is applied against adultery. Some people in Britain would consider her adultery immoral; others, possibly including her husband, would not see anything wrong. In Europe, the US and elsewhere, the great, great majority of people would assess the punishment of stoning as horrendous and deeply wrong. Some say this shows that such matters are relative. What she did was wrong relative to her culture, yet not wrong or not so wrong, relative to modern Western culture. Relative to that country's Muslim morality and law, she was rightly punished.

Many years ago, in a school debate, I spoke in favour of the motion 'Down with the mini skirt!' Supporting the motion enabled me to engage in the schoolboy humour of the *double entendre* 'down with'. At the time, miniskirts were fashionable; a few years later they were out. Fashions come and go – as do words for the fashionable – 'chic', 'cool', 'groovy', 'trendy', 'wicked', 'with it'. What we find attractive, daring, acceptable or offensive is relative to its context. Once, it is said, men swooned at the glimpse of a lady's ankle. Consider how red wine tasted to you as a child (nasty?) with how it tastes now. Contrast the reactions to grilled canine *bleu* served in Korea with those to the same dish served in Britain; to sexual relationships involving boys in ancient Athens with those to such relationships in the West today; or the reactions of Scots to bagpipe music with those of the English to such noise – I mean, sounds.

Cultural relativists typically extend such relativities to morality. What is morally right or wrong is, they claim, relative to society. Expansive relativists (as I term them) expand relativity further, some even to all truths. They say, for example, 'God exists' is true for believers, but false for non-believers; or 'the Earth is flat' was true for most people in the Middle Ages, but is not true for us now. They may argue that when I try to say that something is true absolutely – that is, not relatively – all I am doing is saying what I believe. I cannot get out of my own skin and find out how things really are. Some relativists argue that there is no 'really are' at all. It is all relative.

Are all values and truths relative?

Relativism, arguably, seems more persuasive when the seeming truths are to do with morality – with what we morally ought or ought not to do – than when those seeming truths are to do with the world around us. Moral relativism is supported by many Western secularists. Such relativists, considering the stoning discussed above, sometimes mistakenly infer that it is wrong for us to interfere with the practices of that other country. If that conclusion is put forward as a non-relative claim, namely, that interfering is wrong 'full stop', then it contradicts the relativists' claim that all moral judgements are relative. Such relativists cannot consistently hold to their position. That is a clear reason to reject *their* relativism.

Perhaps moral relativists are saying that it is wrong, relative to a group's values (presumably, their group's), to interfere with another country's (relative) values. If that is the story, I may find it interesting but, as it is only a relative matter, on its own it provides me with no good reason to accept their values.

Although relativism may seem naturally to go with a liberal toleration – as far as possible, do not interfere with others – there is no good reason why. Relativists cannot coherently tell nations, sects or individuals that they are wrong 'full stop' when they impose their values on others, for those nations, sects or individuals may well value the spreading of their (relative) values to others. That all moral judgements are relative does not justify our drawing the conclusion, even if taken relatively, that therefore we in this country *ought not* to interfere with the practices of another country, just as it does not justify drawing the conclusion that therefore we *ought* to interfere in the practices of another country.

Once morality is taken to be relative, there is the question: relative to what? To the society in which we live? To sub-groups – sects, political parties, unions, clubs – to which we belong? To some other authority? To me? Whatever the answer, we should then ask the relativists: is your answer just relatively true, that is, just true for you or your group? If it is, why should I pay attention to it? If not, then you are no true relativists.

Students sometimes profess a belief in relativism. They confront the folly of their professing when it is pointed out that if they are right, they ought not to complain that it is wrong for me to give them low marks. 'Our essays are good,' they insist. 'Absolutely,' say I, 'but as absolute non-relative values do not exist, your essays deserve low marks, relative to how I feel right now.'

Many left-wing radicals are drawn towards moral relativism because they want to respect other people's cultural identities. This leads them into the quagmire of trying to square their relativism with their judgement (surely correct) that women ought not to be forced to be veiled, undergo genital mutilation or be literally stoned to death. Of course, let me hasten to add, there are many ills in Western societies: women often feel pressured into having children, having a man or, indeed, having no man at all; both men and women are often made to feel failures, these days in Britain, if not on career ladders or if lacking home ownership or needing to travel by bus.

Respect for culture and tradition ought not to be taken to imply that all cultures and traditions should be respected. Such respect does imply that some respects are right absolutely, not merely relatively. A puzzle is where to draw the lines or, in fact, where to find the lines drawn.

$$\gamma$$

The ancient Greek sophist, Protagoras, is seen as the key source for fully expanded expansive relativism. 'Man is the measure of all things,' he said. His position seems to be that what is true is always a matter of what is true *for* someone. There is no such thing as truth 'full stop'. A quick (and correct) response is to wonder about the status of Protagoras' claim – just as we should wonder about the status of any argument put forward to defend relativism. 'All truths are relative.' Is that relative or non-relative? If the latter, then it is self-refuting, so we should reject it. If the former, if it merely means, 'For me, Protagoras, all truth is relative,' we should answer, 'That is all very well Mr Protagoras, but why should we take any notice of what you say? After all, you're only talking about how things strike you, not thereby how they are.'

Mr Protagoras stamps his feet and shouts, 'But I am the great Protagoras who has thought about these things and who has seen...' At this he hesitates – what he needs to say to influence us he cannot consistently say, for he needs to say that his arguments are better than others' and not merely relatively so for him. He needs to be saying that he has seen... er... er... the truth. Full stop.

Place a moral relativist in front of a screaming, innocent child being tortured. Ask her if she still thinks that what is being done is only relatively wrong.

Place an expansive relativist on the tracks before an advancing express train. Ask her if she really does think that it is only relatively true that she is about to die.

21
THE DANGERS OF HEALTH

You are a surgeon — and a bit of a philosopher. You are the head of a first-class team of organ transplant specialists that has an immaculate record of successful results. On your waiting list are four young people, all desperately ill and urgently in need of transplants without which they will soon die. Andrea requires a liver transplant, Barry a heart, Clarissa a pancreas and Donald a set of lungs. No donors are available. You are in despair. You did not enter medicine for money; you wanted to help people and improve their lives, yet here you are, watching four people die. These people have done nothing wrong; they would have long and happy lives ahead, but for their illnesses. If only organs were available, all would be well – for you have overcome the problems of tissue matching, rejection and so on.

As you are about to tell your patients there is no hope, you note the arrival of the new receptionist – a young man, namely, Eric. You know from his medical records that he is healthy. Your eyes light up. You ask Eric to accompany you into the operating theatre, to show him around, of course, of course... Your quiet reasoning is:

> I want to do my best for as many people as possible. By killing Eric, I am in a position to distribute his organs to Andrea, Barry, Clarissa and Donald, saving their lives. True, the world no longer has Eric; but the world has gained the other four lives. Four for the price of one is an excellent deal.

Killing Eric would be illegal, but what is *morally* the right thing to do? Killing Andrea or one of the others for the organs would not help, given their organs' conditions. If we do nothing, we lose all four, but, true, Eric lives on. If we sacrifice Eric, we lose his life, but gain four. In terms of quality of life – relationships, contributions to society – all the individuals are similar; so, the moral question seems to rest on quantity. Yet, curiously, many people are horrified at the thought of killing one innocent individual, to save a greater number.

Morally, ought you not to kill one person to save the lives of others?

Most of us, as noted with earlier quandaries, are pretty inconsistent in our views on the importance of *life*. (Let us assume, by the way, that we are here speaking solely of human life.) In war, many people readily accept that innocent civilian lives will be destroyed to secure the greater safety of others. Or, bringing the concern closer to home, many people will die sooner than they otherwise would because governments, instead of increasing spending on health care, keep taxpayers happy with low taxes. Further, some tax revenues fund the arts, prestigious sports projects and government entertainments. Were that money not so spent, it could be used to improve care for the elderly and poor, reducing the numbers that die each year. Our current society is such that many lives are lost merely to ensure a better quality of life for others.

You, the surgeon, are proposing, though, to kill Eric to *save* four lives, not merely to increase their quality. Hence, ought we not to support your reasoning? If we think that we should, we may be following, somewhat crudely, the moral doctrine known as 'utilitarianism', in which the right action is that which will (or is likely to) bring about the greatest happiness of the greatest number. Is that what we should seek? Most people would say 'no' to the idea. 'No one has a right to use my organs against my will,' they insist.

ᵧ

Many announce that we simply have rights over ourselves – self-ownership – and that it is morally wrong for anyone, against our consent, to invade us, take our organs or kill us, unless we have ourselves done wrong. Some push this further, arguing that we also have rights over our labour and the results of our labour; hence, most taxation is a form of theft. Such rights form the bedrock of morality and such a morality makes the individual king. That is the idea.

If the individual is king, it is morally wrong to bring about an innocent individual's death as the means to something else, however worthy, such as saving the lives of four others. Eric's death, though, *is* required for the others to live. Of course, sometimes killings happen as a result of doing what is morally right, yet they are unintended, even if foreseen. The killing of innocent civilians is not usually an aim of war; rather it is (or is said to be) a very unfortunate side effect. Such unintended killing of civilians is justified in a just war, it is often argued, and is morally different from the killing of civilians that is the intended aim of some terrorists and, for that matter, sometimes the intended aim of nations at war, increasingly desperate.

In contrast to making the individual king and distinguishing between intended outcomes and foreseen side-effects, the utilitarian ideal gives top priority to the overall outcome being maximum happiness. Whether deaths are side-effects or deliberately intended, if the outcomes are the same, then, for utilitarians, there is no morally relevant difference: there is no moral distinction between, for example, acts of war and acts of terrorism, *if* the consequences are the same. That is the basic utilitarian line, prior to refinements.

Even if we adopt the utilitarian stance, we may fault the surgeon's argument. Healthy individuals would feel highly insecure (as they do from indiscriminate terrorist acts), were there a policy of kidnapping and killing them to use their organs. Remember, those who benefit from the treatment may themselves become victims. Because of this insecurity, total happiness may well decrease in a society with such surgeons. Of course, this is so only if people know the policy is in operation. Suppose it were kept secret? Well, this is where too much utilitarian reasoning may damage our health – and politics (see page 313).

Looking healthy? Perhaps 'tis best to avoid walking too near a transplant hospital.

PART III: LOGIC

So much for reason...?

Do I contradict myself?
Very well then I contradict myself,
(I am large, I contain multitudes.)
Walt Whitman

Logic is often viewed as scary. At heart, though, it is simply concerned with good reasoning and avoiding contradictions – resisting the assertion, for example, that something is both true and false. If Socrates is a man and all men are mortal, then logically it follows that Socrates is mortal. That is a valid argument. If the premises are true, we should accept the conclusion. To conclude, instead, that Socrates is immortal would be to contradict those premises.

Certain little puzzles also rely on simple logic. Three logicians walk into a bar: 'Do all of you want a drink?' asks the barmaid. 'I don't know,' replies the first logician. 'I don't know,' replies the second. The third simply says, 'Yes.' The third rightly reasons that Logician One and Logician Two must want a drink, but do not know if he wants a drink; hence neither One nor Two knows if all three want a drink – whereas he now knows the truth about 'all three', given he knows that he is in need of the refreshment.

The simple points above are fine until we ask whether all statements are either true or false; until we wonder whether contradictions can always be avoided when thinking about what we know and intend; until we are reasoning about what others may be reasoning about *our* reasoning: look out for the game of 'Chicken!'

This Part III includes some famous paradoxes – perplexities that appear to enmesh us in contradictions – the Liar, Russell's Paradox and the mysteries of Hilbert's Hotel. The paradoxes continue to fascinate and worry philosophers, with ever greater delvings. The following tale is therefore worth bearing in mind; it was related by an excellently named John Wisdom, who was much influenced by Wittgenstein.

When an isolated community was introduced to the telephone, its expression for what the telephone delivered, translated into English, meant 'messages on poles'. Later, when the wireless became available, the expression for what the wireless delivered meant 'messages on poles without the poles'. What may appear contradictory, once explained, need not be contradictory.

We set off, though, with some fun – of a Princess and her suitors. Paradoxically, that fun relates to the serious business of nuclear deterrence. It is a splendid problem – if a problem can be splendid – but let me, here, own up to my favourite: the Card-Sharp Camel with her enigmatic smile, while dealing the playing cards. Now, how can we sort out the reasoning there?

22

ON THINKING TOO MUCH *or*
HOW NOT TO WIN A PRINCESS'S HAND

Cast ourselves into a kingdom, a kingdom ruled by the king and queen, a kingdom with jesters, princes and princesses, with dragons, dreams and damsels in distress. In our kingdom, there is a beautiful princess, the king and queen's daughter; yet there is stalemate: which young man should gain the princess's hand? The king wants his daughter to marry Prince Clever, who is indeed clever, though neither exactly handsome nor strong nor possessing a prince's charm. The queen backs a rival, Prince Not So Clever, who is assuredly not so clever, yet is handsome, manly and charming. Both young men are enchanted by the princess. And the princess's love concerning the young men? Well, she wisely lets it be known she could love either; she does not want to make enemies of her father or mother. Such is love in those days – and such is parental authority.

'We must set the suitors a task,' declares the queen, 'to see who displays the greatest devotion to our daughter.'

'What a good idea,' agrees the king. 'Let it be a mathematical puzzle and one that...'

'Of course not,' insists the queen, knowing Prince Not So Clever would fail any such test. 'They must slay a dragon. The first suitor to return with a dragon suitably slain shall have our daughter's hand.'

Now, that is not as impossible a task as it may sound; this is a kingdom with convenient dragons ready to be slain. Our princes, though, lack eagerness toward the proposal – after all, dragon-slaying is hard work and can be quite a heated affair – but, if it has to be done, it would be worth the effort for the princess's hand. The king is very unhappy at the proposal; his preferred candidate would be highly unlikely to win.

The king and queen argue until the princess pipes up. 'Let it be that one of the men needs *only* to *intend* to slay a dragon, while the other must actually slay a dragon.' At this, Prince Clever quickly bags the 'intention only' option, thinking that would obviously be so much easier than all the messy effort of slaying. Prince Not So Clever sighs, accepting that his slow-wittedness means that he will have to do the slaying.

'This is pointless and silly,' thunders the queen, then muttering, 'Prince Not So Clever is bound to lose – *intending*, which is all Prince Clever has to do, is so much easier than actually doing.' Yet the princess kicks her, politely of course, silencing her – such is daughterly authority in those days.

And so, it is decided that the winner of the princess's hand will be the one who completes his task first, be it the intending only, sincerely of course, or the actual slaying, starting at sunrise tomorrow. Before readers ask, the king and queen have a court mind-reader who can easily read minds for sincere intentions. If this worries readers, we pop into the kingdom future brain scanners that readily detect psychological states such as intentions. Now, the question is:

Who is more likely to win the princess's hand?

The puzzle centres on rationality and affects our everyday lives. In our question, we have added the caveat of 'more likely' as protection from readers who rightly note that we have said nothing about how strong the local dragons are, exactly how clever the suitors are, whether they remember the task next morning and so on. Assuming all is straight-forward, other than the tale's oddness, the answer, as readers may have guessed, is that Prince Not So Clever wins. He gets on with his task, slays the dragon, and marries the princess. What goes wrong for Prince Clever?

Prince Clever was, of course, eager to accept the condition whereby merely intending was sufficient to win the princess's hand. As the queen thought, merely intending to do something seems so much easier than actually doing. Indeed, we may well sincerely intend to perform feats, yet fail. Prince Clever mused upon this point.

'I need only to intend to slay a dragon,' he reflected. 'The actual slaying is hard work; so it would be silly to do any slaying, once, at sun-rise, I have already intended to slay… Ah, but that means that I would not be sincerely intending to slay after all — if I know that I won't then bother to slay.'

Prince Clever thought more. 'Ah well, I'd better slay the dragon after all,' he reflected miserably, but then hesitated. 'Hold on, that would be crazy, for I don't need to do that, once I have had my sincere sunrise intention to slay. Yet as I am aware of that, once again I should have failed to have formed the required sincere intention. Okay, I had better go and slay — but hold on…'

And so Prince Clever's reasoning looped round and round — and as the sun rose he still found himself unable to form a sincere intention. Whenever he said 'I intend', trying to mean it, his reason reminded him that he would not need to do what he intended — and he would have good reason not to do it, when the time came. Of course, Prince Not So Clever lacked all such quandaries; he went out and slew the dragon. Mind you, it was a little dragon.

And so it was that Prince Not So Clever married the princess. The princess pretended surprise, while within she smiled wisely. Such was princesses' wisdom in those days.

♈

Had the mere 'intention' requirement also been given to Prince Not So Clever, he might still have won. Being not so clever, he might not have become enmeshed in the clever reasoning of Prince Clever. The puzzle arises because, at times, it is rational to commit ourselves to doing something that, later on, it will be irrational to do. When we reflect on this, we see how rationally we should lose the motivation to do the irrational, once that 'later on' comes, thus undermining our commitment now to performing the task in question.

Had Prince Clever been cleverer, maybe he could have persuaded himself the requirement was that he really did have to slay the dragon rather than merely intend to slay: he would have been better off having that false belief. Or perhaps he could have committed himself to behaving irrationally in the future.

A particular instance of commitment to irrationality exists when nations hold nuclear weapons with the professed policy of 'mutually assured destruction' (MAD). 'If you strike first, we shall strike back, destroying the human race.' Now, we may need the enemy to believe that is our intention; yet we (and they) may doubt the rationality of our keeping to that intention. Hence, can we truly intend such mass destruction? Perhaps we need to persuade the enemy that we are sufficiently irrational to carry out the intention, yet rational enough in other respects. 'Chicken!' (Chapter 24) explores related problems.

The general puzzle here concerns binding ourselves over the future. Prince Clever needed to bind himself to carrying out his intention, blocking his ears from reason's nagging little voice, reminding him that he would not need to do the slaying, if only he could intend to slay. In more everyday scenarios, things are a little different. Reason may tell us that we should arrange circumstances to prevent ourselves from yielding to future temptations; yet paradoxically we may know that, when faced with those temptations, we shall see things differently and fully favour succumbing.

There is the ancient Greek tale according to which Odysseus knew that, unrestrained, he would yield to the sirens when he heard their melodious and beguiling song. Hence, he told his sailors to bind him to the mast and stop their ears with beeswax, ensuring that they would hear neither the sirens nor his orders to be released, when tempted by the song. Thus it was that, paradoxically, Odysseus intentionally prevented himself from doing what he would later want to do.

These days we rarely encounter sirens seeking to sing us to the grave. We may, though, somewhat more prosaically, be aware that, as the evening draws on, we are likely to eat too many chocolates or drink too much wine – manifesting weakness of will, as examined in Part VI with cream bun temptations – so we deliberately avoid buying these goods of delight on the way home. Yet we know that we shall soon be regretting that earlier decision. Did our past selves, so to speak, have a right to bind us to this sober, chocolate-less evening?

And as we puzzle that question, we may more urgently puzzle whether the local supermarket is still open – or whether, hold on… Isn't there some whisky tucked away upstairs?

23
IRRATIONAL PREFERENCES
or HOW TO PUMP MONEY

'What flavours do you have?' asks Lucinda, contemplating the home-made ice creams.

'Chocolate, cherry and coffee,' comes the reply.

Lucinda ponders for a moment or two, not exactly happy with a choice so limited. 'I'll have the coffee,' she decides.

The waiter takes her order, but as he turns to walk away, he remembers, 'Ah, we also have plum, peach and passion-fruit.'

'Splendid!' says Lucinda. 'I'll go for the cherry.'

〰

We all have preferences, often different preferences – and what we prefer depends on context, on the options available. Now, the Lucinda story generates a smile of bafflement: how can knowledge of the plum, peach and passion-fruit options lead her preference to switch from coffee to cherry? That seems paradoxical.

It does seem paradoxical; but we can tell a tale and the paradox vanishes. We hypothesize that Lucinda was initially unhappy with going for cherry, but only because it appeared to be the sole fruit flavour available. 'Maybe the ice cream maker lacks expertise in flavouring by fruit,' she pondered. On learning the availability of other fruits, Lucinda gained confidence in the maker's fruity abilities. With such confidence, she could go for her top preference, namely, the cherry – but only when other fruits are available. Her preference for coffee gains top place, when only one fruit is available. Context affects her preference between coffee and cherry.

With that background point to the fore, let us see if it helps with some preference paradoxes. First, I introduce 'transitivity'.

If I prefer apples to bananas and bananas to clementines, then I should surely prefer apples to clementines. That is, the preference relation is transitive. Many relations are transitive. If Maynard is taller than Naomi and Naomi is taller than Oscar, then Maynard is taller than Oscar. In contrast to such transitive relations, 'kiss' is intransitive. If Maynard kisses Naomi and Naomi kisses Oscar, it does not follow that Maynard kisses Oscar – far from it. And although Maynard loves kissing Naomi and Naomi loves kissing Oscar, it does not follow that Maynard loves kissing Oscar.

If you are rational, your preferences should be transitive – or so it appears. The classic Preference Paradox challenges the appearance. Suppose the following:

I prefer opera-going with Lucy to attending investment seminars alone, yet I prefer attending investment seminars alone to watching football with Sid. This makes perfectly good sense: I delight in opera and Lucy's company. In contrast, I dislike football and find Sid uneasy company. Rationality suggests that I should obviously prefer opera-going with Lucy to football with Sid. But does it? Paradox arises because I may none the less prefer the Sid football option to Lucy opera – and that could be a rational preference. Yet how? Let us set out the question in abbreviated form.

If I prefer Lucy opera to seminars and seminars to Sid football, can it be rational to prefer Sid football to Lucy opera?

Circumstances can be described where the correct answer is 'yes' and hence where, it seems, preference is not transitive. Suppose that I strongly need to overcome a claim by Sid that I am elitist; and suppose that Sid knows the choice is between Lucy opera and football with him. If I choose the Lucy option, I shall be exposed to Sid's elitist charge. Hence, I choose the Sid option, even though I prefer opera with Lucy to seminars and seminars to football with Sid. Rational preferences, it appears, need not be transitive.

Perhaps the paradox is no paradox at all. Perhaps preferences are no more transitive than 'likes', 'loves' and 'licks'. The problem with acquiescing in that conclusion is the danger of bankruptcy. More accurately, if we have intransitive preferences, then money can, in theory, be pumped from us – until it is all gone – with our gaining nothing in return. It cannot be rational to succumb to that. Here is the money pump at work.

In summary, I prefer opera to seminars and seminars to football, yet, intransitively, I prefer football to opera. Attending opera, seminars and football costs money – and let us pretend the same cost. Suppose that I have a ticket for the football and you hold tickets for the seminar and opera. As I prefer seminars to football, I should surely trade my football ticket for your seminar ticket – and pay you something for that trade, say, £10, seminar attendance being more valuable to me than football. The trade completed, you have the £10 and the football ticket. You still have the opera ticket. I now have the seminar ticket. Here comes the next stage.

I prefer opera to seminars, so I should be prepared to offer you the seminar ticket and, say, another £10, to secure the much preferred opera ticket. I do so. I now have the opera ticket, but am down by £20. You now have the football and seminar tickets and the £20. Here comes the final stage.

Because of my preferences' intransitivity, I yet prefer football to opera, so I should be prepared to trade my opera ticket and £10, for the football ticket that you accepted from me in the first place. The outcome is that I am back to square one, holding just the football ticket, but £30 down: that is not good. You are back with your seminar and opera tickets, and a £30 gain and no doubt a big beam. As you now have tickets that I prefer, you and I should commence trading all over again, with more money pumped from me – until either the money runs out or I see sense, either ceasing to trade or dropping my intransitive preferences.

The money pump demonstrates an irrationality in holding intransitive preferences, unless preferers enjoy loss making. Of course, someone with intransitive preferences, but otherwise rational and resisting bankruptcy, should refuse to trade; then, though, we must ask what justifies the refusal, for the preferences also provide good reasons to trade. Assuming that rationality does demand transitivity, we are cast back into the Paradox of Preference.

Let us recall Lucinda and her ice cream preferences. We thought of Lucinda as irrational, switching from coffee to cherry, until we understood the relevance of background fruit flavours. In the Lucy/Sid tale, the background, once entered into the preferences, may save me from intransitivity and hence from pumping dangers. Once the preferences are spelled out in greater detail, arguably the puzzle evaporates. Here are the preferences:

First: Opera with Lucy, no elitism displayed to Sid.
Second: Seminars alone, no elitism displayed to Sid.

But if they are unavailable, I may be driven to:

Third: Football with Sid, no elitism displayed to Sid.

Worse options would be: opera with Lucy, elitism displayed to Sid; and football with Sid yet somehow elitism still displayed. Whether I can secure my first preference depends on whether the choice on offer is between football with Sid and opera with Lucy. If that is the choice, and known by Sid, then I end up with my sad third preference – but that is better for me than declining Sid and appearing elitist, opera-going with Lucy.

ϒ

In the above, we have tied rational preferences to transitivity. What is disturbing is that we hit a new puzzle, when combining individuals' rational preferences, even when individually transitive. Consider an example of voting preferences.

Abe prefers tax reduction to increased overseas aid and prefers increased overseas aid to increased arts funding.

Ben prefers increased overseas aid to increased arts funding and increased arts funding to tax reduction.

Clem prefers increased arts funding to tax reduction and tax reduction to increased overseas aid.

Counting up the preferences of our three voters, we see that tax reduction defeats increased overseas aid: 2 to 1. Increased overseas aid defeats increased arts funding also 2 to 1. So, given the need for transitivity, tax reduction should surely defeat increased arts funding 2 to 1 – yet it is the reverse: increased arts funding defeats tax reduction, 2 to 1.

Paradoxically, even when members of a group are individually consistent in their preferences, there is no fair and rational means of combining the preferences to ensure no inconsistency can ever arise in the group's preferences as a whole. But should that be surprising? After all, even though separate groups of preferences of an individual may be consistent, there is no guarantee that the totality of that individual's preferences must be.

An individual – a human being – typically has a chaotic medley of beliefs, aims and memories, yearnings, hopes and anxieties, some to the fore, others submerged. As is discussed further, when meeting Fox and Hedgehog (page 286), some people are keen to straighten their lives – all elements must cohere – while others live with the chaos. Some homes are tidy, everything being in its 'proper' place; others are stacked with papers, paintings and panic. It may be difficult to choose between the two ways of living, but it is surely worth reflecting that order can be boring, whereas some degree of disorder, of chaos, can at least be fun.

24
CHICKEN! CHICKEN! CHICKEN!

'Chicken' is a game played by the rough and tough; well, only the rough and tough can face playing this version. Our players are two macho young men, Angelo and Berto, motorcyclists, bare chests bedecked with gold chains; lovers of revs and roar; of leather, rubber and heat; men out to impress the chicks; men who cannot face losing face; mean macho men of mean machines.

The game is simple. From opposite ends of a long straight road, they accelerate towards each other, chests puffed out with confidence and conceit, hair streaming in the wind. (Helmets? Not for true macho men!) They come at each other fast, driving along the central white line, getting closer and closer to a head-on crash. The one who veers away into the correct lane first (left, in Britain) is 'chicken' – fear, or good sense, finally taking over. The worst games are those in which the chicken chickens out pretty early on, quite a few seconds before a possible crash. We shall ignore degrees of chicken-icity.

The best outcome for Angelo is the one in which Berto veers away while he, Angelo, roars on, making Berto the chicken and Angelo the hero, receiving appropriate rewards from the chicks. The worst outcome for Angelo is that he chickens out, leaving Berto the road. The second best outcome (for both) is that they veer away at the same time into their respective lanes, just before it is too late. Some may argue this leaves them both chickens, but wiser counsel is that they both merit congratulations for their nerve, judgement and final good sense. The only remaining possible outcome is a stupendous crash – not exactly good for either but, in their macho world, not as bad as being the sole chicken.

Apart from the risk of that stupendous crash, what is the problem? 'Rationality' is, paradoxically, the answer. Yes, we are, counter-intuitively it is true, making Angelo and Berto rational individuals, as far as that is possible for people who play this game.

Angelo reasons: 'Either Berto will chicken out or he won't. If I keep my nerve, he might well chicken out before me; if he does, I win. But suppose Berto is not chicken: then for me to chicken out would be the worst outcome for me; remember, my machismo leads me to prefer a crash to such dishonour. So, whatever Berto ends up doing, I should hold my nerve, drive on, no veering.'

Berto reasons likewise. Reason tells both of them not to veer away, leading them to their worst but one alternative – and to the hospital (or the mortuary). There is a better option for both: to veer away just before crashing. Why not do that? Because if Angelo reckons that is what Berto will do, he may as well drive on and win; but Berto reasons likewise, if thinking that Angelo will veer away.

What if they secretly promise each other that they will both veer just in time? If Angelo is sure Berto will keep his promise, why should Angelo keep his? Macho men are ashamed of chickening but not of lying. Of course, Angelo would be aware that Berto would also be thinking that he, Berto, need not keep his word. Once again, a crash looks inevitable, if the players are rational.

Is it ever rational to co-operate?

This is no silly game. Imagine: Andorra and Bermuda are nations at loggerheads in an arms' race, in possession of the same conventional weaponry. Andorra wants to be militarily stronger than Bermuda: it plans to develop nuclear weapons. For Andorra, the best outcome is Andorra with such weapons and Bermuda without. That is the worst option for Bermuda; it wants just the reverse. The second-best option for both is for neither to develop nuclear weapons: nuclear weapons are costly and, if they both end up with them, nothing of value is achieved. Both having nuclear weapons is a worse option than neither having nuclear weapons. Co-operation is in their mutual interests; they should agree not to develop nuclear weapons. But why should either party honour such an agreement? From Andorra's perspective, if Bermuda sticks to the agreement, Andorra would be better off secretly breaking the agreement, developing nuclear weapons and achieving its desired superior position. And if Bermuda secretly does not stick to the agreement, then Andorra needs all the more to be breaking the agreement and going nuclear.

These are examples of the prisoner's dilemma, so-called because it is typically put forward in terms of two prisoners. We shall call them Al and Belle. Al and Belle are being interviewed separately by the police, who are seeking confessions to their joint crime. Al and Belle do not know what the other will say, yet each must decide whether to confess. If neither confesses, their sentence will be a couple of years in prison: if one confesses and the other stays silent, the confessor is released and the silent one will receive ten years; if they both confess, they get five years each. Without trust, they will both confess and end up with five years each in prison — just as, without trust, the motorcyclists end up crashing and the nations pointlessly developing nuclear weaponry.

| | **B** | |
	Keeps central Goes nuclear *Confesses*	**Veers away** No nuclear *Stays silent*
Keeps central Goes nuclear *Confesses*	**Crash** Futile expense *Five years prison*	BEST FOR A WORST FOR B
Veers away No nuclear *Stays silent*	WORST FOR A BEST FOR B	SENSIBLE SECOND-BEST FOR BOTH

A = **Angelo**/Andorra/*Al*; B = **Berto**/Bermuda/*Belle*

The dilemma is how to gain the mutual advantages of co-operating, if – as it seems – such co-operation involves the risk of the other party not co-operating. Is that risk a genuine risk? Reasoning through the alternatives leads us to do something that *seems* to be in our own best interests, whatever the other party does, yet it fails to give us the best result.

♈

These are theoretical examples, in which the players seek to be rational by way of seeking their individual best outcomes rather than the mutual best outcome. Yet explanations by way of such self-interested rationality, so simply applied, fail to account for much of our social behaviour, even if self-interest remains at the core. We get to know people and learn how they react in a variety of circumstances. As a result, we often have reasons to think that others are trustworthy and likely to act co-operatively. Importantly, we are often aware that if we fail to co-operate or break our promise, it is less likely we shall receive co-operation from others when we need it. The likelihood of repeated prisoner's dilemmas gives a boost to our selecting the co-operative choice, the sensible second-best choice, in the examples.

Reasoning about repeated cases, however, does not provide a watertight solution to such dilemmas. Sometimes we know that no future cases will arise and even when we know there will be an indeterminate number of future cases, we are still taking something of a risk in a decision to co-operate and trust the others involved. Many of us, though, do find ourselves taking co-operative risks. Doing so is often to our benefit, even if it is irrational from the perspective of a single self-interested individual – and it at least avoids the head-on crash towards which Angelo and Berto, the rational bikers, are heading.

25
'DON'T READ THIS NOTICE'

Unthinking students often ask in lectures, 'May I ask a question?' Quick and witted replies are 'Too late' and 'Was that the question?'

If the 'Don't read this notice' sign refers to itself, then it too is too late in its warning, just as is the notice that says 'Do not enter the blue room,' which is displayed in the blue room rather than outside. Those thoughts may help us to handle a couple of paradoxical classics.

There once was a barber, of Alcala, a Sicilian village, who, it was famously said, shaved all those inhabitants of the village who did not shave themselves. It was added that he shaved no others; he shaved only those who did not shave themselves – and he shaved all of them. So far, so good, until someone asked, 'Did the barber shave himself?'

Either he did or he did not. Suppose he shaved himself: then he was not one of the inhabitants who did not shave themselves. But we are told that the barber shaved *only* those who did not shave themselves. So, he did not shave himself. Therefore, from the supposition that he did shave himself it follows that he did not – which is a contradiction. 'Con-tra-diction!' we could sing. Presumably, then, he did not shave himself; so let us consider this alternative. If he did not shave himself, then he was one of those inhabitants who did not shave themselves, but as we are told that the barber did shave all such inhabitants, he must therefore have shaved himself. 'Con-tra-diction!'

What is to be done? It is not possible for there to be a barber who both does and does not shave himself. When we said that either the barber shaved himself or did not, we were presupposing that such a barber existed. The answer is that there can be no such barber. The presupposition is false.

And now for something completely different – or is it? It derives from Eubulides, but a closely similar problem is associated with Epimenides, centuries earlier. Both were of ancient Greece.

Suppose someone says, 'I'm lying' – and says nothing else. When people utter such words, they are typically referring to other things that they have said; but in this case the speaker is referring solely to what he is saying when saying, 'I'm lying.'

Is the speaker who just says 'I'm lying' speaking the truth?

As with the Barber, let us consider the two alternatives: that he is speaking the truth and that he is not. Suppose he is speaking the truth: then it is true that he is lying; but if he is lying, he is not speaking the truth. We have a contradiction. Suppose that he is not speaking the truth: then, as we assume he knows what he is doing, he is lying and so, as he says that he is lying, he is speaking the truth after all. 'Con-tra-diction!'

With the Barber, we said that there could be no barber. With the Liar?

The speaker who says that he is lying both exists and utters the words 'I'm lying', but we may reasonably challenge the assumption that he expresses something that is true or false. Just as the Barber paradox led us to conclude that there could be no such barber, so the Liar paradox may lead us to conclude that there is nothing that is being expressed by the speaker which is either true or false.

That answer does not reach the heart of the problem, for we can strengthen the paradox, with the speaker saying that what he says is not true. Would he not be expressing the truth that what he says is not true? If so, again the contradiction arises. This has suggested to some that we should resort to a stronger claim, namely that there is nothing at all that such a speaker is expressing when he says, 'What I am saying right now is not true' – despite the words forming a coherent sentence.

We need to handle the above response with care. Quite what grip have we on the notion of 'expressing' such that we can tell that such a speaker is expressing nothing at all? He certainly seems to be expressing something more than someone who is silent or who utters nonsense words. Let us leave that thought lingering, to be picked up later.

~~~

A notice can sensibly instruct people not to read a different notice, just as the sign that warns of dangers in the blue room can be sensibly placed outside the blue room. Futility arises when the notices involve elements of self-reference. A barber in Alcala can readily shave all and only those who do not shave themselves in the next village, say, Balcala. The contradiction arises if that barber moves to Balcala. Metaphorically, he goes up in a puff of smoke or a froth of shaving soap. In more literal mode, were the barber to move from Alcala to Balcala, then what was true of him about his shaving clientele could no longer be true.

A liar may say of someone else, without paradox, that that someone else is lying; it is when he says it of himself that paradox flies forth. True, he may sincerely think that he expresses something, but he is merely uttering words and failing to express a complete thought. By analogy, someone is not successfully telling you the meaning of 'blibble' if, when asked what she means, she can say only that by 'blibble' she means 'blibble'; not even God can blibble (please see Chapter 71).

Notices and sayings usually need to point away from themselves, rather than referring to themselves, but we need to be wary of mirrorings; wary of what is said being reflected back, indirectly generating some self-reference. Consider the following:

1. What I express by the next sentence is true.
2. What I expressed by the previous sentence is not true.

The first sentence is used to tell us about what is expressed by the second but that sends us scuttling back to the first, with paradoxical results – unless we insist, once again, that, one way or another, nothing is being expressed.

Self-reference continues to feast philosophers' minds. Some self-reference seems fine. For example, this sentence is printed in black. My use of that sentence expressed a truth. But we may question whether that sentence involves self-reference. What is expressed is about the sentence (the printing) used; it is not about what is expressed by means of that sentence; that is, it is not about itself. What is expressed is not the sort of thing that can be coloured. A word can be printed in black, but the meaning of a word cannot be printed at all. The same belief may be expressed by both German and French speakers, but their utterances would be radically different – as is sometimes the case with the English and American, to say nothing of the differing sounds from a Glaswegian and Geordie who are yet expressing identical views.

When a speaker announces, 'What I am saying right now is not true,' quite what is it that he is saying is not true? It is whatever is referred to by his use of 'What I am saying right now' – yet what is that? It is not the words, but whatever is expressed by the words – so, what is expressed? It seems that we are in a position akin to the emptiness of 'blibble'; there is nothing there about which to speak. We may now clarify the claim that nothing is expressed by the use of such self-referential sentences. The truth is that nothing is being referred to by the speaker in his speaking. Although the concepts of 'saying' and 'being true' are being expressed – they are not being expressed *about* anything.

♈

Philetus of Cos, *c.*300 BC, received the epitaph:

> *Philetus of Cos am I,*
> *'Twas the Liar who made me die,*
> *And the bad nights caused thereby…*

Liar versions continue to cause some philosophers to wrestle during sleepless nights – and probably nights even when fast asleep – though these days such troubling logical paradoxes result not in death, but in more and more articles in learned journals. The logical spinning spins on – and on.

26
THE UNOBTAINABLE: WHEN 'YES' MEANS 'NO'

We often seek the unobtainable – a tribute to human pertinacity, or is it perversity? Jack has a great passion for Jill, but only so long as she remains aloof and unobtainable. Were she to say 'yes' to his marriage proposal, his desire would evaporate. We may sum this up by saying that Jack wants Jill if and only if she does not want Jack, that is, if and only if she does not say 'yes' to his proposal. No contradiction arises, just the misfortune of our perverse human nature.

Let us now add that Jill is a sensible and romantic woman. She will say 'yes' if and only if Jack wants her. Now, if she says 'no', then Jack wants her; so, then she should say 'yes', but that ensures that Jack does not want her – as a result, she then does not want Jack, which brings Jack back round to wanting her – and so on. The reasoning loops round and round. Let us bear this in mind, as we bring forth a little legal controversy involving Protagoras, the ancient Greek relativist we engaged with earlier when resisting – well, er – relativism.

Protagoras gave legal training to Euathlus, an impoverished student. The condition set was that Protagoras would receive his fee, once Euathlus won his first court case. Euathlus, after his studies, gave up on the law, deciding instead to go into politics. Protagoras worried about his fee, but Euathlus pointed out that he was not required to pay until he had won a court case. So, Protagoras sued Euathlus for the fee – and lands us, seemingly, in a logical mire.

Should Protagoras get paid?

Protagoras argues that, whether he wins or loses the case, either way, Euathlus must then pay him. If he, Protagoras, wins his case for the money, then that simply means that he should be paid. If he loses the case, then Euathlus would have won his first case – and hence, by the contract's terms, he should get paid. Hence, he, Protagoras, cannot lose. Why even bother to have the case? Of course, lawyers are typically unhappy to have that last question raised.

Euathlus pursues a different line. 'If I lose the case, then I still have not won my first case, so obviously I should not pay. If, however, I win the case, then the court ruling says that I should not pay. Either way, I should not pay. Why even bother to have the case?' Of course, lawyers etc....

We note that Euathlus is defending himself. Were someone else defending, then they would be winning or losing. So, if Protagoras lost the case, Euathlus personally would not have won his first case – and so would not need to pay. And there would seem no grounds for Protagoras to win.

Protagoras and Euathlus present two different approaches, reaching conclusions in conflict, so something has gone wrong – but where? Perhaps the contract is itself inconsistent and hence impossible to fulfil: it seems to be saying that if Protagoras wins, then he loses, as well as allowing that if he wins then he wins – and similarly for Euathlus. Yet that criticism is itself open to criticism. The contract specifies what happens if Euathlus wins a case; it says nothing about what happens if Euathlus loses and a court rules that he should pay. We could clarify the contract by saying that Euathlus should pay Protagoras *when* and *only when* he wins a case. Let us hereafter deal with that clarified contract.

What happens if, for example, Euathlus wins the court case in which the judgement is that he should not pay? That is a contradictory situation in which, it seems, he wins and yet does not win; he should not pay, yet should pay. A similar contradiction arises if he loses the court case in which the judgement is that he should pay. The judges may anticipate the contradiction that arises whichever way they judge; they would do well to have a third way, of passing no judgement. There is, though, no reason for seeking a fence-sitting way out.

We need to attend to the saga's temporal element. Judges are being asked whether Euathlus should pay. He should not pay until he has won a case. Hence, the judges could reason that he has not won yet, until they pass judgement. Hence, they pass judgement on the basis of his not having won a case yet, and so their judgement is in his favour – and he wins. Protagoras can then take Euathlus to court again. All will then be well for Protagoras. He now successfully argues that Euathlus has indeed won a case and so needs now to pay. All would not be well if the judges had ruled that Euathlus should *never* pay; but they would have no good reason to do that.

♈

The puzzle is akin to the Liar paradox (see previous chapter) – but with a key difference. Let us recall the Liar. Someone sincerely announces, 'I am lying,' meaning that he is lying simply in saying that he is lying. With various caveats, if what he is saying is true, then he is not lying – hence, contradiction. If he is lying and so not telling the truth, then he is telling the truth because he says he is lying – contradiction again. With the Liar there is no easy temporal escape route from contradiction; that contrasts with the legal contract above.

Groucho Marx would not join a club that would have him as a member; and women may desire men, wanting them to propose marriage, yet once they propose, the men lose their desirability. We often want the unobtainable. The unobtainable is sometimes unobtainable because of practical matters, but sometimes because of deviancy in our wanting.

When I saw a fine burgundy velvet jacket in a sale, I dithered: was the colour too strong, fitting too tight, price too high? When the jacket appeared to have gone, the balance was tipped: I wanted it, regretting my earlier dithering. Yet when it turned out still to be available, dithering restarted. If available, jacket not wanted; if unavailable, jacket wanted.

We often engage in activities, seeking achievements – reaching the mountain top, discovering how the story ends, satisfying yearnings of passion – yet also we resist reaching the ends, for, having achieved them, there is the anti-climax, the sadness, the emptiness. If only the bracing climb continued; if only there were another volume to the novel; if only the passion persisted… And so, in writing the final words of this chapter, there is the pleasure of completion, yet also some loss, some sorrow, some post-chapter'd *tristesse* – well, for the author, if not the reader.

27
BEAUTY AWAKE

There is more to this puzzle than meets the eye, but let us meet the eye – and then touch the more. Sleeping Beauty has a walk-on part, or, more accurately, a sleep-on part, for her role is merely to be put to sleep and then awoken in the following little game.

It is Sunday. Beauty is truthfully informed that she will shortly be popped to sleep. What then happens – and she knows this – depends on a coin's random spin. The coin is fair. If it lands heads, she will be woken, just once, at 6.00am for ten minutes, on only one of the next five days, randomly chosen; and then returned to sleep until the end of the game. If it lands tails, she will be woken at 6.00am for ten minutes, every day of the game, then popped back to sleep, each time her memory wiped each day of any previous awakenings. The game ends on Saturday, when she is woken, her memory fully restored. Before that Saturday waking, whenever she is woken, she remembers everything about the game's set-up; but she is not told how the coin landed. Furthermore, as said, she fails to remember any previous awakenings.

So, if the coin has landed heads, then she wakes up once – obviously not remembering any prior waking. If the coin has landed tails, she wakes up five times, once each morning, but not remembering any other awakenings during the game. Speaking roughly, tails for *total* possible awakenings; *heads* for hardly any.

The puzzle is: when she wakes up during the game, what assessment should she make that the coin landed heads – or that it landed tails? This is a question of what it is rational for her to believe, given the evidence.

What should Beauty believe
when she wakes up?

A few argue that it is obviously a fifty–fifty matter. When she wakes up, she has no new information, just the information given at the game's start. At the game's start, she knew that heads and tails were equally likely. She also knew that she was bound to wake up, whether heads or tails. So, now she is awake, how can she possibly conclude that tails must have been more likely? She has nothing new to go on.

Others argue that she should believe it more likely that the coin landed tails. If she bets on tails each time she wakes, then, over a series of such games, she is more likely to win overall than not. Suppose the game runs twelve times, one game per week: she is likely to lose the tails bet six times because there would, on average, be six awakenings resulting from heads coming up six times out of the twelve weeks. Regarding the other six weeks, the weeks of tails, her tails bet would occur thirty times, leading to thirty wins. That is, with the twelve weeks, on average, tails should come up for six games, and there are five awakenings for each of those six — hence thirty bets on tails when in fact it is tails.

This type of consideration leads some to the conclusion that, whenever she is awake during the game, it is rational to believe it is more likely a tails awakening. Yet, we may doubt whether that is quite right, at least regarding what to believe.

Here is a route into the puzzle. I am walking along a long bendy road, with a thousand turnings, a tree at each, but I can see only one tree at a time – mind you, I am not paying attention to them. I know that I have taken either a road (Max route) with a thousand goats, one tethered to each tree, or a similar road (Min route), but with only one goat tethered to a tree, independently of anything to do with me. The Min route is certain to have a goat at a tree, but it is a one in a thousand chance to which tree it would be tethered. In other words, Min is guaranteed to have an unlikely feature – just as a lottery may be guaranteed a winner, but it is a one in a million chance against any particular player being the winner.

My chosen road has been randomly chosen, perhaps by a fair coin's spin. I am on the road and just happen to pay attention to a tree. A goat is tethered to it. I think: although it is certain that Min has some tree with a goat, it is highly unlikely that the one I just happen by chance to look at should be that tree. With Max, it is certain that I see a goat whenever I look at a tree. Hence, I should judge that it is highly likely that I am on Max rather than Min.

Suppose, though, that my goat love is so great that whenever I pass a tree, I am bound to pay attention to it if, but only if, it has a goat tethered. Perhaps the goatish scent attracts me. Then, whichever route I walk, the first experience of tethered goat points equally to Min as to Max. Of course, if I have a second goat sighting, then that makes Max certain. If, however, I am always utterly forgetful whether I have seen a goat tethered, then I have no idea whether a sighting is a later one or a first; so, I am back to being unable rationally to judge one route as more likely.

In this traveller's tale, we have mentioned two features that may coincide: my paying attention to a tree and its having a goat. When it is just by chance that I attend, then, for all I know, I may see a goat or no

122 • THE BIG THINK BOOK

goat: it could go either way. That it goes one way rather than the other is relevant evidence for me, when judging which route I probably travel. But when my attention is determined by goatish scent, then, whichever route I am on, there is no surprise in my finding a goat, when I pay attention. And so I cannot use the first goatish sighting as evidence either way regarding which route.

With Beauty, when she awakes, there is no surprise at two features happening to be conjoined, such as attending to a tree and seeing a goat. It is not as if there is a coincidence between Beauty's being awake and noticing that she is awake. Whichever way the coin came down, she is guaranteed to have the experience of waking; and, with the memory loss, all awakenings seem a first awakening. So, on any game's awakening, she has no good reason to change her initial assessment; she should continue to believe that her being in the tails game is no more likely than her being in the heads game.

What of arguments that it is rational for Beauty, whenever awake in the game, to *believe* tails is the more likely outcome? Some present detailed probability considerations, but perhaps – note the hesitation – the puzzle shows how rational betting can separate from what it is rational to believe. Whenever Beauty is awake, she has no more reason to believe that tails came up than that heads came up. Having said that, if she is awake because tails came up, then she has five opportunities to bet on tails and be right; but if she is awake because of heads, she has only one opportunity to bet on heads and be right. If she bets whenever awake, she should therefore bet tails. This is not because tails is more likely than heads, but because the tails outcome offers more betting opportunities than the heads outcome.

We may now reflect that if, whenever awake, she believes it is a tails game, she would have more correct beliefs over a run of games than if she believed heads. But that does not justify the claim that what is believed is more likely to be true. The evidence justifies neither the belief that it is a tails game nor the belief that it is more likely a tails game. If Beauty wanted to increase the number of times it is likely that she believes something true, and if she could, *per impossibile*, switch on beliefs at will – Chapter 45 reflects on that impossibility – then she should believe she is in the tails game, but that does not mean it is rational to believe the game is more likely to be tails than heads.

$$\gamma$$

Sleeping Beauty has its source in work by Arnold Zuboff, leading him – all of us, apparently – into a marvellous metaphysics, one whereby all experiences are *my* experiences, where we are all one and the same person. Zuboff presumably would accept the thought experiment of Chapter 56, with its unacceptable conclusion of Issie and Aussie both being Sir Isaac Newton. Before you turn to another chapter, nodding your head sadly at some philosophers' craziness, reflect on the following.

My existence, according to the usual view, required a certain spermatozoon and ovum; and their existence depended upon a sequence of a vast number of highly specific events stretching back over generations and into evolutionary mists and mysteries. A sneeze, a delayed coach, a wrong foot, so to speak, centuries ago – and my great-great-great grandparents, for example, would not have been conceived; hence I should not have been conceived. Is it not an amazing coincidence, on the usual view, that the very specific requirements for my existence should have come about?

Of course – though paradoxical sounding – it is often highly likely that unlikely things will happen: witness the lottery example above. But, on the usual view, we have no reason to think it highly likely that the unlikely event of *my* existing would have happened. That I exist, if I am a person distinct from others, is akin to the unlikeliness, when on the Min route, of my randomly looking up and seeing a tree with a tethered goat – but where there are trillions of trees yet still only one goat. A far more reasonable hypothesis, according to Zuboff, is that my existence occurs in a Max version of a consciousness creation. Whenever any experiences come about, they are mine. Indeed, the only factor that makes an experience mine is its first-person character; and every experience has that. If this is right, then that is what we all think, being all one individual consciousness – and yet do not think, because, in some way, consciousness is segmented.

Philosophical reflections can set minds reeling. Our reeling here requires thought on unlikeliness. The one-person view is struck by the seemingly highly unlikely coincidence of the conditions required for my existence being the conditions that arose. But we may then comment on the highly unlikely coincidence of the conditions required for this book's existence being the ones that arose. Does that show that there really is only one book? The response is: of course not, unless the book were conscious. Were it conscious, then its existence would be a coincidence *for the book*. So, the one-person view hangs a lot on my existence involving a coincidence *for me*; but what is so special about the 'for me' concerning unlikeliness? Consider a lottery where it is certain that someone would win: it is still highly unlikely that the individual who won would be the winner, even if she, the winner, is unaware of having won. We may also wonder how the one-person view accommodates the fact, seemingly unlikely, that, for example, *these* experiences, when writing these words, appear to be only within the experience of Cave and not Zuboff.

What is this 'me' to which I – and you – refer? That baffling question arises in more traditional ways in Part VI. Here, though, we close with the reflection that while our existence on the usual view is vastly, vastly unlikely, it may still be more likely than the truth, or even sense, of the one-person view. 'Who knows?' And here we have as much perplexity with the nature of 'who' as with that of 'knows'.

28

A GAZELLE, A SLOTH AND A CHICKEN

Here we have some mixed-up logic – well, at least, some mixed-up thinking resulting from logic – but we approach it by coaxing some mixed-up creatures into a race. There is good reason for this. Our creatures are a gazelle, a sloth and a chicken. So, we have two mammals and one bird. True, this is an unlikely combination. Mind you, the logic will be impeccable.

The race is fair, the creatures positively motivated, no drugs taken. Now, we have excellent reasons for thinking that the gazelle will win. We also have excellent reasons to think that the sloth will come last – she is true to her name – and that the chicken will be in the middle, coming second. Let us set out our beliefs more determinedly.

We firmly believe that the gazelle will win. We know that the gazelle is a mammal; so, a little piece of reasoning leads us to believe that a mammal will win. If we are willing to bet on the gazelle winning, then – were bookmakers to take bets in terms only of a mammal winning or not – we ought to bet on a mammal. If we are certain that the gazelle will win, we must be certain that a mammal will win.

The chicken is a bird and no mammal; so, of course, in believing that a mammal will win, we do not believe that the chicken will win. Now consider:

Premiss 1: If a mammal wins, then if the winner is not the gazelle, the winner will be the sloth.

Surely we are committed to that claim. If – *if* – a mammal wins our little race, and if it is not the gazelle, then it must be the sloth. After all, the chicken is no mammal. Furthermore, we do firmly believe:

Premiss 2:   A mammal will win.

Therefore, we ought to believe:

Conclusion: So, if the winner is not the gazelle, the winner will be
the sloth.

Yet that Win Conclusion is just what we do not believe. We believe
that if, for some reason, the gazelle fails to win, then the winner will
be the chicken – with the sloth a very long way behind, slothfully
slothing.

Whatever has gone wrong in this simple argument?

Our little piece of reasoning employs *modus ponendo ponens*, abbreviated
to *modus ponens*. It affirms a conclusion by affirming the 'if' part of the
first premiss. It would be tragic to be forced to accept that *modus ponens*
sometimes fails to work. It is the bedrock of our reasoning. Here is a
modus ponens at work, where we affirm the conclusion by affirming the
second premiss:

Premiss: If there is lightning, there will be thunder.
Premiss: There is lightning.
Conclusion: So, there will be thunder.

The conclusion follows from the premisses: if the premisses are true,
then the conclusion is true. Here is another example of impeccable
reasoning:

Premiss: If no umbrellas are available, then if it rains, the guests
will get wet.
Premiss: No umbrellas are available.
Conclusion: So, if it rains, the guests will get wet.

Our problem is that using similar, seemingly impeccable reasoning about the creatures' race, we reached the paradoxical conclusion that, if the winner is not the gazelle, it will be the sloth. How odd.

One approach to our paradox is to expose an ambiguous use of the term 'mammal' in Premisses 1 and 2. The expression can mean: some mammal or other. We may colloquially say: *any ol' mammal*. The expression may, though, mean: a particular mammal or type of mammal – in this case, a gazelle. We believe Premiss 2 understood as 'A particular mammal, a gazelle, not any mammal or other, will win.' But Premiss 1 is baffling if read as 'If a particular mammal, a gazelle (not any mammal or other), will win, then if the winner is not the gazelle, the winner will be the sloth.' With Premiss 1 baffling us, we have no good reason to accept the argument's conclusion.

Arguably, the above approach fails to solve the paradox. Our belief that the gazelle will win surely supports the more general belief that a mammal – some mammal or other – will win. If I believe that Edgar kissed Elaine and I know that Elaine is a raven-haired woman, then surely I should believe that Edgar kissed some raven-haired woman or other. That latter belief may well be true, even if my grounds for it are lousy because I confused Elaine with Zelda. Zelda is also raven-haired – and it was Zelda who was kissed.

To resolve the paradox perhaps we need to distinguish between an argument's premisses and our acceptance of, or belief in, those premisses. Yes, if Premisses 1 and 2 are true – if those two propositions are true – then the Win Conclusion is true. That is indeed straightforward *modus ponens*; but is our acceptance of Premiss 1 straightforward?

> *Premiss 1*: If a mammal wins, then if the winner is not the gazelle, the winner will be the sloth.

We believe – we accept – that a mammal will win only because we believe that the gazelle will win. So, on the supposition that a mammal wins, if we then suppose that the winner is not the gazelle, we are supposing 'what if' we lack our belief that a mammal wins. If that supposition is consistently applied across the argument's premisses, we lack good reason to believe Premiss 2's 'A mammal will win.' Hence, although the Win Conclusion follows from the two premisses – the argument is valid – that does not justify our accepting the argument's conclusion.

Here is a blatantly extreme example of what is going wrong. Holding fast to our belief that the gazelle will win, what happens if the gazelle does not win? We do not know what to make of that question. It is like asking what happens if the gazelle wins and yet does not win.

The moral of this paradox is not that the formal logic of *modus ponens* is wrong, but that the logician's premisses, conclusions and their relationships are not the same as reasons, beliefs and their relationships. The formalizations of logic are not what they are sometimes cracked up to be.

♈

Suppose we invent a new classification – 'chickelle' – which applies only to items that are chickens or gazelles. We believe that the gazelle will win; so, we should believe that a chickelle will win. Now, consider the following argument structurally similar to our mammalian one.

Premiss 1: If a chickelle wins, then if the winner is not the gazelle, the winner will be the chicken.
Premiss 2: A chickelle will win.
Conclusion: So, if the winner is not the gazelle, the winner will be the chicken.

In this example, we do believe the conclusion; but this ought not to be solely because we have a valid *modus ponens* argument with premisses which we believe independently to be true. After all, the mammalian argument possessed such features – certainly, it initially appeared to – but it failed to persuade us of its conclusion's truth.

Why the chickellean argument works is because if we suppose the winner is not the gazelle, we do not undermine our belief that a chickelle will win. In contrast, in the mammalian argument, the supposition that the winner is not the gazelle did undermine our belief in a mammal winning. The mammalian classification was a red herring, so to speak, regarding the argument and the relevant beliefs about the race's runners. The chickellean classification was designed to be relevant.

Arguments are sound when premises are true and conclusions follow; but whether such conclusions should be *believed* depends on whether the premises jointly can be believed. Jokes hang on the way that you tell them; what you do hangs on the way that you do it – and belief in conclusions hangs on the way premises come to be believed to be true.

29

JESTERS, BERTRAND RUSSELL AND PARADOX

The jesters were not happy. They put their heart into jesting, joking and clowning at the various courts of their employment; but never were they invited to join in and dine at the banquets at which they jested. Rebellion was in the air – their jesting bells jangled – but instead of rebelling, they planned their own banquet, the Jesters' Banquet. More accurately, they would hold a banquet for all and only those jesters ineligible to join in banquets at which they performed their jests. To be eligible for the banquet you must not merely be a jester but also one who jested for people who would not permit you to join in their banquets. All such jesters could join the Jesters' Banquet.

The Jesters' Banquet would be as grand as those of the great courts – dining on swan, with singers and song, even the odd glass of champagne. Arrangements were made, all going according to plan. One day, a thought crossed their jesting minds. 'We must find ourselves a jester to jest for us at our banquet. After all, we don't want to jest ourselves – that would be too much like work.' An excellent idea, they agreed; and, as luck would have it, they happened upon a fresh-faced lad looking for his first jesting job. 'You shall be our Jesting Junior.'

All went well, so well – until today, the banquet day – for here we are, listening in to the singers and song, as the jesters dine and wine at their splendid Jesters' Banquet. They are, of course, somewhat solemn-faced, not wanting themselves to risk working as jesters. Jesting Junior, though, has just performed some fine japes, jokes and jests.

'Come and join the banquet, Junior,' the jesters cry – well, all of them apart from Jesting Stickler, the most stern-faced jester of them all.

'Our banquet is just for jesters ineligible to join in banquets at which they jest,' says Stickler firmly. 'So, Junior, I'm afraid, cannot join us.'

'Oh yes, he can,' answer the others. 'Oh no, he can't,' replies Stickler, with Junior looking suitably baffled.

With the 'can's and 'can't's becoming more ferocious, the argument clearly turning into a fracas, a fight forthcoming, we tiptoe away and reflect on the puzzle.

Is Jesting Junior eligible to join the Banquet?

There is nothing contradictory in jesters being employed to perform at banquets, yet ineligible to indulge and dine. There is nothing odd about such jesters feeling unloved, even aggrieved, and hence making their own banqueting arrangements as described. Trouble arises with the jesters employing their own jester.

If Jesting Junior is employed by those who do not permit him to dine, then, as the banquet is for all those who work for such stickler employers, he is eligible after all. But if he is eligible to join in the banquet, then, as the banquet is open only to those not allowed to join in the banquets at which they jest, he is surely ineligible.

In summary, the conditions of the banquet mean that Jesting Junior is eligible if and only if he is ineligible. That is contradictory. Typically, logicians would conclude that the banquet cannot exist for it has contradictory membership rules. In humility, we resist such a quick response.

There can exist – no doubt there do exist – institutions, banqueting clubs, corporations, constitutions, with contradictory rules, rules that cannot be consistently applied in all possible circumstances. They may go unnoticed, for circumstances may not arise which exhibit the inconsistencies. Now, if the existence of our Jesters' Banquet hangs on its conditions determining for all *possible* individuals, without contradiction, whether they are eligible to banquet or not, then indeed the banquet cannot exist. The banquet's conditions fail to give a consistent answer regarding the eligibility of any possible jester. We have brought this to light by actually having a jester, Jesting Junior, jesting for them.

In reality a banquet or institution or club's existence does not hang on its rule book lacking contradictions. We can tell that the Jesters'

Banquet exists by the wining and dining. In similar vein, many of us unwittingly hold contradictory beliefs; yet we get through life undefeated by such contradictions. It is even possible (really?) that this book contains the odd contradiction or even quite a few – yet it exists. The Jesters' Banquet exists, but it has a contradictory condition of attendance, *if* the condition is intended to provide a 'yes or no' answer in all possible circumstances. Related puzzles arose in Chapters 25 and 26, where we met Alcala's Barber, the Liar and, somewhat casually, Groucho Marx; but a more disturbing conundrum now comes along.

≋

Our Jesting Tale is a lead-in to Russell's great paradox which concerns classes or sets. Classes and sets are abstract entities, unlike banquets and jesters.

You are a human being, so you belong to the set of human beings. The set is not itself a human being: it is not made out of flesh and blood; it is not a messy fleshy combination of all humans. It is abstract – as are numbers and the concept of justice. We may meet and eat three apples, but the number three is not something that we can meet and eat.

Whether items are members of the set of humans simply hangs on whether they possess the feature of being human. Pianists, philosophers and princesses are members, but pianos, peacocks and porcupines are not. All members of the set of philosophers are members of the set of humans. The set of philosophers is hence a 'subset' of the set of humans.

Now, the set of philosophers itself is not, of course, a philosopher – a set cannot philosophize – so, it is not a member of itself. The set of pianos is not itself a piano; so it is not a member of itself. Many sets are not members of themselves.

As there are sets that are not members of themselves, there may well be some sets that are members of themselves – and there are. Consider the set of items that are not pork-eaters: it includes some people, lots of other creatures, also turnips, trees and treacle – and also itself. The set of non-pork-eaters is itself a non-pork-eater; so the set of non-pork-eaters includes itself. Were sets containers, then we would doubt that a set could ever be a member of itself – how can a container contain itself? Well, a container cannot contain itself; but sets are not containers.

Time to give Bertrand Russell, Cambridge philosopher and logician of the early twentieth century – also a political activist – a run for his money. By the way, we met him in the Prologue.

Russell proposed a set, hereafter the Russell Set. The feature that determines membership of the Russell Set is that members be sets that are not members of themselves. The Russell Set contains the set of readers, the set of berets, the set of cannabis users, for no set is itself a reader, a beret or a cannabis user. The Russell Set does not contain the set of non-pork-eaters, for that set is a member of itself. Now, here comes our jesting and troubling question. Is the Russell Set a member of itself?

Suppose that the Russell Set is a member of itself: then it belongs to the set of items that are not members of themselves; so it is not a member of itself. Suppose that it is not a member of itself: then it qualifies to be a member of the set of items that are not members of themselves; so it is a member of itself. Paradoxically, the Russell Set is a member of itself if and only if it is not a member of itself.

The Russell Set leads us into contradiction, as did the Jesters' Banquet. With the Jesters' Banquet we made sense of how the banquet could exist yet with contradictory conditions for attendance: after all, we could see the banquet in full flow. In contrast, we cannot make sense of the Russell Set existing, albeit with contradictory conditions. We can pick out a set only by the conditions for determining whether items are members or not. Contradictory conditions fix nothing. If given the contradictory instruction, 'Right now, both turn off and don't turn off the light,' there is nothing possible you can do correctly to obey: you are baffled. Similarly, the conditions for the Russell Set fail to determine a set.

Russell's contradiction arises from the feature 'is not a member of itself'. That feature, though, usually gives no trouble. It is intelligible – witness the simple examples given of it above – and it is used to provide perfectly acceptable mathematical results. So, arguably a continuing puzzle is how best to handle the feature – how to justify restricting it – to avoid the paradox.

♈

When, in 1902, Russell discovered the paradox of his Russell Set, he revealed it to the German logician Gottlob Frege. The paradox undermined a basic assumption held by Frege; and Russell's communication led to Frege abandoning his approach to logic and mathematics. Russell later commented:

> As I think about acts of integrity and grace, I realize that there is nothing in my knowledge to compare with Frege's dedication to truth. His entire life's work was on the verge of completion, much of his work had been ignored to the benefit of men infinitely less capable, his second volume was about to be published, and upon finding that his fundamental assumption was in error, he responded with intellectual pleasure clearly submerging any feelings of personal disappointment.

Russell was evidently greatly moved by Frege's commitment to truth; and, despite (or maybe because of) Russell's chaotic personal life, Russell too sought after abstract heavens of mathematics, untainted by contradiction.

For Russell, mathematics should possess eternal truth and supreme beauty: 'a beauty cold and austere, like that of sculpture'. Russell's discovery of his paradox was therefore highly unsettling, probably more so for him than for Frege – for the paradox gave but the foothold of shifting sands. And the sands of attempted solutions continue to shift.

30
INFINITY, INFINITIES
AND HILBERT'S HOTEL

Travelling one seasonally festive day, we encounter some marvellous maids a-milking and lovely lords a-leaping. 'I bet there's the same number of maids as there are lords,' announce I, ignorant of traditional numbers in such festive matters. 'I bet not,' responds my travelling companion.

Bets taken, we could count the maids and lords; but my companion points out that we can, instead, pair off the maids and lords. If one maid or one lord or more are left over, unpaired, we know that the maids and lords differ in number.

The task, easy to do in theory, is not so easy in practice, in view of the leapings and milkings; but eventually we manage – and, sure enough, I lose. We find that some lords are left a-leaping, unpaired with maids a-milking. Clearly, there are more lords than maids. That should be the tale's end, except my companion, an itinerant mathematician, is bearing a gleeful smile, aware of my lack of mathematical skill.

'Of course,' smiles she, 'If you have a group of items and then take some away, you are left with fewer items than the original number.'

I readily agree. Even I can see that.

She now directs me to the whole numbers – 1, 2, 3, 4, 5 and so on – and then starts to remove the odd numbers. I casually remark that the remaining even numbers, 2, 4, 6, 8 and so on, would be fewer in number than the original set of 1, 2, 3, 4, 5… The '…' means 'and so on, without end'.

'Caught you!' Her mirth magnified way beyond justification. 'Look,' she says, 'you can pair off all the original numbers both even and odd, with just the even numbers – without end.'

THE NATURAL NUMBERS	THE EVEN NUMBERS ONLY
1	2
2	4
3	6
4	8
and so on...	...and so on...

'Paradoxically, there are as many even numbers as there are even and odd numbers together. If both groups, maids and lords, were each infinite in number, there would yet be as many maids as both maids and lords.'

I see the point. Although the set of even numbers contains just *some* of the even and odd numbers, the set of even numbers is the same size as that of the even and odd numbers combined. My companion has shown this by 'pairing off', 'matching', 'corresponding'. She tells me that two infinite sets are equi-numerous, equal in number, if there is at least some order such that the two sets *can* be paired off with each other, without remainder.

On that understanding, the squares of numbers, namely, 1, 4, 9, 16... and the cubes of numbers, namely, 1, 8, 27, 64... are also equi-numerous with the positive whole numbers 1, 2, 3, 4... as are many, many more series.

'All very interesting,' yawn I, 'but then infinity is endless – so these series are bound to match. You can't have anything bigger than infinity.'

My companion's smirk shows that to be a *faux pas*, a faulty step indeed.

'Some infinities are bigger than others,' she announces. And I am left wondering:

Can anything be bigger than infinity?

The question is whether some number of items exceeds an infinite number. The quick answer is 'yes'. This was demonstrated by the great mathematician Georg Cantor who developed 'transfinite' mathematics, dealing with differently sized infinities.

Pairing off the items of certain sets and series with the infinite series of whole numbers, 1, 2, 3, 4, 5... still leaves some items remaining unpaired. Let us focus, for example, on the decimal numbers – the 'real' numbers – between 0 and 1. They are infinite in number.

There are, of course, the decimals that derive from the fractions one-half, one-quarter, one-eighth… represented as 0.5, 0.25, 0.125… There is an infinite number of them. There are also fractions such as one-third, one-sixth, represented as recurring decimals 0.333… and 0.16666… These latter two examples clearly have decimals that are endless. There are others, for example, one that derives from the square root of 2, with 1 deducted. This cannot be represented as a fraction: it is an endless decimal: 0.4141…

Now, pop this infinite number of numbers, in whatever order you like and pair them with the natural numbers, 1, 2, 3, 4… Here is an arbitrary scattering, with highlighting yet to be explained.

THE NATURAL NUMBERS	THE DECIMAL NUMBERS
1	0. **3** 3 3 3…
2	0. 1 **4** 2 8…
3	0. 1 2 **5** 0…
4	0. 4 1 4 **1**…
…	…

The infinite series of decimal numbers goes down the page without end – and is paired with the infinite series of natural numbers. Whichever decimal numbers you put, in whatever order, there exist some decimal numbers that are bound not to be included. We can spot some 'missing numbers' by deriving them from the highlighted numbers showing diagonally, with a systematic change.

The decimal formed from the diagonal above, if no change is made, is 0.3451… That number may occur further down in the series for all we know. But suppose we make the following change, creating an 'extra number':

Whenever we encounter a '3' in the diagonal, we replace it with '1' and whenever we encounter anything that is not a '3' we replace it with '3'.

Our sample extra number starts off, then, as 0.1333... We are guaranteed that the decimal being formed is not in the infinite series given, for we know that the 'missing number' differs from the first row's number by having a '1' instead of a '3'. It differs from the second row's number by having a '3' instead of a '4' — and so on, infinitely so on, down the diagonal. We can create more such missing numbers by different replacements. The set of decimal numbers between 0 and 1 certainly has more numbers than the set of natural numbers, even though the natural numbers are infinite in number.

♈

Differently sized infinities seem highly paradoxical; but we should remember that we are talking of abstract entities and ways of comparing them. After all, in the realm of chess, the bishop moves only diagonally; yet that tells us nothing about bishops in life and nothing about how wooden pieces labelled 'bishops' can be physically moved. Yes, infinity does have application to the world. It also has misapplications. Let us see, by returning to infinities that are the same size as the whole number series, 1, 2, 3...

Here is Hilbert's Hotel, introduced by another brilliant German mathematician; this one is David Hilbert, whose ideas and questions set off considerable mathematical research throughout the twentieth century. Hilbert's Hotel has an infinite number of rooms, numbered 1, 2, 3... Every room is occupied. Yes, every room is occupied. No room is vacant.

A traveller arrives. Paradoxically, he can still be accommodated, insist mathematicians of the infinite. Room 1 occupant is moved to Room 2, Room 2 occupant to Room 3 — and so on — for there is always a higher numbered room to move any occupant you care to mention. Room 1 is now available for the traveller.

Even if an infinite number of travellers arrive, accommodation is no problem. Regarding the people already occupying the rooms, Room 1 occupant moves to 2; Room 2 occupant to 4; Room 3 occupant to 6; Room 4 occupant to 8; Room 5 occupant to 10; and so forth. Thus, the infinite number of even numbered rooms sweeps up all the established occupants, leaving the infinite number of odd numbered rooms free for the infinite number of travellers.

It is, though, baffling to describe a hotel with *all* rooms occupied, with every room filled, yet which takes new guests. With the infinite, 'every', 'all' and 'size' need to be understood differently from normal. As for making sense of an 'infinite hotel'...

Imagine meeting a weary Charlotte, walking the last few yards of a mile-long race. She started 1,760 yards away; and is panting the final yards: 3, 2, 1. That is fine; but it would surely be nonsense to think of Charlotte – or anyone – as having started an infinite number of yards away, now sighing out the final 3, 2, 1.

It is not a mere medical limitation that we cannot finish walking an infinite number of yards. It is not a mere architectural and material difficulty that prevents our building Hilbert's Hotel. And arguably it is not all that surprising that abstract infinite series generate paradoxes if applied to the world of hotel rooms, maids a-milking and lords a-leaping.

31

HOW TO GAIN WHATEVER YOU WANT

An eminent British philosopher gave a lecture in the United States about fifty years ago. The lecturer was J. L. Austin – John Langshaw Austin – a master of the nuance, of grammatical felicity and infelicity in the English language, a philosopher whose writings consisted of finer and finer linguistic distinctions. In his lecture, Austin made the point that an interesting fact about the English language is that a double negation makes a positive – if he did not *not* take the money, then it looks as if he did take the money. Yet a double positive, 'yes' added to 'yes', does not make a negative. Immediately from the audience came forth the sceptical mutter, 'Yeah, yeah.'

With the above background, consider the following two puzzles, seemingly of impeccable reasoning. Allow me to orientate one in which you lose; the other in which you win. You could, of course, always be the winning participant – or the loser.

Here is a 'lose everything' puzzle. A woman, sitting at a bar, offers you the following deal, wanting to know if you are happy with its conditions.

Accept this offer of a holiday in Venice – you can take someone with you – and all you have to do is pay me £10; everything else is free. There are no strings about the holiday: return first-class tickets, first-class hotel and so on. Here is one further condition. If what I say next is true, then I keep the £10 and you have the holiday at no further cost; if what I say next is false, then you must accept the £10 back, but still have the holiday free.

How can you lose? There are no snags about the holiday. You would like to go to Venice, see the art – and so forth. Either way, you are surely bound to have the splendid Venetian break. At worst, it costs you a mere £10. And you may even have the £10 returned. Rational man that you are, you eagerly accept. She takes the £10, with a coy smile; and then says:

Either I shall return the £10 or you will pay me £1 million.

Before we examine what has gone wrong, here is a 'win everything' similar puzzle. Find someone – say, Melissa – with some valuable item that you crave. Maybe you want her fine yacht. You ask her:

Q1.   Will you give the same answer, 'yes' or 'no', to this question as to the next?

Melissa hesitates. She has no idea what you are going to ask, so it would be foolish to commit either way. You reassure her, saying that you are happy for her to decide which way to answer *after* you have asked the second question; but would she merely agree that she will answer truthfully 'yes' or 'no'. If she still hesitates, slip her some fivers to agree – after all, it is easy money: she is free to answer either 'yes' or 'no'. She agrees. You now ask her:

Q2.   Will you give me your yacht?

She may immediately answer 'no'; but can she give that answer truthfully? After all, how is she going to answer that first question now? Logic can indeed puzzle us.

How have you lost a million, yet gained a yacht?

We tackle the 'yacht' tale first. Melissa has agreed to answer the first question 'yes' or 'no'. If she answers 'yes', that commits her to the same answer, 'yes', to the question about giving you the yacht. 'Yes' to *the same* keeps us with 'yes'. If she answers 'no' to the first question, that commits her to not answering the same to the yacht question, hence also making a 'yes'. 'No' to *the same* switches us to 'yes'. The offer, of 'yes' or 'no' answers, appeared to be leaving her with alternatives, but it did not. 'No' repeated is 'no' to 'no', that is 'yes'. 'Yes' repeated – 'yes' to 'yes' – also delivers 'yes'. Of course, maybe saying 'yeah, yeah' sceptically as a response could leave us baffled as to whether it is a 'yes' or a 'no' – but that was not an option.

How about the £1 million puzzle? She says, 'Either I shall return the £10 or you will pay me £1 million.' Suppose what she says is false: for it to be false, just considering what she says, she must not return the £10. But conditions are that she does return the £10, if it is false; hence, there is a contradiction, whether or not you pay the £1 million. So, what she says cannot be false. Therefore, what she says must be true. But if it is true, then that must be because either she returns the £10 or you pay her the £1 million. It cannot be because she returns the £10; the conditions state that she keeps the £10, if what she says is true in her statement. Hence it can only be true because you pay her the £1 million. So, you are £1 million down. Once again, conditions have been rigged to ensure a 'yes', an affirmative, a 'true', to what is wanted.

♈

Lurking in many paradoxes are presuppositions deserving challenge. A dangerous presupposition is that having to answer 'yes' or 'no', or 'true' or 'false', is a fair request. In a classic case, the police ask the suspect, 'Have you stopped beating your wife? Yes or no.' Answering 'yes' implies that you indeed used to, although you are now reformed. Answering 'no' implies that you did – and tells us that, bad character that you are, you continue to beat her. The suspect is afforded no opportunity to challenge the presupposition. He is not first asked, 'Did you beat your wife?' Then, only if he answers 'yes' should he be asked, 'Do you still?'

We should be wary of 'yes or no' demands, of surprising offers however attractive they may seem. A 'yes or no' insistence should make us pretty suspicious; and an offer that sounds too good to be true is, almost certainly, too good to be true. When contemplating matters abstractly, though, that is easy to say; but when confronted by tempting offers down here on Earth, well, we can be easily seduced into giving them a clearly affirmative 'yes, yes', instead of being rightly sceptical with the 'yeah, yeah'.

32

THE CARD-SHARP CAMEL *or* 'YOUR NUMBER'S UP'

Encountering a camel, when in the desert, is to be expected, but finding a humped card-sharp, sitting at a table outside a Soho club, wearing shades, smoking a cigar – well, we are, to say the least, a little surprised.

'Here's a little game suited for you two, suited because I can see that you are perfectly rational individuals, able to work things out – unusual for round here,' smirks the Camel. With that she deals us two cards face down, one for my friend Ariadne, one for me, telling us that they are cards from a pack of one hundred, numbered from 1 to 100.

I look at my card, Ariadne at hers; but we cannot see the other's card.

Camel adds, with a glint in her eye, the glint sneaking out from behind puffs of cigar smoke, that we cannot tell just by reasoning, reasoning separately from each other, who has the lower number. Well, with the flattery of rationality seducing us, we each quietly reflect, to see what we can conclude from Camel's comments, I from the card before my very eyes, and Ariadne from hers. Camel is insistent that we should do our very best by way of reason, but quietly and separately.

A moment's muse tells me that Ariadne clearly has not found herself with card number 1 – after all, she would then know straight away that she has the lower card. Camel would not have dealt her number 1 – and indeed I do not have card number 1.

To make the set-up vivid, I own up to readers, but not to Ariadne, that I find myself with 29. Maybe Ariadne has 63, though, to repeat, I am ignorant of which card she has been dealt. Clearly, in such a case – and there are many more – both Ariadne and I would readily agree that we are unable to figure out who has the lower.

JUST THINK RATIONALLY—
IGNORING THE FACT THAT I'M
A CAMEL, OF COURSE...

I can see my number, number 29. Moving on from my reasoning that Ariadne cannot have number 1, I reason that Ariadne will also have reasoned that I cannot have number 1, otherwise I would know that I have the lower.

So (it seems) we must both know that number 1 is ruled out. Now, if Ariadne has card number 2, then that must be the lower number. We both know, though, courtesy of Camel, that we cannot tell who has the lower, so obviously Ariadne lacks number 2; and she will have ruled out my having 2.

And so the reasoning continues, with each of us (separately, silently) ruling out 3 next and then 4 and so forth. By such reasoning, we should rule out our having any numbered cards at all. Yet that cannot be right: we have two distinct cards, one of which is the lower numbered. That the reasoning goes wrong will be before my very eyes, when it reaches as far as ruling out 29. Yet, how does the reasoning go wrong? No wonder Camel smiles smugly – well, for a camel.

What goes wrong with the reasoning?

We have Camel's clear statement, which we summarize as:

C: Neither of you can work out who has the lower card.

We each have that statement to consider, against the background of our being rational, seeing one card each, keeping quiet, no peeking and so forth.

Suppose I were to have card number 1, then I would rightly judge that C is false. The evidence of my eyes easily outweighs what I heard from Camel – not because I have better eyesight than hearing, but because there are better explanations for what I heard being wrong than for what I see being an illusion. Now, I do not have card number 1, but how do I know that Ariadne lacks that card?

Were Ariadne to have number 1, then that would show to Ariadne, but not to me, that C is false. So, before the paradoxical reasoning can move up the numbers, we both need to recognize that neither of us has number 1.

The mutual recognition that neither of us has 1 could be secured by our publicly announcing it or by Camel, flicking through the remaining cards, displaying card number 1. Were 1 to be ruled out in such a way, we should then possess common knowledge: that is, not merely would we mutually know that neither has number 1, but I would also know that Ariadne knows that I know that she knows – and so forth – that we both lack card number 1.

Possessing such common knowledge, our reasoning would move to: 'What if one of us has card number 2?' As with card number 1 being ruled out, so card number 2 could be ruled out by public announcements or Camel's display of that card, drawing it from the pack's remaining cards.

And so on…

If cards, one by one, are gradually ruled out in public, with Ariadne and I recognizing this, then Camel will look more and more irritable through her puffs of smoke, for, at some stage, the 'and so on' of the paradoxical reasoning will be blocked. Ariadne or I will be unable to confirm lack of the relevant card. One of us will have it – and will know it to be the lower because all lower numbered cards will have been eliminated. At that stage, Camel's C claim would be shown to be false. This, though, only comes about because of the public displays whereby we both know that the other lower cards are ruled out as held by us.

Arguably, the above discussion shows that common knowledge is required for the paradoxical reasoning to be justified in ruling out the cards. So, the paradoxical reasoning goes wrong because it illegitimately assumes such knowledge – when such knowledge is absent. If nothing is said by either of us, we have the possibility that the other has card 1 and that Camel has misled us in saying that neither of us can tell who has the lower card.

Suppose, though, that we both truthfully and clearly announce at the beginning, 'Well, I cannot tell who has the lower card.' I now know that Ariadne knows that I know… – and so on – that Camel spoke the truth and that neither of us can work out who has the lower card. That tells us that we, in common, both rule out our having card number 1, but does it show that we both rule out having cards 2, 3, 4, 5? Neither of us would know how many cards the other would rule out in that way. It is indeterminate. Hence, neither of us can be justified in succumbing to the paradoxical reasoning, ruling out cards one by one, on and on.

$$\Upsilon$$

'Here,' says Camel, 'We're starting again. See, I've just dealt you a single card, face-down, from a pack numbered 1 to 100. It is the lowest card that I can deal and which you cannot work out which one it is – without looking, of course.'

We wonder at Camel's confidence. We can surely work out some things. Camel would not have dealt us card 1, for that would be the lowest possible card. So, it would not be the lowest card she could deal us, without our knowing it to be the lowest. We guess the lowest must be card number 2 – and we start to utter the word 'two', when we hold back. We realize that we should then know that 2 is the lowest. So, 2 is also ruled out.

We feel queasy. We see how we could run through all the cards. None seems to satisfy the conditions set. If we reason that a particular card is the lowest one, then that fact rules it out, for we would then know – or so it seems.

Camel smiles at the disquiet on our faces. She coolly turns over the card: it is number 1.

'But we did think of that…,' we stumble.

'And so, you ruled it out.' Camel completes our sentence.

We realize the moral. The lowest card Camel could deal was card number 1 – and we knew that. But we used her claim, that we could not know the lowest card, to rule out 1; and hence it was ruled back in – but if we saw that, then we would be ruling it out again. We ought to have stayed our hand, insisting that it was card 1, showing that Camel had been mistaken in saying that we could not work out the lowest card. Well, we would have shown that, unless she had taken our reasoning into account and had dealt us card 2. But then we might have taken all that also into account.

And so it is that some things that we can be told disorientate us – for by ruling them out, we must rule them back in and then back out – and so on.

PART IV: METAPHYSICS
What is there – really?

———

Metaphysics is a dark ocean without shores or
lighthouse, strewn with many a philosophic wreck.
Immanuel Kant

When unearthing the works of Aristotle – so the story goes – papyrus scrolls were found entitled *Physics*. The next work lacked a title; it became *Metaphysics*, 'meta' meaning 'after'. True or not, the title was apt, for the book dealt with the very nature of 'being'.

Metaphysics, it has been said, is the systematic study of the ultimate constituents of the universe. It includes ontological questions of what fundamentally exists as well as questions of the most basic relationships such as causality. Hence, we confront classic paradoxes of space and time and whether, in reality, there are distinct objects. Perhaps reality 'out there' is not out there at all, but depends upon our thoughts, perceptions and classifications. That raises the metaphysical perplexity of mind – the self, the 'I' – a perplexity so great that it merits a separate part, namely, Part VI.

Here is a 'reality' question, courtesy of Elizabeth Anscombe, when worrying at a Cambridge seminar, many years ago. She had met a chocolate with a wrapper that read 'fruit or nut'. Now, she reflected, a chocolate can be fruit chocolate; it can be nut chocolate. It can be chocolate that is fruit *and* nut. But what is there about reality that could make it fruit *or* nut? Such indicates the puzzling intermingling of our language, concepts and reality.

Puzzles in this Part IV certainly raise difficulties in our understanding of the identity of objects, of what constitutes an object being one and the same object over time. A little tale is that of the treasured axe that has been passed from generation to generation in a family. True, over the decades, its blade has often been replaced; true, over the decades, its handle has often been replaced. Still, it is the same treasured axe – or is it?

Before we encounter the deeper problems of identity – deeper than that of the much loved axe – problems that transport us from rivers to goats to degrees of decency, sea and sand, we meet the most famous tortoise in philosophy, here presented as the wealthy Mr T. Mr T needs to be handled with care.

33
THERAPY FOR TORTOISES

Allow me to introduce you to Mr T, a wealthy tortoise from lands of Ancient Greece. Speak forth, Mr T. Explain how you became so wealthy.

'Being but a humble tortoise, I was always laughed at for my slowness of gait. When I tried to run, the laughter turned to ridicule, sometimes even crude mockery. Other creatures sped by me, waving, cackling, calling me "Speedy Gonzales". I was downtrodden; I felt truly rotten and rubbish. But then, my life changed. I discovered Professor Zeno of Elea: "Zany", to his friends.'

Would you explain yourself, Mr T?

'Zany (well, I called him "Professor" at the time, of course) set up a mile-long race between Mr Achilles and me. Mr Achilles was the fastest runner in Athens. At first, I thought the Professor was intent on making a fool of me – pulling my leg or tap-dancing on my shell. But that was not so. You see, I was given one hundred yards' start. That was only fair, as Mr Achilles ran much more quickly than I did. Let's pretend, just twice as fast – so that I may easily explain.'

But how did the hundred yards' start help? Presumably Achilles still won the race.

'That's what everyone predicted. I got amazing odds when having, as I thought, a mad moment and putting my faith in the Prof., I placed some large bets on Mr Achilles never catching me.'

What happened?

'The starting gun was fired. But before Achilles could win the race, he had to overtake me, you see. And before he could overtake me, he had to get level with me.'

True enough – but that was just a hundred yards.

'Achilles raced forward to the point where I had been. By the time he'd completed that hundred yards, I had moved fifty yards further, running at half his speed.'

So, he had just those fifty yards to run to catch up.

'Indeed. But by the time he ran those fifty, I had gone another twenty-five.'

Well, so then he ran those extra twenty-five.

'Quite so. But by the time he'd done that, I'd gone twelve and a half further.'

Yes, yes – but the distances for him to run are getting smaller and smaller.

'Don't you see? Achilles could never catch me, let alone overtake me. Whenever he got to where I'd been, I'd moved a little further. Half, then quarter, then one eighth, then one sixteenth of that initial hundred yards' start. That's an infinite series. Those proportions, though ever-decreasing, go on endlessly… Endlessly… Endlessly…'

Ah, so that accounts for your wealth, Mr T? Presumably, you collected your winnings?

'Indeed I did sir – and in cash – all thanks to Zany Zeno. He's brought me right out of my shell – and as for that cash, invested over the centuries, growth upon growth… Well, I'm digressing, sir.'

How can we ever manage to move at all?

Zany, I mean, Zeno, gave us four famous paradoxes of motion, in support of his teacher, Parmenides, who argued that all motion and change are illusory. To reach Mr T, Achilles needed to complete the endless series of half, then quarter, then eighth and so on. For you to walk to the wall opposite, you must go half the way, then half of the half, then half of that half: again, an endless series. Of course, Mr T has the same problem. He keeps tortoisely quiet about that, slipping back into his shell. How can he move to a place or even slip back into his shell? How can an endless series ever be completed? Yet complete such series, it seems that we must, whenever we move.

Mathematicians often think they have the puzzle solved. They tell us that many series, for example the one just mentioned, are indeed infinite, yet partial sums of the series converge within a limit. The series of half plus a quarter plus an eighth plus... – take the series as far as you like – well, whichever ones you take, they can be shown to converge towards one. Achilles ran one hundred yards, then half of one hundred, then half of that half and so on; hence, at the two hundred yard point, he drew level with Mr T. Similarly, the times taken to run those distances became progressively shorter, the partial totals also converging to a limit. The reducing size of the spatial distances was matched by the reducing size of the temporal durations.

Many philosophers are dissatisfied by this mathematical solution, for there remains the philosophical puzzle of how we can ever complete an *endless* number of runs or other movements, even if, indeed, the spans of time are also reducing in length. It is all very well to talk about mathematically converging to, or within, a limit, but that is no explanation at all of how in the physical world we reach the limit.

♈

Movement is not at the heart of the paradox. Similar difficulties arise concerning anything extended, whether in space or in time. Consider an unmoving object, existing through any span of time. For it to have lasted for an hour, it must have completed an endless series of time spans: for example, half an hour, a quarter of an hour, an eighth, a sixteenth and so on. Or ignore time and consider an object extended in space, say one foot long: somehow that foot is made up of half a foot and a quarter and an eighth and a sixteenth – and so forth. There is also the puzzle of how anything can even get started in its existence through time or movement through space. Take any time span: the object must first have existed through half of that time span. Now consider that half time span: it must first have existed through half of that half and so on.

One thought is that we need to be careful about what we mean when we speak of endlessly dividing or dividing to infinity. Talk of infinity may wrongly lead us to think that infinity is a place we can reach; think of the bizarre claim that parallel lines meet at infinity. Just because we can conceive of any mentioned distance as being further divided, we must not leap to conclude that an infinity of divided distances actually exists.

Perhaps the direction towards a solution is to distinguish between abstract mathematical representations and what is represented. A similar thought occurred when facing Hilbert's Hotel (Chapter 30). Consider a portion of any distance. The portion may be accurately represented by, for example, the fraction of one third – 1/3 – of the whole. That would seem to pose no problem. But it can also be represented by the endlessly recurring decimal number 0.333..., causing our bewilderment about how that physical distance could contain an endless flow of distances diminishing by a tenth.

It is all very well for Mr T to bathe in his wealth and paralyzing perplexities – we meet him again in Chapter 97, where he challenges a misunderstanding of logic – but if we cannot resolve the puzzles over the divisibility of space and time, all movement, all division, all separateness – all tortoises, all shimmering tortoise shells, all fluttering pages of philosophy books – are but illusions. Indeed, all is one.

All is one?

34
TENSIONS IN TENSE

While you read these words, the Earth orbits the Sun. A long time before your reading of these words, various rock formations changed and continents drifted, occurrences with long names with which only geologists are familiar. Numerous eclipses, comets trailing and stars a-shooting will occur some time after your reading, details of which only astronomers are competent to predict. In summary, things *are* happening, *have* happened and *will* happen. Saying the same thing, but differently: many events are in the present; many in the past; and many the future.

Now – and we should be careful with such (un)timely terms – delete all conscious beings from the events. Let us have only non-conscious happenings: geological changes and movements of clouds, planets, comets and the like. Even (and happily) ignoring the complexities of relativity theory, there are puzzles. When no conscious observers exist, are some of those events still in the present? Are some past? Some future? Or, for anything to be in the present, past or future, must it, at least, be related to individuals having experiences, having a viewpoint?

Presumably, we should insist that, even without conscious beings, events certainly occur. And if events occur, changes occur. Some states and events come after other states and events – after those which went before. In a universe without conscious beings, there would still be temporal relationships of 'before' and 'after'. But would there be any temporal properties of 'present', 'past' and 'future'? Would there be tenses? Would there be truths to the effect that things had happened; things are happening; and things will happen?

Perhaps we are inclined to say 'no'. The existence of a past, present and future requires a point of view, a view from where things are, indeed, past, present and future. If there are no conscious beings, there is no viewpoint; there are just events in a 'before and after' sequence.

Were we inclined to agree that, at the very least, we need a viewpoint for there to be any sense in the idea of events being past, present or future, we may become even more suspicious of 'past', 'present' and 'future' concepts. What is this talk of 'viewpoint'? Perhaps all that can be rightly meant is that some events are before, some after and some simultaneous with any given viewing event. If the viewers are speakers, then when they say that certain geological changes occurred in the past, all they are really saying is that those changes occurred *before* their current utterances. The eclipses and other changes that will occur – future eclipses and other future changes – are examples of happenings *after* their utterances. Further, some of the Earth's movements are occurring at the same time as their utterances – 'occurrences now' or 'occurrences in the present'.

There is the metaphysical question here: are 'past', 'present' and 'future' nothing more than our ways of referring to events that are before, simultaneous with or after someone doing the referring? More simply:

Is talk using tenses just talk about what is before, after or simultaneous with the talk?

When we speak of 'talk' we are, of course, alluding to any event – a thought, a hope, a speech – whose content involves reference to what is taken to be past, present or future. Many philosophers have argued that 'past, present and future' talk (and this applies to tensed talk) is simply reducible to 'before, after and simultaneous with' talk, hereafter referred to as 'before and after'. 'Past, present and future' gives us nothing more than that. Can this be right?

If talk of the present or 'now' is merely a matter of saying that some events are simultaneous with this talking, are we not missing the fact that these events simultaneous with this talking are indeed *now* – and not past or future? There are more problems: events, occurrences, happenings – events causing other events – all involve change. Does an understanding of time purely in terms of 'before and after' capture change?

Although there has been some recent publicity for Wittgenstein's poker – a controversy over whether, at a 1940s Cambridge Moral Sciences meeting, Wittgenstein, brandishing a poker, threatened Karl Popper – there is another, more significant, Cambridge poker, courtesy of McTaggart, a few decades before the brandishing dispute. (For more McTaggart, please see Chapter 91.)

Consider a poker: coloured red at one end and black at the other. Although it possesses these different colours, the possession does not carry with it the idea of its *changing* colour, merely that it *has* different colours. Similarly, that the death of Plato occurred *after* that of Socrates and *before* your reading of these words fails to capture the change we have in mind, when we speak of Plato's death once having been in the future but now being well in the past.

Consider now a black poker placed in a fire: it becomes red at one end because of the heat; still black and cold at the other. As the heat spreads, the black cold end will also turn to red hot – a change through time. The change is that the end that presently *is* cold and black, *will* become hot and red and, once hot and red, it is then true that it *was* cold and black.

Events involve change and change involves an item's properties – such as being hot and red – being future, then present, then past. If that is so, what account can we give of events changing from possessing the property of being in the future to possessing the property of being present and then past? A natural way of understanding such talk is, as said, in terms of how the events stand in relation to the speaker. But that, seemingly, involves merely the 'before and after' relation – and that fails to carry any implication of temporal change.

Your reading of these words is after certain historic geological changes; timelessly and always after those changes. You are reading these words before the Sun burns out; timelessly and always before that burning event. Events do not change their position in the 'before and after' series; so it is difficult to see how that series can be all there is to talk of past, present and future – for events do change their status as being past, present or future.

♈

Time, and the idea of time, present many such troubles. McTaggart settled for time being an illusion. He argued that time does indeed essentially involve past, present and future, yet he, McTaggart, could make sense only of events standing in the 'before and after' relation.

To say that time is an illusion immediately generates its own paradox. Even illusions seem to involve time; even if it is an illusion that the tortoise is moving (recall Zeno, page 152), there are changes in that illusion, such that some experiences, as if the tortoise were at point A, are in the past, while at present the tortoise seems to be at point B.

Here is another thought. I call it the 'paradox of time-taking'. It is quite common to accept that, one way or another, what is happening now in the universe (at least at the level of planets and trees and clouds) has been caused by, and is in some way explained by, what happened in the universe just before. The thought is that the state and events of the universe a little earlier are sufficient – enough – to bring about the state and events of the universe now. Were they not sufficient, we should need to postulate something else to explain why the things that are happening now are, indeed, happening now. So, we have the picture of the universe in state C being sufficient to bring about the universe in state E. If that is so, there is a puzzle about why it takes time (and the particular time it takes) for E to come about, once C is present. Why is E not instantaneous with C? If there is a time lag, then it shows that something else must have been required, as well as C, to bring about E.

The puzzle that results from the above reasoning is as follows. We are inclined to think of the states and events of the universe as standing in causal chains, over time. Yet this simply cannot be so – for such a chain would have to be an instantaneous 'everything happening all at once'. A big bang, bigger, indeed, than any big bang dreamt of by the scientists.

That's philosophy for you! And we didn't even leave our armchairs.

35

COCKTAILS, RIVERS AND...
SIR JOHN CUTLER'S STOCKINGS

A cocktail unshaken or unstirred can quickly cease to be a cocktail, for the ingredients separate. When wanting a gin and tonic, your want may not be divisible, such that you want a gin, whatever the outcome regarding the tonic, or vice versa. A gin and tonic needs to be mixed – and it is the mixture you want. Those simple examples remind us that some items are what they are and remain the same only if they have parts with some swirl, some mixing of ingredients. Even if the parts remain constant, the items may not – and that can be simply because of absence of swirl, absence of mixing.

The cocktail ceased to be; yet the ingredients remained. Rivers remain; yet the ingredients change. An oft-cited remark in connection with this is from the early fifth-century BC ancient Greek philosopher, Heraclitus:

You cannot step into the same river twice.

Quick-fired responses have been that you cannot even step into the same river once. They may depend on a logical point that stepping into *the same* implies stepping more than once. They may, though, be relying on the fact that the waters are forever changing, whether you step once or twice.

What may have intrigued Heraclitus – and what has intrigued later philosophers – is that when Heraclitus first bathed in the river, he was indeed bathing in some water. The river consisted of just that water and nothing else. Yet the next time he bathed in the same river – because the waters had flowed – he bathed in some different water, even though the river was the same river.

How can the river be the same, yet the water be different?

The river is, of course, extended in space; so, at one and the same time, two different people may be bathing in the same river yet in different patches of water, just as two people may be seeing the same mountain, yet one sees its bare rock to the south and the other its forests to the north. Some would then urge that the river be thought of as stretched not merely in space but also in time, as having not merely spatial but also temporal parts. We may then account for how bathing at the same location, in the same river, but at different times, may involve bathing in different waters.

Strictly speaking – a dangerous expression – Heraclitus bathed in one temporal slice of river, identical with a patch of water, at one moment on one day; he then bathed in a distinct temporal slice of the river, identical with a different patch of water, at a later time. The first temporal slice is not identical with the second, but both are slices of the one temporally extended river.

Thinking of items, such as rivers, pokers and people, as collections of temporal slices, though, seems to lose the idea that one and the same thing endures yet changes.

A more obvious response to the Heraclitean aphorism is to resist the identity of the river with its waters, making instead the common sense observation that a river is *composed* of water. One and the same river is composed of ever-changing waters – otherwise it would not be a river, but perhaps a long thin lake. What makes something one and the same river does not depend on its possessing the same composition, the same watery ingredients, over time – and, with cocktails in mind, even when something has the same ingredients, it does not follow that it is the same item. Heraclitus, in his thinking, may have simply been making, albeit enigmatically, that common sense point. Indeed, he offers a cocktail example: 'The barley drink disintegrates if it is not stirred.'

Changes in composition can be essential to the identity of a thing. That the river yesterday is the same river as the one today does not amount to its having the same composition. But then, what does make it the same river?

$$\Upsilon$$

Sir John Cutler, of the seventeenth century, was much attached to his black worsted stockings, so attached that, as holes developed, his maid would darn them, with silken thread. Eventually, his stockings no longer consisted of the original material, but of silk. The composition of his stockings was clearly different. Yet, it could reasonably be said, they remained the same stockings, in that they possessed a continuity through space and time and were used by Sir John to cover his legs to fine effect. What made them the same stockings did not depend on material sameness, but on continuity, ownership and function.

And what makes something the same river depends on location, usually a long geographical continuity, and changing waters flowing into a sea. A river may be the same river over time, even if during a period it runs dry, but is later replenished. And there will be times when we are unsure what to say, when rivers flow into each other. It may seem not to matter until, so to speak, it matters – as when there may be disputes about land or irrigation or fishing rights.

Here is a much discussed further example. As the parts of Duke Theseus' ship wore out, they were replaced, plank by plank, sail by sail, rope by rope, until – as with Sir John's stockings – not one of the original parts remained in the ship. The tale of Theseus' ship, though, has a twist. Suppose scavengers hoarded all the worn-out planks and other parts cast asunder, and then reconstructed the original ship, admittedly excessively shabby and unseaworthy. Which is really Theseus' ship – the one now composed of new parts, yet in Theseus' continual ownership, or the shabby one consisting of the original materials?

We may again be tempted by the thought that there is no 'really' about it, just a matter of decision. Here, though, it is a decision with consequences – especially if Theseus' new-looking ship is lost at sea, yet insurance companies refuse to pay out, claiming that the ship insured was the one composed of the same material, not the one now lost.

Identity itself can make us feel bewildered, at sea, especially when we raise the question of the identity of ourselves. It is all very well speaking of its just being a matter of stipulation, of decision, of words, which ship counts as Theseus', or when a river counts as the same river; but when we think of a person continuing over time, yet also changing, whatever makes her or him the same person? Now, that does matter — and is highly puzzling. Look out for the awakening of Isaac Newton, if Isaac Newton he be.

36
A GOAT WITH GAPS

I have a goat – one goat only. She sits quietly and still on my left, listening to Purcell. In front of me is a doorway. Through the doorway wanders a creature – a goat. She looks like mine. I can still spy my goat to the left; so the doorway goat is no goat of mine. What I saw afforded me no evidence that the entering beast is my goat; mine still sits, quietly and still, on my left. One goat cannot wholly be in two spatially distinct and discontinuous places at the same time. One goat cannot be two.

I have a goat – as before. She sits, quietly and still, on my left, listening to Purcell. I nod off. When I wake, a few minutes later, no animal is there to my left. A creature wanders through the doorway – a goat. She looks like mine. What I see affords me *some* evidence for thinking the doorway creature is my goatish beast. With no other goat in the vicinity – I check – I conclude that the goat wandering in is indeed mine. One goat can change its location over a period of time.

One goat can change its location over a period of time; but must there not be spatial continuity and proximity between its locations over that time? Must it not be possible to trace a spatially continuous line, through time, of the goat's locations from, in this example, its position on my left and its later position in the doorway? Such spatial continuity is, of course, expected; but *must* such spatial continuity exist for my goat to be one and the same goat over time? Puzzlingly, many people think so.

Must my goat exist without gaps over time?

Suppose the nodding-off scenario as before, yet with absolutely no sign of my goat having tiptoed round my sleeping form; no sign of my goat having skipped through an open window, then having raced round to

the doorway; no sign of the house having been de-roofed, a crane having lifted my goat, the goat then being dropped unharmed and unfazed at the doorway (the roof being neatly returned to the correct position). To sum up, there is no sign at all of continuous movement by the afore-mentioned goat from my left to the doorway. Yet various signs – love of Purcell, birthmark near left hoof (front), familiar dulcet tones – all point to the beast that now enters being my goat. Why should we insist that, for her to be my goat, the selfsame goat, she must have travelled across continuous spatial locations from my left to the doorway?

Some insist for the following reason. Suppose the discontinuity were to occur: perhaps for some time my goat ceases to exist, then seemingly re-appears in a new location without passing through adjacent locations. Assuming such discontinuities are accepted, we could then conceive of different circumstances after my goat vanishes: for example, two goats subsequently appear, one to my left, one to my right. They both look just like mine. Without spatial continuity there would be no good reason for my believing my goat to have re-appeared on the left rather than on the right. And my single goat could not now somehow manage to exist in two places at once.

Because of the above replication possibility – and we could expand the story from two to any number of goats, and to vast distances between them – the single goat now appearing in the doorway, after a discontinuity, cannot be mine. A single case of discontinuity brings about a conceivable case of multi-goats – and with a twosome or more, there would be nothing that made one of the resultant goats my original goat.

Can we, though, uncover a feature that, outweighing the lack of spatial continuity, preserves the identity of the goat as my goat?

We return to my goat. I know her well. I take her for walks; I listen to Purcell with her. She is pretty and a pretty constant companion. To date, she is a regular goat. One day an odd thing happens. As she frolics in the field, she vanishes before my very eyes. Her disappearance is for but a few minutes. Perhaps I was distracted; perhaps I have imbibed excess whisky and am tired. Thereafter, every few days, similar gaps in her life – goaty gaps – occur; perhaps they even become prolonged. Others notice the gapping. Here, we could develop different stories. After each disappearance, she reappears in exactly the same location and state as before, or maybe she is a few minutes' distance further on, at average goat travelling speed. Her goat's goatee is in the exact position relative to her body as a few minutes earlier – or maybe it is now more ruffled, in line with the blowing of the wind.

Scientists investigate. They are baffled. Their tests show that in all respects, despite the gaps, she is qualitatively the same goat. Two £1 coins, though, are qualitatively the same; yet one is mine, the other is yours. The coins are numerically different. So, is the goat that appears *my* – numerically the same – goat each time?

There could be motives for different answers. On the one hand, maybe my goat has just won the annual goatish prize, with a lucrative contract. So, this goat appearing after a few minutes' delay, or this goat coming through the doorway, had better still be mine. On the other hand, maybe I have an insurance policy that pays out on my goat's demise; so I would prefer this goat before me not to be deemed mine.

But whether this goat is my goat is surely not an arbitrary decision or deeming. There must be some facts of the matter.

What facts can there be, once we have run through shape, hoof-prints and bleat patterns, through genes and iris scans? The answer, given earlier, is: spatial continuity. But why should that be thought a necessary condition for numerical sameness? In learning the term 'same' in the sense of 'one and the same individual', spatial continuity is typically present – but that does not show that it is essential to our grasp of 'one and the same'.

My gappy goat, frolicking in the field, retains a regularity in activity and structure, despite the gaps. When I feed her, even if some goatish gaps then occur, she remains fed (for a bit); if she becomes 'with kid', her pregnancy continues roughly for the typical duration – and so on. To deploy a suggestion from the great seventeenth-century Leibniz, for there to be the same continuing individual, there must be an active principle of unity. Unity through regularity is the key. In our regular world, this regularity underlies the usual gap-free continuity; but, as our goat tale shows, such underlying regularity is consistent with spatial gaps. My goat remains a unity, albeit with gaps.

When regularity has gone, we doubt sameness of item. When the bottle is smashed, destroyed, the smithereens do not perform as one. After the mother gives birth, the behaviour of the child soon lacks spatial regularity in relationship to mother. It is the regularity in behaviour that holds an item – a creature – together as a unity. Such regularity leads us to think of a swarm of bees, even a flock of sheep, as items with some unity. Contrast with the 'hand and book' (page 189).

$$\Upsilon$$

The proposed 'active principle of unity' for an item to remain the same, even a gappy one, may itself appear exposed to replication puzzles. After a gap, two or two hundred and two goats could appear, all exhibiting the same regularity with the original. We should be unable to determine which one is my goat.

The replication argument, though, could also be used against the sameness of any standard spatio-temporally continuous entity, such as a goat. We could dream up thought-experiments whereby a regular goat spontaneously divides into numerous goats all like the original. We could therefore argue that even with a single goat, the existence of a goat a moment later cannot be taken to be the existence of the same goat. Yet that conclusion would be absurd – for we should have lost all idea of one and the same entity persisting through time.

Of course, gaps could get out of hand. We could imagine goats ceasing to be, then popping up years later in different parts of the universe. We may then anguish philosophically whether they could be numerically the same goats. In such cases, the required principle of unity would seem to be lacking – though who knows quite what is being imagined in such bizarre cases?

Thought-experiments need to be handled with care. Our concepts are grounded in this world to date. If possible replications are to be treated seriously, they cannot be used to undermine our normal understanding of items remaining numerically the same through time. Our modest gappy goat tale is a thought-experiment, but it is not one thought too far. It makes perfectly good sense. My goat may continue as my goat, numerically the same, even with the gaps.

Thus we see how what makes a creature one and the same creature over time is neither spatial continuity nor arbitrary linguistic decision. Rather, it is a question of how well the creature, the biological chunk, hangs together. Pondering further, we should see that that applies as much to human beings as to goats. For your human life to be the self-same life through time – well, how well do your values, memories and intentions, your character traits, physical features and abilities, hang together?

37

WHEN ONE MAKES TWO: DRESSING UP

Variety is the spice of life – or so it is said. Maybe that saying leads a few to change their identities. More often the change has evasion in mind, perhaps because of bigamy charges, evasion of tax or police in pursuit. Avoiding embarrassment can motivate changes in names – parents, take care when naming your young. Some changes are turnings on pathways to fame: Norma Jean became Marilyn Monroe. Or, for that matter, they occur after seeing the light: bound to Damascus, Saul became Paul. Yet double lives become the outcome for some – and such lives may spell some logical trouble.

David delights in variety; he delights so much that he often dresses in a womanly fashion – as Lady Davinia – playing the lady role exceptionally well. When out in public, and not dressed as Davinia, he is masculine and mean – 'Dave', so rough and so tough. The girls swoon at Dave the tough, yet are unmoved by Davinia the cool. Men dismiss Dave as 'Jack the Lad', but yearn for kisses from Davinia so cool, so elegant. David's changes in persona always take place in private. People, if observing his apartment, often see Dave, dressed in the usual leathers, disappearing indoors; sometime later, Lady Davinia appears, her long blonde hair shimmering, dress sparkling and stilettos so sharp.

Many things, it seems, are true of Davinia, yet not of Dave. Men open car doors for Davinia, but never for Dave. On particular occasions, Dave, not Davinia, enters the home; later Davinia, not Dave, exits. We may add complexity by commenting about David, but allow him to drop out of the picture, until required again. Consider how we may reason:

Premiss 1:   Girls make dates with Dave.

Premiss 2:   Dave is Davinia.

Conclusion: Girls make dates with Davinia.

The two premisses are readily accepted as true, yet we – even we in the know – may well resist accepting the conclusion. After all, girls do not really date Davinia. Yet if they do not, we hit the puzzle that follows:

As Dave and Davinia are one individual, how can some things true of Dave not be true of Davinia?

We may have wanted to ask, 'How can some things be true of one, yet not of the other?' – but, while we have the 'one', we lack the 'other'. 'They' are one and the same person, identified by two names. If we have two names for the same item and know which item that is, we can surely substitute one name for the other, without altering the truth of what we say. Lewis Carroll was Charles Dodgson. It is a truth that Dodgson died in 1898; so it must surely also be true that Carroll died in the same year.

One line of thought, the Identity Line, stresses that the same things really are true of Dave and Davinia. The line needs, then, to explain why we tend mistakenly to think otherwise. Another line, the Difference Line, accepts that there really are some differences between what is true of Dave and of Davinia – and that is because we misunderstand use of the names.

According to one Difference Line, everything that persists is really a sequence of temporal stages. Why it is true that girls swoon at Dave and not at Davinia is because the temporal stages differ: the Dave stages differ from the Davinia stages. In Premiss 1 and the conclusion, we are not directly referring to the same individual, but to a person's different stages in time: a 'Dave' stage in 1; a 'Davinia' stage in the conclusion.

In criticism of the Difference Line, is a continuing life really just a sequence of temporal stages? Maybe it is, when natural and significant developments occur. Yes, the tadpole is a temporal stage of a creature that has the later stage of frog. David, though, keeps switching between

Dave and Davinia: the temporal stages of Dave lack continuity. For that matter, David, the generator of the persona changes, would also need to be fitted into the temporal tale.

The Difference Line demands linguistic juggling. It is not obviously true that girls swoon at temporal stages of a man. More accurately, it is not obviously true that female stages swoon at male stages. Maybe 'swooning' needs understanding afresh. Further, perhaps girls speak to rough-voiced Dave on a mobile, while peering through the apartment's curtains, seeing Davinia on the phone. That is, David is dressed as Davinia, yet speaking as Dave: the temporal stage is the same, yet both Dave and Davinia are present. The Difference Line also needs to explain why Premiss 2, Dave is Davinia, seems true. Perhaps 'is' sometimes needs special rendering as 'is a temporal stage of the same person as'. Yes, much juggling is required, as seen earlier, with Heraclitus not stepping into the same river twice.

The Difference Line is problematic. How fares the Identity Line? This line keeps faith with the thought that Dave and Davinia really are the same individual. So why do we make different assessments about what is true of them? Maybe the conclusion, 'Girls make dates with Davinia', is true; but we resist assent because assent would mislead people unaware that Davinia is David, and that David is appearing as Dave, whenever girls date him.

Here is an analogy. I truthfully announce that the Queen appeared on television and was sober. You wrongly conclude that she is not usually sober. Why would anyone mention her sobriety, unless it was unusual? Even though what I say does not logically imply that the Queen is usually drunk, my comment may convey an alcoholic royalty; my comment carries a 'conversational implicature'. A little similarly, we hesitate in saying that girls date Davinia because we realize how, in many contexts, to assert it would mislead. Here, of course, we have already exposed David's lifestyle; so, here, asserting our conclusion that girls date Davinia should not mislead. More explanations, though, are needed; and more problems duly arise.

♈

We want to say that girls do not date Dave *as Davinia*. Girls make dates with Davinia, not as Davinia, but *as Dave*. Maybe Premiss 1 is truthfully saying, or implying, that girls make dates with someone personified as Dave – with the conclusion read as saying that they make dates with someone personified as Davinia. That line seems to make the strange commitment that girls make dates with personifications or aspects. Can you date a persona or aspect? If David's cross-dressing ways are revealed, girls may truthfully say, 'Wow, so sometimes Dave is dressed as Davinia, a woman.' But that does not amount to saying that David personified as Dave is sometimes dressed as David personified as Davinia. David, when personified as Dave, certainly is not dressed as Davinia.

The above approaches to the cross-dressing puzzle generate more and more difficulties. Perhaps we fail to see the wood for the trees, even though – dare I say? – the wood is identical with a collection of trees. The puzzle has arisen because we have two different names and a story – a story that provides two different sets of thoughts and pictures, one set associated with one name, the other set with the other name. We hold two separate files on David, for we know about the double life. Which file we handle depends upon which name is being used.

'Do girls make dates with Davinia? – yes or no.' Resist being bullied into giving a 'yes' or a 'no'. Let our answer be, 'In a way, yes; and, in a way, no.' Which file (dossier, cluster) is in play (see page 408)?

'Did you meet your husband before you married him?'

'Yes.'

'So, he was your husband when you met him?'

'No.'

Let us try the question again. 'Did you meet your husband before you married him?'

'Well, no.'

'So, you just went and married a perfect stranger, you poor thing. I'm so sorry.'

38
PIN DROPPING

Things may be so quiet that you can hear a pin drop; but, for that hearing to take place, you need not merely a pin and the drop, but also a conscious observer to hear. Such a thought should silence the wonder of whether, when trees fall in a forest, there is any sound if no one is present to hear. 'No observer; no sound' may be the principle. If so, the universe is a fine and quiet place, when lacking conscious creatures. Recording apparatus, if magically existing before creatures came to be, would still register the vibrations of those forest 'snaps', 'crackles' and 'thuds'; but, on playback, there would be no sounds to play back, if still no creatures to hear.

There is no good reason to stop at sounds. If no one is present, salt, it seems, lacks any taste; roses lack the scent of roses, and, as for the colours of rainbow, could anything be coloured, if no one exists to perceive the colour? Such considerations led a certain Bishop Berkeley, a powerful reasoner of the early eighteenth century, to argue that for anything to exist at all, there must be observers, perceivers. 'To be is to be perceived' was the good Bishop's mantra – well, part of his mantra. Perceivers are also beings and yet are unperceived, being not perceivable bodies but minds or spirits; so the mantra in fullness is 'To be is to be perceived or to perceive', with 'perceiving' covering the five senses, seeing, touching, hearing, smelling, tasting, as well as thinking.

In speedy summary, material things, themselves no spirits or minds, cannot exist if understood as items unperceived – well, thus argued the Bishop. What we think of as material objects – tables, chairs, mince pies and mountains – are just collections of qualities, of colours, shapes, weights, tastes, softness or hardness; and such qualities depend on perceivers perceiving. To one perceiver, the bathwater feels hot; to another,

tepid. The mince pie is salty to one; sweet to another. From one angle, the table looks oval; from another, circular; and so forth. These 'physical' objects are not matter, existing independently of mind – a repugnance, a contradiction, according to Berkeley – but collections of ideas, that is of mind-dependent perceptions.

There need be no worry, though, about tables and chairs popping out of existence when we leave the room (and the room popping out too) and popping back upon our return. We need not fear for the existence of unseen bodily organs and the movements of legs and arms that come and go out of existence, depending on whether they are perceived, be it inwardly or outwardly. There need be no fear, for Berkeley ushers in God, the greatest perceiver, upon whose mind all objects depend. God is all seeing and always seeing. Thus came forth the limerick:

> There was a young man who said, 'God
> Must find it exceedingly odd
> That this tree I see, should continue to be
> When there's no one about in the Quad.'

and the divine reassuring reply:

> *Dear Sir:*
> *I am always about in the Quad.*
> *And that's why the tree*
> *Will continue to be*
> *Since observed by*
> *Yours faithfully,*
> *God.*

To answer Berkeley's puzzle, let us resist refuge in God. How may we combat Berkeley's position that tables and chairs, mountains and mince pies are mind-dependent collections of ideas?

Are there sounds in a forest when no one is present to hear?

Can things exist when there are no observers?

To quell Berkeley's argument we should distinguish between the ideas that we have, the mind-dependent entities, and the mind-independent entities that cause those ideas. We sometimes conflate the two because of ambiguous language. When we speak of sounds, are we speaking of experiences or of vibrations in the air? When we speak of the pie being hot, are we speaking of hot sensations or of the pie's molecular motions that cause the sensations? Experiences differ from what the experiences are experiences of. Experiences are mind-dependent; the vibrations and molecular motions are not.

The above is an answer to Berkeley; but Berkeley has a reply. What are the vibrations or motions or qualities that allegedly are distinct from our experiences? One person experiences the water as hot, another as tepid. Which is it? Look at the sky with – then without – rose-tinted glasses: its colour seemingly changes. What qualities do the water, the sky, the mince pies and so on really have? And what do we know about vibrations and molecular motions, save how our senses are affected?

The general point is that our experiences, we casually believe, result from an interplay between the objects and our perceptual apparatus. Our perceptual apparatus contributes to what we take the objects 'really' to be. A cat's apparatus gives it different experiences; a Martian's apparatus (were there to be such creatures) different too. How can we possibly reach out to anything other than our experiences?

According to Berkeley, we perceive just ideas, experiences – and they are mind-dependent. According to others, behind the veil of ideas exist the material or physical objects that cause the ideas. As there is no possibility of lifting the veil even ever so slightly, Berkeley's stance is that talk of such objects behind a veil is idle talk. Mind you, as mentioned, Berkeley does end up with something behind the veil: God. We continue here, though, without God.

$$\gamma$$

The line of argument above can reach a radical conclusion, for my knowledge of other people is based on nothing more than my experiences; so, I am also unjustified in believing other people exist, save as ideas dependent on my mind. I could land in the position of believing that only I and my ideas exist: 'solipsism'. Here, let us return to common sense. Common sense can often help.

Berkeley had us seeing, touching – hearing, smelling, tasting – ideas. That immediately set us on the wrong path. The particular senses need to be treated differently from each other; but, risking the general, we often accept, as a matter of common sense, that we see and touch – and so forth – physical objects. We see the cat, smell the cat, stroke the cat, even accidentally kick the cat. When we see the cat, we have visual sensations; but we do not see the sensations. The sensations, the ideas, are what, arguably, we have when seeing the cat – though we may wonder about the relationship between the cat and those sensations.

If the cat is white, we have sensations of whiteness, depending on lighting conditions. Of course, such visual sensations are lacking, when no one is around to see the cat. Does that mean that the cat lacks a white colour, when unseen? Well, it depends what is meant by 'white'. One quick solution is to argue that an item is white if the following is true: were it to be seen by typical human beings, or maybe discriminating experts, under agreed 'normal' conditions, then the perceivers would have certain visual sensations, namely those of whiteness. Is that visual sensation in the cat? No. Is the cat white? Yes.

The approach, details to one side, seeks to understand qualities such as colours and shapes, tastes and smells, as dispositional: that is, they are understood in terms of which sensations would occur *if*... When we say salt is soluble, we do not mean that it is dissolving right now: what we mean is that, *were* it to be placed in water, then it would dissolve. When we say salt is white, we do not mean that there are experiences of a whiteness right now, if no one is looking: what we mean, or at least imply, is that, were it to be viewed under normal conditions, then certain visual sensations would occur.

We return to the forest bereft of sentient beings. The winds howl, the trees crash and the lightning is followed by thunder. Were there to be humans present, they would hear those things. So, just as oceans and mountains, shapes and sizes, densities and durations surely existed before sentient beings existed, we should acquiesce in accepting that the deserts were coloured, oceans were salty – and forests were filled with sounds.

Yet does that sound quite right?

39
IN NO TIME AT ALL

Many people quite naturally accept that the future does not exist – by which they mean that future events, being in the future, are not yet existing. Similarly, it may seem obvious that the past does not exist – by which is meant that it does not exist now. It once existed, when present; but it no longer exists. Those chocolates, our tasting them and delight in them, once existed, but exist no more, being now in the past. Right now maybe you are looking forward to the future, to your next summer holiday; so, the holiday does not exist now, but it will exist. Of course, your looking forward exists; the looking forward is in the present.

All this seems obvious. The further thought, also obvious, is the conclusion that anything which exists can exist only in the present, only now. But what is the present? What is *now*?

People impressed with the above thoughts may yet slip into giving an answer by way of duration. *Now* lasts for a few minutes, or a second, or a split second – and so on. But anything suggested which has duration hits the buffers of the reflections above; well, so it would seem. If it has duration, it has parts, a beginning and end. If we are at the beginning, then the end must be in the future and hence fails to exist. If we are at the end, then the beginning must be in the past and hence fails to exist. We, here in the present, are squeezed into no time – into *no time* at all.

When we reflect on these arguments, we see the present as metaphorically going, going, gone. Nothing is left. But if neither the past nor the future exists, and if the present gets squeezed into nothing, can there be anything – just anything – that exists in time?

Can anything exist in time?

The above argument has led us to think of the present as a boundary, a boundary between past and future. Yet, if neither past nor future exists, how can a boundary exist between them? And if this supposed boundary is without duration, then quite what existence does the boundary possess — and hence quite what can possibly exist in the present? We may also wonder what happens to time itself in all of this. We seem to run out of time, for time itself seems to be squeezed out of all existence.

For many philosophers, the paradox arises because we are misled by our language of 'past, present, future', the language of tenses, with talk of what *was*, what *is* and what *will be*. Perhaps, instead of thinking of such tensed time as basic, we should understand time in terms of events happening *before* and *after*, or *simultaneously*, with certain other events. On this latter view, as seen in the earlier 'Tensions in Tense' (Chapter 34), if I say that the goose is now cooking in the oven, then that amounts to making the point that it is cooking simultaneously with my saying.

If time is properly captured simply by events being in the before–after series, then the events are equally real, equally exist, whether or not we describe them as being past, present or future. A tree extended in the three spatial dimensions, with length, breadth and height, has time as a fourth dimension; its roots are spatially below its branches and its temporal stage of being a sapling is before its temporal stage of being a mature oak. This is the tenseless view of time.

On the tenseless view, our talk in terms of tenses arises out of the fact that the different judgements we make stand in different positions in the before–after series. Time is being seen as a fourth dimension: the past, present and future are then usually considered to be in the same boat, all existing. The future is some temporal distance away from us *now* — just as Pluto is some spatial distance away from us *here*. Future events, years away from us, exist, just as events millions of miles away from us exist. It is simply that we lack easy access to events a long way away, be they 'away' in space or in time.

Were the tenseless view of time correct, then there should be no puzzle about events existing in the present: they are as real whether they exist in the present or past or future. With the tenseless view, though, we confront different puzzles. We may wonder why it is that we cannot perceive – see, hear, smell – those events that are existing further along the before–after sequence, in either direction, in what we think of as the past and the future.

There are, of course, answers – even acceptable answers. Causes operate in one direction in the before–after series: events *before* cause events *after*, and not vice versa. Events after your reading this page, events 'in the future', cannot cause events before them. That is why, even though those future events exist, they cannot affect us now; that is why we cannot, for example, see which football team is winning next week.

What of events that occurred before your reading of this page? On the tenseless view, they too exist. And, in fact, we do perceive some of those events, events that are existing in the past. Think of the spatial distance of planets and stars. Given that light does not travel from A to B instantaneously, the changes that we see are ones that occurred at points in the time dimension well before our seeing them; they caused our seeing them. Indeed, if we think that A's causing B always takes some time, however short, then we are always experiencing things that have already happened, that are, at least a little bit, in the past.

The biggest problem with the tenseless view of time is its failure to do justice to change. The cooking goose is changing colour, changing from being raw to cooked. This is not merely a variation akin to the way in which the goose is spatially variable, with skin on the outside, bones within. Spatially, a cake may be chocolate on the outside and cream inside, but the cake is not thereby undergoing a change. Think of how different the chocolate *changing* into cream is from there simply being chocolate next to cream.

Returning to the goose, the change as it cooks seems to make essential reference to tenses: the goose was raw, but will be well done. Yet, if we are back with time understood as involving tenses, involving change, we are back with our initial puzzle.

♈

Arguably, some of the puzzles to do with the present can be dispelled, by separating out features of time that are easily confused. Events and actions – the cooking, the handshaking, the crashing tree – take time to occur, yet they may be in the present; they are happening now. That would be impossible, were the present just a boundary or instant. Right now, you are reading this book; the present century is the twenty-first; and your present age is... – well, complete at your discretion. What is present now is typically understood as being more than a moment. Perhaps this should lead us to accept that the present in a way includes at least portions of the past. If so, then the past, at least to some extent, and also the present certainly do exist.

That the present century is the twenty-first does not, of course, imply that we are experiencing the present century now from beginning to end in one go. What we experience as *now* is of very short duration, but still has duration. What we experience as now also differs from the period that we are able to keep before the forefront of our mind. This latter period is often known as the 'specious present', though characterizations of the specious present vary.

We can hold before our minds durations, the specious presents, that are longer than what we experience as now. Yet the 'now' durations that we experience should still be distinguished from any durationless boundaries. These distinctions, though, do not save us from bafflements about time. We now meet bafflements about the relationship between the specious present, the experienced present and any durationless boundary.

One way of feeling the power of puzzling time, and how time strikes us, is to wonder quite what is going on when we listen to a piece of music. We are listening to a symphony, a song or even some techno, yet are we listening to all of it, right now? Well, no, we are hearing some notes now. Presumably we must also be remembering or holding in our mind other notes, in order to identify the melody, the rhythm, the movement. Or must we?

St Augustine of Hippo (now part of Algeria), writing in the late fourth century, early fifth century, seemed well-informed on original sin, divine grace and the City of God; yet his certainties fell away when thinking about time. Augustine is he of the 'Lord, make me chaste – but not yet' request. As well as his confessions of personal lapses, he confessed, more relevantly for this chapter, 'What then is time? If no one asks me, I know what it is. If I wish to explain it to him who asks, I do not know.'

Well, even when no one asks me, I fear I do not know what time is. What is it, though, that we are seeking to know? Presumably, we seek more explanation, yet in order to explain quite what? After all, as we argued when facing Achilles and our tortoise Mr T, just because in the abstract we can talk of dividing any duration again and again – infinitely so – it perhaps is a mistake to impose such divisions on time as we experience it. The mistake is akin to thinking that if a computer programme properly models changes in the weather, we should expect the computer sometimes to be wet with rain. In our quest for understanding, we can go far, when applying abstract models and representations to our everyday lives in space, in time, even in love – we can go far, but only so far.

A comment from Wittgenstein in a different context is, 'The difficulty here is: to stop.'

I stop, at least on this topic of time – just in time.

40
SAND, SUN, SEA AND...

Bikini-clad Sandy stretches out on hot sands, idly reflecting on their vastness. 'How many grains on this beach?' she wonders. 'Many more than one thousand.' But her eyesight alone is not sufficiently discerning to distinguish between one thousand and one thousand-and-one grains, unless she starts counting. Sandy, being but human, is unable to see the difference between a large number of grains and that number with one more added or one taken away – purely by looking, as opposed to, for example, popping them, one by one, into an urn and counting.

'I can tell, just from looking around me, that there are more than a thousand grains. Just by looking, I cannot spot the difference between a thousand and a thousand with one grain more, so I must be able to tell, on the basis of what I see and my bit of reasoning, that there are more than one thousand-and-one grains.' Thus, Sandy moves from the truth that there are at least one thousand grains to the truth of there being at least one thousand-and-one.

'So, I know that there are at least one thousand-and-one grains, but I cannot tell the difference between that and one thousand-and-two, merely from looking; so I know that there are at least one thousand-and-two.' Sandy continues thus, going on, grain by grain, into the higher thousands. Of course, at these low numbers, she can tell, without any of the reasoning, that the beach has more grains than such low numbers of grains. After a while however, some uncertainty would cut in, unless she deployed and was convinced by the line of reasoning just outlined. And the reasoning, going up one grain at a time, would lead her to the millions, billions, trillions, trillion trillions and even the number which is the number of electrons in the whole universe, as being at least the number of grains on the beach. Somewhere *en route* she would have moved from truth to falsehood, for even though the beach is big and sandy, the grains do not reach the trillion trillions. Where does this reasoning go wrong?

A couple of grains of sand, every now and then, are blown off a nearby sandcastle, yet a couple of grains cannot make the difference between a sandcastle and a mere sandy mound. Remove a couple of grains and it would surely remain a castle; remove a couple more and it must surely remain a castle – and yet? Somewhere, if continued, that reasoning goes wrong, for it could leave us insisting that the castle remains when there is no castle left at all. Furthermore, Sandy is aware that she would be unable to distinguish the castle as it is right now from the same castle with a few grains missing. Remove a couple of grains and she will see it is a castle still. Remove a couple more and she must surely still see it is a castle – and yet...

A rock's shadow darkens her thighs. Twenty minutes earlier the shadow had only touched her toes. Even had she paid careful attention, she would not have noticed the shadow's gradual movement during one minute. Although she cannot spot the shadow's movement each minute, somehow she spots it over twenty; yet the twenty consists of twenty non-spotting temporal spans. She now notices how much closer the lapping waves are to her feet; yet she failed to detect the slight changes of their drawing closer.

A man stares at her. Her bikini top has slid off her breasts. It must have been gradually slipping; yet neither she nor the man could have spotted the teeny movement of skimpy material each second. Of course, they spot the cumulative effect. Sandy is excited, until she takes in the man's official uniform. She is on a puritan beach and, via imperceptible stages, has moved from decency to indecency. She is prepared to pay the fine, but then realizes, from the man's gaze, that there may be an alternative...

If teeny changes make no difference, how can big changes make a difference when big changes are just collections of teeny ones?

The motif in our tales derives from Eubulides, from whom we heard in Chapter 25. There, he worried about the Liar; here his worries are these

Sorites ('heap') paradoxes. Eubulides reflected that a heap of pebbles is still a heap even after one pebble is removed. First find a heap: remove a pebble and a heap remains. As it is still a heap, when we remove another pebble it remains a heap. Perform as many pebbling removals as you wish; according to this reasoning, we keep a heap – yet manifestly we do not. Similar reasoning should lead us mistakenly to conclude that the sandcastle remains a castle, however many grains are blown off.

Before saying that none of this matters, reflect on biological examples. Minute by minute a foetus develops, leading to baby, child, adult – with resultant different permissible treatments, moral treatments about which there are extremely strong disagreements, as touched upon in Chapter 3. Even Sandy's move from decency to (perceived) indecency has significant consequences for her – and others.

The puzzle rests on some objects and concepts lacking sharp boundaries. At which point (if any) does a sandcastle cease to be a sandcastle? Let us acknowledge that there are grey areas concerning such sandy matters; but must there then not be sharp boundaries between the clear and the grey areas? It would seem not: so how do clear cases transform into the less clear? How can a grain of sand make a difference between what is a definite sandcastle and a vague or grey borderline sandcastle? These sandy slopes are slippery slopes.

There is also the question of what we know and how we perceive: witness Sandy and the lapping waves, moving shadow and number of grains making up the beach. Sandy cannot spot the difference, by feeling or sight, between the extent of the shadow cast on her thigh from one second to the next; yet, after repeated seconds, she notices that shadowy movements have occurred. She cannot sense a small slide of her bikini top; yet further small slides enable her to be aware of her topless state. If the small changes make no noticeable difference to her, how do they somehow add up to a noticeable difference? If a grain's difference cannot affect what she knows and can see, how can added unnoticed differences make a difference to what she knows and can see? How can she be justified in switching from judging that the pile of sand is a sandcastle, to hesitating a little, hesitating more, then to being certain that it is no sandcastle at all, when a single grain difference goes unnoticed?

♈

I often know how to do something without knowing quite how I do it. I know how to cycle, open an awkward gate and drink a glass of wine, without knowing quite how I do these things. Some golfers just 'know' how to hole the ball without being able to explain how. People who have 'blind sight' sincerely report that they cannot see anything beyond a certain edge, yet give correct descriptions (more often than randomness would dictate) of what lies beyond that edge, without anything further to go on than what they, so to speak, 'cannot see'.

We speak of what Sandy can and cannot discern, yet we need to recognize that she can discern things without knowing that she can or how she can. Teeny changes, be they to do with sand, shadowy movements or bikini tops, are below Sandy's conscious awareness and hence imperceptible to her (if perceptibility demands awareness); but that does not mean that they do not register on her central nervous system. We detect some small changes without knowing that we do. This raises questions of how small neural changes, each of which leaves no conscious mark, eventually give rise to conscious awareness; and how some teeny changes in sandcastles affect the eye and optic nerve and brain while other teeny changes do not.

These thoughts offer no direct answer to how we manage to use vague terms – except to remind us that what we cannot consciously detect, we may yet be able to detect without conscious awareness. It remains puzzling, though, how undetectable minuscule changes give rise to our detecting, consciously or otherwise, greater changes. That there is, though, such detection explains why, at certain stages, we start hesitating about whether the castle is still a castle, whether the shadow is in the same position and whether the bikini slippage now exposes us – well, Sandy – to an indecency charge and fine.

41

DO WE MAKE THE STARS?

'If the prisoners move, shoot first; ask questions later.' So came the instruction to Smart, the new guard. What a pity that Smart was a stickler for accuracy – and knew his astronomy. Later, as the other guard stared down at the dead prisoners, horrified, Smart explained that he had to obey orders and shoot. 'Don't you realize,' Smart smartly said, 'we're on Earth, so the prisoners were moving pretty fast – orbiting the sun.'

$$\approx$$

Whether or not something moves is relative to something else, taken as fixed, as platform. What that else is depends on context. Really, Smart was no stickler for accuracy, just obsessed with heliocentricity, with the sun as platform. Such relativity works well with motion, but surely not with the existence of objects.

Whether people are celebrities – pop stars, film stars or just stars for being stars – depends on us; but whether stars of the sky and other heavenly bodies of non-human ilk exist is different. Of course, some things do hang on taste, are relative to taste-buds, but stars of the firmament do not. True, we may see the man in the moon – children may take the expression literally – but really there exist only configurations seen by us as fascinatingly facial. Did that face exist before humans identified it? Not at all – the face depends on our patterning inclinations; the moon and its craters do not.

Two opposed arguments lurk here:

Mind-Struck: Someone guides your eye across the night sky, pointing to constellations: there's Orion's Belt; here's the Plough – ah,

Cassiopeia. Did those star patterns exist before humans existed? Certainly no one, prior to humanity, saw some stars as forming a letter W, or as being a lady with head hanging. Without such 'seeing as', would there have existed a W pattern? And the star patterns could surely have struck us as grouped differently. The groupings depend on us. There is nothing 'out there' in the night sky that brings those stars together into a W – just as there is no man in the moon.

Star-Struck: That is all very well. No doubt in some way we construct the patterns, in that the patterns we see are partially determined by what strikes us as resemblances and of interest – but those patterns are still limited by the stars and where they are. Certainly we neither made the stars nor decided where they would sparkle. We did not fix the number of planets orbiting our sun.

Mind-Struck: Until recently, that number was nine. Now, it is eight, with the sad demotion of Pluto. How many planets there are depends in part upon how we classify heavenly bodies. The planets, the stars, are but patterns of gases, chemicals, explosions, swirling molecules and atoms. Those patterns also depend in part upon the fact that we group things in certain ways. Had we not done so, there would not have been stars…

The general question is:

How independent of us is the universe?

It is crazy to think that the solar system – and indeed sunsets and oceans and forests and trees – were made by us. Certainly they were not physically crafted by us – and we have evidence that they existed long before we did. Surely, Star-Struck is right. And yet…

Does not Mind-Struck have a point? Without human beings, there would have been no carving up of the world into solar systems and galaxies. It is because of our interests and the way that we perceive things that we apply terms such as 'trees', 'oceans' and 'stars'. Some differences we proclaim; others we ignore. We could have seen and carved things differently. The joints between things, so to speak, are of *our* making.

Did the wooden chess pieces, carved from a single tree, exist before we carved them? Well, no, but the tree did. Gold was not valuable until human beings bestowed value, but it existed before human beings. Did the states of the US and countries of the European Union exist before frontiers were set and treaties ratified? True, we shaped the boundaries – but the land was there, ready to be shaped. Perhaps Mind-Struck is merely reminding us that some truths arise because of human activities, interests and conventions; but that does not mean that all facts of the universe depend on our conventions and carvings.

And yet – that is not all that Mind-Struck is suggesting. Mention any fact and you will deploy descriptive terms; but those terms result from how we see, carve and regard the world. The world comes to us unchopped – yet what then becomes of the world?

Look at this book. Is it one object or many? Well, it is one book, a collection of many pages, and a vast collection of electrons and other sub-atomic particles. These are different ways we have of carving the book; but is there one correct way of identifying objects, such as books, birds and birch trees? Should we, for example, think of the tree as 'really' just a collection of cells or as one genuine unity? And the same question arises regarding the universe: is there one correct way of understanding it? Or is it undifferentiated, until we humans commence carving?

Mind-Struck is questioning whether there is just one right way of seeing things – or, at least, whether some ways get us nearer to reality than others. After all, some have seen lightning as divine thunderbolts, others as electric discharges. Surely, though, we know that one is wrong, the other right.

The playful Jorge Luis Borges described an ancient Chinese taxonomy, a classification, of animals into fourteen categories: belonging to the emperor; embalmed; those trained; suckling pigs; mermaids; fabulous ones; stray dogs; those included in this classification; those that tremble as if mad; innumerable ones; those drawn with a very fine camel hair brush; et cetera; those that have just broken the flower vase; and those that, at a distance, resemble flies. Even without the circularity of the self-referential (recall Russell's Set, Chapter 29), we should recognize the divisions as lacking grounds in nature. Contrast with the reports by physicists. While we, in everyday affairs, consider that the table is solid, physicists say that 'really' it is mainly space and sub-atomic particles. Perhaps, though, the conflict merely displays an ambiguity in the term 'solid': we can produce evidence to show how in one sense the table is solid, in another sense, it is not.

One approach to the quandaries is via predictions. Similarities between star patterns and shapes of the alphabet and myths concerning the gods and ancient classifications have not generated predictions of value. Seeing books as distinct from the knees they rest upon and the hands holding them provide us with stabilities for successful predictions. We might have tried to see the hand and book as itself a unity, but that single unit so quickly and easily consists of parts, widely separated – when we move. Of course, Mind-Struck may argue that what counts even as regularities and success in prediction are also just matters of our worldly carvings, concepts and language – a thought explored further in Chapter 52's gruesome affair.

♈

The starting point for this puzzling picture is already a distortion. We speak of 'we' as if we are distinct from the rest of the universe. If we are, ought I not to begin the story from just me? Do I carve the universe up in such a way that I make other people?

Of course, this is crazy. I did no dividing. My awareness of the world and of myself developed within, and because of, a pre-existing community, with others using language, interacting with me. Thinking and language presuppose a world common to us all of independent perceivable objects – that is, medium-sized, reasonably stable objects. Only further investigation leads us to postulate atoms, electrons, waves or worse. Only further reflection leads us to wonder whether the world could be seen in different ways. That does not mean that ultimately anything goes. Mind you, the question of what does – or does not – go maintains much mystery. It is worth remembering, though, that physicists, to construct their theories of quantum mechanics, the indeterminacy of events and reality's nature, quietly rely on stable, objectively observable monitors, testing equipment and also coffee to stay awake – as well as on memories of previous experiments, today's news and the certainty that by tomorrow their offices will not have transformed into peacocks chanting in Sanskrit. Their theories of the strangeness of underlying reality have no impact on their lives, save with regard to employment, salary levels and possible Nobel prizes.

Nelson Goodman, an influential twentieth-century American philosopher – we meet him again, 'gruesomely', in Chapter 52 – was much taxed by puzzles of how reality is represented as carved and, indeed, by related puzzles in the arts. So, let us end on a more relaxed note, using his wry humour.

Goodman tells of someone being stopped for speeding. 'But look,' says the driver, 'relative to the car in front I was not speeding, but stationary.' The cop stamps on the road, stressing that movement relative to the road is what matters. 'But,' persists the driver, changing his tune, 'don't you know that Earth is spinning eastward; I was driving westward – so I was going even slower than those parked cars.' 'Okay,' says the cop, not to be tricked, 'you get a ticket for more or less parking on the highway – and the parked cars get a ticket for speeding.'

PART V: KNOWLEDGE

Drowning in seas of doubts?

Why am I deemed the wisest man of Athens?
Because at least I know that I do not know.

Socrates

We know many things – from our way back home (well, usually so), to the movement of the planets (at least if with astronomical tables), to the cost of milk (unless a government minister). We know full well that Paris is the capital of France, the number eleven is a prime number – and this book will not transform into oysters. Yet, how do we know? Paradoxically, must we not first know what knowledge is?

We are entering epistemology, a term derived from the Greek for 'knowledge'. Epistemology, the theory of knowledge, is largely concerned with how our beliefs about the world can be justified by evidence and reason – such that we are possessors not merely of beliefs, but also of knowledge. Much of our knowledge, of course, is derived from what others tell us, be those others, teachers, family or guide-books, doctors, lovers or even (well, it is possible?) tabloid newspapers and internet tweets. How reliable are our sources of information, of testimony – or are they sources of misinformation and hence no transmitters of knowledge at all?

Philosophers bring forth the Sceptic, a philosophical figure who doubts whether we can know, or have good reason for believing, virtually anything. After all, do you know that you are not dreaming right now? Mind you, there is no need to lapse into such overwhelming scepticism to sense puzzles here. We worry about cults, religions and schools indoctrinating individuals. Investment houses print the regulatory mantra 'the past is no guide to the future' – despite displaying past performance figures, encouraging people to invest on the basis of those figures.

With those background thoughts, we shall soon be meeting Humpty Dumpty, some remarkable scientific investigations without even leaving the bed, and the perplexity of how our understanding of reality determines what that reality 'really' is. First, though, we deal with the basic perplexity of quite what constitutes knowledge. The dealing takes us from the great Socrates, the wisest man of ancient Athens, to a tale about the recent British playwright Harold Pinter.

42

PINTER AND ISABELLA: TETHERING THEM DOWN

Certain statues of people are so lifelike that they dance around rather than remaining still and unmoving. In Greek mythology that was so of the statues carved by Daedalus for he was such a fine craftsman. Socrates spoke of how the statues of Daedalus would run away like runaway slaves – a revelation of some social interest – unless they were tethered down.

Let us keep the above thought in mind, when musing upon knowledge.

≈

You are walking along a country lane and Isabella, gazing across the field, notices an animal, and says, 'Ah, there's a donkey grazing in the field.' You mumble a response, uninterested, yet trying to show politeness: 'I didn't know you knew about such farming matters.' You hope that donkey talk will not squeeze out the intended romance of the stroll.

Now, what is needed for Isabella to *know* that a donkey is grazing – or, for that matter, for her state not to be one of knowledge? We are, by the way, assuming that Isabella is speaking sincerely, believes what she says – and indeed speaks the truth. The field really does contain a donkey grazing. In other words, Isabella has a true belief; but do true beliefs count as knowledge? Can we add features to the scenario to show how, perhaps, true belief is not thereby knowledge?

How does knowledge differ from true belief?

Why is knowledge more important than true belief?

Isabella gazes at an animal. Now, the animal, in fact, is not a donkey but a goat. Yet Isabella speaks the truth in saying that the field contains a donkey because, unbeknownst to her, a donkey lurks in the corner out of eyesight. Isabella has got things right – but by luck. She lacks knowledge of there being a donkey. She takes a goat to be a donkey.

This may suggest that, for Isabella to *know* that there is a donkey, the donkey needs to feature in the explanation of why she spoke as she did. If we ask her though, she would justify her donkey claim by pointing at a goat – hardly a good justification. Her mistaken thought about the creature that she sees explains why she says that there is a donkey; but the actual donkey in the field has nothing to do with her thought that there is a donkey. She pays no attention to the donkey.

Now, to bring out a further point, let us consider the following scenario, a true one concerning Harold Pinter.

> Pinter was lunching at the House of Lords, at the invitation of his father-in-law, Lord Longford. Various lords and dukes chatted to Pinter. A Hackney lad, son of a Jewish tailor, Pinter had grown up in London's East End and had made good as a playwright. 'And do you know the port you're drinking?' asked a Lord Donaldson. 'Dão 1963,' came Pinter's reply, although he had neither seen the bottle nor been told. The waiter was called over. He confirmed Dão 1963. The lords were suitably impressed by Pinter's knowledge: he may be just a playwright, but he's a good judge of port.

Pinter, in our example, paid attention to the port. He was not tasting some other port and mistaking it for Dão 1963. He tasted some port that was Dão 1963; but, as he later confessed, Dão 1963 was the only port he knew. Whichever port he tasted, he would give the Dão 1963 answer. Pinter hit lucky, as did Isabella.

The brief tales of Isabella and Pinter show two different ways in which we may reach the truth by means of good luck, and hence not possess knowledge.

Perhaps knowledge is grander than true belief in that it needs the belief to be appropriately linked to what makes the belief true. The true belief needs to be tethered down, to use Socrates' metaphor at this chapter's very beginning. The tethering down could be by means of the knowing individuals being able to give good reasons for what they claim – or by there being appropriate external links, causes, between what is believed and what makes the beliefs true.

∿

Let us now consider Isabella in a different scenario. She first really does see the donkey (and not the goat) and as a result says, 'There's a donkey.' So, what she sees – the donkey – is involved in the explanation of why she believes that there is one. There is an appropriate causal link between what she believes and what makes her belief true. The donkey features in the story about how she came to have certain visual sensations that led to her belief. Indeed, Isabella can justify what she believes. She can truthfully say, 'I can see a donkey right there,' pointing at the donkey.

Does our Isabella, in this scenario, now know that there is a donkey in front of her? Well, it is true that there is one; and she thinks that there is one – and the donkey figures in why she has her belief. Let us, though, have Isabella looking round more intently. She now sees the goat and says, perfectly seriously, 'Ah, another donkey.' Suppose she walks on, turns a corner and exclaims, 'There's another donkey,' but she is now looking at a sheep. She hit lucky with the first case – of seeing the donkey and getting it right – for clearly and surprisingly she cannot distinguish between donkeys, goats and sheep.

The interesting outcome here is that even if Isabella does not walk on and does not make mistaken comments about goats and sheep, she still lacks knowledge in the first place concerning the donkey. This is because of the following truth: were she to be asked about these other creatures, goats and sheep, she would announce that they too are donkeys. She is unable to discriminate between such creatures – just as

Pinter was unable to discriminate between ports. She is liable to make mistakes about such creaturely matters.

♈

Isabella and Pinter, in our tales, lack knowledge because their beliefs about the relevant matters are unreliable. Pinter is no reliable guide, if asked to judge port vintages. Isabella clearly is not to be trusted: if you order a donkey from her, you may end up with a goat or sheep.

Knowledge requires that those who know can be relied upon about the matters in question: they need to be reliably right, though not infallibly so. It is the 'reliably right' feature that makes knowledge so valuable. Were infallibility always demanded, knowledge would quickly become a will-o'-the-wisp. Knowledge of my friend Pelham, here and now, does not usually require my possessing the ability to distinguish him from a fake Pelham, were we to imagine such existed – or from a twin, were such to be shipped over from another land.

Which possibilities need to be ruled out in judging whether someone is reliable and hence has knowledge depends on context and information sought. If a Pelham twin is not on the cards, there is no need for a knowing me to possess the ability to distinguish between the Pelham twins. If, though, we fear the arrival of the twin – he is a gangster eager to 'take us out' – then things are different; we need to know whether benign Pelham or gangster twin is in town. An informant, to be reliable for us in those circumstances, must be able to distinguish between the twins, before we should credit him with knowing that, say, gangster twin has not flown in.

A good guide knows how to find the right path; a port connoisseur knows how to distinguish between vintage 1963 and '73; and Isabella, if knowledgeable about animals, should at least be able to sort out the sheep from the goats – and from the donkeys.

43
'DON'T TELL HIM, PIKE!'

In the BBC television series, *Dad's Army*, a part-time British Home Guard platoon helps defend Britain in the Second World War. The local bank manager, Mainwaring, is the platoon's pompous captain. Pike is a young and gullible private. No doubt by mistake, the platoon is holding captive a few German soldiers. After Pike makes some offensively childish remarks, the English-speaking German leader demands that Pike reveal his name, so that he can be dealt with when the Third Reich secures victory. Quick as a flash, Captain Mainwaring shouts across – in front of the listening enemy – 'Don't tell him, Pike!'

The scene is one of British television's most popular for comedy. Part of the humour derives from Mainwaring's attempt to ensure that the enemy is not informed of Pike's name – by means which ensure the enemy is so informed. Although Mainwaring does not *state* that the private's name is 'Pike', his use of Pike's name in telling the young man to keep quiet gives the name and hence the game away. His action is *contra* his intended *diction*. His action is enemy informative, whereas his purpose is to render the enemy uninformed. His instruction gives rise to an informational absurdity.

Now for something which may seem to be completely different. Consider the following statement about my good friend, Zoe: 'Riga is the capital of Latvia, but Zoe doesn't think it is.' The first part, about Riga, is true and is conjoined to a second part, about Zoe's view on the matter (and let us assume that that is indeed her view). Now, let Zoe try to tell us the same truth: 'Riga is the capital of Latvia, but I don't think it is.' We are both saying the same about Riga and, it seems, about Zoe's view on the matter: what she thinks or believes. What comes from my lips is sensible, but from Zoe's it is absurd. Try getting yourself into the position of sincerely asserting that something is so and so, yet sincerely asserting also that you do not think it is so or do not believe it is so.

There are exceptions. Sometimes no absurdity arises: you may, so to speak, be speaking with two voices. As train announcer, you say 'The train will be on time,' yet softly add, 'I don't think it will.' 'I don't believe it' can also be a way of expressing surprise: 'I won the lottery, but I still don't believe it!'

How can saying something true be absurd?

In 1940s Cambridge, G. E. Moore presented the puzzle in terms of belief. Wittgenstein highlighted its significance, claiming that it showed that my relation to my own words is wholly different from other people's to those words. We may readily talk about Zoe's psychological states, using expressions such as 'Zoe thinks this,' or 'She doesn't believe that,' but when Zoe is speaking, in the first person, present tense, for example saying 'I think Wittgenstein gave away his inheritance,' she is not describing her psychological state; rather, she is expressing, with some hesitation, something about Wittgenstein.

Consider this case. It is raining and you are wondering whether it is worth waiting for a bus. A woman at the bus stop discusses this with you and finally says, 'I'm certain the bus will be here in a few minutes.' After some time with no bus, you challenge her, pointing out that she had got things wrong and had misled you, presumably unintentionally. It would not go down well if she responded, 'I was merely telling you about my psychological state – my state of certainty, belief and what I firmly thought – not about the bus's likely arrival.'

Use of 'I think', 'I believe', 'I am certain' – and also, 'I don't think', 'I don't believe', 'I'm not sure' – is typically a means of expressing something about the world, with varying degrees of certainty or hesitation. Zoe's statement that seemed to be about both Riga and her lack of belief is more akin to her saying: 'Riga is the capital of Latvia, but [hesitantly] Riga is not the capital of Latvia.' The second part is Zoe speaking (albeit hesitantly) against herself in the first part. Captain

Mainwaring's instruction generated an informational absurdity; so too does Zoe's utterance.

♈

The peculiarity that Moore noticed and Wittgenstein stressed occurs with many first person present tense uses of psychological terms but not with past and future tense uses. 'Riga is the capital of Latvia, but I used not to believe so' is not absurd. A feature of belief is that if you believe that something is so and so, then you believe that it is true that that something is so and so. Hence, there is no use, in the first person present tense, of 'falsely believing'. Maybe I falsely believed that Riga was the capital of Hungary, but I cannot sensibly say, 'I falsely believe that Riga is the capital of Hungary,' though others can sensibly say it of me. A related oddness is, 'I am modest' (presented in Chapter 55).

The peculiarity of first person present tense uses has been much explored since Wittgenstein, notably by J. L. Austin. 'I name this ship *Bathsheba at Sea*' is to perform a naming, not merely to describe what I am doing. 'I bet', 'I promise', 'I order' are further examples of what have become known as 'performatives'.

Consider, 'I assert that Riga is the capital of Hungary.' You tell me that I am mistaken: Riga is not the capital of Hungary. I reject your accusation of error. 'I merely said that I *assert* that Riga is the capital of Hungary, not that Riga *is* the capital of Hungary.' Is that a fair riposte?

Is prefacing remarks with 'I assert that...' a way of always speaking the truth? If 'yes' is the answer, then all this book's words, for safety's sake, should be prefaced with 'I assert that' – or perhaps they ought not, for the added words may alert readers of some dubiety. After all, politicians who say 'Trust me' may engender only suspicion; please see Chapter 82. Here comes another example.

Groucho Marx announced with a flourish, 'These are my principles.' We are impressed – a man of principles – until he adds, 'If you dislike them – well, I have others.'

44

THE PLACEBO:
AN OFFER YOU CAN ONLY REFUSE

Some offers, it is quipped, *The Godfather* in mind, are offers you cannot refuse. What may be seen as kindly offers, by those in the know, are nothing but mean and nasty threats or tricks – but no treats at all. When the gunman asks you to unlock the safe, well, were you to play for time, pondering the invitation, you know without doubt that your health is at risk. When cops solicit your company down at the station – 'A few questions, sir' – it would be foolish and pointless to decline their kindly request.

There are, though, offers that you can only refuse – or, more accurately, they cannot logically be accepted. Suppose that you feel unwell, rotten and feeble; so, off to the doctor's you go. To your surprise, she gives you a choice of cure.

> There's no problem in making you better. There are two ways to health. You could either take this medicine four times a day for a week. True, it tastes nasty and may well give you headaches; but you'll definitely get better. Here's an alternative. Simply believe that you'll get better. What's wrong with you merely requires your belief that you will be well; the belief is as effective as the medicine. No need, then, for the nasty medicine. And this is not mumbo-jumbo. There's vast evidence that beliefs often aid recovery; after all, beliefs have some basis in states of the brain and brain states affect the rest of the body.

The doctor smiles; she adds that the 'belief' option is surely the rational one to choose. You agree: obviously you would rather follow the recommended belief route, thereby avoiding the medicinal. Yet can you simply choose to believe something? Is not that an impossible offer to take up? The answer is: It is – as the next chapter shows.

Let us, then, revise our medicinal tale a little. You accept the medicine, believing it will make you better. In fact, un-beknownst to you, it lacks all curative properties in itself – and the doctor knows this. Perhaps it is just water – with an additive that provides the nasty taste and colour. It is a placebo. Its sole role in the explanation of how patients become better is that they falsely believe its chemical composition possesses curative powers; and so they believe they will get better. It is this latter belief that then causes the recovery. Now, the doctor may truthfully murmur what she knows to be true:

> The medicine will make my patient better only in so far as he believes it will make him better.

If you overhear the comment, believing the doctor to be truthful, then you are now about to believe:

> The medicine will make me better only in so far as I believe it will make me better.

Yet, in the circumstances given, you cannot believe that – well, not rationally so. Paradoxically, the doctor can, but you cannot, believe the truth about the matter – a paradox of self-believing.

Why should learning the truth about your belief undermine that truth?

You believed that the medicine would make you better because of its pharmaceutical powers. Learning that it lacks such powers, you lack the belief that it will make you better; hence, you lack the resultant belief that you will get better. Lacking the belief, you obviously cannot get better because of the belief.

The Placebo Paradox, here on display, arises because what is true cannot survive, cannot remain true, upon your discovery. So long as you do not discover that the medicine is a placebo, your belief that you will get better is true. Upon discovery, if only you could hang onto your belief that you will get better, all would be well in your getting well; and hence your belief would be true. The discovery, though, pulls the rug from under your belief. Your belief that you would get better was grounded solely by belief in the medicine; with that grounding, that reason, now gone, your belief has gone too.

In contrast, the doctor's belief that you would get better was grounded on the efficacy of patients' believing they get better through, for example, taking placebos not believed to be placebos. Now, an optimistic patient, without placebos, may believe in any case that he will recover; but his belief that he will recover, while the reason why he does recover, cannot logically be the reason for his *belief* that he will recover. Your believing that so and so cannot be the reason for your believing that so and so. A reason needs to be different from what it is a reason for.

In fact, placebo prescriptions can work even when patients learn placebos are prescribed and know what 'placebo' means; adverse side-effects can also arise. Our paradox, though, set off with you, the patient, believing that you will recover because of the efficacy of the medicine – for that reason alone.

$$\gamma$$

The Placebo Paradox has something of a self-defeating air. If you learn why you will get better, then you will not get better, given the circumstances set out. The learning defeats, so to speak, what is learnt. The paradox does not involve some simple self-defeating in the way that shouting out 'No one is shouting' is self-defeating. It may be more akin to that of a schoolgirl being told that she is very bright and will pass the examination; this leads to her over-confidence, or indeed nerves, such that she subsequently fails the examination.

A reason for a belief, to be a reason, needs in some way to be independent of that belief. Religious believers sometimes justify belief on the basis of scripture. 'But why believe the scriptures?' 'Because they are God's word.' 'Why believe that?' 'Because it says so in the scriptures.'

Reasons offered in support of beliefs need to stand independently of the beliefs and not themselves be supported by those beliefs. Independence can be important in various ways. In health, for example, if told that your heart is fine, you would reasonably think that your life was not about to be cut short because of your heart – that any early death would at least be initiated by some factors not dependent on a poor heart. With that sensible thought in mind, we may spot the ambiguity and wit in a splendid W. C. Fields' quip. Here it comes.

'Don't worry about your heart; it will last you as long as you live.'

45

INDOCTRINATION: WHEN BELIEVING GOES WRONG

Here is a little challenge:

> Try sincerely to believe that Beijing is the capital of Britain, that $2 + 2$ makes 5 and that it is right to torture children for the sheer fun of it. Try sincerely to believe that promethium has atomic number 61.

For the sake of the puzzle here, let us hope that you cannot believe the first three suggestions. And, unless you already have knowledge of the periodic table – or believe this book to be an authority on such matters – let us hope you cannot just believe the final suggestion. The point is that people cannot simply switch on a belief; people cannot believe at will. Beliefs are switched on by the world, often by years of schooling. Let us consider outlines of three school teachings, deliberately presented in a stark, extreme manner – to afford focus.

> A certain Fundamentalist School teaches that the Bible holds the truth regarding the world's creation, how we ought to live, and how God judges behaviour and offers eternal life. If pupils question these claims, the teachers point them to some historical evidence for the Bible's accuracy, the authority of the Church – and the need for faith.

> A Science School teaches evolutionary theory and that religious texts are not to be relied upon for scientific fact. If pupils question, the teachers point them to some fossil and genetic evidence, some extracts from Darwin and mention the authority of eminent working scientists. The ultimate authority is scientific investigation.

A Nazi School, at one stage, forced Jewish pupils to sit separately from German pupils. If pupils questioned, they were told that Germans had superior blood running in their veins. The pupils were taught of Germany's glory and its destiny for expansion, taking over Poland and Russia. The Führer knew best.

Most people consider the Nazi School as indoctrinating. Some people view the Fundamentalist School as engaged in some degree of indoctrination. These schools contrast with the Science School. Yet some would claim that the fundamentalist teaching is no more indoctrination than the science teaching. All schools rely on approved text books; they have teachers with certain views, sometimes with an official state line to promote. Pupils typically lap up what they are taught – as many did in Nazi Germany.

As adults, we are not immune to our beliefs being manipulated – 'coaxed' – by various authorities. When women pay exorbitant sums for wonder creams, convinced of rejuvenating powers, executives rub hands with glee at their advertising success. If politicians receive increasing support because of stories placed in the press and slick advertisements, they trumpet (well, to themselves) their persuasive skills.

In addition to the above ways of coming to believe – ways that may have a feel of indoctrination – there are the blatant examples of indoctrination, of brainwashing, where victims are broken down psychologically. The victims find themselves simply accepting and believing, it seems, whatever they are told. Such examples are reported by certain survivors of North Korean and Soviet prisons, and others.

How, then, should we learn about the world?

How does education differ from indoctrination?

The difference lies not in the content. We may be indoctrinated with the truth; and education is likely to include some mistaken beliefs. The difference lies not in the perpetrators' intentions, for both indoctrinators and educators may intend the best for recipients, by way of access to perceived truth, flourishing lives and even afterlives.

Indoctrination 'proper', it has been argued, involves force. The recipients' psychological states have been caused by certain external factors, drugs and torture. In the school context of weak indoctrination, the causes may be charismatic teachers, restricted reading and repeated mantras.

Resting indoctrination's distinctiveness on the beliefs *being caused* deserves challenge. Most beliefs have, in a way, been forced upon us – by experiences. Turning your head, you see the train approaching, and, as a result, believe that it is indeed approaching and you had better move quickly. The belief has been caused by what you saw. Someone might even have forced you to look, to warn you. Causes, even blatant force, can be benign, giving us true beliefs – causes can also be the opposite. Consider the following.

I tell my friends that Prince William has relinquished his right to the throne after Charles and is living in a tent. Friends look baffled – then they twig. 'Ah, you fell for that April Fools' report. Mind you, you were drunk.' I should then be irrational in clinging to my belief, now learning of its causal source.

Whether I should stick with my beliefs depends on the evidence, and that includes taking into account how they arise. We may now relate that thought to the difference between indoctrination and education.

The psychological states – how they feel 'from within', the phenomenology – may be the same, whether resulting from indoctrination or not, whether they have been blatantly forced by drugs or simply the Bible or *Scientific American* readings – or by directly experiencing the world. Further, the indoctrinated and regular believers may appear the same 'from without': that is, they behave similarly. There is, though, one big difference in potential behaviour; namely, their responses to evidence that runs counter to their beliefs.

Indoctrination provides a protective belt, a belt that shields believers from counter-evidence. Education encourages an openness to evidence. Whether the indoctrination be political, commercial or religious – be it glorification of the state, Western belief in free enterprise and that no child should be without a PlayStation, or the Qur'an interpreted as justifying stoning – the outcome is a block on questioning, criticism and further investigations.

The indoctrinated yield to no challenge to their belief: any challenge is reinterpreted, explained away or simply ignored. Indeed, we may value this stance to a limited extent in certain areas: witness how blind – and delicious – love can be. Yet, to get around the world – to flourish in the world – we have to be responsive to the world, to the evidence and to changes. Full-blown indoctrination is designed to prevent such responsiveness. Education is designed to embrace it. That is why education is preferable to indoctrination.

♈

Indoctrination comes in degrees. Religious believers often allow room for criticism, but within certain boundaries. On some subjects the Pope's word, for example, is treated as infallible. A newspaper gives space to opposing opinions, yet ensures that its news presentation is appropriately politically slanted.

When indoctrination is at the extreme, we may wonder whether indoctrinated 'beliefs' are beliefs at all. If you properly believe something, you believe it is true – even though it may be false. Beliefs aim at truth: we cannot just decide to believe something, though we may act *as if* we believe. Try to believe that the stars are even in number – or odd. If atheistic, try to believe in God. Beliefs cannot be switched on or off.

Because of the truth-aim, beliefs to be beliefs need to be responsive, sensitive, to evidence. Being open to evidence, to hearing opposing views, does not mean, though, that all views deserve equal respect.

All views certainly do not deserve equal respect. Some are false; some are morally horrendous. In line with J. S. Mill's liberalism, though, it is better to have them aired than silenced. They may even stimulate us to find and assert the truth – though, sadly, that lacks guarantee.

46

HUMPTY DUMPTY ADVISES MS TURKEY

MS TURKEY: Isn't the world a wonderful place! Fast food delivery service each morning, courtesy of good friend Farmer McDonald; sustained gobbling throughout the day; well-fed night's sleep – up and ready for next morning's delivery at first cock crow.

HUMPTY DUMPTY: Ah, but I have to tell you, Ms T, past farmer performance is no guide to the future.

MS T: How on earth do you know?

HD: Over the years, I've known lots of your relatives. Initially, things go splendidly for them, but… Well, speaking as a friend, let me just say that, were I you, Ms T, I'd quit the farm once December's snows snow, sleigh bells sound, and fairy lights sparkle on fir trees high.

MS T [gulping]: Thank you, HD – I understand. But you're still relying on past performance as a guide for your kindly advice; yet you said the past was no guide at all.

HD: Your mistake is in thinking that I meant what I said. As I told that silly girl, Alice – she once met me through the looking glass, you know – when I use a word, I make it mean just what I want it to mean.

MS T: Isn't that terribly confusing?

HD: Maybe it is; maybe it isn't. It all depends on whether you take past meanings to be a guide to future meanings.

MS T: But, but, but…

〜

Let us, for the moment, skate round questions of whether meanings are frozen or fluid (more in Chapter 52). Here is a basic question:

Is the past ever a good guide to the future?

This puzzle is most closely associated with the eighteenth-century philosopher David Hume. Hume was Scottish; but English philosophers sometimes bathe in his glory with Hume as 'British'. Of course, when it comes to John Locke, who was English, well, he is often allowed to remain English.

Just because various things have regularly happened it does not follow that they will carry on, regularly so, into the future. Famously, crudely yet rightly, over perhaps centuries, Europeans observed swans – always white swans. From those experiences, they concluded that all swans are white. But, had they nipped to Australia, they could have encountered black swans. From the fact that all observed swans are white, it does not follow that all swans are white. From the fact that I have been breathing for many years, it does not follow that I shall always be breathing.

The puzzle is not solely of what justifies our moving from past cases to future, but what justifies us in moving from some observed cases to the unobserved. At heart, the puzzle rests on the gap between 'some' and 'all' – 'these' and 'those'. It is the problem of induction. Whatever the number of instances of experienced combinations, are we ever justified in expecting similar such combinations, and, if so, why? This is an 'epistemic' question, one concerning knowledge or belief. The underlying metaphysical problem – one of 'what there is in the world' – is: if there are certain regularities, over here, or in the past, is the world such that they are likely to be repeated over there or in the future?

Sometimes people – even philosophers – cheat. 'That big black bird merely *looks* like a swan. Its feathers are not white, so it's not really a swan.' In that move, we are making 'having white feathers' a necessary condition for being a swan. But if swans are defined as being white, then earlier searches to see whether all swans were white turn out to be pointless. We met that move before (in Chapter 2), when seeing how people sometimes insist that we are all selfish, all self-interested, all of the time.

Accidental associations, white and swan, for example, may well not continue into the future or the spatial elsewhere, but perhaps there are some necessities in nature. Consider: all glass is brittle. Under standard conditions, glass smashes when struck by concrete blocks. We may insist that, if this transparent pane does not smash, then it cannot be glass. Well, all right, let us accept that; but we have merely swept the puzzle to elsewhere. We were wondering whether we could be sure that the next piece of glass we encountered would smash. Now, we know that it will, if – *if* – it really is glass. The new puzzle is: how can we be sure that this transparent material is glass, until we see whether it smashes? Once again, we have to make a leap to what will happen.

♈

MS T: I see that we ought not to reason from the past being a certain way to the future continuing that way. There's a gap. Perhaps we should just rely on our experience that often things have continued in the same way. The reasoning – inductive reasoning – has typically been successful in the past; so, it is reasonable to expect its continuing success.

HD : Circularity, dear Ms T. How can past successes of inductive reasoning justify future ones?

MS T: Well, I guess we just accept that they do. You continue to balance on that wall, HD – as you know in the past that you can.

HD *[looking nervous]*: Well, sort of… But, yes, that excellent egg, Hume, made your point. Habit is key. We simply have certain expectations. Perhaps that we have evolved with such expectations is a mark of their reliability.

MS T: That success, though, is only success to date. It may not be success in the future. The human race has expanded over the past, but who knows about the future? Think of current tales of climate warming; yet, who knows? Think of past predictions of global freezes and population explosions.

HD : Point taken, Ms T. But, without reliance on the past, how can we make informed judgements about the future, about fine wall-balancing by eggs such as myself, about tastes of unopened pinot noir wine – and the succulence of the yet to be carved roast turk… Ooops! Sorry Ms T.

MS T: An easy enough slip, HD. But are we getting confused? Just because past regularities are no guarantee of similar future regularities, may they not offer some likelihood? Is that not reasonable? Mind you, in the investment world, many advertisements proclaim that the past is no guide to the future, yet display fine past performances. Some claim that the past is not *necessarily* a guide.

HD: Yes, even if the past does not have to be a guide – is not necessarily a guide – it may still happen to be one. After all, humans do not have to be so keen on roast potatoes and turkey, yet they… Sorry, I've put my egg-head in it again.

MS T: My, this is getting to be a habit, HD. I'll soon be eggs-pecting it – on the basis of your past performance. Perhaps we simply need to accept that, in this world, past regularities do happen to be pretty good guides to future ones.

HD: We may even toy with the brilliant thought that the past is necessarily a good guide to the future. If things have been irregular – highly higgledy-piggledy – in the past, that is evidence, though not conclusive evidence, pointing to irregularities in the future.

MS T: I'll need to think on it further…

HD: I shouldn't hang round, thinking for much longer, Ms T. Whatever we may *think* about the past not properly justifying beliefs about the future, I know, just know, that you should listen out for those farmer footsteps with some trepidation, when those December snows snow. And you'll be right to listen – because of what has happened in the past.

MS T: Just as, in view of your past performances, I am justified in believing in your wall-balancing abilities, HD. Musing more, that I understand your words is a tribute to the fact that the past guides us. We cannot even speak or think about these matters without accepting the linguistic past as guide to the future, maybe even necessarily so after all, and…

[*Crashing sound, as HD falls to the ground.*]

47
FOR ALL YOU KNOW...?

You know how it is. Tiring day at work, then journey, so slow, so slow, as homeward and boringly bound as ever. Long wait for crammed train, fiddling with coins (parking meter, you see) while rain it rains, so much rain it does. Arrive home – to rest, oh bliss, to drink, wind down. 'Mmm... things aren't that bad.' Stretch back on sofa – and transported you are... You're walking on air, blue skies above, entwined with lover(s); then, mysteriously racing, with tigers, tigers so stupendously striped, flying across oceans, landing back in the office but now making a speech, rapturous applause, telling bosses how hopeless, sacking them all. That lottery win's a boost, big boost to your ego, big boost to you. And it is all so real – so real, at the time, at the time; yet, of course...

It is all a dream.

You drift back to reality, wine glass dropped, stains on your shirt, ache in your neck (must replace this dreadful sofa), need to get organized. There's bed yet to come, early start in the morning.

Now you're reading these words. It's the cold light of day. You're back on the train (I hope not driving the car). Or maybe you're holiday bound, airport lounge lounging, flight delayed, seat booking all wrong, but smiling at girl's smile opposite. Or perhaps, right now, you're thinking hard, drinking coffee so awful, wondering where this is going. Whatever, wherever, whoever, you know full well that now you're awake, wide awake now. This is no dream.

Yes, you surely can tell when you are truly awake. You well know that often, in dreams, you fail to realize that you are dreaming, but you know, well enough too, from how everything looks, how everything feels, that right now and here, you are alert and awake, well awake at that. The things around you – the book, the pages, the coffee, your head – are no mere figments of dream-like life. No erotic encounters, no running naked through crowds. Yet, even if there were such events, you would surely be able to tell right now they were real.

So, here you are, reading these words, in this all too orderly and mundane world, as undream-like as possible. And the next moment?

The alarm goes off; the cat licks your face; you have overslept – and you realize you have been dreaming, dreaming about reading a book, a chapter on dreams.

How do you know you are not dreaming – not dreaming right now?

The dreaming puzzle was most famously presented by the seventeenth-century French philosopher, Descartes, the so-called 'father' of modern philosophy who made famous 'I think, therefore I am.' His answer to the question relied on his having already proved to his satisfaction that God exists; but it is difficult to believe that God's existence needs to be established before we can ever know that, on many occasions, we are not dreaming. Let us drop God. It is simply true that often we are utterly convinced – and indeed know – that we are not dreaming; but should we be convinced? What justifies our conviction? For all you know… for all I know… we may be fast asleep right now.

If asked to reflect on what makes us so sure that we are wide awake and not dreaming, we may point to the orderliness of our experiences, how they cohere with our memories and the constancy of the objects around us, an orderly world of home, family and friends. We are also aware of how vivid real life experiences are – how hard the wall is, how drenched we are from the rain, how painful the headache. Yet, any features we come up with, as being distinctive of being awake and not dreaming, may be challenged in two ways. Are they distinctive of being awake? And, even if they are, may we not merely be dreaming that our experiences right now have those features?

Suppose you think that the sheer orderliness of real experiences tells you that you are not dreaming. Is that true? Can you not have extremely orderly dream experiences? If that is so, then maybe this is one of those cases, of a very orderly – mundane – dream. But let us suppose that orderliness of experiences is the distinctive mark of being awake. This raises the question: how do we know that we are not merely dreaming that things are orderly? Whatever feature – call it 'F' – that we say our experiences must have in order not to be dreaming experiences, how can we ever be sure these experiences have F? How do we ever know that we are not merely dreaming they have F?

♈

The mere possibility that, for all we know, we are dreaming is enough to make many people sceptical about what we claim to know. Descartes, and others, have tried to take things much further, supposing it is possible that we are being misled, not merely through dreaming, but perhaps courtesy of an evil demon intent on deceiving us as far as possible, or courtesy of mad scientists who have our brains in vats, feeding us experiences via electrodes (explored in Chapter 59). Film producers have taken such thoughts further, in virtual reality tales, such as the incomprehensible *The Matrix*.

The dreaming possibility gives a boost to philosophical sceptics, those who doubt whether people know what they reckon to know. Here is one simple sceptical argument:

Premiss 1: If I know that I am reading a book right now, then I know that I am not merely dreaming that I am reading.

Premiss 2: I do not know that I am not merely dreaming that I am reading.

Conclusion: Therefore, I do not know that I am reading a book right now.

The conclusion does indeed follow from the premisses. The argument's form is *modus tollens*; we use it every day. 'If she's going to be late, she would have phoned. She's not phoned. Therefore she's not going to be late.' If we accept the premisses, we should accept the conclusion. Another basic valid logical form is *modus ponens*, which the gazelle, sloth, chicken race sought to undo (in Chapter 28).

As the conclusion follows from the premisses, if you are to reject the conclusion – that is, if you are to accept that you do know that you are reading this book – you are committed to at least one of the premisses being false. Premiss 2 seems unassailable: have we not already shown that we cannot know that we are not dreaming? Perhaps Premiss 1 is at fault. Is it possible that, to know things, we do not need to know that we are not dreaming them? How on earth can that be? How can you know that you are reading this book and not merely dreaming that you are reading, if you cannot rule out that you may be merely dreaming that you are reading?

Even if you feel you can be sure about whether you are dreaming and can know, in some cases, that you are not – that is, even if you reject Premiss 2 – the sceptical argument can be revised, replacing the dreaming possibility (as already noted) with that of a powerful demon or a mad scientist, out to deceive you as far as possible. If I know that I am reading a book, then must I not know that I am neither dreaming nor being deceived into thinking that I am reading when I am not, be it by a powerful demon or mad scientist stimulating my brain, so that I am caused to have these misleading experiences?

The possibility of a powerful deceiver – Descartes spoke of the possibility of an evil genius – perhaps gives us a deception too far. Suppose the deceiver is so good in her deceivings that we can never tell when we are being deceived: it still seems to us as if we go to work, read books, fall in love, take holidays, have a family, drink too much at parties, sing out of tune and so on. If any deceiver is that good at her deceptions, what becomes of the deceptions? They go up in a puff of smoke – or, better, they collapse, giving us the real world just as we know it – for is there any content to such universal deceptions? Deceptions that cannot, even in principle, be spotted by us are no deceptions at all. In contrast to such extreme seemingly deceptive possibilities, dreams often do take us in, yet we can eventually discover our mistakes. After all, we wake up – and sometimes we know it.

Here you are, indeed, in your waking state, knowing that you are reading this book and knowing full well that no morning alarm is about to go off in the next few seconds to wake you up…

Brr… Brrrr… Brr… Brrrr…

48
JUST HANGING AROUND

Logical Lo knew it was a mistake to holiday in Wild West parts, where cowboys and sheriffs were laws unto themselves – and to visitors. Here sits Lo, sentenced to death by hanging – a hanging with a twist, a very strange twist, in its noose. The sheriff had taken a dislike to her when she had rebuffed his advances, denounced him as sexist and danced a jig on his ten-gallon hat.

'Tis now Sunday. The sheriff has just announced to Lo that she is to be hanged, at noon, one day this coming week – either Monday, Tuesday, Wednesday, Thursday or Friday. Saturday is *siesta* day, when no one hangs around. The hanging will be a surprise: on the morning of the hanging, Lo will have no good reason to believe that the hanging will take place that day. Perhaps, for example, she will undergo the noonday noose on Tuesday: if so, on Tuesday morning (and before then) she will have no good reason to believe that the hanging will be on that day. Lo knows, she just knows, that the sheriff speaks the truth.

Things look bleak. Lo is too young to hang. Distraught, she settles in her cell, but then she starts to reason and reflect. After all, she is Logical Lo.

If I get through to Friday morning, unhung and hence unhanged, my neck still intact, then the hanging would have to occur that day at noon, for there are no other days left. So, for the hanging to be a surprise, it cannot occur on Friday. Friday is ruled out. Mind you, there are still all the other days. Hold on – as Friday is ruled out for the hanging, then, if I get through unhanged to Thursday morning, I'd know the hanging would have to be on that day's noon. That's the only day left, given Friday is no real possibility; hence, I can rule out Thursday…

So Lo reasons, ruling out Friday, then Thursday, then Wednesday and so on down the days, ruling out Tuesday and Monday by similar reasoning. Smugly, she concludes that the sentence announced by the sheriff cannot be implemented. 'My neck is safe,' smirks Logical Lo, in confident mode, ravished by reason.

Then, one day that week, perhaps Wednesday or even Friday, the hangman intrudes upon Lo's confident complacency and hangs her. She is both hanged and surprised or, more accurately, surprised and hanged.

Surprise hangings, surprise parties, surprise school examinations, can be given, yet if both the spectrum of possible dates and the fact that the event will be a surprise are guaranteed, did Lo not prove that, paradoxically, such surprises cannot occur?

Where does Lo's argument, that there can be no surprise hanging, go wrong?

A natural way of handling the paradox is to point out that when someone is told of a surprise under such conditions – and schoolchildren often are given surprise examinations in this way, though currently not hangings – what is meant is that the event will be a surprise, *unless* it happens on the last possible day. If you have reached the last possible day, then obviously you will not be surprised, so the backward reasoning does not get started and the puzzle evaporates. It is then no more puzzling than being told that we shall be unable to work out which of four face down ace cards (Clubs? Diamonds? Hearts? Spades?) will be turned up last, until three have had their faces turned up; after three are shown, we may easily work out which ace remains unturned. The puzzle also is no puzzle if Lo knows that the sheriff could be having her on; for then possibly no hanging will take place. Once again, the backward reasoning cannot start. It starts once Lo believes that Friday is a possible day for the surprise hanging – for then, what can she conclude?

The puzzle bites if you have excellent reason to think the sheriff is telling the truth. If he is – and if you suppose you get through to Friday morning – then there is a conflict in your reasons for what to believe. He tells you that there will definitely be a hanging; hence, on Friday morning, you think that it must occur today (it is the last possible day). Yet he also tells you that it will be a surprise, so, now on Friday morning, you think his overall announcement cannot be true: maybe the hanging will not occur. But then you realize that you now are not believing that there will be a hanging; yet, in that state of mind, you can reflect that his overall announcement could well be true after all: you do not believe there will be a hanging, so now it can both occur and be a surprise. That reflection reels you round into again believing that a hanging will happen – but in that state of mind it will not be a surprise to you; and so you go through the reasoning again. Such reeling means that no stable belief can be reached. The reasoning loops round and round.

$$\gamma$$

We should question whether Lo can have good reason to believe that the sheriff is right in predicting both that there will be a hanging and that she will not believe that there will be one, if she is left hanging around, unhanged, until Friday. How can the sheriff predict her state of mind? Perhaps he could for people who are unable to grasp the reasoning – but Logical Lo is logical, her reasoning both seemingly impeccable and also reeling her between thinking her neck will meet the noose and thinking it will be noose free. Hence the sheriff cannot know what she will believe just before a hanging on Friday and hence he cannot be certain that she will be surprised. Logical Lo, who will also have worked this out, should realize that she has no good reason to believe that the sheriff's announcement must be true with regard to both the hanging and its being a surprise.

To be true, the sheriff's announcement means that if she is left hanging around, unhanged, until Friday morning (or if she projects herself to Friday morning), she will think 'My hanging will take place at noon, but I don't believe my hanging will take place at noon.' What she thinks has the same structure and absurdity as the thought in Moore's Paradox (encountered via Private Pike, Chapter 43). Surprisingly, the puzzle neither results from the sheriff's telling Lo of the surprise hanging, nor from there being a surprise hanging, but from Lo's believing what the sheriff tells her.

And so, as seen, some paradoxical perplexities of philosophy may be dissolved by questioning the authority and reliability of the speaker in question. Logical Lo has no good reason to believe that the sheriff is right about what she will end up believing at a moment before the hanging; and you, dear reader, have no good reason to believe that I am right in saying that you are reading or hearing these words on this page – or do you? After all, I am right. Or am I?

49

SLOTHFUL SLOTH SPEAKS: 'WHAT WILL BE, WILL BE'

Meeting a sloth, deep in sloth, and a butterfly, fluttering by in a South American jungle, is no surprise, but hearing the name of a Roman orator, Cicero, dropped into the conversation – well, how could I resist listening? I had been hacking through creepers, heat and undergrowth, perspiration pouring, so, in any case, I needed a rest.

'But, but, but,' said Flutterby, settling on Sloth's snout, 'being so slothful and lazy, why, you may starve to death, whatever you've been reading in Cicero.'

'What will be, will be,' sighed Sloth, hanging upside down from a branch.

'That may well be so,' buttered Flutterby, 'But what will be, does not *have* to be.'

Sloth sighed, slothfully of course, but the butterfly tickled him into saying more.

'Look,' said Sloth, 'If it's fated that I shall dine this afternoon, then I shall dine, whether I go hunting for food or not. If it's fated that I shall starve, then I shall starve, whether or not I go hunting for food.'

'Ah, the Lazy Argument,' interrupted Flutterby. Sloth, though, was in full, albeit slow slothful flow.

'And either it is fated that I shall dine this afternoon or it is fated that I shall not. So, either way, it is a waste of energy to go searching for dinner.'

'You should have read more Cicero,' fluttered the butterfly, 'for fallacy rests in your reasoning.' And in her excitement, she fluttered around, landing on Sloth's outstretched tongue. As Sloth gulped her down, I heard him murmur with a satisfied yawn, 'So, clearly it was fated I'd have at least a teeny hors-d'oeuvre.'

If it is true that things are going to happen, are we not powerless to prevent them?

When in times of distress, despair or even guilt, we may sigh, 'What will be, will be.' People sing the words, often in Spanish tongues, 'Que sera, sera.' Such sighs, such songs, such tongues, may manifest hopelessness. We cannot affect the future. Or, if we are sighing over the past, there was nothing that we could have done to have made things turn out differently. The events in question are fixed – determined by the stars or hand of fate, or some sort of divine predestination.

'Don't bother to smarten up for the interview. After all, either you'll get the job or you won't.' 'There's no need to revise for the examination. Either I'll pass or I won't. Let's party instead.' Such reasoning has, indeed, been well-named: the Lazy Argument.

Is it true that what will be will be? If it is, does it lead to fatalism, the belief that certain things are going to happen regardless of how much we try to prevent or encourage them? If or when you meet, or fail to meet, the man or woman of your dreams, was it just meant to be?

Showing fatalism to be true cannot be as easy as muttering, singing or sighing, 'What will be, will be' — and, nodding wisely, grasping how true that is. True, if something will be, then it will be. If something will happen, then it will happen. But the butterfly is right: it is not at all obviously true that we are all fated, that we cannot affect the future. What will be will be — true. What will be, *must* be — well, that is a radically different claim, one that has not yet been justified. Sloth's Lazy Argument, though, seems to have more going for it than the weary sigh of 'what will be, will be'. Here is another example of his lazy reasoning.

> You are ill. Well, either it is fated that you'll recover or it is fated that you'll not recover. If it is fated that you'll recover, then there's no need to bother visiting the doctor. If it is fated that you'll not recover, then it's pointless visiting the doctor. Either it's fated that you'll recover or fated that you will not. Either way, don't waste time visiting the doctor.

As it stands, this can hardly be welcomed as a good argument for fatalism; after all, it assumes straight off that things are fated — either you are fated to recover or fated not to recover. Why believe that?

♈

We are, though, being unfair to Sloth. Here is a modified Lazy Argument.

> Either you are going to recover from the illness or you are not going to recover. If you're going to recover, then there's no need to see the doctor. If you're not going to recover, then it's pointless seeing the doctor. Either way, therefore, don't waste time seeing the doctor.

Well, what do we make of that? For a start, it does not presuppose fate.

There are many events over which we are powerless. Whatever we do, we shall not affect the orbit of Pluto, the nature of snow and the colours of rainbows. You and I are unlikely to find a reliable plumber late at night or make the trains run on time. But surely we often do influence our recovery from an illness, getting a job, or passing an examination.

The Lazy Argument's simple mistake is to assume that if something is going to happen, then it is going to happen regardless of what we do. Maybe it is true that we are going to recover from the illness; but this may be because we do see the doctor. Of course, some of us, sceptics that we are, think that recovery is more likely if we avoid doctors. Perhaps you are going to be offered the job after the interview, but only because you do polish your shoes, sound eager and smile brightly at the boss's jokes. Perhaps you will find the lover of your dreams, but finding her or him is more likely if you keep your eyes open.

'What will be, will be' does not logically lead to 'what will be, will be, whatever you or I do.' Concerning many factors that affect our lives, we cannot pass the responsibility buck to fate. We do have inputs, though it is true that few inputs guarantee desired outcomes.

If we want to avoid responsibility for what happens, we should have more success turning to the unexpected events that hit us in life – the chances, the contingencies, the good or bad luck – rather than to some mysterious notion of fate. Indeed, your chancing upon the Lazy Argument may tempt you to try it out, when looking into his or her eyes, declaring that your getting together was simply fated to be – and so all resistance is futile.

Good luck.

50

CREAMY PHILOSOPHERS:
WHO KNOWS WHO KNOWS...

Allow me to introduce you to the importance and nature of common knowledge by way of a puzzle.

Suppose ten philosophers, attending an international convention, are sitting in a semi-circle at the dining table, having just finished some gorgeous creamy dessert in which they all delighted. They can see everyone's face, except their own. No mirrors, no squinting allowed; and they are not permitted to confer. You are the draconian waiter, gazing at them all. No philosopher knows that he has cream on his lips; he cannot see himself. Just two of them have been messy eaters this time, their lips all creamy; the others, surprisingly, are sparklingly clean. For ease, let us call those with cream on their lips 'creamy'. Naturally, all of them, being philosophers, are perfectly rational reasoners – despite the flow of wine – ready to obey instructions.

You say to them, 'Hands up all those who know that they are creamy.' They can all see at least one creamy philosopher. That there is at least one creamy philosopher is universally known, mutually known. Not one of them, though, knows that he himself is creamy. So, no hands go up. Importantly, no hands go up, if you ask the question repeatedly. No philosopher can work out by reason alone that he must be a creamy one.

Now, suppose the same set-up, except that, before any instruction, you announce, 'At least one of you is creamy.' Of course, they knew that in the first scenario: they could all see at least one creamy philosopher. Your announcement, though, magically it seems, alters what will happen. You now instruct, 'Hands up all those who know they are creamy.' No hand is raised. You make the same demand again,

'Hands up all those who know they are creamy.' Amazingly, the two creamy philosophers, and only those two, do now put their hands up. Your announcement, albeit of what they each already knew, made all the difference.

Why did the creamy philosophers now raise their hands?

A philosopher with no cream on his lips can see two creamy philosophers, say Alo and Zeki. He reasons that why neither Alo nor Zeki raised their hands at the first instruction was because they each thought it possible that the creamy philosopher they could see was the only creamy philosopher.

Creamy Alo, for example, can see only one creamy philosopher, namely Zeki. Alo reasons that clearly Zeki did not raise his hand first time because he must have seen a creamy philosopher. But Alo can see no creamy philosopher other than Zeki; so, after the first instruction with no one's hand raised, Alo rightly concludes that he must be creamy. Zeki reasons similarly. Hence, when the instruction comes the second time, both philosophers, having each worked out that they must be creamy, raise their hands.

Your announcement made all the difference. Through your announcement, Alo learnt that Zeki knew that at least one philosopher was creamy. Prior to the announcement, although Zeki knew that at least one philosopher was creamy, Alo did not know that Zeki knew. The philosophers' knowledge of the other's knowledge came about through your announcement. Alo and Zeki both came to know that the other knew that there was at least one creamy philosopher. They possessed knowledge of each other's knowledge to that small degree – to degree 2, namely, knowing that the other knows – and so they could reason accordingly.

Our creamy philosophers' tale has just two creamy philosophers. Assuming your announcement is made, it can be proved that when there are n creamy philosophers, those creamy philosophers will all raise their hands on the nth occasion of the instruction to raise hands if creamy. Without the initial announcement and hence the required level of knowledge of knowledge, no hand-raising occurs.

Try a case of just three creamy philosophers, Alo, Zeki and Bob. At the first instruction, no hands go up, and Bob can see why: it is because Alo sees Zeki, and so, Bob thinks, Alo may think Zeki is the sole creamy philosopher. Bob reasons similarly regarding what Zeki may think. So, on the second instruction, Bob still does not raise his hand – but now seeing that, for example, Alo also does not raise his hand, Bob knows that must be because Alo sees a creamy philosopher in addition to Zeki. Bob now realizes that that additional creamy philosopher is he, and so he raises his hand on the third instruction. Alo and Zeki also raise their hands, having argued in like fashion.

With our creamy philosophers, the public announcement by you, the waiter, starts the philosophers on the path of knowing that the others know that there is at least one creamy philosopher. And we may move further along that path – of knowing that they know that others know that they know – and so forth. Common knowledge possesses, it seems, that feature of possible endless reiterations of knowledge, though, for example, with just the two creamy philosophers, Zeki merely needed to know that Alo knew there was at least one creamy philosopher – and vice versa.

Of course, most of us are not logicians, and none is a perfect reasoner, yet paradoxically in our daily lives we depend on common knowledge or, at least, common belief. It is paradoxical because we are finite creatures, yet common knowledge and common belief appear to enmesh us in potentially infinite reiterations. Here is an example.

In Britain, safety requires us to drive on the left. When, on a narrow road, I see an approaching vehicle, I should steer to the left – assuming that the other driver knows the convention. But not just that – he needs to know that I know the convention. Yet not even just that addition, for I need to know that he knows that I know the convention. And so on… Without common knowledge, common belief, or at least acting as if we possess such, there would be no language, no social living, and at best (or, more accurately, at worse) we should be isolated hermits living no recognizably human life at all.

ϒ

John Maynard Keynes told of a newspaper competition in which competitors had to select the six prettiest faces from a hundred photographs. The winner would be the one whose choice was closest to the average preferences of the competitors. In order to win, therefore, a competitor had to choose not those faces which he himself deemed prettiest, but those which he thought likeliest to appeal to the other competitors. They, of course, were all looking at the problem from the same point of view – and so, there are further moves to be made. Let us see some.

To win, do not judge who is the prettiest. To win, do not judge those which average opinion genuinely thinks the prettiest. To win, you must devote your intelligence to anticipating what average opinion expects the average opinion to be about the matter. But, of course, winning is more likely secured if you can move to the fourth level of correctly judging what the average opinion expects that the average opinion expects the average opinion to be about the matter – and even further levels could be sought.

Thus it is that lurking in our social behaviour – in public announcements, in conventions – are the reiterations of common knowledge and belief, though in practice, of course, we get by without infinite iterations. Now, that is puzzling; or would it be puzzling only if we were perfectly rational – only if we were perfect philosophers?

51

TIME FOR ZOOLOGICAL INVESTIGATIONS – FROM THE BEDROOM

Sophie and Suzie looked out of the lodge's window; gloom, misery, despair swamping them. The rain was torrential; cold winds howled. It was the first day of their school field-trip. They were meant to be out and about, from early morning, clad in unseemly Wellington boots, anoraks and hoods, wading through swamps – and for what purpose? To collect evidence to support, or not, a froggy hypothesis, the hypothesis that all frogs are green.

'Who cares about frogs and their colour?' muttered Sophie.

'I bet the teachers already know the answer,' added Suzie.

'It's all pointless – unless the point is to make us suffer,' they groaned in unison, staring at each other despondently.

A bright smile suddenly crossed Sophie's face. 'Look, Suzie, don't you remember our logic lessons the other week?'

Suzie groaned at this memory of another torture. 'Don't mention logic to me – all those 'A's and 'B's and 'if so and so, then such and such' and this following from that – and that from this.'

'Sorry, Suzie, I'll try to avoid the 'A's and 'B's, but this is worth thinking about. Look, suppose all frogs are green.'

'Here we go,' thought Suzie. 'Suppose this; suppose that. But, okay, I'm supposing away.'

'Well, if it really is true that all frogs are green, then it must follow that if we see something that is not green, it cannot be a frog.'

'Even I can grasp that; but so what?'

'I may as well add that if is true that all non-green items are not frogs, then it follows that all frogs are green – so, any frog we meet would have to be green.'

Suzie groaned; but Sophie continued. 'You see, to say that all frogs are green is the same as saying all non-green items are non-frogs.'

'Okay,' yawned Suzie, 'all very interesting; but we'd better get out of bed and get those horrible rubber boots on and face that dreadful rain.'

'You haven't worked it out yet, have you, Suzie? Look, we don't need to leave our beds and this warm lodge at all. There are numerous items around us, right here indoors, that help support the hypothesis that all non-green items are non-frogs – and that means that those items help support the hypothesis that all frogs are green. The two hypotheses amount to the same thing. We can do our zoological researches without getting out of bed.'

And with that, Sophie started writing entries in her research book, listing the evidence she could see in favour of all frogs being green:

One teddy bear (non-frog): pink (non-green);
Two pillows (non-frogs): purple (non-green)

– and so forth.

Suzie caught on, and was soon making her own list – 'After all, we don't want to be accused of cheating,' she giggled.

Wardrobe/brown. Cat/black. Lampshade/purple. Mouse/grey.

'Mouse?' the girls both squealed – but that's another tale.

How can pink teddy bears be evidence –
for all frogs being green?

Let us offer a little background: the ground is that of inductive reasoning – met earlier via Humpty Dumpty. Past regularities frequently lead us to expect the regularities to continue into the future. In spotting regularities, we spot similarities in some respects, ignoring various dissimilarities; we also take into account the circumstances of the regularities. Just because all the people we know live in Europe, we ought not to conclude that all people live in Europe. We have been exposed to a biased sample, if we have never reviewed what exists outside Europe.

Inductive reasoning needs handling with care; yet, however great the care, there is no logical guarantee that the regularities noted will continue into the future. Notwithstanding that point of logic, some scientists and logicians – and our common sense – accept that certain past regularities constitute *some* evidence, indeed, sometimes excellent evidence, in favour of those regularities continuing. If you encounter many frogs in a variety of environments and each one is green, you have some evidence in favour of the universal generalization 'All frogs are green.' Those noted froggy instances 'support' the generalization, even though only to some very small degree.

Our paradox – well, Hempel's paradox of confirmation – arises because we assume that instances do support universal generaliza-tions. Consequently, instances of non-green things that are non-frogs – instances such as pink teddy bears, purple pillows and black cats – support the generalization 'All non-green items are non-frogs.' That generalization, though, seems equivalent to 'All frogs are green.' Hence, finding a pink teddy bear appears to point as much to the 'All frogs are green' generalization as finding a green frog. Yet that is highly paradoxical.

What can be done to overcome the paradox – or should we succumb to the conclusion? Well, are we happy with the equivalence between 'All frogs are green' and 'All non-green items are non-frogs', the latter being the 'contrapositive' of the former? When we read those sentences, we focus on different items, frogs with the first, non-green items with the second. Yet, with some reflection, we probably accept that they are saying the same thing about the world. So, what is good evidence for one is, it seems, good evidence for the other.

The paradox, as said, assumes that a generalization is supported to some extent by its instances. That again is highly plausible. How else do we come to accept that these pages can burn, your hands will not turn into copper, and your head will not transform into a yellow balloon tomorrow?

Perhaps we should just accept the paradoxical conclusion. The pink teddy bear, the purple pillows, the black cat, all offer support for the generalization 'All frogs are green.' Or can anything further be said to avoid this conclusion?

♈

Lots more can be said. Here is a little more. Perhaps we have been amiss in casually speaking of support for a generalization, a hypothesis, a claim. Perhaps we should be speaking of the support there may be for our coming to *believe* that the hypothesis is likely to be true. Once in the territory of possible beliefs, we need to attend to pre-existing beliefs and knowledge.

What we already know is that the number of non-green non-froggy items – which include the aforementioned teddy bear, pillows and cat, but also billions of insects and trillions of atoms – vastly exceeds the number of frogs. Further, we accept that frogs form a natural grouping, whereas teddy bears, pillows and cats do not. Further still, in finding certain non-green non-frogs – say, some pink teddy bears – we are as likely to be supporting beliefs such as 'All frogs are yellow', 'All frogs are blue', even 'All frogs are disguised llamas.' Hence, although 'All frogs are green' and 'All non-green items are non-frogs' are equivalent, it does not follow that a pink teddy bear and a green frog provide the same degree of justification for our coming to suspect that all frogs are green.

How should we set about things, when seeking evidence for a proposed universal generalization? Well, in the case at hand, finding some frogs that are green has some value; but, in the right circumstances, finding the pink teddy bear also helps.

Suppose Sophie and Suzie trek out into the swamps, where there are numerous frogs, all ones seen so far green. Sophie then notices something distinctly un-green that is bobbing around: it is pink. It would be useful to establish whether it is a cast-off teddy bear and so no frog. It is worth discovering the item to be a teddy bear – otherwise it could be a pink frog and a counter-example to the froggy hypothesis. Scientific research can involve seeking to refute a proposed hypothesis as much as garnering support.

Paradoxically, instances of a generalization sometimes undermine support for the generalization. Suppose the hypothesis is, 'All green frogs live outside the estates of the Queen.' Well, we encounter lots of frogs outside the estates and indeed they are green. Unless and until more information is available, these frogs would be evidence for green frogs also living within the estates, not their absence. Frogs are no respecters of property rights.

What does all this show? Well, simply that supporting our beliefs about *all* this or *all* that is far from simple – yet we get by, day after day, holding such beliefs; and that is pretty paradoxical.

52
HOVE AND LATE: A GRUESOME AFFAIR

Even the closest friends may possess little quirks. Although Miranda was a close friend, my girlfriend indeed, her little ways of calling blue things 'bleenly' coloured and green things 'gruely' irked me, though I tried to see them as sweet linguistic quirks rather than irks. I had no reason whatever to think things appeared differently to Miranda than to me; well, no more so than anyone else. After all, she called the sky 'bleen' and the grass 'grue'. And when she wore her aqua-marine dress – was it really green or blue? – she wondered whether it was really grue or bleen.

What do I care, I mused, about her linguistic ways? Mind you, I thought it best not to discuss whether she considered this or that person was grue with envy; and, when we engaged in musical reflections, I resisted asking her whether she liked the bleens. My silence on such matters turned out to be sensible – for we were about to have sufficient troubles.

Ah, yes, there was one other little quirk. Whenever we were in romantic mood and I was declaring how much I loved her, she expressed her love too – save she said how much she hoved me. And curiously, when she expressed dislike of abstract art, football crowds and champagne breakfasts, she would speak of lating them.

One sultry summer's day, having fallen asleep on the green grass, out in the sun, under clear blue skies, I awoke, with Miranda tugging me. She was astonished – even distressed. 'Why, what's wrong?' I asked. 'Don't you see?' she cried, 'The grass is now bleen and the sky grue – whatever am I to do?'

I was baffled. They looked the same to me. 'But, Miranda, do they look differently from how they used to appear to you?'

'Well, I suppose they must – I guess. I am not really sure what to say. The sky, though, certainly is no longer bleen; I can tell that. And I haven't suddenly changed what I mean by my words.'

I looked at the calendar: while we were asleep, there would have been a rare comet crossing the sky at the same time as a partial eclipse of the sun.

And I wondered. I wondered whatever did Miranda mean all along by 'grue' and 'bleen'? Certainly, it seemed that, after all, she failed to mean what I meant by 'green' and 'blue' – for I still used 'green' of the grass and 'blue' of the sky. But she had now switched her applications of 'grue' and 'bleen', consistently – for all blue things, she now called 'grue' and all green things she now called 'bleen'.

So, what did Miranda mean?

A quick response may be that at least Miranda must have known all along what she meant and that her meaning contained a time element. The point about time is met below. Let us recall Wittgenstein's dictum about philosophy, mentioned in the Prologue – 'take your time' – and so, let us not rush in, thinking the puzzle is nonsense or easily solved. The puzzle is leading us into wondering quite what is involved in knowing what we, and others, mean.

As a small step, we need to remember that what strikes some people as 'the same' colour or shade strikes other people as different colours or shades; yet this difference may not be exposed for years – and only when the particular colour happens to be encountered by the people in question. When teaching a child how to multiply numbers, what may strike the child as going on 'in the same way' may not be what we meant by 'the same way'; and we may not discover this until much later on.

Our puzzle 'gruely' derives from American philosopher Nelson Goodman, whom we met in Chapter 41. The puzzle remains in the philosophical news. People, suggested Goodman, may have the colour term 'grue' and mean by it all items that are examined before a certain future time and are green; and otherwise items that are blue. In our story, we have orientated the date to an astronomical coincidence, now just past. Because we have passed that date, we can tell that something has gone awry with what we assumed Miranda meant.

On the surface it certainly looks as if, bizarrely, by 'grue' she meant what we mean by 'green' before that astronomical coincidence, otherwise what we mean by 'blue'. One unclear feature of the story is whether she experiences the grass differently. She certainly describes it with a different colour term – it is bleen, no longer grue. Another question is: given that only now have we discovered that she certainly did not mean green by 'grue', who knows her future linguistic uses?

The tale is not a play on language. Goodman initially introduced 'grue' when questioning inductive reasoning. We saw the basic induction problem in our encounter with Humpty Dumpty and Ms T (in Chapter 46); but there the assumption was that at least they knew what they meant, what counted as something being the same. Goodman's 'new riddle of induction' casts that assumption into doubt.

Some reject the puzzle, arguing that the special terms are not genuine colour terms; you have to check the occurrence of the comet and eclipse – the clock, the watch, the time – before you can tell whether something is or is not coloured grue or bleen. The reply is that someone who spoke in 'grue' terms and wondered what 'green' meant could pass a similar comment. To understand use of 'green', a gruesome speaker would learn that 'green' applied to observed grue things before a certain date, or before the astronomical coincidence, otherwise to bleen things. We could resort to wavelengths, and scientific theory, in explaining our colour terms; but similar problems can arise. A Goodmanian riddle could be created by introducing bizarre terms that applied to certain wavelengths before a certain time, but to others otherwise.

The gruesome speaker projected 'grue' into the future, believing that things that were grue would remain grue; that is, according to us, would turn to blue. Why was that any more unreasonable than our projections? Did we not just have to wait and see?

♈

I have presented an easy version of the riddle, but complexities have been added; the riddle has been embellished.

We had the word 'grue' to mean grue and 'bleen' to mean bleen; but suppose that Miranda – or some tribe we encounter – uses the word, the sound 'green', to mean grue, and the word, the sound 'blue', to mean bleen. We may be unable to tell that Miranda and others mean something different from us by those terms, until the key time is passed. After all, Miranda, in our original story, points to the same things as 'grue' that we call 'green'; she believes they will carry on being grue – and so on. She could do just the same, using the word 'green', but *meaning grue*. We just have to wait for her surprise when, one day, she announces that grass is no longer green, sky no longer blue. Or maybe that will be a day when *we* are surprised, suddenly thinking the sky has changed to green, the grass to blue – while Miranda insists nothing has changed, still calling sky 'blue', meaning bleen, and grass 'green', meaning grue.

We may really put the cat amongst the pigeons – poor pigeons – by asking our final gruesome question. How do we know what *we* mean when we use the word 'green'? Well, we point and say things such as, 'The colour of this grass is green – and other things are green that resemble this.' But how do we know how we shall react tomorrow, when we look at the grass? The puzzle is: what makes it the case that any one of us means one thing with a word rather than another?

Returning to our little story, I am now rightly nervous about Miranda's use of 'late' and 'hove'. Perhaps she does not mean love by 'hove', but love up to a certain date and then hate. So, in hoving me, Miranda at some future point will be hating me – yet speaking in terms of 'hoving' me still. Perhaps that is just the way that she is biologically built.

Of course, am I in any better position? How do I know what I mean, when I insist that I love Miranda and will continue to love her?

And so it is, when we say something remains the same, are we sure we mean the same when using the word 'same'? How can we tell?

PART VI: THE SELF

What am I?

Life can only be understood backwards;
but it must be lived forwards.
Søren Kierkegaard

'As Gregor Samsa awoke one morning from uneasy dreams he found himself transformed in his bed into a gigantic insect. "What has happened to me?" he wondered.'

Kafka's beginning to *Metamorphosis* sets the scene for a highly baffling puzzle. What makes me the same person over time? I worry about *my* future, look forward to the holiday, yet not the dental treatment; I recall *my* escapades last year. What, then, makes me that same person continuing – with a past that is mine, now living forwards into my future?

Descartes, as seen in Chapter 47, doubted whether his body and brain existed – he could be deceived – yet he still existed. So, he asked, what am I? What is the 'self'? Is it just a set of experiences? 'Everything is what it is, and not another thing,' wrote Bishop Butler. Perhaps the self is irreducible – and 'not another thing', not really just something else. Perhaps it is a persisting something, a soul, in which experiences come and go.

Isaac Newton is wheeled in for initial focus on the self and the theory that what makes me me is the continuing stream of consciousness, not some underlying persisting soul. What, though, is that consciousness?

One day, could biological automata be constructed, behaving just as regular human beings behave, yet lacking conscious experiences? Look out for Chapter 57 and the bafflement of Miss Doll. Further bafflement reigns, if we take seriously the proposal that thoughts and experiences are 'nothing but' neurological changes. Beware, once again, the 'nothing buttery'.

Before engaging with the tangles above, we turn to everyday temptations that affect our future. As we well know, we can succumb to cream buns, another drink or romantic liaisons, while knowing full well, it seems, that they end in unwanted weight gain, hangovers or tears. Straightforward actions, and emotional states such as modesty and shame, may also tie us in knots. As for poor Ass with his bales of hay – Ass raising a deep puzzle about reasons, actions and causes – well, too much reasoning can be fatal. Or so it seems. Still, the cream buns are waiting to be delivered.

53

RESOLUTIONS, GOOD INTENTIONS – AND CREAM BUNS

When Jane eats the big cream bun, her New Year's good intentions to stick to her dietary plan now have a bun-sized flaw. She knows that the planned diet is best for her health, but she is weak when faced with cream and bun. She has shown weakness of will. She is weak-willed.

Actions, though, speak louder than words – or so it is said. And Jane's bun-clasping action must surely mean that, at the clasp, her belief was that, all things considered, one bun would do no significant harm. She must have judged that, taking everything into account, the bun-eating was the best thing, right then, for her to do. If she did not so judge, she would not have chosen to succumb to temptation.

Paradoxically, though, the thought that actions speak louder than words can rule out weakness of will, even its possibility. Whatever we do, when acting freely, manifests what we take to be for the best, all things considered – or, as Socrates argued over two thousand years ago, 'No one willingly and knowingly does what is wrong.' Obviously, we may make mistakes about what is best; but we always do, given the circumstances, what we take to be best. Well, that is the idea.

True, Jane sincerely believed that she needed to lose weight for the sake of her health; true, she wanted to be slim; true, she was well aware that big cream buns would not assist that project. But pressed against those considerations were her desire for the immediate cream-filled pleasure and her belief that one bun would not undermine her dieting project. So, all things considered, bearing in mind her desires and beliefs, she was surely acting rationally, and displaying no weakness of will at all. Yet is that right? Can weakness of will be shown so easily to be illusory?

We ask that question for our everyday experience tells us that we often do suffer from weakness of will. We may seriously intend to study all evening for the examination the next morning, yet instead we meet up with friends and watch the snooker. We know we ought not to have a drink as we shall be driving; but we soon find ourselves with drink in hand and in mouth. Yet, if weakness of will genuinely occurs, what moves people, if not their intentions based on their beliefs and desires? If weakness of will does not occur, what is the right explanation of those cases that seem to be instances of the will's weakness?

How is weakness of will possible?

Cases of weakness of will – or what are taken to be such – differ from cases where the individuals concerned act under compulsion. If Jane is force-fed a bun, that clearly does not manifest weakness of will on her part. It is not weak will, if Jane suffers from a compulsive disorder with no chance of resisting the buns. Cases of weak will are ones in which, it seems, the individuals could resist whatever should be resisted – the gluttony, the lust, the sloth – yet they do not.

Returning to Jane as weak-willed, the following could surely be true. She truly wants to keep strictly to the diet; she recognizes that one bun now could easily pop her on the slippery slope to many more. Further, she sincerely values the project of dieting. And yet she still chooses to eat of the bun and savour the cream. She fails to act on her belief and desire concerning the diet: she acts against her better judgement. She could have exercised self-control, yet did not. That is weakness of will *par excellence*. It is sometimes known as 'akrasia': *kratos* being Greek for power, the *a* negating the power. It is also known, somewhat unattractively, as 'incontinence'.

Jane's actions, say many philosophers, cannot be explained, if they do not issue from her beliefs and desires. If so, we may be led to a revised understanding – the revisionary approach – of what Jane is truly committed to, when finally choosing the bun.

The Socratic approach, for example, is that the sight of the bun leads

Jane to become, metaphorically, short-sighted: she is unable to see the future value of health clearly enough; it is too distant. The value of future good health appears small compared with the value of the immediate creamy pleasure; so, whatever Jane is saying about her dieting commitment, her current genuine belief is that eating this bun right now is better overall than resistance.

Another suggestion, in that spirit, is that although Jane genuinely believes that sticking to the diet is valuable, it is conditional, depending on circumstances. In these very circumstances, of the bun immediately before her, she now believes it is better to eat than not. Of course, later on she may well regret yielding to the bun-shaped temptation.

There is a simple challenge to the type of approach above. Except for trying to explain away weak will as illusory, why must we hold that Jane believes bun-eating on this occasion is better than not? True, she *may* believe that 'just one bun' does not matter; but she may insist that she knows that she ought not to be eating even the one: that may be her sincere belief. The man who takes another drink before driving off may believe that the risk of accident is worth taking; if so, he is reckless, but not weak-willed. He may, though, have no such belief. His belief may be that he ought not to have the extra drink, yet drink he does. We have all, no doubt, had experiences of such weakness. Evaluative judgements – what we believe best and our resultant intentions – are not always aligned to motivational strength.

Intentions, be they good or bad, do not get things done. Just because I intend to do something, it does not follow that I do it. I need to act on the intention. Weakness of will occurs when I fail to act on my best intentions: hence it is, allegedly, an irrational state for the agent. Quite how best to explain that failure remains obscure. Models are given of the self as divided within – with desires in conflict with reason and duty – but such models raise their own puzzles. With which division of the self do I most readily identify? What or who, indeed, is the 'I', the self, that judges between the conflicting parts?

ϒ

We have deliberately left open what is involved in the judgement that something is 'best'. We may judge what is best purely with regard to self-interest; but we may also take into account what we consider to be our duty, of what morality dictates, or, for that matter, of what our commitment to particular causes demands. Weakness of will can be readily seen when the agent recognizes that, for example, she really ought to help the distressed child or denounce some fraudulent behaviour, yet does not. Just as Jane could not stick to what she sincerely thought best for her health – instead she succumbed to the bun – so we often fail to stick to what we sincerely think is the right thing to do, but succumb instead to perceived self-interest. We are weak creatures indeed.

The 'weakness' in 'weakness of will' suggests that it never deserves recommendation. Now, when individuals develop characters so weak that they fail to follow their true intentions, fail to stick to their principles, we tend to lack respect for them. But sometimes it may be best – for others and even for themselves – if they are weakly willed. Would that those who firmly believe in genocide be weak-willed and, instead of being true to their belief, be driven by humanity, compassion and fellow feeling. The highly principled and those with strength of character are not always to be admired; weakness of will has its place.

Yes, the will's weakness has a place, though not one, when surrounded with free offers of cream buns or – let us not be biassed – mille-feuilles, Black Forest gateau or endless pourings of champagne.

54
MARY, MARY, QUITE CONTRARY

Whenever possible, Mary will do something different from what you expect. If she is deciding whether to take her holiday next week and you point out all the good reasons for her so to do, concluding that she is therefore bound to take the holiday – well, Mary will perversely stay at home. 'Mary, you'd doubtless like a cool drink; it's such a hot day.' Not much of a chance; she may well go for steaming hot tea. Mary, Mary, is, indeed, quite contrary. And Mary likes being contrary – to show you, to show all of us, that she is free. She is free to choose what to do, however irrational, however well we all know her. She may think that deciding to act irrationally shows that, unlike timers, thermostats and tea-making machinery, she and others possess free will.

For her knowingly to do the contrary, Mary needs to be told what you predict. If you predict that she will act somewhat perversely and tell her so, she will do the opposite. Naturally, there are some things outside Mary's power or so dangerous that she will not make your prediction false. When you tell her that she will continue to breathe over the next ten minutes, she is not so silly as to undermine that.

Many philosophers – also neurologists, geneticists and psychologists – believe that all our actions are ultimately caused and are, indeed, determined by outside factors. Even if indeterminacy reigns at the quantum level much discussed by physicists, statistical laws hold firm. There is, indeed, increasing evidence that, away from the quantum and at the level of human interactions with the world, our actions are causally determined by factors beyond our control. These factors include our genetic characteristics, our conditioning as we grow up, the culture within which we live – and direct impingings of the environment upon our senses. In one way or another, these bring about our desires, speech, movements and much more; hence, it is exceedingly difficult to find any room for what is usually thought of as free will or free choice. In sum, what we do is determined by our nature and nurture, neither of which we choose.

In slightly more detail, Mary's actions – the movements she makes, the words she utters – are caused by electrochemical changes in her brain which themselves are caused by other electrochemical changes and impingings via her senses, and so on, and so forth. Were scientists to know everything about genes, about how brains work and how they are affected by the environment, and about Mary's particular circumstances, they could predict everything that Mary, even Mary in contrary mode, would do. The scientists could place their predictions of Mary's behaviour in a sealed envelope and Mary would be unable to undermine those predictions. This would seem to show that Mary is not free and, for that matter, not free, whether or not anyone bothers to do the predicting.

But... but... but... Does not the following possibility remain? Were the scientists to make their predictions and were Mary to learn what they predict, is she not free to decide not to do what they have predicted? If they predict that she will choose the red dress, then she can choose whether to make their prediction false. She could go for the blue.

Are we not free to undermine predictions based on all the facts about us?

Acting contrary to what people expect of us – even what scientists predict about us – may seem to show that we are free. Mary's contrariness vividly brings this home. But is that freedom mere illusion? It is true that, typically, Mary can act otherwise than as people predict, but given her neural networks, she cannot act otherwise than as those networks cause.

If scientists tell Mary about their predictions, that is a causal input that will affect her neurological happenings; and so, those predictions may well affect what she does. Suppose we are the scientists who have learned all there is to know about her neurological states to date. We make our prediction of what she is going to do; whether she will choose the red dress or the blue. If we *tell* her that we predict the red, we need to take that feedback into account. In principle, it should be possible to anticipate how that feedback will affect Mary if thus fed back. On some occasions, we may know that, if she learns of our prediction, she will then act differently from what is predicted. Let this be such an occasion; let us see what happens.

We know that if we tell her of our red dress prediction (call this 'Prediction One'), she will choose the blue dress – and may even think this shows how free she is. We could secretly have predicted that of her (call this 'Prediction Two'). If she learns of Prediction Two – 'Mary will choose the blue because we told her we predicted the red' – we know that she will revert to red. That would generate Prediction Three, a prediction of which we are confident, unless Mary learns of it. If she does, we know how that will affect her and how she will respond. That could lead us to make Prediction Four, which would turn out correct, so long as she does not learn about it. And so on – with more and more predictions about how she will respond, given the inputs of the previous predictions.

This shows that, were we to learn all there is to learn about Mary and were all her actions completely determined, on some occasions we may know that it is impossible for her to learn of our correct predictions and they remain correct. It would also seem to show that Mary cannot learn all there is to know about herself such that she correctly predicts her own actions, yet is able to choose to act otherwise. This may be marked by the big distinction between our intending to do something and our merely predicting that we shall do it. (Chapter 66's boxing puzzle can be related to that distinction.)

Maybe all there is to free will is the mere feeling and true belief that we would sometimes have acted differently from what was predicted, if told of the predictions; but it does not follow that we could have acted differently, given the particular causal inputs on us that remain outside our control.

♈

The problem of free will and determinism haunts many people. I have suggested that acting freely is not possible, if all our actions are events that are determined, enmeshed in deterministic causal chains of events, with the causes stretching back into the past, before our birth and hence beyond our command – but, consider the alternative. Suppose that, after looking through brochures, discussing with friends and reflecting alone, I choose to holiday in Bucharest rather than Budapest. As with many free choices, I have my reasons for the choice. The difficulty is that, had that choice been causally determined, then – we are told – it would not be a genuine free choice. The alternative to the causal story is that such causal determination is lacking. My choice would then amount to being causally random – at least, that would seem to be how it came about, whatever I say about my reasons.

To act freely, however, is not to act randomly. Typically, we are held to account for what we freely do, but if our choices and actions result, in some way, from randomness, we should not usually be so held. If our choices and actions come about randomly, then they seem to be as much beyond our control as choices and actions resulting from causal chains extending to times before we even existed. Whether our choices and actions are caused or random, what scope is there for making sense of what is surely so: namely, that we often act, freely act, on the basis of reasons?

The resulting bafflement should lead us to examine more carefully what we are seeking, when seeking the subject, the 'I', that does the choosing, deciding or acting, and that gives reasons for the choices, decisions and actions. If 'I' lacks all characteristics and character, then what we are talking about is baffling. It is also mysterious how whatever it is that we are talking about could make choices at all, including, therefore, any choices of what characteristics and character to develop, as well as what actions to perform. Jean-Paul Sartre, French existentialist and political activist, famously associated with Simone de Beauvoir, seemed to hold that baffling position while being unbaffled. We remain baffled; yet if characteristics and character are granted to 'I', then we naturally look for causes outside the 'I' which brought about those characteristics and character, hence undermining our free action. Whichever way we approach the matter, we fail to find anything like the free choices, decisions and actions which we apparently want, namely ones which are ours, under our exclusive control and for which, indeed, we can usually give reasons. We are left bewildered – as bewildered as we are when reading Sartre who seems to claim that it is our 'nothingness' that somehow enables us to make free choices.

A common response to the bewilderment is that 'acting freely' is more to do simply with our getting what we want or having *our* reasons for what we do, without reference to neurological causal stories. This would indeed be compatible with such actings being determined and within causal chains. Of course, the cry then goes up, 'But I am not free to choose my wants.' Well, on what basis would you choose them?

What is it that we choose? Well, the red underwear (oops!), *Seinfeld* DVD and a holiday in Venice. As scientists uncover more laws to explain movements, moods and tendencies to drink, do we expect laws of underwear, *Seinfeld* and holidaying abroad? Let them predict Mary's eyelids' flutter, but is that an action of flirting, signalling a gin – or just a twitch?

As a footnote, let us note that arguments about whether our behaviour is explained by our genes or by our upbringing and environment are irrelevant to the problem of whether we act freely. Philosophically, it does not terribly matter which is more prominent. If the threat to freedom is having our actions caused by things outside our control, then, if indeed out of our control, it is irrelevant whether those things be genetic or environmental, nature or nurture.

55

MODESTY AND SHAME: A CAT AND MOUSE TALE

'Know thyself,' said the ancient Athenian philosopher Socrates, deriving the injunction from the Delphic Oracle. Many of us would hesitate to obey, from fear of what we may uncover. Yet there are cases where we cannot obey, or so it seems, without losing characteristics that we should be pleased to uncover. And, by coincidence, in a Delphi Taverna, a cat and mouse engaged in a debate that raised precisely such matters.

≈

CLATEO CAT: I bet you wish you were me. Feel my silky coat – yes, I've just won the International Feline Beauty Contest. And did I mention how I received special commendation for my thesis 'Prowling at night: reflections on Socrates'? And in the marathon, I...

MENA MOUSE: Oh dear – *so* immodest, Clateo, with all that boasting. Wouldn't a little modesty become you?

CLATEO: Nothing wrong with immodesty; after all, I merely tell it as it is. No point hiding my light under a bushel – or in a mouse-hole. Follow my example, Mena. True, you're just a grey mouse, but I hear on the grapevine that you have many achievements. The fastest mouse in the house, in the taverna...

MENA: That's nothing – the competition is poor...

CLATEO: Not what I hear, Mena – and there's your Cat–Mouse Reconciliation Project. Also your excellent work with asylum-seeking mice and...

MENA: But that's just what any mouse would do...

CLATEO: Mena, you at least have to admit you're excellent at being modest, don't you know?

MENA: I'm not being modest – just telling it as it is.

IF IT'S ANY CONSOLATION, I FEEL **SO** ASHAMED ...

Immodest Clateo tells it as it is. He is immodest, given the telling; but he would also be immodest merely in thinking so highly, so proudly, of himself. Clateo knows that he is immodest, but what of Mena Mouse? Mena certainly sounds as if she is modest; and let us assume that she is. Why does she find it difficult to recognize that she is?

Can modest individuals know that they are modest?

We may know that we are kind or mean, courageous or cowardly. We may know that we are conceited, proud and immodest – yet can we know that we are modest? Modesty, here, of course, concerns our achievements, our good features, not our resistance to flaunting the body bared.

To put it paradoxically – the Modesty Paradox – if we know we are modest, then we are not. Modesty requires that we do not over-estimate our achievements – but it requires more than that. Clateo Cat may be accurate in the estimate of his achievements, yet is clearly not modest. Modesty, it appears, needs us to underestimate our achievements, diminishing their importance, yet not reflectively and deliberately so. Were we to underestimate deliberately, conscious of that fact, we should be falsely modest: we would be well aware of our achievements, yet pretending they are not that great. That would be a pretence at modesty.

Modest individuals, such as Mena, genuinely see their achievements as less significant than they really are. They see their kindness or generosity, or being the fastest mouse in the house or taverna, as not especially impressive. Paradoxically, modesty – usually taken as a virtue – requires some sincere yet poor evaluation of one's qualities.

Assuming that modest individuals cannot know that they are modest, Mena Mouse could not acknowledge her modesty, saying 'I am modest.' Others, though, could truthfully describe her as modest, as indeed Clateo did. Paradoxically, Clateo can say something true about Mena that Mena cannot say about herself. Moore's Paradox, as seen in Chapter 43, has a similar feature.

The above needs a caveat. Modest individuals may occasionally take a detached attitude about themselves, step out of their skin, and reflect that they have modest tendencies. Even if that is so, that is far removed from, on particular occasions, consciously underplaying what they are. A man – or mouse – who proclaims modesty acts immodestly.

≈

MENA: I forgive your immodesty, Clateo, but I'm not so sure about forgiving you for chasing my little friends the other day. They were really scared. Didn't you feel any shame?

CLATEO: Funny you should ask. Yes, I felt ashamed; but then, being aware of that feeling, I felt rather good about myself – at being the kind of cat who feels bad about his chasing behaviour. That, though, lessened my feeling of shame, so I felt ashamed of that lessening. But then...

MENA: Don't tell me – you felt good about yourself at being the sort of cat who could feel ashamed about that. I suppose you started feeling bad again as a result and...

CLATEO: By that stage, I was so befuddled, swaying to and fro from bad to good – well, I slept it all off.

~~~

Mena cannot be modest and be aware of her modesty. Now, Clateo was aware of his shame, yet that awareness seemed to undo the full extent of his shame; so we are led to the question:

Can I, if reflective, ever be properly ashamed?

Sensitive individuals, when they wittingly do something bad, should surely feel shame, remorse or regret. Yet in feeling shame, they are not as bad as shameless individuals, individuals who do not care. Once sensitive individuals are aware of this, the paradoxical result is a reduction in their shame – for they are now feeling a little better about themselves.

We need not stop there. Now feeling a little better about themselves, the individuals may feel ashamed of this feeling better, for it detracts from their feeling bad about whatever they did; and, reflecting on this new level of shame, they feel a little better about themselves again. And so on. Whenever feeling better about themselves at feeling ashamed, they move to a new level of shame; but that awareness spirals them into another level of feeling pleased with themselves at being so ashamed.

There is nothing odd in having feelings about feelings. You may feel harassed, and feel irritated with yourself at feeling harassed. You may blush with embarrassment and feel embarrassed at blushing, thus blushing more. There is nothing odd about reflecting on your feelings. In as far as you reflect – human psychology being as it is – you may be distracted from the full immediacy of the feelings upon which you reflect. That is one reason, relied upon by certain therapists, why talking about feelings can reduce your direct involvement in them, thus reducing their intensity. The puzzle of shame, though, does not rest on simple distraction.

Shameful Clateo, on reflection, recognizes that his being ashamed possesses some moral merit. The result is that it is impossible for him to catch the full extent of his badness about which to be ashamed. Although he appears to have a grip on the badness, his reflection on the virtue of his being ashamed leads to a diminution of that badness. That is because he now recognizes that he has the worthy feature of being ashamed. Yet he may be ashamed at how he has, apparently, diminished his badness in that way; thus he spirals.

Clateo cannot know the full continuous extent of his shame, for if he seems to catch it, he loses it. Of course, others may know that he is truly ashamed of his behaviour, and merits some praise for being so – but that is what he cannot know, without destabilizing the shame.

♈

'Know thyself' is all very well, but Socrates might have added that there are some good things about ourselves – being modest, feeling ashamed – upon which it is best not to reflect and hence not to know.

Socrates claimed to know only of his ignorance; but in stinging people's complacency with unsettling questions, Socrates was a philosophical gadfly – arguably a shameless and immodest one – one so good at puncturing the immodesty of others. No doubt deliberately, did he highlight the immodesty of the immodest, intending to deflate them and bring them to heel. No doubt he sometimes highlighted the modesty of the modest; but, in making them aware of their modesty, he, albeit unintentionally, may have endangered that very modesty.

56

'HI, I'M SIR ISAAC NEWTON –
DON'T MENTION THE APPLES'

'Hi, I'm Sir Isaac Newton – don't mention the apples,' says the man in the bed, waking up, rubbing his eyes with seeming disbelief.

We must suppose this happens quite recently, certainly in no seventeenth century. The words astonish those who hear them – for the man in the bed is just a regular guy, with the slightly irregular name of 'Ossie'. His wife and children are amazed, and then irritated, as they, understandably so, think their Ossie is having them on, pretending to be Newton. Ossie is speaking in flowery old – ye olde – English. He looks around, amazed. 'Where am I? Where are my servants, my books, and alchemy records? What's this strange lantern glowing in the ceiling? How are words being spoken out of this magical box?'

We could go on in this vein, but happily shall not. Suffice it to say that the individual – Ossie – continues, seemingly in all sincerity, to know nothing of his life as Ossie, but manages to say lots about Isaac Newton as if, indeed, he is Isaac Newton, somehow inhabiting poor Ossie's body – as if, indeed, Isaac Newton is living here in Soho, London, and not dead and buried in Westminster Abbey.

At first we assume Ossie is playing a big game. Yes, we all know the story of Newton, who, it was mistakenly claimed, hit on gravity when apples hit upon him. Ossie could have secretly studied Newton's life, practised the sounds of old English, reflected that Newton would be tired of apple jokes and so on; but could a time come when it is rational to accept that, hey, maybe after all, somehow or other, Newton has been reincarnated? We should then have lost Ossie. Where indeed is Ossie? But that is a different puzzle. Let us focus on the individual here, this Ossie or Newton, the general question, a question of some gravity, being,

Could it be rational to believe that a deceased historical figure is living again?

We speak of 'could', of what is possible. This does not commit us to saying that it will happen or even is likely to happen. We simply wonder about the sheer possibility, whether there is anything contradictory in the idea.

Who is this man who looks like Ossie, yet speaks like Newton and claims to be Newton? Let us call him 'Issie' – just so that we are leaving things open at this stage, concerning who he really is. If Issie really is the reincarnated Isaac Newton, he must at least describe many events of his past as '*I* experimented with this, wrote that' – and so on. He must speak of Newton, himself, in the first person – and let us suppose that Issie does. We may still doubt whether Issie is Isaac Newton; Ossie could have learnt the historical facts, transposing them into the first person.

Suppose Issie speaks of events unknown to anyone living, yet which can be checked. Maybe he speaks of burying some papers and biblical items in a secret vault under King's College Chapel and in a chest buried under an ancient beech tree at the Gog Magog Hills outside Cambridge. Experts examine the sites, find that they have not been disturbed for centuries, dig away, and discover the items. With such evidence – good evidence, surely – maybe we should think, 'Yes, somehow Newton has been reincarnated in Ossie's body. Issie is Isaac Newton.'

Bodily continuity – having the same body over time – is not essential, it seems, for Newton, or for anyone else, to survive. Issie – I mean, Newton – agrees. 'I keep telling you that I am Isaac Newton, though I can't get used to this body with which I now find myself. Ossie didn't keep himself in trim, I can tell only too well.'

But... Consider a further possibility. Unbeknownst to us, Bruce, sleeping on Australia's Bondi Beach, also woke up one afternoon, saying, 'Hi, I'm Sir Isaac Newton – don't mention the apples.' This individual knows nothing about what has been happening regarding Ossie. Bruce goes through similar astonished declarations to those of Issie – maybe greater astonishment in light of the bikini-clad Bondi Beach. To register our uncertainty about the identity of this man whom we thought of as Bruce, but who is now claiming to be Newton, let us call him 'Aussie'. The evidence for Aussie being Newton ends up being just as strong as the evidence for Issie being Newton. So, if we are right in thinking that the evidence showed that Issie was Newton, then we should also believe that Aussie is Newton. If so, we seem committed to the belief that Aussie, the individual in Australia, is identical with Issie, the individual in London. Yet that is surely impossible. How can one and the same person be both in Australia and Britain at the same time, knowing nothing of what each other is doing? Has Newton been reincarnated as a split personality inhabiting two different bodies?

♈

We could, without logical contradiction, have twenty-seven, or twenty-seven thousand, such individuals all waking up, announcing sincerely that they are Newton, all with equally strong credentials. With the single awakening, the Issie case alone, it seems reasonable to believe that Newton is alive and well. With the multiple cases, we should be baffled. The mere possibility of the multiple cases does not count against Newton being reincarnated in the single case. But although that is true, the possibility of multiple cases does appear to count against psychological conditions alone being sufficient for what it is for one and the same person to be reincarnated.

Let us return to the single case of Issie. Let us assume that Issie is indeed Isaac Newton. If so, then Issie might have been Newton even though he was unable to give any impressive evidence about buried papers to establish the fact, not least because he, Newton, performed no such burials. We – and Newton – hit lucky with our reincarnated Newton; he possessed distinctive knowledge to pass on. We also hit lucky because he was not confused; he knew who he was – but it is possible for a person still to be the same person yet to have forgotten a huge amount about his identity. Suppose Newton, when he awoke in Ossie's body, was having his own psychological problems. Just as he, so to speak, invaded Ossie's body, so he, Newton, felt that his mind was being invaded, an odd collection of mistaken memories, thoughts and attitudes, squeezing out his own…

And so it is possible – or is it? – that our tale could have coherently been of Newton waking up in Ossie's body, utterly confused about who he is. Indeed, if we dare press logical conceivability even further, may not poor Newton have woken up in Ossie's body, even more confused, thinking himself to be a man called 'Ossie', waking up in the twenty-first century? If so, then, as we nod to a man in a bed, humouring a poor and possibly confused Ossie – as we see him – in fact the man in the bed is Sir Isaac, unaware of who he really is. Indeed, perhaps I am Sir Isaac – perhaps we all are Sir Isaac – a Sir Isaac with a very poor memory of earlier living.

And so it is that we learn that we should not push possibilities too far, yet the puzzle then is: how far is too far?

57

'I AM A ROBOT'

'I am a robot – a mechanical woman, a mechanical doll indeed. Well, so I have just been told. I thought I was like everyone else – a person, with thoughts and imagination, intentions and memories, pains and pleasures – but apparently this is not so. Certain philosophers have explained that there is a huge difference between people and me. People have private experiences. I do not. How can this be? As far as I can tell, I differ in no crucial way at all.

'"Ah, yes, as far as you can tell," reply silver-tongued philosophers, "but you have been cunningly created, to appear like a person; yet you are no person at all."

'Well, I am made from biological material. My mechanism does not consist of crude wheels and pulleys but of electrochemical activity in a neural system, just as in people's. I am humanly shaped – rather desirably so, if I may modestly add. I have brain and heart and womanly pulsations – laughs and talks and coquettish walks. Tears fall from my eyes when onions I peel, when I lose at the races and when I see my lover(s) dancing too closely to others. My voice is unsteady after a little red wine – how I do prefer champagne! – and my heart skips when some handsome gigolo meets my gaze.

'That is how it all seems to me but, apparently, I have no conscious life, no experiences, no true "seeming to me" at all, if "seeming to me" involves conscious experiences. I use the right words for consciousness, experiences and the like; I react as people typically react – but all this, I am told, is not because of any awareness or consciousness or feeling on my part.

'Tread on my toe – and I jerk my foot away, wince and cry "Ouch!" Yet, so they say, I experience no private painful sensations. Everything that goes on inside me is open to scientists observing my neural and other bodily changes. And however deep within me they peer, they spot no thoughts, no images, no pains, no pleasures. You, reader(s), by contrast, have private sensations and thoughts, such consciousness that I, apparently, lack. Although I can, as well as any regular person, discriminate between hot and cold, light and dark and loud and soft (and act accordingly), I am, it seems, no better than a complex thermostat, light sensor and sound apparatus rolled into one – and certainly they lack feelings of heat, sensations of sight and experiences of sound.

'I break down at this news. I am terribly hurt by what these philosophers say about me. My distress proves nothing at all, for – to them – it cannot be a distress that involves my having sensations. They congratulate themselves on how much like a real person I am.'

Is there more to *you* than your behaviour, body and brain?

Are your experiences different from the physical things happening within you?

What are we to make of Miss Doll, who spoke so movingly? Might someone, who speaks and reacts almost exactly as we do, be without conscious experience?

Some philosophers – and even some sensible people – believe such robots to be logically possible. They argue that conscious experiences are over and above – are different from – what goes on inside brains and bodies and the movements that get done or are likely to be done. Therefore, they add, there is no contradiction in there being an individual such as Miss Doll who is, in all relevant respects, like us, except that she ('it'?) lacks conscious experiences. She performs as we all do but when she and we are reading these words, we have visual experiences, whereas she has none. Such creatures, who seem like us yet who lack experiences, are called by some philosophers, somewhat misleadingly, 'zombies'.

Other philosophers argue that, as Miss Doll is the same physically as we are and acts in the same ways as we act or are likely to act (apart from her recent discovery of seemingly being a robot), she is, indeed, a person with experiences – and it is sheer nonsense for her, or us, to believe otherwise. Some stress that having the same neurology is all that is required for Miss Doll to be one of us: in some way, experiences are identical with brain events. A difficulty here is to grasp how our experiences – pains, visual impressions and how things seem to us – can be just chemical or electrical changes in the brain. And why insist that creatures which lack our neural structures – maybe creatures from distant planets – cannot have experiences?

The way we assess whether others are in pain, keen for a drink or just happy, is not by their neurology but by what they do or say and tend to do and say. This leads some to identify experiences with behavioural tendencies. We may think that this approach muddles the way in which we *tell* whether something is so – for example, that someone is in pain – with its *being* so. If, though, this is the right approach, then, again, Miss Doll is definitely one of us. A difficulty here lies in making sense of the idea that my experience of pain simply is identical to a tendency to want to cry out and escape from the perceived cause. And, of course, 'wanting to cry' and 'perceiving' also need to be understood in ways related to further behavioural tendencies. Yet we may well doubt whether all our psychological concepts can ultimately be adequately grasped solely in terms of the behavioural and dispositional.

♈

Miss Doll raises the questions of what minds and experiences are and how they relate to the body. How things seem and feel to me – do they not possess a privacy? My experiences cannot simply be physical events open to public gaze.

'What is it like to be a bat?' That question is one way of raising the difficulty. However much we humans learn about the behaviour and neural structures of bats, however much crazed philosophers hang upside down from church towers, flapping their arms, is there not something that we miss – namely, how *bats* experience the world? Plausibly, we should answer 'yes'; yet such an answer pushes us further, into thinking that we also can neither directly know how other humans experience the world nor, indeed, how we experienced it previously (nor, for that matter, whether other humans experience the world at all). Perhaps other humans are, in fact, nothing but many Miss Dolls, if Miss Doll is, indeed, nothing but a senseless robot.

Thus, we hit the problem of 'other minds'. If I possess direct knowledge of only one example of a mind, an experiencer, me, what can justify me in my firm belief that there are other experiencers? Can I even make sense of there being experiences other than mine? I know only *my* experiences. Can I make any sense at all of a mine/thine distinction? What do you think, Miss Doll?

'These ways madness lies. I thought (if I may use the term) that things were bad enough when you scientists and philosophers tried to persuade me that I lack all experiences. With this "other minds" problem, I may argue that I alone am the one individual who has experiences. Madness indeed. Let's try sense. I use words such as "experiences", "thinking" and "feelings" in the usual way. In view of that, it is impossible for me to grasp that my use is somehow phoney – and that, in fact, I lack experiences. I guess you have all been raising an empty problem for me.'

Miss Doll, if you are a senseless robot, then you are just parroting such words without any understanding of those words and with no experiences at all.

'And how do you know you're not?'

58
UNIQUELY WHO?

A strange thing happened the other day. I glanced at the man by the bar, just as he glanced at me (but this is no tale of gay love at first sight). It struck us both how similar we looked – as if we were identical twins. We laughed, got talking and discovered the same interests. It transpired that we had been born in the same town. A little later, amazingly, it came out that we had the same birth date. Coincidences happen. We pursued matters further. Imagine my astonishment when he announced the exact time and place of his birth. Identical to mine! He named and described his parents. 'But they're my parents!' I said. He looked at me, his stare and my stare alike with incredulity. We found ourselves exploding with indignation, each exclaiming, 'But I'm Peter Cave. You're just pretending you're me.' We were embarrassed at making a public scene, so we got up and left. Bizarrely, we headed back to the same address. 'Ah,' I thought with some triumph, 'I have the only keys.' The triumph quickly subsided, as I saw him yanking out similar keys from his pocket…

The tale could be continued in various ways. The two sets of similar keys could open two similar houses containing two similar families – in exactly the same location? – or perhaps we returned to one and the same house, met one and the same family and so on. What it illustrates is that, however similar someone may be to me, surely he can never be me. Am I not unique? What is it that makes me *me* – and makes this me continue to be me?

Uniqueness applies to any object. There are many copies of this book; they could be very, very similar – the same creases, the same shaped coffee stains, in the same unread, dusty state – yet, none the less, each copy is distinct because, even if all their features are the same, they are in different places or, if in the same place, in the same place at different times. The distinct copies consist of different sets of molecules – more colloquially, different lumps of physical stuff. The particular lump that makes up this copy cannot be both here and over there, at the same time.

So, what makes me *me* – and makes me continue to be me?

Is what makes me *me* the particular physical stuff out of which my body and brain are formed, just as this particular book is made from this set of molecules? If so, then maybe my continuation demands the continuation of the same physical stuff. Yet I can have heart, lung and liver transplants and still be me. New tissue can be injected into my brain and old tissue removed and yet I remain the same self, the same me. All my molecules are naturally replaced over the years.

Perhaps what makes me continue to be me is not being made out of literally the same physical stuff but there being a continuing, developing neural structure or organism, continuous in space and time. Or perhaps what is essential is not the same neural structure but the same continuing consciousness, with memories, desires and intentions developing, coming and going, with some appropriate degree of connectedness. After all, does it not make sense – at least, it seems to make sense – to conceive of waking up, with a different body and brain, as we saw with Isaac Newton in a previous puzzle and as happened to the central character in Kafka's story, *Metamorphosis*, quoted in this section's introduction?

Some have conceived the possibility of another universe, a duplicate or 'identical twin' universe. Speaking loosely, in that universe there is another 'me', or so it seems, with the same neural structures as I have in this universe and with the same memories and desires; the same relationship to bar, house and keys. Yet that could not actually be *me*.

I am a particular item. Whatever stories are told of items having all the same properties and qualities and memories and relationships as I have, I cannot make sense of any of those items being me, apart from one – *me*. I make sense of myself continuing over time: I have a past and a future – and these past and future selves (as we may call them) must bear some special relationship to me now. Perhaps that relationship is, as some have suggested, one of psychological continuity, involving some connectedness. The psychological continuity answer gives rise to its own puzzles: it needs to be able to handle cases of amnesia – and paramnesia, where people sincerely think they remember doing things which they have not done. If the psychological disruption is so great, perhaps that does indeed amount to the death of the person, of me. If all my memories have gone, all specific desires and plans and hopes, what is left of what can properly be identified as me?

Consider this: I am shortly to undergo some severe and prolonged pain. Perhaps an evil scientist is about to torture me. Being no masochist, I do not at all look forward to this future. If the scientist promises, 'I'll make things a little easier for you. I'll wipe your memories just before I begin the torture,' would my fear be reduced? My fear should surely be at least as great. I shall still be suffering the pain, even though I shall no longer know who I am. How would that help to stop its being me undergoing the pain? Aware of my distress, the scientist adds, 'After I wipe your memories, I'll give you a set of false memories. Maybe that will help.' Will it? I shall end up being mad as well as tortured. Surely, it will still be *me*, even though I shall remember nothing of my past and shall doubtless have a completely different personality.

The tale challenges the thought that what makes me me is the retention of psychological continuity. Suppose the new memories and character that I am given are those of someone else whose body and brain are receiving my psychological states. That does not seem to help me to conclude, 'This body, soon to be tortured, will no longer be mine, so I shall not feel a thing, for I shall then be inhabiting that other body.' Perhaps one simple truth is that what makes me me over time must, at a minimum, be one of either psychological continuity or physical continuity – but when these criteria come apart, we are unsure how to respond.

♈

Maybe one day it will be possible to put me to sleep and transport me to different planets. Maybe all the physical and psychological information and neural structures that make me me – my complete specifications – are copied, leaving on Earth at most a lifeless blob, the lifelessness resulting from the copying procedures. The information is beamed to a distant planet called 'Distant Planet', where it is used to reconstitute me – a speedy form of interplanetary transport. True, the stuff is different on Distant Planet, but we have already seen that the actual physical stuff even on Earth changes, yet I may remain. I awake on Distant Planet, with everything relevant – same structured memory, desires, body, brain – intact. I say: 'Yes, it's me, Peter Cave; it wasn't at all painful. I wasn't really worried about its not working.'

At first sight, the above tale of scientific advance generates no problems, *if* the procedure in some way involves my body's destruction, down here on Earth. But suppose advanced procedures require no such destruction. I should awake on Earth and also on Distant Planet. How can I be in two places at once? Indeed, if I can be copied, so to speak, onto Distant Planet, I could be similarly copied onto multitudinous planets. The concept of my self demands that there be solely one, solely one *me*; yet everything about me seems open to replication – and hence more '*me*'s.

Suppose that I wake up on Earth, go to my favourite pub and sitting there is the Peter Cave – that 'me' – who, as a result of a beaming, should have been re-created on Distant Planet but due to a misdirected power surge is here on Earth and – having my memories and desires – has gone to his favourite pub and we get chatting...

59

THE BRAIN *or* WHERE AM I?

I've recently lost my appetite. That's unsurprising, I suppose, given that I'm just a brain in a vat – well, so they tell me. In fact, I reside in a precious Grecian vase, size large, and not just any old vat. At first I thought they were making fun of me, but then my experiences started to go haywire. Sometimes they cut out completely and I just experience a blank. They tell me not to worry. I'm in good hands. They promise to let me see me one day, but currently they feed me experiences as if I were at home, gazing through the window, feeding the pigeons – or out dancing and prancing, drinking champagne with young men of my dreams. Ah, that's the life.

Of course, I do worry. I sometimes dwell on my vase-free days, when I was more than just a brain. But that way of looking at things is mistaken – so they insist. I've always just been a brain – but now I am a brain in a vase and not a brain in a typical human body. 'Typical' did they say? I'll have them know that mine was highly desired and desirable, more so than any Grecian vase, however precious.

I guess we all knew that things like this could happen. Years ago, when my arm was chopped off, I continued to have experiences as if I had an arm, despite being armless. I experienced what is called a 'phantom limb'. Technology was developing fast, and I soon had an impulse machine plugged into my nervous system. By tinkering with the machine's settings, I could give myself experiences as if the missing arm, the phantom limb, were in the right place, even as if it were holding a book. With my body's deterioration – more bits falling off – neurologists thought it best to concentrate on preserving my brain. That is how I, brain, ended up in a vase – antique, let me remind you. I undergo experiences – they seem real enough – which the neurologists judge to cohere with my former life. The experiences result from their stimulating my brain's cells.

So, here I am. Well, I am not sure what that means these days. I am here in the vase, but my experiences are, as I said, mainly as if I am carrying on normally. And I do have a say in what happens. They can tell from the neural activities how my vocal chords would then be moving, if I had any, to express what I am thinking and wanting.

News has, though, just come in of an incident. My brain was accidentally sliced in the night, right down the middle. Apparently, that's no problem. They had contingency plans. The neurological changes transmitted from one hemisphere to another continue – this time by some wireless transmitters attached to each hemisphere. They have sorted out the right speed of transmission. Mind you, I am feeling queasy. What if such accidents happen again – and again…?

Can a brain have experiences?

Many believe that we essentially are our brains. Hearts, livers and lungs can be transplanted; arms and legs can be chopped off. What is responsible for my continuing to have my experiences is my brain. Science fiction and horror stories of the 'brain in vat' ilk abound. As philosophers, we are concerned with whether the idea even makes sense.

Some cells in the brain die, but the millions that remain end up, through nutrition, having their molecules, atoms and electrons changed over time. The particular brain stuff is not important to our identity; what seems key is the configuration of electrical activity, properties and chemical levels. Let us sum this up: experiences depend upon various neurological changes occurring in certain sequences. If that is true, then why should it matter whether the brain is kept as one unit, or sliced – as happened to poor Biv, 'Brain in Vase', as we may call her? All that matters seems simply to be the right configuration of billions of neurological changes of the right type. How the individual changes are brought about is irrelevant – so long as they are brought about. After all, particular changes do not have impressed upon them how they have been caused.

The above line of thought brings trouble. To see how, let us reduce the billions of neurological changes a little – well, radically – down to three changes, A, B and C, that are of the right configuration, intensity, and so on, for Biv to have a certain experience. We can rebuild the complexity by multiplying what is said about A, B and C billions of times.

A particular experience results from A being followed by B being followed by C. If we think of A, B, C being of certain types, then perhaps that type of experience for Biv results from an A-type change being followed by a B-type and then a C-type. That event A causes B and B then causes C does not seem essential to the story, but just that A, B and C occur in the right sequence. Of course, usually such events occur inside a single human body. For Biv, though, such events now occur in a vase; but, in theory, it seems, A could have been in America, B in Britain and C in China. So long as the neurological features are of the right type, manifested at the right time, then the relevant experience should occur for Biv. Any A-type change cannot tell, so to speak, how close a B-type is – and so on. Thinking more, is the time sequence even important? After all, A, B and C do not register the existence of each other as being before or after.

We could take further puzzling steps. Given the billions of neurological changes happening in each human being and the billions of human beings, do we need even to contrive the special existence of A, B and C? Will not changes of those types be occurring in the skulls of populations in any case, maybe A in American Angela's brain, B in British Bernie's and C in Chinese Chou's? If that is so, then our Biv is undergoing experiences without the need to retain even her brain, however much broken and dispersed. Indeed, a whole mishmash of experiences must be occurring for a vast number of unknown people with neither bodies nor brains. What an incredible and crazy thought.

Modesty and humility – well, the conclusion's bizarre features – suggest that the reasoning is radically faulty. One obvious thought is that, for experiences, we need the body after all; but that alone does not save us from weird results. We could imagine a brainless human body linked in the right way, by wireless, to neurological changes such as our

A, B and C thousands of miles away. That body would then be moved by the wireless transmissions, as if a brain undergoing those changes were present within it. Does a person with experiences result?

See the depths and intrigues of philosophical reasoning – and the dangers when philosophers fear not the darkness lurking within those depths.

♈

The error would seem to be the casual separation of a human being, a person, into parts. Yes, we can amputate limbs, and engage in organ transplants, while retaining the same person. Having said that, we need to make clear that it does not follow that a brain in a vase would have experiences, even if the brain were undergoing the same internal changes that, when properly humanly embodied, would have ensured experiences for a person.

We confront bizarre puzzles, even without 'brain in vase' tales. Consider some of your current experiences, of the sight of chairs, the taste of coffee, the sounds of rustling papers. Experiences of the same type and configuration, it seems, could well be occurring elsewhere. If they are distinct experiences of the same type, what makes them someone else's rather than yours? What makes *your* experiences yours?

Perhaps when two people have the same thought, there really is just one thought, one thought shared by two people. That approach, even if right for thoughts, would seem simply wrong, if applied to pains. My pain, however similar to yours, is still the one that I experience and you do not. But could human biology have been differently constituted? Might human biology have been such that you, for example, could experience headaches located in the Queen's head – and the Queen also experience those very aches? Consider Siamese twins, joined at the hip. They could both experience the 'same' pain at the join, that is, the same type of pain; but, however similar, must there be, in fact, two distinct pains?

The answer is probably 'yes'. A pain is not logically separable from the individual experiencing the pain. It seems impossible, logically impossible, that my experiencing the pain in the Queen's head could be numerically identical with the Queen's experiencing.

Mind and body – psychological and physical states – are intermingled; and, when we seek to untangle, we hit perplexities. Letters of the alphabet scattered around the universe do not make words and sentences. Neurological changes, similarly scattered, do not make a person's experiences. With some matters of mind, what matters, it seems, is as property owners say: location, location, location.

60
MAN WITH PULLEY:
WAVING OR DROWNING?

We may wonder whether the girl at sea is waving or drowning, though even if drowning, she may be waving for help; and when you look up at the scaffolding, a man about to land on your head, you may reasonably wonder whether he was pushed, blown by the wind – or jumped, having taken a dislike to your panama hat, shortly to be flattened by the fall.

The puzzle is: what do we do when we do something? What is going on when we jump rather than fall, when we deliberately wave at friends rather than have arms automatically flapping when drowning? The puzzle is important for when we do things, we are usually held responsible – in contrast to when things just happen to us, when, for example, we sneeze, blush or are pushed.

To attain more focus, there is the tale of the irritated soldier who, when asked by the doctor to clench his teeth, could not resist the retort, 'No, you clench them,' at which he removed his false teeth and popped them onto the desk.

There are different ways whereby bodily parts get moved. Even when the teeth are original and true, a clenching may occur because you do it directly, or because you yank your jaws together with your hands, or because it is an involuntary twitch. Let us zoom in closer to the puzzle.

A man is in bed. When asked to lift his leg, he pulls at a string with his hands, a string which runs through a system of pulleys and is tied to his leg. Hence, he lifts his leg – and no one else is involved. That is one way of his lifting his leg, but he is not lifting it directly. When he raises his leg directly – with no strings attached, no people pulling it, no gale blowing it – what does he do? The leg goes up, but that movement

alone does not amount to his directly lifting his leg. If we, so to speak, subtract the fact that his leg goes up, what remains? What makes it his direct lifting?

What do you do when you raise your leg?

There is a tendency, because of the specific example, to compare the successful case of someone who directly raises his leg with the unsuccessful case of someone who cannot, because of injury or being tied down. In unsuccessful cases we may picture the man trying to raise the leg, some effort involved. If we see the effort as muscles tensing, then we may next imagine a man paralysed, so that not even the muscles tense; yet still he tries to move his leg. Trying becomes viewed as a conscious willing, a mental happening. If such mental activity occurs in the odd and unsuccessful cases, when the leg fails to move, we may answer our puzzle, regarding successful cases, by saying: when someone directly raises his leg, a mental activity – a *willing* occurs – which causes the leg's upward movement.

The term 'action' is often used for what we do, 'movement' for the physical change that occurs. The leg moving up, on its own, is a movement; it is an action if brought about not via strings, but directly by the person concerned. Human actions, then, have often been seen as consisting of a mental component – a willing – and the resultant physical movement. That picture, highly influential, is found in the works of that Monsieur Descartes whom we encountered earlier, in Chapter 47, with the 'dreaming' mystery.

What puzzles me about the 'willing' approach is why so many people readily accept it. Think of the thousands of things you do every day. Have they all involved mental events – little willings? You shouted at your partner, slammed the door – not a good start to the day – went to work, to college, to a film. You curled your hair round your fingers. You walked across the room, opened this book, sliced the bread, poured the coffee. True, you sometimes wonder about what to do and how to do it; but is it true that, in all your actions, willings must have been involved that caused the movements? That certainly is not obviously true to your experience.

'Ah, there must have been unconscious willings.' But why be so convinced? Further, if willings must occur for bodily movements to be actions, what are we to say about those willings? They are usually thought of as being actions themselves, actions of the mind; but if that is so, then it looks as if those willings must be preceded by earlier willings – but then those earlier willings would need to be preceded by earlier ones still. For example, it looks as if your lifting your leg requires you not only to will your leg to move, but also that you will that you will your leg to move – and will that you will that you will... and so on. Something has surely gone wrong with the assumptions or reasoning.

Suppose the 'willing', as a mental happening, is part of what an action is. What is the content of the willing? What do you will? Do you will that your leg moves? Well, how do you do that? I bet you have no idea how to will a movement of an object – we draw a veil over Uri Geller.

Try this. Stare at an item nearby – a cup, a glass, a pen – however light you want. Concentrate on it. With all your will, try to make it rise, without touching it. I suspect it has not moved. Now, with whatever form of willing you engaged just then, focus it on your leg – concentrate hard – and see if you can will your leg to move. I am confident that such concentration will fail. If a willing occurs when you move your leg, it is not that you will that your leg moves – for that would be ineffectual, as just seen. Also, you do not will that certain neurological changes occur; you do not know how to do that directly. We know how to cause neurological changes indirectly: we move a leg, sure that some neurological changes must have happened – but we did not will them directly to happen. We do not 'do' the neurological changes.

♈

Although we often think and plan what to do, although we often want to do things, although sometimes we try hard to do things, there seems no good reason to believe that typically our actions consist of mental events, of willings, that cause the physical movements. We have been working with a distorting picture, in thinking that we must find some added mental events to the leg's movement. Perhaps an action usually does not require a psychological element that precedes and causes the movement, even though when we fail to do something, some mental trying or willing may have occurred.

What do you do when you raise your leg? Answer: you do nothing except raise your leg. What is involved in that? Answer: your leg goes up. How does that differ from the case with the string and pulleys? Answer: the string and the pulleys – and maybe the pressure of string on the flesh. How does your raising your leg differ from when it goes up in spasm? Answer: in various ways, depending on circumstances; you may be surprised and embarrassed at what has happened. You may apologize to the nurse who was struck by the misbehaving leg, saying, 'Sorry, I don't know why that happened.'

If someone asks you why you raised your leg, you rightly say, in a spasm case, that it wasn't you who raised it; it moved of its own accord. When you have directly raised your leg, then you take direct

278 • THE BIG THINK BOOK

responsibility – and may give reasons for why you did it. 'I was seeing how far I could stretch. I was trying to touch the ceiling.'

Now, as you read these words, raise a leg, wave a hand, or wiggle your ears. If you're in public, people, of course, may stare, wondering if you need help. Simply say, 'Don't mind me, I'm just seeing what I do, when I do what I do – I am, after all, a philosopher philosophizing.'

They may smile kindly – and move away.

61
A BALE OF WOE

While wandering across centuries past, o'er hill and vale, came I upon an ass, so thin, so scraggy, that I felt concern, so overwhelming, for its health. 'Oh, Ass,' said I, 'you are so thin, so forlorn, so pale; why eat you not? Are you blind? There is, just here, right here, towards your left, a bale of hay – the straws are golden – and, with steps a few, that whole bale yours will easily be.' As I spoke, I noticed how his eyes swivelled repeatedly from left to right, from right to left.

'Kind sir,' replied Ass, 'would that things were as simple as that. Indeed, I can see that golden bale of succulent hay to my left so well but, can you not see? There is another bale, equally golden and with a degree of succulence the very same, exactly the same, to my right.'

'That is true,' replied I, 'but that is all the better – is it not? – for poor starving and skinny you. You have two bales upon which to dine instead of one. Are they not equally tempting, my dear, dear Ass?'

'Precisely the problem, dear Sir,' moaned Ass, eyes ever swivelling between bundle left and bundle right. 'They are indeed equal in all their features, save one to my left does sit and, the other, my right. They are equal in succulence, in weight, in size, in goldenness, in all respects indeed. They're the same distance away from me too.'

'Yes?' questioned I, looking baffled and lost, not least because baffled and lost was I.

'You see,' sighed Ass, 'I need a reason for choosing to eat one rather than t'other – but I have no reason. The bundles are equally attractive, so equally so.'

'Eat both!' I snapped, teenily tired of Ass's bleak groans.

'Don't be angry with me, Sir. I am an ass of reason. I need a reason for choosing which to eat first.' And as he brayed, he visibly weakened yet further, still further, with hunger, so weak was he, so weak.

'Well, act without reason,' declared I.

'Sir, rational beings need reasons for actions. What else could motivate them?' came his woeful reply.

'Hunger,' I muttered but, by then, I knew reasoning with Ass was foolish. He was a fine and upstanding ass, despite falling to the ground, moaning most pitifully, yet courteously. Action was required. I would bring just one of the bundles right up to him, so he would have a reason to eat of that first, for it would require no walk, unlike the other bundle that would remain in place some distance from him.

My eyes swivelled from left to right and right to left and suddenly I realized that I could not decide which bundle to fetch.

Do we always need a reason for choosing one course of action rather than another?

Jean Buridan, a French medieval logician, is linked to this puzzle; hence it is traditionally known as 'Buridan's Ass'. Centuries after Buridan, Leibniz put forward his principle of sufficient reason, his 'apex of rationality'. There must be a sufficient reason for everything that happens, including what we do. Incidentally, Leibniz uses the principle to argue for the existence of a being that necessarily exists, namely God. God's necessary existence is the only reason that is sufficient – enough – to explain the existence of the universe. What is the sufficient reason for God's existence? Well, he necessarily exists and so he is his own sufficient reason – explorations of which occur in Part VII.

Buridan's Ass has more ramifications than are usually recognized. Suppose I had managed to give Ass just one bundle: he would still need to choose which straw to bite into first. True, one straw may be a little closer or thicker than the other but would that be sufficient reason to choose one over the other? It is not just a matter of finding a difference between the alternatives – the original bundles had different locations;

one to the left, the other to the right – but of finding a difference that is relevant to what we want. Is it true that, to be rational, we need a sufficient and relevant reason for everything that we do?

The answer is that we can, and often should, act without reason. To be rational, we should on some occasions act irrationally, or, better, non-rationally, that is, without a reason for every feature of the actions performed. Ass has a splendid and sufficient reason to eat – to avoid starvation – and that is sufficient reason to eat either the left bale or the right. His mistake is to think that he also needs sufficient reason for choosing either the left bale over the right or the right over the left.

♈

This answer may yet be inadequate, if we think of reasons as motivating forces – the oomphs! – that get us moving. Without a reason for choosing the left rather than the right (or vice versa) we lack the oomph to get our legs stepping off one way rather than the other. This is, though, to mistake reasons for causes. We may certainly wonder about which events cause our bodily movements and how they are related to the reasons that we give – as we did with Mary, Mary (Chapter 54). We may be inclined to believe that everything that we do has causes and those causes have causes. It is possible that two bales are sufficiently similar that they have the same causal effects on us, causing neurological changes such that we equally incline towards the left as towards the right, leading to a paralysis such as Ass's. As Spinoza quipped, we should be asinine to be in that position: being human, we can still choose, even when choices are equally balanced in significance. Or can we?

Try this. When you next are unable to choose between alternatives, yet you have to do something, what happens and how does it happen?

62

A PILL FOR EVERYTHING?

Consider this little dialogue.

'Madam, may I help you?'

'I doubt it. I so want that red dress, but it's way, way too expensive, way beyond my means.'

'Madam, how about the blue? It's equally attractive, yet so much cheaper – I mean, more competitively priced.'

'Mmm, I could afford the blue; but I never feel comfortable in blue – even though people always tell me how it suits me. I'm always happier with red.'

'No problem at all, madam – with the blue comes an optional pill, take the pill and you'll find you like the blue.'

'Not sure. I don't like popping pills – artificial stuff, not me.'

'Not really, madam – if I may be so bold to disagree. You would like the blue dress, if only you could overcome your discomfort with the colour. The pill is merely helping you to get what you truly want.'

'That's true, I suppose. Some people don't want to be smokers, yet cannot give up smoking, without some external assistance.'

'Exactly, madam.'

'That's all very well, but I still don't like the idea of using external help such as pills.'

'No problem at all. We can give you a pill to overcome that.'

'But that's missing the point. I'm not the sort of person who wants her system meddled with in these ways.'

'May I ask: are you satisfied being that sort of person? Wouldn't you prefer to be the sort of person who doesn't mind about these things?'

'Yes, perhaps.'

'If so, then take this other pill – it will help you to be that sort of person you would prefer to be – and look, it has a nice red colour.'

'But I can't decide what sort of person I'd rather be.'

'No problem, madam. We have a pill which will make you decide firmly one way or the other.'

'But which way is that?'

'Well, that depends which pill you take – the red or the blue, madam?'

When do I get what I truly want?

We could have added 'or the yellow, or the green, or the white' – and so on – for there are many, many ways our lives would be changed, for better or worse, by outside interferences. Yet do we have any clear idea of what counts as outside and inside? Of what counts as being truly what *I* want rather than what is imposed upon me? This is the puzzle at the heart of the Pill Puzzle. We tend to think of impositions as external physical obstacles or threats, yet sometimes we feel buffeted by our own desires, yearnings and longings; we would prefer to be without them – be they sexual lusts, gluttony or obsessive fears.

Consider smokers: they want cigarettes. Their desires may result from years of advertising combined with genetic dispositions or rebellious youth. They are smokers; yet some do not want to be smokers. They want not to have their smoking wants. There is a second-order want: a want about their first-order wants. Maybe we – friends, society, the government – should help them to become non-smokers. We could ostracize them, bar them from lighting up, but that does not directly quell their smoking desires. Maybe we could inject them with drugs that destroy the smoke-filled yearnings. What can be wrong with that, given that they do want to stop smoking?

Their freedom to smoke – the opportunity, the 'negative freedom' as it is known – is interfering with their second-order desire becoming satisfied, the desire to be non-smokers, their 'positive freedom'. We may restrict their negative freedom – place obstacles in the way of their smoking – in order to promote their positive freedom, to be non-smokers. This is when we may quip: we are forcing them to be free – but it is not really a forcing. After all, they do explicitly own their second-order desire to be non-smokers.

That may be all well and good; but now consider smokers who seemingly lack the second-order desire to give up smoking. We may insist that really they do possess that second-order desire: at least, *were* they fully informed of health hazards, rationally grasping their best interests, they would be wanting to be non-smokers. This, however, is where 'forcing someone to be free' seems but rhetoric to justify forcing people to do what they do not want to do, even though, maybe, they ought to want to become non-smokers.

At times we do force people to behave in a certain way, in their best interests. Parents and other authorities do this with children, the mentally disturbed and some drug addicts. But we need to be careful when we take this step: it is better to call a spade 'a spade'. These people are often being compelled to do what they really do not want to do; however, once changed as a result, they may be thankful.

♈

We have spoken of first-order and second-order desires. We could dream up more orders. Some end up regarding a person as consisting of battling selves. A third self, so to speak, may enter the picture, adjudicating between, say, the conflicting desires of the self who wants to smoke and the self who wants to give up. We may then picture a fourth, trying to referee between the first three – and so on. That is an unhappy way to view things. Perhaps we need simply to see ourselves as often possessing conflicting desires which we reflect on, trying to decide which it is best to satisfy – though how that reflection and decision can be understood, without there being another desire thrown into the pot, remains mysterious.

Talk of second-order desires may slip us into treating them as 'higher' in the sense of 'better'; but that need not be so – and, even if the second-order are somehow more worthy, the individual may still not identify with them. A woman loves dancing and jazz, yet her extreme Protestant church tells her that such things are sinful. As a result, she develops the second-order desire not to be someone who loves dancing and jazz. Yet it is far from obvious that satisfying that second-order desire is in her best interests. She may be true to herself, if she resisted that second-order sermon-based desire. Of course, that expression 'true to herself' raises the question of which of our desires are truly ours.

There is a tendency to believe that science can solve everything. If you are unhappy about complexion and bust size, have cosmetic surgery; if addicted to gambling, pop into the addiction clinic. Surgery, pills, therapy – numerous treatments are available to give us what we want, assuming the ability to pay. Dangers arise when treatments are applied to give us what we *truly, deeply* want, whether or not we know of that want. Think historically of the many authorities that have forced people to change their behaviour 'in their best interests'. Think of authoritarian religions and political regimes that compel people to 'realize' that they do not truly want to be homosexual or atheist or promiscuous or capitalist or socialist or Protestant or Muslim… The list could go on. Protestors who would otherwise be cast into gaol – a bad enough outcome – find themselves in psychiatric units, minds, not just bodies, undergoing change and restraint.

Neither medicine nor religion nor governments – nor the moon and the stars – can ultimately tell us what we truly want. For that matter, we cannot tell what we truly want, *if*, in order to do so, we must find a 'self' – what I truly am – that has not resulted from outside causes. This is not because the search is so difficult, the self so elusive. It is because there is not a something, a self existing, unburdened by a past, uncaused by an outside.

We are layers of criss-crossing imprints and reflections; imprints from parents, schoolings and chance encounters; reflections when planning, yearning and remembering. We can be whirlpools of conflicting emotions and passions, of decisions and agitations, of admirations and jealousies. When the chaos is widespread and embracing, we are not in control; that is when we agonize about what we 'truly' want. Yet, once we begin to see structure, once we identify with projects and stances, we gain a sense of what we truly want, of what sort of character we truly are. To search after something more in 'truly' wanting, in 'truly' being, is to search after a chimera, an illusion, an impossibility. And, being an impossibility, it is not only impossible to have, but also not worth the having. Far better to focus on bringing order to any chaos in our lives — or, even, better still, let us simply embrace the chaos.

When encountering irrational preferences (in Chapter 23), we reflected upon how an individual typically has a *mélange* of desires, yearnings, beliefs, assumptions, commitments, projects, hopes and fears, at varying levels of conscious awareness. It is no wonder that if they were all lined up, numerous inconsistencies, irrationalities and irrelevancies would be revealed. Yet think how austere and monotonous lives would be, lacking vitality, zigzags, creases and swerves, were we to have that *mélange*, that mishmash, ironed out, all its elements pointing in one direction.

'The fox knows many things, but the hedgehog knows one big thing.' That line from Archilochus, an ancient Greek poet, came to fame through Isaiah Berlin, the twentieth-century Oxford intellectual, a Russian Jew, born in Riga. He, rather playfully, proposed it as a way of dividing thinkers: some have one overriding central vision; others embrace the variety, the scatterings, the diversity. Well, at the level of everyday living, the distinction also has application. As hedgehog, we may seek to mould the *mélange*, discarding some elements, revising others, to secure one coherent pattern of living; as fox, we may welcome and celebrate the diversity.

The fox/hedgehog proposal itself manifests something of the hedgehog stance. In fact, most of us in our lives are probably to some degree fox, to some degree hedgehog. And so, for representation of human lives as actually lived, the prize goes to the fox.

63
THE FROG, SCORPION AND GOD –
or 'THOU SHALT NOT'

FROG: I have a feeling of déjà vu, swimming across the river, with you on my back, Ms Scorpion. I guess I shall come to a sticky end – well, a wet and drowning end.

SCORPION: I fear you're right, Mr Frog; but 'tis kindly of you to be carrying me to the other side.

FROG: Remind me, though: why do you sting me *before* we're safely across the river? It's most odd as it leads us both to a watery demise.

SCORPION: It's in my nature. It's something that I cannot help.

FROG: Never been sure of this tale, often misattributed to Aesop, for it is surely not in my nature to give lifts to scorpions. Still, there it is. If only, Ms Scorpion, you could control your nature…

SCORPION: At least until I safely reach the other side – instead of dooming me as well as you. No doubt there's an evolutionary explanation for these things.

FROG: No doubt – and I note your revisionary thought that evolution should have delivered you a better sense of self-interest, with your reaching the other side before stinging me. But, self-interest to one side, have you not heard of morality, of kindness, of fairness? Of how morally you should treat me well, instead of using and abusing me?

SCORPION: You've been listening to those human beings, haven't you, Mr Frog? Yes, they burble on about such matters – though without much concern for scorpions and frogs – but from whence does that morality derive?

FROG: Good question. After all, we non-human creatures lack any sense of morality. Ah, but we are mere evolutionary products of natural selection.

SCORPION: And humans are not? They're as much part of the natural
world as are we. And you're right, Mr Frog: there's no morality in
nature. Witness my forthcoming sting.

FROG [shuddering]: Perhaps those human beings are right – those who
insist that they're made in God's image. Perhaps the moral sense is
a spark of the divine. It cannot be a spark of nature, for nature tells
us how things are, not how they ought to be.

SCORPION: Forget about divine sparks. Human's moral sense is
just another product of evolutionary advantage. If you listen to
evolutionists' babble, they increasingly explain how creatures of
certain types, possessive of moral concerns, are more likely to
flourish than others. Well, their genes are the ones more likely
to proliferate.

FROG: You mean that, in the end, acting morally is just natural instinct,
accounted for by certain genetic survival advantages?

SCORPION: Yes, a species – and hence its genes – is obviously more
likely to flourish, if the members tend their young, help others and
show special concern for close relatives. Even we small creatures do

that to varying degrees. And think of ants and bees and meerkats: self-sacrifice appears to happen, but there's no morality there. They aren't judging that helping others is what they *ought* to do. It's just what they do.

FROG: I see. There are no moral *oughts* in nature, even human nature.

SCORPION: At bottom, human kindness, self-sacrifice and appeals to justice, are no more divine, no more supernatural, than my natural instinct to – well, I'm sorry about this – but to sting… *[splash, glug, glug]*

From whence comes morality?

Morality puzzles many people, even those who feel that the existence of the universe has no need for God or gods. The existence of moral truths – of what we morally ought and ought not to do – leads many, though, to turn to a divine source such as the Bible's Ten Commandments: thou shalt not kill, thou shalt not commit adultery and so forth. In fact, there are many, many more divine commandments – apparently 613 in the Torah (the first five books of the Old Testament) – but most tend to be overlooked these days.

Morality, it is judged, is a matter of God, the divine law-giver, telling us what we ought to do. Human beings – in contrast to frogs and scorpions – possess the privileged capacity to understand the divine law. So, the assumption up for challenge is:

If there are objective moral truths, then there must be God who commands them.

With that assumption, the argument goes one of two ways. Either you believe that there are objective moral truths, hence you conclude that God must exist – or you reject God's existence and so you reject the existence of objective moral truths.

Must the assumption be accepted? The answer is 'no'. There may be a third way – a third way between morality as divine and morality as delusion. First, let us look at the divine answer and then turn to whether there is a third way, distinct from the delusion.

Consider the proposal that goodness (including rightness) is what is commanded by God: to say that protecting innocent human life is good is to say that God commands it. The idea is that goodness is determined by some supreme authority which we should obey. The natural question that follows is: how does God determine what is good and hence what to command? Here, we have two possible answers.

One answer is that goodness exists independently of God – and so God, being of a certain character, chooses to command the good. On this understanding, God commands the good because it is good; the good is not good because God commands it. If we follow this path, objective moral truths do not ultimately depend on God. It is therefore possible that we human beings can uncover those truths without any need for God. Certainly, they exist independently of God.

The other answer is that what counts as being good is fixed by God. Whatever God ordains as good is, by definition, good. Were he to command killing the firstborn – allegedly did he not once command such in Egypt? – such killing would be morally good. Were he to command men to treat women as slaves, then to do such would be good. The objection to that line of argument is that it gives an outrageous understanding of what morality could be. The reply by godly believers is, of course, that God could never ordain such things – because he is all good. That reply, though, swings us back to goodness being identifiable as something distinct from God, otherwise whatever God is like would count as good.

Sometimes it is proposed that God is identical with Goodness. This, though, ends up explaining the source of goodness as being Goodness, which is no good explanation at all. If the response is, 'But God also cares about human beings,' then the puzzle becomes how Goodness could have such personalized characteristics.

Tying morality to God, it should be noted, does not help us to know what is good, what is bad. Ancient texts deemed 'holy scriptures' lead to conflicting answers: witness the disputes between religions and within a single religion. 'It is written thus' is no reliable means for discerning morality, for discerning what we ought and ought not to do. We need, first, to judge which ancient texts are worthy of following; that requires evaluating the moral acceptability of their contents.

If the divine theory is rejected — we have given only a flavour of the debate — are we left with objective morality as delusion, as outlined by Ms Scorpion?

$$\gamma$$

The proposed third way is that moral truths need be neither divinely grounded nor delusory. Truths exist about climate changes and the Earth's orbit of the Sun. Such truths are objective and independent of what humans think. Now, it would be most peculiar if, in nature, there existed empirical facts such as 'Killing is morally wrong' or 'You ought not to break promises'; so, how can morality be objective?

We should, though, stretch our eyes and minds. Think of mathematical truths, usually treated as independent of human beings, yet not necessarily pointing to God. They are objective necessary truths; yet when wandering through forests, we meet trees, beer cans and rabbits, but not numbers, right-angled triangles and abstract syllogisms. Maybe, as with mathematical truths, moral truths can yet be objective, without divine resort. True, moral truths, unlike mathematical truths, tell us what we ought to do, but that just is their character. True, we are sometimes blind to morality, but there is much of the natural and mathematical worlds to which we are blind.

The many disputes in morality may indicate lack of objectivity, but the disputes usually concern applications of morality; and disputes also arise about the application of mathematics to the world. Many, many people, from many different societies, see that, other things being equal, innocent people ought not to be killed, promises should be kept, and people should be treated fairly. Dilemmas arise when circumstances bring such principles into conflict and when facts are in dispute — for example, whether a human foetus is a person, whether fox-hunting is cruel, and whether you should break a promise if it would ease someone's pain.

In contrast to scorpions and frogs, we are intelligent creatures who can reflect, reason and plan for the morrow: such attributes provided us with evolutionary advantages. Evolution's natural selection, as Darwin emphasized, just is, though, about betterment at survival, not betterment in a moral sense. Yet, possessed of intelligence, we can also spot abstract mathematical truths and discern moral truths; we may appreciate beauty and have feelings for harmony (discussed in 'The Life Model', Chapter 84). Now, the ability to uncover such truths, to appreciate beauty and so forth, may or may not aid survival. Evolutionary explanations can account for what is advantageous for survival – but the advantageous may also carry features unrelated to survival.

One day, there could be evolutionary explanations of certain human characteristics (perhaps aided by commercial competitive ploys, also with evolutionary explanations) that give rise to further features in certain types of individuals, especially the young – namely, the seeming inability to exist without the loud 'beat, beat, beat' of mindless music and mobile ring tones, impervious to the effects on others; but those explanations would say nothing about the value (or, more relevantly, disvalue) of those features.

There is no doubt an evolutionary explanation concerning the survival value of our having the ears that we have. An added feature of ears is their ability to support the arms of spectacles; but the evolutionary explanation for the existence of ears says nothing about spectacle-supporting functions, be it advantageous or not. And evolutionary explanations of how and when we do or do not cooperate say nothing about what morally we ought, or ought not, to do. The plight of Mr Frog and Ms Scorpion reminds us of that.

PART VII: RELIGION

Looking beyond this world to...?

If cows and horses had hands and could draw, then horses
would draw the form of gods like horses, cows like cows...
Xenophanes

The existence of the universe appears – initially so – as an immense mystery. That mystery leads many to demystify – to demystify via belief in God. Perplexities and new mysteries then come to the fore: whatever is the nature of divine existence? An all-powerful being generates apparent contradictions: can such a being create a shield so strong that it resists all possible forces, including those of that deity? Can an 'all-knowing' divinity know everything? Does such a being know what it is like to be forgetful, regretful and riding a bicycle? Can such a being experience lusts, lists and laughter? Is divinity capable of empathizing with those who suffer?

Those perplexities to one side, some believers, as we shall see, produce arguments for God's existence; others rely on revelation or faith. Yet others judge it prudent to believe in God, 'just in case', discussed in Chapter 69 via Pascal's Wager. That prudent encouragement to believe has its own problems, not least those of how to catch hold of the right belief and hold fast to it, when aware of the suffering in the world.

That there is so much worldly suffering, so much evil in the world, strikes many people as extremely disturbing and puzzling – certainly so, if a deity exists, a deity that is morally good, loving and caring for humanity. If the universe has been divinely created, how do we know that the creator is not a malicious demon, irritated by believers who think he is all good – or perhaps delighting in their mistaken belief and worship?

Commitment to God, whether or not he exists, generates perplexities over the moral motivation of believers and how they handle the apparent cultural relativity of their religious beliefs. Their beliefs often hang on whether they are, for example, born into Judaism, Christianity or Islam; so, ought not awareness of that undermine their belief or, minimally, suggest some revision?

In reply, religious believers of different traditions sometimes insist that they are all worshipping one and the same god. That raises the question: where is the evidence? Believers committed to one understanding of God and his commands often condemn – with support, as they take it, from 'their God' – those believers who think otherwise. That is a worrying state of affairs that mystifies many.

The nature of prayer and God's grace also mystify, touched on here through tales of perfect punishment and the 'One Two Box' television show. First, though, we encounter a couple of famous, much discussed arguments in philosophy for God's existence; both at times have received official blessing from the different religions of the one God. Thus, we turn to God as 'the greatest being that there is' and then to the existence of miracles as evidence for that one God. Here comes 'the greatest'.

64

'I AM THE GREATEST' *or*
'THERE AIN'T NO SANITY CLAUS'

G: I am the greatest.

I: The greatest what?

G: The greatest being.

I: Ah, you mean *God*.

G: That's right – or *Allah* or *Yahweh*. Names don't hurt me, whatever people say. I am, after all, the greatest – the greatest being than which nothing greater can be conceived, dreamt of, imagined.

I: So I hear, but you don't exist.

G: You're talking to me.

I: I talk to myself.

G: That's true – and even true now. Being the greatest being I have no need for chat. This is a dialogue with yourself; yet, if you reason correctly, you'll realize that I must exist – and not just in your mind, imagination or dreams.

I: How come?

G: Look, you agree that my existence is not straightaway ruled out. You can make sense of my existing.

I: I'm not sure, once I start thinking about it. But let's suppose that I can – that there can be a being that is all powerful, all knowing, even all perfect, that created the universe. Having said that, still there's simply no evidence for you, O greatest conceivable one.

G: That's true. Despite what many believe, I left no signs in the world. Don't focus on the universe. Don't even focus on your self. Focus on the very thought of me.

I: Okay, I have the idea of the greatest conceivable being – I think.

G: Indeed, that being than which nothing greater can be conceived – excellent. Now, suppose that I do not exist.

I: I don't need to suppose. You don't.

G: Let's pretend that is true. Then, were I to exist, it seems that I should be greater than the greatest conceivable being, according to your idea of the greatest conceivable being.

I: Ah, a contradiction.

G: Well, only a contradiction if your idea is really of a being that both lacks existence and is the greatest conceivable being – for such a non-existent being could not be the greatest conceivable being. How could such a being be the greatest, with such a glaringly obvious defect as non-existence? Perhaps you now grasp that I exist.

Must God, Allah, Yahweh, the greatest conceivable being, exist?

Our little dialogue is a version of the ontological argument put forward by the eleventh-century St Anselm of Canterbury. Ontological arguments, in one form or another, have received considerable support, yet also considerable rejection – and recently, mainly rejection. Major philosophers have lined up – some for; some against. Descartes for; Hume against. Leibniz for; Kant against.

One challenge is: how can any reflections, based solely on the meanings of words, on which ideas we possess, lead to conclusions about reality? We have ideas of unicorns, mermaids and Santa Claus, yet we need to search the world to establish whether such items exist.

Should we be impressed by that challenge? After all, from analysing our ideas, we conclude that certain things can *not* exist in reality. Once we grasp the nature of squares and circles, we conclude that there are no square circles. Furthermore, once we understand the number series, we can conclude that a prime number *must* exist between seventeen and twenty-three. Of course, these examples are distinctive: they concern abstract entities, entities that we, in any case, cannot experience through the senses or gain evidence for via scientific investigations. We may, though, also show, by reasoning alone, that certain hypothesized everyday empirical entities cannot exist – for example, a creature that at the same time is both capable and incapable of flight.

Some suggest that ontological arguments muddle the *idea* of X with X. Our idea of an elephant is of a creature with a trunk, but the idea does not itself sport a trunk. The arguments' seeming force, the suggestion runs, rests upon a threatened contradiction, resulting from such a muddle. We see this, when we present a key stage in some of the arguments.

> If we suppose that the greatest conceivable being fails to exist, then, were he to exist, he would be greater than the greatest conceivable being – but that is a contradiction.

The mistake here lies in treating our idea of the greatest conceivable being as itself a contender for such greatness. Yes, were the greatest conceivable being to exist, he would be greater than our idea – indeed, greater than *any* ideas – existing in our minds, but it does not follow that he would be greater than what our idea is an idea of – for our idea simply is of the greatest conceivable being. So, there would be no contradiction.

Our godly dialogue, though, does not appear to involve the alleged muddle. God's argument is that if we reflect on what we mean by 'the greatest conceivable being', we should see that it involves existence. To take matters further, here comes Santa Claus.

I: But Santa Claus, you don't exist.

SC: You're right, given your understanding of 'Santa Claus'. But consider, instead, a Santa Claus with maximal generosity, most perfect white beard, best possible 'ho, ho' – and so on.

I: I'm trying.

SC: Call him, 'the greatest conceivable Santa Claus'. Then, were he not to exist, we should be able to conceive of a greater Santa Claus, namely one that exists, and so...

I: Go on, tell me – 'and so therefore the greatest conceivable Santa Claus exists.'

SC: By Santa, you've got it!

I: But then the greatest of numerous, numerous things exist – the greatest cat, chimp and chameleon; the greatest Zilli's ice cream.

SC: The universe – 'tis great indeed.

I: So great that, if such reasoning works, there exists not merely the greatest good God, but also the greatest evil Devil.

♈

What is meant by 'greatest'? Sometimes it is understood as perfection, sometimes as maximal independent reality. Whatever the version, it includes existence and excludes features lacking in greatness. So, the greatest conceivable Santa Claus involves a contradiction because, being Santa Claus, however great, he must still be finite, limited, in many ways – for example, he must fit regular chimneys and deliver presents to human beings. For similar reasons, we need not judge that the greatest being has perfect eyesight, Estonian language skills, and tango-dancing ability. Despite that, in the spirit of ontological arguments, could we not argue that we at least have the idea of a great Santa Claus, great in that he possesses the feature of existing? So, were such a Claus not to exist, then we should have landed ourselves with a contradiction.

Here is one way of trying to expose the error in such arguing. Were you to describe the woman of your dreams to a dating agency, you would be unimpressed if the agency suggested someone who satisfied the descriptions you gave – the predicates listed – yet who was fictional. 'Oh, but you didn't specify that she should exist' would not quell your 'money back' demand. Yet, had you added 'and exists' in your initial requirement, that would not have been another feature, but simply that the agency produce a woman as described by the descriptions, the predicates, first listed.

With the dating agency example in mind, let us return to God. From the idea of the greatest conceivable being, we may infer that such a being has features of being all powerful and so on. But to infer 'and exists' is simply to say that there is a being that has those features. Whether there exists such a being depends on whether any item in the world satisfies the given descriptions or predicates. And how could we find that out, save by investigating the world? This line of thinking is grounded in the slogan, 'Existence is not a predicate.'

Quite what does exist, though, is not without controversy. The characters Romeo and Juliet exist – or so we may insist. In the Shakespeare's play, they are flesh and blood; they live, love and die. Atheists could accept that about R & J; and so, in the R & J sense, atheists could accept that God exists and is, for that matter, a creation of man. But, according to believers, God is, of course, no mere fictional existent and no human creation.

When we investigate the world, fictions now to one side, we encounter items that only happen to exist. This book, that tree, the sun and the moon might not have existed – well, so it seems. And it is difficult to see how putting together a set of descriptions or predicates could establish that there is a thing that merely happens to exist. Yet, as said earlier, we do conclude, by reasoning alone, that round squares cannot exist and the number nineteen must exist. These examples concern *necessary* existence, what *must* be so. Perhaps the idea of the greatest conceivable being points to something that necessarily exists – that has an existence akin to abstract mathematical entities. We may now wonder whether we do really possess a coherent idea of the greatest being involving necessary existence.

The greatest number cannot exist. Mention a number and greater ones can always be mentioned. Perhaps the idea of the greatest conceivable being – the greatest power, the greatest love – is as incoherent as the idea of the greatest number. Further, even if we can make sense of such a being and are led to think that there *must* be one, it would seem to be an abstract entity, akin to the mathematical.

Abstract entities lack causal powers. They cannot create, love and judge; so, the greatest conceivable being, God or Allah or Yahweh, understood in that way would lack divine features as traditionally listed. And, for that matter, even if some silver tongues could persuade us that the greatest Santa Claus and greatest ice cream *necessarily* exist, such a Santa Claus could not deliver presents in our non-abstract, concrete world – and such an ice cream could not be licked by our non-abstract tongues, be they silver or otherwise.

65
THE GREATEST MIRACLE?

Water has been turned into wine – well, so some believe. The dead have been brought back to life here on Earth; someone has walked on water. Miracles, it is said, occur at Lourdes – by 2015, sixty-nine, according to the Catholic Church and one way of counting.

Many, many people have believed in miracles. Many, many people do believe. But what is a miracle? Sometimes people speak of miraculous happenings merely when very surprising and fortunate events occur. A mother who finds her child alive in an earthquake's wreckage, when hundreds are dead, may perceive the life as a miracle. She thanks God, or gods, for her child's lucky outcome, yet, were she to reflect, she should also temper her thanks with blame for the deaths of the others. Such 'miracles' though – as when difficult surgery goes well or weak candidates pass examinations – are normally accepted as in accord with the usual and natural ways of the world.

Let us focus, for the moment, on miracles as divinely caused events. That is one feature; but some believe that everything that happens is divinely caused. So, to avoid everything being miraculous, we need to add the condition that the events differ from what usually or naturally happens. In some way, miracles interfere with the laws of nature. Water is not the sort of stuff that turns to wine; corpses, according to known natural laws, do not suddenly sit up, alive again.

Often people believe miracles occur because they already hold a religious faith which accepts miracles; and then, certain events, which would otherwise be explained naturally, are taken to be miracles, sustaining that faith. This is, to say the least, a little self-serving. The reasoning loops round.

Some people reject miracles, even the possibility of miracles, on the grounds that any events that violate what we take to be the natural laws simply show that we have failed properly to grasp what the natural laws are. The laws are more complicated than we first thought. This rejection too is self-serving, serving those sceptical of miracles, ruling miracles out virtually 'by definition', as some may seek to rule out black swans by defining swans as white.

Is it ever rational to believe in miracles?

The question is puzzling because some people are certain that it can be rational so to believe, whereas others flatly deny it. The philosopher most famously associated with a 'no' to the question is the eighteenth-century philosopher David Hume – we met him with Humpty Dumpty in Chapter 46. In fact, a certain Thomas Woolston, writing a little earlier than Hume, outspokenly attacked biblical accounts of miracles; he pointed to their many absurdities and improbabilities. Woolston ended up in prison, where he died. Hume, despite being labelled 'The Great Infidel', was much luckier – and, it would seem, less inflammatory.

Let us now shelve the 'divine intervention' feature of miracles and focus on whether it is ever rational to believe that some remarkably unusual events, going against the natural laws, have occurred. For ease, hereafter we refer to such events as 'miracles', adding 'divine', when the feature of godly intervention in particular is being addressed.

Hume's position is often seen – probably mistakenly seen – as the following: while miracles are possible, it is *always* irrational to accept as reliable any reports that they have occurred. We seem to have a paradox here. Although it is recognized that a type of event is possible and can be witnessed, it is argued that it is bound to be irrational to believe any events of that type ever happened. That sounds paradoxical. After all, it is not as if we are discussing events that can only occur when human beings did not exist. There are observers of the alleged miracles.

Why may it always be irrational to believe in miracles? Well, we have considerable evidence for our beliefs that laws of nature hold. For example, none of us, despite wishes, has ever seen water turned to wine. True, many things happen to water – freezing, steaming – and theories have been developed explaining such changes. We have, though, no evidence at all to think that water can have the intoxicating transforming possibilities reported as having occurred. Indeed, it may be partly because water has not, in the experience of billions of people, ever turned to wine that we are confident that water naturally lacks such possibility. Now, what could lead us to think that a few times, centuries ago, some water was turned into wine?

Well, a few eyewitnesses reported such a change. Could their testimony, testimony passed down, make it rational for us to believe that water underwent such change? Let us assess the different evidences in play.

On the one hand we have considerable evidence in favour of water not turning to wine – from centuries of everyday uniform experience and experimentation. On the other hand, we have considerable evidence that reports of events can be misleading, either wilfully or by accident. We should, of course, apportion our belief to the evidence. Further, very high standards must be set for reports of exceptionally unusual events. Evidence against water turning to wine: exceptionally strong. Reliability of reports of events, of testimony: sometimes low. Hence, without other factors, it would appear irrational to believe in the so-called miracle – and all other so-called miracles, for similar reasons – at least when based on what people say. It is more likely that the reports are mistaken than that the exceptional events occurred.

Are things essentially different if we personally have experiences of the seeming miracle? Again, it may be more likely that we could offer a better explanation for what we experienced than its being a miracle. The exceptional nature of the experience, if a miracle, needs to be contrasted with the well-known fact that we make mistakes, can be misled, tricked, are tempted by the extraordinary – or are just plain tired.

Υ

The overall conclusion is not that we should be absolutely certain that any 'miracle' reports are false, but simply that it is irrational to believe that the reported miracles happened. Further reflection on Hume's discussion suggests that even that conclusion is too sweeping.

Hume supposes people, of different nations, reported a darkness over the planet during the first eight days of the seventeenth century. It could then be rational to believe that that highly unusual occurrence took place, given the number of reports, different sources and so on. This shows that Hume does not argue that it is *always* irrational to believe reported unusual events have happened – 'miracles'.

Maybe Hume's position is that it is always irrational to take the further step and believe the events were divinely caused, were divine miracles. Even here, we may wonder. Suppose that the reports of the eight days of darkness also spoke of a booming voice from the skies, speaking in all languages, telling of the creation of the world, of eternal life, of its being the voice of the one true God to be worshipped... Well, such an extraordinary event may lead us to think that there is some conscious power present, but it would still be a big leap to conclude that therefore the power must be an eternal all-powerful deity who is all good. After all, there is still all the suffering in the world, which at least suggests that the power in question is not all good. That is a problem for those who believe God to be both all good and all powerful. That belief may in fact be a source of distress for the Devil – please see Chapter 68.

It is wise to be cautious of people's reports of miracles, of apparently highly exceptional events. Such caution, though, does not guarantee avoidance of error. In the eighteenth century, the King of Siam had not seen ice. He refused to believe the Dutch ambassador's reports that, during Holland's winters, water became so hard it could support the weight of elephants. Depending on what other evidence was available to him, the King, even though mistaken, may well have been rational in believing the reports false.

As well as an event's likelihood, we need to take into account reporters' motives, their position to judge, and whether similar events would be expected to occur that could be checked. In principle, more and more evidence could be given to the King, showing that, in certain circumstances, water regularly turns to ice.

Hume nicely quipped that religious believers must be conscious of a continual miracle in their person in holding their religious belief. Perhaps that is the greatest miracle. But, of course, religious faith and belief in miracles are very common – so, really, their existence is no miracle at all. Despite the belief's irrationality, it is far from a miracle that people believe in miracles. Indeed, it may be the very irrationality that explains why it is that so many people do believe; the irrational, esoteric and mysterious can possess considerable appeal. Witness the Christian belief in Transubstantiation where, when celebrating the Eucharist, the bread and wine offered is, in some mystifying way, the actual body and blood of Christ.

And so, the irrational yen for irrationality and similar, it seems, is no miracle at all. After all, many believers accept that rationality alone cannot lead them to God; rather, they commit themselves to leaps of faith – rarely, though, or so it seems, to hops, skips or jumps of faith.

66

GOD, CHOCOLATE AND PRAYER
or TAKE THE BOX?

A paradox seemingly miles away from God and chocolate has fascinated philosophers for the last forty years; it is Newcomb's. Before we connect it with the everyday, here comes the paradox, set in a 'One Two Box' television show.

The show has a mind-reader. You, a contestant, are presented with two boxes. In one, £10,000 is clearly in view. The other, the surprise box, is closed, its contents concealed. What you know is that the mind-reader, after reading your mind, will either have popped £1 million or nothing at all into the surprise box. So, in front of you there are two boxes: one with £10,000 clearly visible; another, the closed surprise box, with either zero or £1 million already there.

You are given the following choice. You may take either both boxes or just the surprise. Thousands of people have been given the choice. Those who have taken both have always found the surprise box empty; they have always ended up with just the £10,000. People who have taken only the surprise box have happily found the £1 million within.

People speculate. Maybe the mind-reader assesses people's characters. If she judges that players are not hugely greedy, settling for the surprise box alone, she rewards them accordingly by popping the £1 million into that box. If she judges players to be greedy, wanting as much as possible, likely to grab both boxes, she leaves the surprise box empty. To date, she has always been right. Who knows how she does it – but she does. It is known that it is possible for her to make mistakes, but she has not made one yet.

You want to get the most money you can. You do not want to risk losing the £1 million; yet you do not want to end up with nothing. The

£10,000 is certainly worth having, but winning the £1 million is better still – and getting both the £10,000 and the £1 million would be best. What is it rational to do?

Which way are you jumping? Try it on friends.

Should you open both boxes or solely the surprise box?

Many philosophers follow the 'already there' approach:

> Look, either the surprise box already contains the £1 million or it's already empty. If it's already empty, then obviously I should take both boxes – in order to get the £10,000. If the surprise box already contains the £1 million, then I should also take both boxes, securing both the £1 million and the £10,000. There can be no dispute. Any rational person – and I, being a philosopher – must take both boxes.

The retort is the 'evidential' approach:

> Consider the evidence. Whenever people have taken both boxes, the surprise box is empty. Who knows how the mind-reader works it

out, but somehow she does. Obviously, the rational thing to do, given the evidence, is to take just the surprise box. Only by my doing that will I secure the £1 million. All I can say about your 'already there' reasoning is: if it's so very clever, how come people who reason as you do aren't rich?

We may reel with the reasoning, between the 'already there' and 'evidential' approaches.

Perhaps, we decide to take the surprise box only; but then reason's teeny voice whispers that the mind-reader will therefore have already filled the surprise box with the £1 million, given the way we have decided. Hence, we may as well take both boxes after all, the 'already there' approach coming to the fore. But now we reflect that the mind-reader, being so clever, would have judged that we would take that next step in the reasoning, switching to favouring both boxes; so, it would be better after all to remain faithful to the original decision to take the surprise box only... But, the 'already there' reasoning cuts in again. And so on... The reasoning loops round.

My approach questions the puzzle's casual beginning. How is the mind-reader so successful? At least, how could she be successful when dealing with rational players? As we have seen, rational philosophers reach opposing or unstable conclusions about what to do. Of course, so-called rational philosophers – heaven forbid? – may end up defending one line of reasoning over another because of their psychological tendencies: risk-takers or greedy, overawed by evidence or cautious, committed to one type of philosophical theory or another. And we can seek to explain other reasoners' choices also on the basis of their psychological tendencies. Paradoxically, though, when assessing what it is *rational* for me to do, I cannot see my own decisions as the results of such tendencies.

The mind-reader, though, is back in business, if decisions, even of so-called rational players, result from players' psychological tendencies; but if they result purely from what it is rational to do – well, players and mind-reader are at sea. Our mind-reader would indeed be a phantasy – though the underlying puzzle is not, in that we now have a deep puzzle of how psychology and biology connect with rational and logical reasoning. We saw that earlier with Mary (Chapter 54).

♈

Whatever happened to God and genetics? Some godly believers, when tragedy has struck, pray or make sacrifices to their God, hoping that, for example, their daughter was not killed in a recent disaster. Maybe they reason that, through prayer or sacrifice now, their daughter *will have been* saved, God having foreseen their actions, their pleas and sacrifices. That is akin to the evidential approach: take the surprise box only; sacrifice the definite £10,000. Some believers, however, may reason that their daughter is already saved or not; so why lose time or money through prayer or sacrifice? That is the 'already there' approach.

Reflective believers, though, may deem prayer for whatever reasons as immoral, patronising an all-good God, as if he would not know what is best for the world, independently of what believers think is best. Prayer, to be acceptable, would need to be just 'thanks' to God for whatever happens. That thought, though, provides a further twist: perhaps what is best for God to ordain depends in part on whether believers give thanks. Thus, we have the evidential versus 'already there' dilemma again – and the question of whether our giving thanks is to manipulate God, hence, undermining the sincerity of the thanks.

Of course, some religious believers hold that it is predestined whether they gain eternal bliss or not – yet they still judge it important to lead godly lives to secure that eternal bliss. In that case, they are rejecting the 'already there' approach and following the evidential approach, while maybe accepting, somehow, that what they do and think is completely divinely determined.

Turning to genetics, suppose there is a correlation between certain genes and proneness to heart disease. Perhaps people so prone also eat lots of chocolate. Therefore, perhaps we should give up our chocolate consumption, hoping that we are thereby unlikely to have the undesirable genetic factor. In such reasoning, we are, so to speak, foregoing the chocolate box, the £10,000 box, in the hope that genetically our surprise box is filled with health. Here, this is a highly dubious argument. It would be better to argue that the genetic factor is indeed already fixed; so, if the factor is the cause of the proneness, we may as well have the chocolate and hope – maybe against hope – that the surprise box is yet filled with health. Of course, it may be that the genetic factor causes the chocolate desire, but it is the chocolate that actually causes the disease proneness; then, it could be rational to try to resist the chocolates.

These puzzles arise because we are uncertain which are causal factors, which irrelevant side-effects and which accidental correlations. We often lack understanding of how nature works. The Newcomb paradox baffles because we lack understanding of how the television's mind-reader works.

Newcomb's weirdness is shown by embellishing the tale, making the surprise box also open to view, with players seeing whether the £1 million is present. We then add to the story: yet, even when the £1 million is present and on view, players take only that box instead of taking both. This highlights the tale's mystery – a mystery present in Newcomb from the very beginning.

Genetic research seeks to eradicate mystery, distinguishing causes from coincidences, but we still live with one central mystery, namely, how causes relate to free choices and reasoning. Richard Dawkins of *The Selfish Gene* fame – we first met him in Chapter 2 – seems to find room for freedom through 'our brains rebelling against our genes'; but whatever does that mean and how does it provide room for free choices? As touched upon with Buridan's Ass (Chapter 61), how causes relate to free choices and, indeed, reasoning, is a deep mystery; and the mystery lurks within Newcomb's paradox, within our praying to God that something has happened, and indeed with our succumbing to chocolate, yet doing so freely. Or not so freely…

67

YOU'LL NEVER GET TO HEAVEN...?

Millions of people believe in a traditional single God, be it the God of the Jews, of the Christians or Allah of the Muslims; and they want to go to heaven. Many, many believe that the way to achieve heaven is to obey God's commands. Perhaps this is to misunderstand the religious texts but our puzzle arises from what many, many religious people believe, whether or not the belief is true. One godly command is a moral one – that we should help others – and, most importantly, that we should help others for their sake rather than as a means of gaining something for ourselves, such as advancing entry into heaven.

The puzzle is that this would seem to leave atheists and agnostics in a better position, with regard to heaven-entry through moral action, than reflective believers in God. Contrast Althea, an atheist, with Godfrey, a god-intoxicated, firmly committed, believer. Althea possesses a strong sense of moral duty; she values improving the lives of others and seeks no reward in return. She is a good person. As an atheist, she certainly is not motivated by desire for, or hope of, heavenly eternal life, yet she would pass any moral test for heavenly entry. (There may be other tests she would fail.)

What of Godfrey? He believes that, if he acts morally, he will reap the benefits of passing the moral test at heaven's gate. We need to break Godfrey down, so to speak, into two versions: a simple and a complex.

Simple Godfrey was a pretty immoral character before he came to believe in God and grasp what God commanded. He began to understand that he must help others, for their own sake, as a necessary condition for his reaching the desired heavenly end. 'But,' he reasoned, 'there is then no point in my helping others, because what is leading me to do this is my desire for heaven (or fear of hell) and that makes the whole point... er... pointless. To pass the heaven test, I need to act morally, without any self-interested motivation, yet I am considering what is best for me to do to pass the heaven test and improve my chances of a heavenly afterlife. That makes anything I do, as a result of such reflections, motivated by self-interest. My simple aim of achieving heaven seems, paradoxically, to prevent my doing what is required for heaven.' A similar worry arises with 'belief' in God 'just in case' via Pascal's Wager (Chapter 69).

Complex Godfrey, in contrast, was already genuinely concerned for others, for their sake not his. He was akin to Althea, in that respect. Since learning that this behaviour apparently helps to secure heavenly entry, he is vexed. He wants to get to heaven and he knows that his moral behaviour aids him in this quest, so maybe his motivation in helping others is no longer pure but is tarnished by self-interest. Maybe his motivation is now a complex and unhappy mixture: what he formerly sought for its own sake, he now seeks, or also seeks, for his own benefit; for the sake of passing through heaven's gate.

Is it easier for atheists to get to heaven than for believers?

There are, no doubt, some entrance conditions to heaven, in addition to those concerning moral motivation (assuming there is sense in the idea of entrance conditions). These conditions may well affect atheists and believers differently. On the one hand, atheists may have an even greater chance of heaven than believers if, for example, God sets lower standards on behaviour for those unaware of his laws than for those who are aware. On the other hand, believers may be better off than atheists because, presumably, conditions for heavenly entry may also include belief in God, worship of God and even certain rituals – all, by the way, rather unfair conditions for atheists who genuinely cannot feel justified in believing in God. One further condition could be that of wittingly obeying God's commands, which raises another motivational puzzle akin to the one already presented: God's commands include our treating others well for their sake – and probably not because God has so commanded.

Being motivated by God's commands and being motivated by a heavenly afterlife need not contaminate being motivated by the plight of others. People can be genuinely motivated to help others for their own sake and be genuinely motivated to do what is required to reach heaven, yet, because they are unaware of the link between the two, there is no puzzle: they simply do not realize that helping others is a means of increasing heavenly chances. Simple Godfrey may be able to take this path of ignorance. He could set about helping people, albeit with the wrong motives, yet, over time, come genuinely to be helping them for their sake because he forgets the link with heavenly entry and how he got started on the path.

More likely, Simple Godfrey would find himself eventually becoming Complex. He ends up helping others – and for the right reason as far as he can tell – but he worries about how this ties in with his behaviour apparently also helping him to get where he wants: heaven. Is there a genuine problem here?

You may be motivated to do X, knowing that X brings about Y, yet not be motivated by Y. That is easily seen when Y is undesirable: you are motivated to visit friends in Zürich, yet know that they will lead you into extravagances and exhaustions, which certainly do not motivate you. But what if the further known outcomes are desirable? For example, in Zürich, your friends will take you to its famous opera house, something that you prize. Is that also part of your motivation? By way of finding the answer, you could consider whether you would still be Zürich bound even if the opera were closed. If you would, that suggests that seeing your friends is at least your primary motivation. Does this line of reasoning help vexatious Complex Godfrey?

For Complex Godfrey to have the right motivation, we need him to help others, even without the consequence of the increased likelihood of heaven – even if, indeed, there were no God. As Godfrey is a seriously committed religious believer, can he make sense of such a possibility: of there being no God; of not wanting to go to heaven? If he is unable to make sense of it, how can he assess what he would still do in, for him, such a senseless world?

The answer perhaps is that no requirement exists for him to be able to carry out the 'Would I still?' test, just that it be possible for someone to carry it out about him. Step forth the atheist – now, arguably (albeit paradoxically) again in a better position than a believer to evaluate the believer's true motivation.

ᕼ

When told that the first shall be last, we should be at sea for, once the first are last, then, being no longer first, presumably the new 'firsts' should be last – and so on. 'Help others, but be not motivated by this command' also has something of the marine queasiness about it. Motivations do not generate puzzles solely for the religious. Many people want happiness, yet believe the best way of securing happiness is by not directly seeking it; so, must they somehow conceal their happiness goal from themselves? John Stuart Mill, who thought that happiness is most likely to be secured if not consciously sought day by day, also argued that, although society's best outcome is the utilitarian one (the greatest happiness of the greatest number), it does not follow that we should be motivated by that desirable outcome. John Austin, a friend of Mill, notes that, although utilitarians approve of love because it accords with utilitarianism, they are far from contending that a lover should kiss his mistress with an eye to the common welfare, to the overall resultant happiness. Were our relationships dominated by such calculations, happiness would assuredly not result.

Some utilitarians have also argued that the greatest happiness would be achieved by people in general *not* believing in utilitarianism but believing instead that there are some moral rules that should never be broken, whatever the outcome. If these utilitarians are right then, as intimated in the voting paradox (Chapter 14) and elsewhere, there are some things that should be kept secret from the public at large – including the fact that some things should be kept secret.

Shh... shh...

68
SYMPATHY FOR THE DEVIL

Once upon a time there was an all-powerful being – and nothing else. Following tradition, we use the pronoun 'he' for such a power. Religious believers would call him 'God', except he differed, in one vital respect, from the traditional God. True, he was all powerful and infinite; true, he was all knowing but, instead of being all good and benevolent, he was all bad and mean. Many may conclude that I have described a jumped-up version of God's fallen angel: the Devil. I shall speak of him as 'Devil' but, to reiterate, he is the *one* all-powerful being. There was no God to create him. He had no beginning.

Devil chose to create a universe, much like ours. It had stars and planets, of which at least one – Earth – had life just like our Earth. In all respects, Earth was the same as ours: it had oceans and mountains, people and nations. There was England, with warm beer, cricket and football; Scots cheering at English teams' frequent misses and losses. There were tigers, suitably striped, and tiger lilies too, alarms so alarming and so without point, mobile phones, designer clothes and techno music. There were petals, porcupines and cooing pigeons; safety regulations, sunbathing gazelles, wishing wells – English National Opera, Wigmore Hall recitals, the Alps too – and so on and so forth.

There were people who argued about how the universe began. Religious texts existed – the Bible and Qur'an – as did churches and synagogues, temples and mosques; and people worshipped a great and glorious and all-good being, God: some even claimed divine revelations of his benevolence, his commands and his concern for each and every one, from sparrow to human.

Devil tried to laugh off this mistaken worship of an almighty good God. He had deliberately arranged for the scriptures to come about but

as a joke. Deep down in his devilish inside, it infuriated and upset him. Even the few devil-worshippers failed to recognize him, Devil, as the *one* almighty being.

What especially annoyed Devil was that theologians, philosophers and even lay people discussed the problem of evil, of suffering. How, given that there is an all-powerful and all-good God (as they mistakenly believed), could so much evil exist, in the form of suffering? Devil had reasoned that if he set the universe going, with so much pain and misery developing over the centuries, reflective people would conclude that there must be an all-powerful, all-bad creator, namely him, Devil. They should be discussing the problem of good. Given that there is so much evidence pointing to an all-powerful bad being – Devil – the puzzle should be why good exists.

Why believe there is an all-powerful, all-good God rather than an all-powerful, all-bad Devil?

Religious believers typically take the universe as evidence in favour of there being an all-good, all-powerful God. They sometimes argue that the world's particular features show that there must be a creator-designer who is, indeed, all good and powerful. Yet, as John Stuart Mill argued in the nineteenth century, if we seriously look around the world in order to work out, by analogy, what features an all-powerful creator must have, we find overwhelming evidence to blacken that creator's name. Millions of people have suffered, are suffering or will suffer disease or starvation, often dying painfully. These sufferings are accompanied by the misery of hopelessness and the misery of being unable to help each other, compelled impotently to look on. Millions of people have suffered war and torture. In more mundane, happier lives, vast numbers of people experience grief as friends and relatives die; vast numbers suffer distressing conditions at work – and so on. Billions of animals are racked with pain as other animals devour them, those other animals suffering when being devoured in turn. Small wonder Devil is upset when he hears 'Praise be to the loving God' and 'All things bright and beautiful'.

Whether we see the problem as that of the existence of good or that of the existence of evil, some have attempted solutions. We should bear in mind that an all-powerful anything – Devil or God – cannot do anything: he cannot bring about things which are contradictory or which, if he performed them, would be contradictory. Can an all-powerful being create an immoveable post? If he is all powerful, surely he can; but if he is all powerful, he can move it, so it is not immoveable after all. Being unable to do what it is logically impossible to do is not a constraint on power. If someone told you both completely to close this book and not to close it, at the same time, there is nothing that would count as doing it, so there is nothing there to be done and hence no constraint on what you can do – indeed, in Chapter 71, God makes that point of logic.

Once we are aware that God or Devil cannot do what is logically impossible (for this consists of nothing at all actual or possible), we may argue that for there to be evil, there must, as a matter of logic, be good. Whatever the force of this point, it would never explain why there is *so much* good (or evil).

A popular move of godly believers is to speak of the value of free will. Free will makes the world a better place: it is better to have free agents than robots, better to have people freely choosing to perform good deeds than being predetermined or predestined to perform them. Naturally, possessing free will, people can choose to inflict evil and they may in fact make such a choice. Devil would, of course, argue in reverse. Free will gives considerable scope for lots of freely conducted evils, maliciousness and injustice – that is why he created free individuals. True, by having such creatures, Devil ran the risk that some would sometimes do good, but that would be outweighed by the evil of people freely and intentionally causing suffering in the world.

The free will defence only works, if it works at all, in regard to goods and evils caused by people. There are puzzles about free will, as seen in previous chapters, but even if we can make sense of it, there is no reason to believe that people have freely caused most earthquakes, volcanic eruptions, floods and diseases. Devil can rub his devilish metaphorical hands: such cruel disasters are evidence for his existence. Devil's problem is to explain why he created sources of happiness: blue skies and sunsets, oceans roaring, mountains soaring; the delights of love, the excitements of sex and the intoxications of music, wine and even philosophy. He may argue that, when things go wrong, these are effective ways of creating huge distress. And even when things go well, other people suffer through envy, jealousy and a sense of unfairness. Furthermore, for the lucky ones, there remains the awareness of the loss of such delights through infirmity and ultimately death.

Let us also draw attention to the despairing uncertainty for some over whether a good God exists. That is itself evidence for the maliciousness of Devil; after all, a good God should not tolerate such despair.

♈

Many people believe that God exists. They often rely on scriptures and religious teachers, but some look for evidence and believe it is found in certain features of the world around them. My suggestion of Devil is a way of challenging the inference from worldly features to an all-good God. Introducing Devil should also remind us that the choice is not simply between a God with benevolence and no God. Those who believe in an all-powerful figure that created and designed the universe need to explain why they are convinced he is all good rather than all bad – or, indeed, something in between. Is it not most likely that there are at least two distinct and powerful powers, one evil and one good? Zoroastrianism is typically taken as proclaiming such a duality. Is it the only sensible religion? Paradoxically, that could explain why hardly anyone believes in it. Mind you, maybe that is no paradox at all. After all, do faith and good sense readily combine?

These days Devil is often left out of the options and out in the cold. Small wonder he is distressed; no wonder he merits our sympathy. The sympathy, though, could be more aptly applied to both Devil and God, to both gods and devils, not because they lack recognition but, paradoxically, because they lack existence – or is that one paradox – and an atheistic leap – too far?

69

ON HOW A LAND WITHOUT CRIME IS BAD, SO BAD

There is a land, far, far away, where no offences against the law are ever committed. No, this is not because it is a land lacking in law. It is not a mis-description of a land where laws are broken, but remain undetected. The people in this land – this land, far, far away – are all law-abiding. People never deliberately park their cars illegally. Tax evasion is unheard of. No one steals; no one murders. Homes can be left unlocked without danger; people can wander dark alleys without fear of attack. This is an ideal land, this land, far, far away.

This is an ideal land, far, far away, yet its crime-free status is neither because the inhabitants are naturally law-abiding, nor because they live so well that none wants for anything. A few would happily evade taxes, break speed limits or commit fraud. No doubt a teeny number would delight in mugging some innocent passers-by for the sheer fun. A few would engage in theft, envious of the lucky wealthy. Some would even delight in smoking while dining out.

Yes, offences would be committed, save that those criminally inclined prefer not to run the risk of detection. This is not because the authorities would be one hundred per cent certain to catch offenders. Likelihood of being caught is, indeed, one highly significant factor in assessing whether law-breaking is worth the risk. The other highly significant factor is the size of punishment if caught compared to the rewards if not; and that factor is in play in this land so very far away.

In the land far, far away, the punishments are severe, extremely severe even for the most minor of offences. Were people deliberately to park illegally, they would have all their property immediately confiscated. Were people intentionally to break speed limits, they would be stretched out on racks for weeks on end. Thieves would be tortured for months and lose various limbs. Murderers would undergo lifetime torment, as would their loved ones. As for smokers in public places, they would be burnt – as were witches centuries ago.

These punishments may strike some as draconian; but are they really, bearing in mind the benefit they bestow? The benefit is the lack of any crime. Furthermore, the punishments never have to be applied. Their severity ensures their lack of application.

What's wrong with this land far, far away – where there is no crime?

Why do we not have laws and punishment as in the land far, far away?

The answer may seem obvious. The punishments are horrendous: how could we tolerate them? Think how brutal the law's custodians would have to be – torturing, amputating limbs and the like. The answer, though, may itself be easily answered. The sanctions are so severe that everyone aims at being law-abiding. Hence, the punishments are never implemented. We assume – for the moment – one hundred per cent deterrence. Yet even with the assumption, people may still object to the land's penal regime.

Punishment is, said Jeremy Bentham, a mischief. It involves offenders suffering, otherwise it would not be punishment. It is, though, surely wrong to inflict unnecessary suffering. The best punishments, therefore, are justified on utilitarian grounds of maximizing happiness, of causing least suffering, while most effectively deterring people from breaking good laws. The authorities of our land far, far away are well aware of that: hence, the severity of the punishments has been fixed to ensure one hundred per cent deterrence. No one suffers the horrendous punishments. What can be bad about that?

Well, it may be replied, the very contemplation of such outrageous punishments is itself morally obnoxious. Even if that reply holds, some morally obnoxious contemplation is a small price to pay in order to live in a land free of crime and free of punishment. Perhaps, comes the new response, the very preparedness to inflict such punishment is so evil that no one would or should be prepared to do so. Again, the reply is how little this evil is – if it is – compared to the gains. Indeed, we may question whether, in reality, there need be any preparedness, in view of the penal threat's effectiveness.

In such a land with such 'ideal' punishment, is there not one highly objectionable feature – that of proportionality? Surely, people who break speed limits do not *deserve* deliberate breakage of their limbs as punishment. What answer may be given by those of the distant land?

Well, do we possess any grip on proportionality? It often is linked to 'an eye for an eye', but few people take that literally. Further, we have no need to worry about proportionality, for the punishments – we are assuming – are not inflicted.

≈

We have been assuming one hundred per cent deterrence. Whether such could be achieved is an empirical, practical objection to the land far, far away. Let us review a little further.

Some crimes are committed when people are in emotional or irrational states. So, even if all citizens are aware of the laws and punishments, sometimes people will be swept along by passions, desperation or madness into breaking the law. One example would be that of people starving, out on the streets: their need to eat may overwhelm them, and so, they steal. The land far, far away handles that potential problem by ensuring sufficient basic welfare provision.

Welfare provision fails, though, to handle those so racked with jealousy that they murder their partners. It fails to prevent certain mentally disturbed individuals from abusing children. Such cases, though, need not generate punishment. Why? By attending to the mitigating circumstances. Being of unsound mind would be such a circumstance – as, indeed, could be ignorance and failed memory.

Our reasoning above assumes that if people do break the law, then there must be mitigating circumstances; so, harsh punishment – any punishment – is ruled out. The reasoning would parallel the famous catch-22 in Joseph Heller's book, whereby applications to avoid dangerous flying missions on grounds of insanity manifest sanity; so, applications inevitably fail. Well, 'successful applications', so to speak, for punishment – that is, law-breaking that merits punishment – need to be deliberate and by the sane, but applicants, in applying, lack the right deliberation and sanity; hence, applications fail.

We ought not to conclude that people in the land far, far away would therefore break the law, cynically relying on 'unsound mind' defences or similar. For a start, the land may ensure that its citizens are ignorant of the authorities' assumption, or at least unsure whether law-breaking would always generate effective defences against the punishments being inflicted. Further, it may be known that those who escape punishment because of unsound mind find themselves in psychiatric units, a result still highly undesirable.

Of course, citizens may feel insecure, fearing accidentally break-ing the law, and maybe fearing the horrendous punishments or the psychiatric institutions, but, even if that is so, is it not a small downside compared to the benefits? Think of the insecurity allegedly suffered by the law-abiding in a society where many crimes – muggings, thefts, gun-crimes – are committed.

♈

The perfect punishment of the land far, far away may appear absurd; yet curiously something similar is accepted by some – *some* – people, namely those who insist that if we fail to obey God's commands on Earth, we face eternal torment. Now, if any punishment is out of proportion, that is surely one. If the possibility of the horrendous punishments of the land far, far away would blight people's lives, then how much more blighted should they be with the fear of eternal torment?

That fear, if taken seriously, suggests that it is in our self-interest to believe in God. Blaise Pascal, major seventeenth-century French math-ematician and theologian, deployed probabilities to draw that prudent recommendation. Pascal's Wager, simplified, is as follows. On the one hand, suppose God exists: then, if you believe, you are likely to attain eternal bliss; if a non-believer, you are probably assured of eternal damnation. On the other hand, suppose God does not exist: then, if you believe, you doubtless waste some time, worshipping and confessing sins; but that downside is as of nothing compared to the chance of eternal bliss, if a believer, and the risk of eternal hell, if not.

Pascal's reasoning is doubtful, not least because of the questions: which god, which scriptures merit belief, which rituals to follow? We need to reach the right answers because, according to many, worshipping the wrong god or in the wrong way can be calamitous, eternally so. Even if we accept the calculation, concluding that we should attend the Synagogue, Church or Mosque, how do we secure genuine belief? Beliefs cannot be turned on at will (as shown in Chapter 45). So, how do we acquire belief in God, if we want the belief? By hypnosis? By contagion? Perhaps we need exposure to believers, in the hope that their belief is infectious; perhaps, through opening our minds to scripture and rituals, we could come genuinely to believe. The difficulty remains of whether the self-interested motivation undermines the belief's divine value. And, with belief of the mere possibility of eternal damnation, sensitive souls may have earthly lives of quakes and anxiety.

Of course, most religious believers live lives perfectly well, unblighted, without quaking anxiously, even when accepting the eternal sword of a divine Damocles. Indeed, despite the eternal danger, a few believers do steal and defraud, harm and murder – as do their non-believing counterparts. Maybe some believers rely on God's grace or divine mercy; if God is all loving, how, in the end, could he justify eternal damnation? Maybe some believers use Sloth's fallacious 'what will be, will be' argument (in Chapter 49). Probably, though, all of us, believers or not, get swept along, in practice, by passions, by apples, enchantments and seductions, being unable to appreciate fully the consequences of what we do; witness, in lighter mode, the cream bun temptations of Chapter 53. Perhaps that suggests that the land far, far away, lacking in crime, is a land of myth, however horrendous its punishments – yet must it be?

70
SAINTS, SINNERS AND SUICIDE BOMBERS

Allow me to introduce you to Hannah and Aminah, two splendid and thoughtful young women. Hannah is Christian; Aminah is Muslim.

Hannah was brought up in a Christian home, underwent no serious youthful rebellion and became more and more personally devoted to the teachings of Jesus Christ. She worships and prays. She speaks, sincerely, of listening to God. She relies on God concerning what is right and wrong, what she morally should and should not do. Sometimes she seeks guidance from others of her faith but they, in turn, rely on their communion with God or the communion of others with God, as described in the Bible. Hannah occasionally has religious experiences, which she describes in terms of 'seeing Christ'. She devotes considerable time to helping the underprivileged. She finds happiness in her religious life; we may say that she is blessed. Speaking somewhat loosely, Hannah is saintly.

All the above holds true of Aminah, save she speaks of Allah instead of God, follows the teachings of Muhammad instead of Christ and relies on the Qur'an instead of the Bible. Aminah too is, speaking even more loosely (given the Christian connotation), saintly.

Had Hannah and Aminah been brought up differently – Hannah in Islam; Aminah in Christianity – their religious beliefs, in all likelihood, would have been swapped. Imagine Hannah and Aminah were identical twins, with the same genetic inheritance, whose mother died at their birth. Through chance, they ended up being nurtured in the different religions: Aminah in Islam; Hannah in Christianity. Had they, as babies, been switched, Aminah would have been nurtured in Christianity and Hannah in Islam.

It would seem that they are irrational in holding the religious beliefs they do, for they know that, had circumstances been different, they

would have held to different religions. Whether or not the irrationality charge stands would appear of little consequence but for the vital fact that believers typically derive their moral beliefs (or think they do) from their religions. Given that different religions tell their believers different things about their morality's content and given that, had those believers been brought up in different religions, they would have adhered to different moralities, we may rightly ask:

How can religious believers rationally base their morality on religion?

We are lucky. Hannah and Aminah understand the words of God and Allah, of Christ and Muhammad, of the Bible and Qur'an, respectively, in such a way that they seek peace, value kindness, perform charitable works and so on. But think how things could have been radically different. Aminah might have listened and heard that she should be a martyr for Islam, become a suicide bomber and kill hundreds of innocent people, as the way to support the Islamic State and build a genuine caliphate. Hannah would be appalled at the thought – but is she in any better position? She also bases her morality on religion.

Had Hannah been in Aminah's shoes (and maybe it is just chance that she is not), she too could be exposed to the injunction to become a suicide bomber. Wearing her Christian shoes centuries ago, Hannah could have been calling for the burning of witches, the slaughter of infidels and the forced conversion of Jews. Wearing her Christian shoes today and listening to the voice of God as understood by some, she could still be supporting bombing raids known to cause tremendous injuries to innocent people. If we start being more specific, we should note the different varieties of Christianity and of Islam; for example how, historically, Catholics tried to force the conversion of Protestants as well as Jews by various brutal methods. Reflect how, even today, many believers have it divinely revealed that homosexual acts are evil, contraception is wicked and a wife should obey her husband – while many other believers deny that God's commands are like that at all.

The most general expression of the danger being addressed in this puzzle is that if people base their moral beliefs – that is, their beliefs concerning how they should treat others and themselves – exclusively on an authority's voice, they run the risk of carrying out some highly immoral deeds and feeling themselves justified in performing them. There is no guarantee concerning the type of actions that a supreme authority may command. The actions commanded could be morally horrendous. Thus, once people recognize that there are conceivable circumstances in which it would be wrong for them to obey the authority, they should recognize that they have some moral beliefs that are independent of that authority. For instance, religious believers who, because of their humanity, reject religious voices telling them to be martyrs for the faith would be sinners in the eyes of the religion, but may well be seen as secular saints, if their rejection means that they refuse to bomb innocent people. It is the fact that many believers have moral beliefs not grounded in religious authority that often explains why they interpret their scriptures in such a way that the scriptures support those moral beliefs.

Believers may reply that even non-believers often base their morality on some authority – on the State, political creeds, parents' teachings or even teachings of philosophers. My reply is that submission to such authorities can be dangerous, unless the authorities are open to questioning, to reasoning and to respecting people and their feelings.

Puzzles obviously persist concerning the basis of moral beliefs but, in general, there is significant agreement among people, in their everyday lives, about what is fundamentally right and wrong; an agreement that has no need of religious backing. That is not to say that non-believers never behave badly. It is not to deny that religious teaching has sometimes helped people to behave well. It is to insist that what is right and wrong, good and bad, cannot ultimately be understood in terms of what God or gods command, a point implied by Plato's reflections over two thousand years ago.

ᕼ

Are Hannah and Aminah irrational in their religious beliefs in general? Consider some non-religious but factual beliefs about the world.

Almost certainly, you believe that, however far you travel on the Earth's surface, you will not fall off the edge. You almost certainly believe that the Earth orbits the Sun. But if you reflect, you will agree that, had you been born many centuries ago, you might well have thought that people could fall off the edge of the Earth and that the Earth certainly did not circle the Sun.

Even though you recognize that you would in all likelihood have held different beliefs about the world, had you been in radically different circumstances, that in no way undermines the beliefs that you hold today. This is because you recognize that, in those different circumstances many centuries ago, you lacked evidence that is now available. Where religious beliefs about God and the afterlife are concerned, based on scripture and revelations, things are different. After all, is there much scope for showing how one set of scriptures or revelations provides better evidence than another? It would seem not – and hence there is the irrationality of believing in one religion, while knowing that another would have been equally convincing. That raises indoctrination problems (as seen in Chapter 45) and how to handle faith schools and children's religious education.

Maybe the puzzle of the variety in religious belief is what motivates certain disparate believers to speak of religious believers all really worshipping one and the same God. It motivates others to speak of 'leaps' (though, as noted previously, rarely 'skips' or 'hops') of faith. Mind you, the leapers do not merely need faith to take the leap, but also faith that their leap is the right leap in the right direction.

Lest we forget: once an ancient scripture, tradition or authority, taken as divinely inspired, is allowed to trump fellow feeling and common humanity, all manner of atrocity can be deemed justified; enslavements, torture and beheadings may be perpetrated against wrong believers and non-believers. Once the appeal to faith exists, any leap, hop, skip or jump – however bizarre, dangerous or morally horrific – would seem to be permitted. That is one clear reason why having faith in faith, pure and simple, may not be such a good idea. Faith, in fact, turns out to be far from simple; and those of faith may yet have a faith far from pure.

71

A KNOWING GOD KNOWS HOW MUCH?

'You know – well, I certainly know, being God and a know-all – that you have only given me this philosophical platform to show me up, as swathed in paradox and mystery. Yes, I am mysterious and in many ways beyond human comprehension; so it is small wonder that you human beings judge it paradoxical that I can be all powerful – omnipotent – and so loving, yet there exist so much pain and distress on your mortal coil. But we shall not be engaging that paradox, I foretell.

'And I am pleased, so pleased, that you are not focusing on immoveable stones. Paradoxically, some of you insist, if I can create an immoveable stone, then I cannot move it – and if I can move it, then I cannot create such a stone. Either way, it is argued, I cannot be all powerful. But you humans should know by now that it is no constraint on power to be unable to perform the logically impossible: that is because the logically impossible is akin to nonsense. People who complain about my inability to deal with immoveable stones should also complain that I cannot blibble, blobble, bleeble. Whatever would it be to blibble, blobble, bleeble, as opposed merely to uttering the words? What would it be to move the immoveable?

'I know very well that you are hoping to make trouble about my knowing everything. Well, go on: see what chaos you can wreak. Of course, I already know how far you will get – because I really do know everything.'

What can God know?

God allegedly is omniscient: he knows everything. That immediately demands the caveat that he knows everything that it is logically possible for such a god to know.

God is usually considered immaterial and without defect; yet, curiously, some believers say that he experiences and knows jealousy and pain, pain through human beings' immorality. It is difficult to grasp how God, a perfect being, can suffer in that way and have such 'personal' knowledge. Presumably, at least, God cannot be scared, dithering or experiencing *schadenfreude*. Perhaps God knows of emotions and feelings in an intellectual, detached way: maybe he can imagine them; maybe he knows how they affect human behaviour. That knowledge would, however, fail to be knowledge in the direct experiential way of humans.

Many people see a puzzle with God possessing foreknowledge. It is sometimes mistakenly argued that if God knows what you will do, then you will not be acting freely. Now, if God knows that you will visit Jerusalem – and he knows this because he determines you to do so – then that could well show that you will not be visiting freely. If, though, God merely knows that you will visit Jerusalem – if he can, so to speak, simply see into your future – then that shows nothing about your freedom.

The error in thinking that God's foreknowledge must undermine human freedom perhaps comes about as follows. Consider an analogous error, using Descartes' 'I think, therefore I am.' If you are thinking, then it necessarily follows – it must follow – that you exist. That is true. It does not, though, mean that if you are thinking, then you exist necessarily: it does not mean that you must have existed. You might not have existed – your parents might never have done funny things with their bodies – and then, of course, you would not have been thinking. We need to distinguish between on the one hand the necessity in a relationship between two items, between thinking and existing, and on the other hand the item, your existence, being necessary. Let us now use the distinction applying it to God's foreknowledge.

If God knows that you will visit Jerusalem, it necessarily follows that you will visit accordingly. That is true. It does not mean that you will visit Jerusalem necessarily – that you could not have done otherwise. If such and such necessarily leads to so and so, it does not mean that so and so is necessary. If the water is frozen, it necessarily follows that it is not boiling; but it does not follow that the water had to be frozen and could not have been boiling. So, God possessing foreknowledge of actions does not mean that those actions necessarily will happen. You can still choose what you will do. It is just that God knows the outcome of your choice.

〰

There remain puzzles about divine foreknowledge, simply because there are puzzles about God possessing any knowledge involving time – if God is taken to be eternal, outside space and time. God is often taken so to be, for were he in space and time, it becomes difficult to comprehend how he could have created space and time, a creation difficult enough.

If outside time, it would seem that God cannot possess the type of knowledge that we possess – or, at least, seem to possess – when we know that today's breakfast is in the *past*, that we are reading a book right *now*, and that we shall see Damascus sometime in the *future*. It may be replied that God could have timeless knowledge of such sequences, of how the breakfast comes before the reading which comes before the

Damascus trip. Although God could not know, as we may know, that the Damascus trip is future, he could know eternally that the trip occurs in the year 2025. He could know eternally that Spinoza is (timelessly) excommunicated in 1656 and dies in 1677. That is, he could have timeless knowledge of dated facts. The dates are built within the facts known.

Even if God can have timeless knowledge of the sequence of dated events – and we may question God's grasp of 'before' and 'after' – he would still lack the type of knowledge that we possess in knowing that it is *today's* breakfast we have in mind, and that the reading is occurring right *now*. You surely need to be in time to have awareness of what constitutes *now* rather than *then*. That is, you surely need to be in time to have indexical, temporal knowledge, knowledge that is grasped from a particular timed location – though it is true, as seen in Chapter 34, that there are puzzles in grasping the nature of the past, present and future, of the temporal indexicals.

As well as lacking indexical knowledge concerning time, if God is outside space he lacks indexical knowledge of the *here* and *there*. If outside space, God cannot know, it seems, what it is like to see things from a certain perspective, to be here rather than there. He cannot have the knowledge you have when experiencing this book as being nearer than the lamp. Being disembodied, he also lacks the knowledge you have of moving an arm or waking up in the wrong bed.

An eternal divinity, outside space and time, encounters difficulties in grasping human indexical knowledge. Yet we humans, of course, encounter difficulties in grasping God's nature. We have no firm grip, if any grip at all, on what God may be able to imagine about finite spatio-temporal lives or may even be able to do by way of actually becoming human. While God cannot be you, having your experiences, perhaps he can imagine, in some way, what your experiences are like.

ϒ

It is hard to reach firm conclusions about God's knowledge, for the very concept of an eternal, immaterial, all-knowing, all-powerful being is baffling. Such beings are not regularly met – well, not by many of us. Suppose, though, that there is sense in an all-knowing being knowing *all* truths. Well, all truths must be infinite in number, if only because the number of natural numbers – 1, 2, 3 and so on – is infinite. Consequently God's knowledge must be without end. Infinities bigger than the number of natural numbers, though, can be described – recall Chapter 30 – and, indeed, it can be argued that God's knowledge must be ever expanding into greater and greater infinities of truths to be known.

We hand back to God.

'Had only you asked, I would have told you straightaway that you shall never grasp the infinite depth of my mystery.'

72

MYSTERIES

'Once upon a time, there was nothing…'

It is not a tale easy to develop. If we continue with '… and then there was something', many would ask, 'How did that something pop into existence? Popped into existence from nothing, did it?' All that we could sensibly reply is, 'It just did.' But that feels inadequate. Some physicists have spoken of the laws of nature 'holding', yet then we should wonder what sense can be made of such laws holding, when there is nothing; we should also wonder what is the explanation of there being such laws, rather than none.

Let us try our tale again.

'Once upon a time, there was something…'

Now we have something to get our teeth into, but many will wonder, 'So how did that something come about?' To that question we may give some answers that momentarily satisfy. We may announce that the something was brought about by something else – and that something else by something else further and so on… That passes the explanatory buck. Whether or not such 'bringing it about' chains can go on, back and back, without a beginning, there yet remains the question of how such chains, endless or not, came to exist, rather than nothing at all.

Let us try starting our tale for a third time.

'Once upon a time, there was everything…'

Now, we probably tend to worry about the 'Once upon a time' over which, so far, we have been silent. We may well point out that not everything is present just at the one time; there are all the things that went before that time and all the things that come after that time – all the things past and all those future. We may muse upon whether only the present exists or whether the past and present exist but not the future – or whether past, present and future all exist. Let us avoid such complexities here; we met them earlier in Part IV.

'Once upon a time' tales possess movement, usually telling us how some events came about as a result of others. So, we could revise our beginning yet again.

'Once upon a time, there was everything that had been up to and including, that time…'

Why are there all the things that there are?
Why were there all the things that there were?

These questions can be raised even if the 'all the things' includes a 'never-ending' chain of somethings having been brought about. The questions could be expanded by adding 'and why all the things that there will be?'

The questions could be divided into 'Why is there – why was there – anything at all?' and 'Why are the things that there are (and were) just those things with those properties?' Let us stay with the first question. In one understanding, it is a question that is frequently asked, in the highest and lowest of circles, with answers demanded and sometimes given. In another understanding, it is one that is shuffled around, in the highest and lowest of circles, with no answer really demanded and no good, clear answer given. The two understandings hang on the 'all' or 'everything'.

The first understanding is that 'everything' covers the whole universe, that is, everything that scientists study: stars, planets, electricity, playstations, cars, central heating, men, women and treacle tart – all things, including minds, including institutions such as money, the law and morality. A terminological complexity needs to be noted: in recent years, a few philosophers, followed by some physicists, have suggested that maybe many universes exist. Our use of 'universe' covers the whole lot.

When 'everything' is so understood, the question is asked, 'How or why did "everything" come about?' Even if the 'everything' consists of a series of things that has no beginning, why is there a series at all? Many feel that to be a genuine question and that, without an answer, we are collapsed into mystery. Many are led to say that, therefore, there must be a creator God (or gods). They say that only with the existence of a creator can the universe's existence be intelligible.

The second understanding is this. 'Everything' is taken, curiously (!), to mean everything. It covers the universe but also any gods or God that exists. How did 'everything', understood really to include everything, come about? Strangely, that does not trouble some people. Their answer is that a creator God (or, maybe, gods), part of the everything, just *had* to exist – and created the rest. Maybe the universe just happens to be, but not God. God *must* be. I and you might not have existed; we are contingent beings, not necessary beings. Had our parents not engaged in funny bodily dealings one day (or, more likely, night) we should not have existed. With God it is different. His existence is not contingent on anything outside of him. He exists necessarily.

How can there, though, be something that *has* to be? Sometimes the answer is that it is a mystery. 'So much,' we may be tempted to reply, 'for telling us that we need to accept God to make intelligible the seeming mystery of the universe's existence.' If we suggest that perhaps the universe itself had to be, with no need of God, heads are shaken: that would indeed be a mystery. But would it? Is it any more mysterious than the mystery of a necessarily existing creator God who moves in mysterious ways?

Maybe these puzzling thoughts arise because of our expectations from explanations. As seen earlier with poor Ass and his bale of woe (Chapter 61), Leibniz advocated the principle of sufficient reason: there must be a sufficient reason for everything. When we give reasons – or explanations – we go beyond what it is that we are giving reasons for. We explain A by reference to B and B by reference to C and so on. So, when we are successful in giving an explanation, inevitably there pops up reference to something else and hence a need for another explanation, one

MYSTERIES • *337*

of that something else. The resort to a creator God is recognition that explanations must come to an end; but once that is recognized, there should be no need to look for a creator of the universe at all. Maybe the universe just happens to be. Maybe, indeed, the Ass can just act, without reason, without being enmeshed in Leibniz's principle.

♈

If this universe just happens to be, might there indeed have been nothing? Or must there always have been some universe but not necessarily this particular one?

That there might have been nothing is a dizzy thought. When we try to imagine nothing, we probably remove, in our thinking, all the items from the universe, yet are we not still left with space and time? How can we remove those? Yet just because we cannot imagine 'nothing' – if it is true that we cannot – it does not follow that there might not have been nothing.

Might there have been empty space and time? Let us focus on time. What counts as time passing, if there are no changes going on at all; no clocks ticking; no movements of electrons; no hearts beating? Perhaps time requires the existence of events, of happenings. And, surely, events and happenings need to take place in time.

Could there have been something that is neither in space nor time? Some tell us that God is neither spatial nor temporal. Maybe we do have a grip on such spacelessness and timelessness: numbers, if they exist at all, do not exist in space or at a particular time. We may, then, suppose that, like numbers, God is timeless. That supposition gives rise to a fresh mystery, namely how God could be a creator, for creating is an event, a happening, which takes place in time. Numbers do not create things; God is usually taken to have created the universe, everything indeed, as we have discussed elsewhere.

There are further mysteries. One that comes to the fore is whether time itself has a beginning. It certainly could not have had a beginning in time, but if time stretches back without end, infinitely, does that mean that an infinite series of time durations, that is, an endless series, must have been completed by now? How is that possible? Recall Charlotte (page 139).

Even if something could exist that needs no explanation, some have insisted that an explanation is required of how there is this *particular* something – the universe with conscious and (occasionally) intelligent life. Is it not highly unlikely that this should have come about without intelligent design – that is, without an intelligent being that 'fine tuned' the constants of the universe such that conscious rational life arose?

It is highly doubtful whether we have any grip on what is likely or unlikely when we are talking of the universe, of which we know so little and of which there is only one. Whatever we conclude about that likelihood, why is the universe's just happening to exist so less likely than a creator God creating this universe? No doubt we shall continue to be told that God moves in mysterious ways; but then it is a mystery why the God mystery is considered less mysterious than the mystery of the existence of the universe.

Enough of these dancing mysteries. Mystery mongering must come to an end, as must explanations – though that does remind me...

Should we seek an ending to the universe's existence? 'In the end, things just stop.' 'In the end, there will be nothing.' 'In the end there is no end.' The focus is usually on the beginning of 'everything', but maybe there are similar puzzles to do with the end of 'everything', even if the universe is to be understood as striving to an end, to perfection, to the Good. More mystery mongering or, at least, mystery, indeed.

PART VIII:
PERSONAL RELATIONSHIPS
What is it to be human?

Only connect.

E. M. Forster

Upon entering the personal realm, we naturally engage with emotions, with loves and lusts, and with fair treatments of others. We often compartmentalize our lives: trustworthy in finance, but not in love. We freely enter into deals, yet some are deemed benign, others blackmail. It is said that we should treat people as people, not as objects; yet do not relationships rest on interacting with others as biological beings? We find some people attractive, desirable and hence desired; others we prefer not to know.

Apart from mysteries of love, possession and commitments – 'we were meant for each other'; 'you belong to me' – there are consequential puzzles about sexual repression, child production and whom to create. We tamper with children by sending them to school, holy services or football matches; so, what would be wrong in tampering with foetuses genetically – to enhance eventual abilities to shine at mathematics, become tennis stars or even believers in God?

Lurking here are deep metaphysical matters, regarding the self and that we view our past and future so differently. They raise fresh puzzles about time, explored in 'Thank Goodness That's Over' (Chapter 74); think, for example, how differently we view our lack of life before birth compared to the lack of life upon our demise. In relationships with others, there is also the problem of 'other minds', and the apparent elusiveness of the thoughts and feelings of others. Paradoxically, in death, we are more at the mercy of others than during life. In death, we have no chance of developing differently or challenging what is reported about us. The others who live on may judge our lives, enhance or ruin our reputations, respect or mock our deathbed wishes, with impunity; in Sartre's terms, we are prey to the Other.

Before we confront the deeper metaphysical puzzles of 'others', we turn to an ethical matter concerning our relationships; we begin, with a distinctive way of securing intimacy – through eating people.

73

WHAT'S WRONG WITH EATING PEOPLE?
or even WHO'S FOR DINNER?

'I could eat you,' she said, she with the sparkling white teeth and devouring eyes, her arms flung round my neck. How could I not be flattered, receiving such warm and welcoming attention, in the club that had just so eagerly admitted me as member?

'Who's for dinner?' some others asked. Well, I was hungry; and present were bright and beaming people – generous to boot, for no membership fee had been demanded. I was an honorary fellow, they said. Naive little me – little did I realize that my enthusiastic 'yes' to dinner would lead me to the cooking pot, not as guest diner or even guest chef, but – *gulp* – as guest 'about to be dined upon'. These people were generous sure enough, but generous to a fault, as I was soon to discover.

Serve Man was the club's motto – and it slowly dawned on me what this meant. Yes, cannibalism was alive and well in the 'gentlemen's clubs' of London's Pall Mall. It looked as if, while I should soon be dead, I should not be much buried – just stewed, with, I trusted, at least a fine garnish.

〰

We may deal quickly with the scenario sketched, once we have the background question: what's wrong with eating people? After all, I had not consented to their gastronomic intentions and was far from wanting to be cooked; so, that was why eating me was wrong.

Jonathan Swift gave satirical voice to eating babies and the young, to stave off impending starvation. The idea has not been much taken up. True, in extreme cases when, for example, survivors of air crashes would otherwise die, people typically accept that eating those already

deceased is morally permissible. Many people, though, would be appalled at the dining habits of our club above, even if members ate only humans recently deceased through natural cause or accident. Yet, many of these appalled people are probably pleased to be blood donors, when alive, and pleased to donate organs on death.

To maintain focus, we cast to one side cases when eating those accidentally or naturally deceased is required because of imminent starvation. Those instances excepted, is something otherwise wrong with the consumption of human remains by humans, even when such cannibalism is voluntarily agreed? After all, many of us enthusiastically eat the flesh of other creatures – fish, fowl and beasts of the field – and sometimes we savour, sometimes unwittingly, snakes, whales and crocodiles, even the odd cat, dog and chimp. Yet only the perverted would defend eating people – it seems.

Whatever is wrong with eating people?

Many creatures – cows, sheep, pigs – would not have existed, but for our husbandry; yet does that give us the right to kill and eat them? Were it to do so, we could return to Swift's proposal and defend farming human babies. The argument is, of course, bad. Just because we created the individuals, we do not possess rights to destroy them — certainly not, if the created possess interests of their own, as arguably animals and babies do. Even a Picasso who creates a great painting, appreciated by millions, may be wrong to destroy his creation.

Many of us, of course, seek to justify the painless killing of non-human animals for food. Maybe a super-species would farm humans, arguing that we humans, a lesser species, suffered little loss, if painlessly killed. That would justify eating people — though not by people. The 'super-species thought' may rightly encourage us not to be so casual in our meat-eating ways.

One man's meat may be another man's person, and there are standard, pragmatic arguments against people-pies, *homo sapiens bleu*, and tinned man or woman.

Were the eating of people to be accepted simply as a pleasurable dish — or maybe not so pleasurable — then, it may be said, we should be devaluing human life in general. Even if such eating were permitted only of those who died naturally or by accident — carrying 'donate for eating' cards — our way of looking at each other could alter for the worse. The looking would be affected by the cooking. After all, some argue that some pornography encourages men to view women as flesh, devaluing their personhood. With person-cooking accepted, maybe we would regard others as lumps of flesh, commodities, rather than persons. But is this likely? Just because we would be treating corpses in one way, why should we slip into a related attitude to living people?

Respect for persons involves respect for their bodies — and such respect extends to a person's corpse. Having human corpses, hanging in butcher shops, or tinned man or woman available on supermarket shelves, merely to provide dining variety, undermines the respect. It certainly differs from using organs of the deceased to save others' lives.

Consider households that keep a few turkeys — Lucinder, Ludwig and Ludmilla — with the intention of fattening them for Christmas. When Christmas comes, not many in the family enjoy tucking into Lucinder and the others. The names have helped to make the turkeys honorary members of our human community.

We de-humanize people, block out respect, reducing their status to mere bundles of flesh, by addressing them, even when face to face, simply by numbers – as done in concentration camps. De-humanization dangers are even present when, for example, patients are known simply as the 'appendix' or 'hernia'. Yet, there are cases and cases. Cases vary, depending on context, intentions and perceptions. People sometimes may rightly be treated as just bodies. Stelarc, an artist, has engaged in street suspension, piercing his body with hooks, hanging his body over New York City. Was he degrading himself? It is not clear that he was; he remained a voluntary agent in that use of his body as apparently artistic object.

We have pictured human corpses dangling in butcher shops; and such scenes would deeply offend. Yet have we really shown anything to be morally wrong with people wishing to be eaten after their natural death – and those wishes being respected, given suitable regulation and discretion? We have a natural repugnance at the idea, but is there anything immoral?

$$\Upsilon$$

Respect may be shown in diverse ways. Consider a society where people may choose how their lives and remains should end. Just as today we respect people's wishes whether to be cremated or buried – and even accept that a few mothers after birth cook the placentas – so, in that society, a choice could be made to be eaten. Perhaps a highly significant and ritualistic dining ceremony exists, with only the deceased's loved ones present. Perhaps the ritual is symbolic of ultimate or eternal bonding, of 'connecting' with the deceased. In such a society, people would feel their lives ended badly if the appropriate ceremonies failed to take place. The dining may be associated with a sense of religious oneness or of the flesh metaphorically sustaining the living. Some could see the eating more as worthy sacrificing to the gods. Others may regard life as a work of art, requiring the right ending, just as do novels and music.

Such rituals, with the justifications offered, would today generate laughter or disgust; they would not be taken in the right spirit. It does not follow, though, that there is anything morally wrong in the proposed society. Let us hasten to add: this is not a slide into moral relativism. It is not a slide at all, for, in justifying the dining practices, we deploy values readily recognized across cultures: respecting people's wishes, connecting with others, manifesting love. It does, though, remind us that respecting people can take different forms.

Eating people could be a significant practice in a highly moral world. E. M. Forster's injunction 'only connect' – here understood as empathizing, bonding, valuing other people's wishes – may now come to mind. It may come to mind with the addition of a more literal rendering than intended. People who, in the circumstances just outlined, value eating people and being eaten are indeed valuing Forster's injunction.

'Only connect.'

74

'THANK GOODNESS THAT'S OVER'

Some people live for the present. Others live in the past. Yet others live for the future. That is a little exaggerated, for we all need to have some concern for all three. Still, doubtless we know of people who tend to focus more on one temporal aspect of their lives than others. Here are some extremes.

Mr Past concentrates on what he has done: how he won that gold medal, built up his business and sported the largest yacht in the harbour – or (or even 'and') he may relive tragedies: the loss of his yacht, his business and his wife. What he is currently involved in, other than remembering, carries little weight. What he is going to do, next year, next month, even tomorrow, has scant impact. This attitude is most common among the elderly.

Miss Present lives for the present – for the moment. For her, no lingering on past successes and failures. Miss Present moves with the present. Projects for the future matter little. She just throws herself into whatever she is up to, in the here and now.

Ms Future focuses on the future. Like Miss Present, she ignores the past. Like Mr Past, she takes little notice of the present. Rather, she lives for what she will be doing, how well or badly things will be going – and so on. She takes great delight in the anticipation of her holiday next month; yet once on that holiday, she is dominated by bleak anticipation of its end.

Mr Past, Miss Present and Ms Future are extreme examples of people's different tendencies, yet if we consider happenings of like intensity and duration, we usually have far more direct concern for our present and future experiences than our past.

Consider this. You will suffer terrible pains resulting from a vital operation. I bet you would prefer them to be in the past, over and done with, rather than in the future. Or, some wonderful experiences are going to enthral you. I bet you would prefer that they are forthcoming, rather than that they be finished.

Why do we prefer pains to be in the past rather than the future?
Why prefer pleasures in the future to those in the past?

Usually, we think of ourselves as being the same selves over time. Memories sharpen and decay, characters develop, circumstances radically change, yet the cry goes up, 'But it is still me!' It is still me, however much my hair turns grey. If I am *me* and as much *me* throughout my life – true, we have met puzzles about this common belief and feeling – ought not I to have the same amount of regard for me, for my existence, at any time? If I am the same self over time, it would seem most rational to have the same concern for past pains as for future ones – and to be as moved by past pleasures as future. Indeed, my *self* that existed ten years ago should carry as much weight for me as my self that will exist ten years hence – and, indeed, my self now. Ought I not to be concerned with my self, *out of time*, so to speak? Ought I not to be a Mr or Ms or Miss 'Timeless'?

Some of our different attitudes to the past, present and future can, in part, be explained by intrusions to do with uncertainty. I am more stressed by the pain I am suffering now than the one I shall suffer next week because I may be able to prevent the latter or, for some reason or other, it may not happen. Were that the key to our different attitudes to past, present and future, we ought also to be more stressed about our past pains – they definitely happened – than future ones. Yet most of us prefer the visit to the dentist to be past than future. With pain, we want to be able to exclaim, 'Thank goodness that's over!'

Undoubtedly, we have temporal preferences. We prefer bad things to be over. We prefer good things to be forthcoming or happening now. Yet it is unclear whether anything can justify these preferences. Indeed, if I am the same self over time, it looks as if these temporal preferences are sheer prejudices – discriminations against my life to date and in favour of my life to come.

Some have argued that we should overcome these prejudices. On this view, if, through loss of memory and medical notes, it is currently unclear whether I suffered painful procedures yesterday or shall be undergoing them tomorrow, it is mistaken to hope that it turns out that the procedures took place yesterday. Either way is as bad for me. If you hear that your children or parents or lovers have been tortured and murdered in some far-off land, but then learn that there is some confusion about whether it has happened or is about to happen, should you not be equally distressed either way (assuming that there is no hope of avoiding the outcome for them)?

♈

Relating the 'out of time' perspective, our being Timeless, to our living 'within time', where future happenings become present and then past, is tricky. Some argue that our temporal preferences do indeed display an inconsistency. Consider your experience of two pains of similar considerable intensity and duration, the only difference being that one occurred yesterday and is all over and the other will occur tomorrow. Are you not inconsistent in being far more concerned about the future pain than the past?

The answer is that the critic is forgetting that you were, no doubt, highly concerned about that past pain when it was yet to come, when it was then in the future and also when it was present and occurring. That past pain is less significant now than a similar future pain because when that past pain was future and then present, you paid as much attention to it as you are now doing to the forthcoming future pain. And the future pain that distresses you so much now – and even more when present – will eventually receive less concern from you, once in the past.

It looks as if we, with our temporal preferences, can avoid the charge of inconsistency, if we step back from where we are *now* in our lives; yet, of course, that does not touch the fact that we still do have the preferences, thinking our future experiences more important than similar past ones, from the standpoint of where we are now. It remains unclear whether those preferences are justified. Maybe nothing more can be said to defend them. Maybe they are indeed mere prejudices – or just how things are.

Our non-existence provides a striking example of our radically different temporal attitudes. Many people fear death, even when they believe that death is annihilation. Their lack of future existence is, so to speak, a cause of great distress. Curiously, they rarely regret their lack of existence before birth, that is, their lack of prenatal existence. Is this also a prejudice? Or is Lucretius, from ancient Rome, right – that we should be as little concerned about being dead as about the time before we were born? In both cases, it seems, we suffer deprivations, deprivations of which we are unaware during the periods of those deprivations. There may, though, be an asymmetry: it is quite easy to picture what it would be like to be me, continuing to live for many years longer than I in fact shall live; it is not so easy to make sense of how it would have been me, this me, to have been born many years earlier. And, it is all the more difficult to make sense of deprivations suffered by those who never get born; after all, they lack the foothold of existence (touched on in Chapter 3), so, how can we sensibly worry about them? The area of concern does, though, have consequences for how we view decisions about which children to create (discussed in Chapter 83).

If, though, prenatal non-existence is on a par with being dead, then – pessimist that I am – I wonder whether the distress we feel at the loss of our life at death should not also darken our feelings about the lack of life before birth. Should we be troubled by what we missed out on before we were born? Are we born too late? Do we die too early?

We saw, in Chapter 9, how we may be harmed, even though unaware of the harm – for example, through peeping Toms and betrayals never discovered. Extending that thought: just because, when deceased, we lack existence and lack awareness of what we are missing, it does not follow that the deprivation of more life has not harmed us. We noted earlier (page 72) how even if the grave is 'a fine and silent place', we may yet become parents; well, however fine and silent is that place, we may yet be harmed, be it through lies being told about us, promises being broken, or simply missing out on the goods of life.

We could end this thought on an optimistic note. Our lives may reap benefits, even when, paradoxically, we are no more: fought-for projects may come to fruition; loved gardens may continue to be tended; the whale may be saved.

Optimistically or otherwise, a timeless perspective is required to grasp properly the overall value, the shape and features, of a whole life. That is why unkindness, rages and arguments with loved ones, as death draws near to them, ought not to be viewed as determining the nature of lifelong relationships. 'Last words' are not definitive of all words. Our own last words, thoughts and personal summations are also not thereby the true revelation of our lives in total. Sadly – or, more likely, fortunately – when it is possible for the whole of our lives to be viewed timelessly, no longer is it possible for us to do the viewing. After all, then, we are no longer around.

75
THE BOTTLE IMP – FOR SALE

Allow me to introduce you to Miss Imp. She is a genie of immense power and lives in this bottle in front of you. With a 'Buyer beware' tag yet to be explained, she is, for the first time, on the market, on offer – for sale. Buy her, and she will bring forth everything that you want, be it fame and fortune, sex and success, or just a comfortable life, tending your garden. This is known to be true. Furthermore, her purchase price is any sum you care to name. Miss Imp will give you whatever you want; so, you do not even have to part with the money right now. An IOU is readily accepted. Once you own her, she will conjure up whatever sum you require for payment.

Now, let us face the 'Beware'. The snag, the caveat, is that whoever owns the imp must at some stage, to avoid eternal torment, eternal damnation, sell her for less than he or she paid. Any potential purchasers must be told of this vital condition. Bearing all that in mind, how much would you pay for Miss Imp?

Obviously, you would not pay the lowest unit of money – a penny or a cent. You could never sell her for less than that; and so you would be eternally damned. (We assume that you and others are not otherwise so damned.) Would you buy her for two pennies or two cents? Well, you would then have to sell her, at some point, for one penny or one cent – and a potential purchaser would be crazy to buy her for those sums, for how could the imp ever be sold on?

Of course, you could take a risk – a big risk? – buying her for £1,000, thinking someone would surely take her off your hands for £999, for that someone could think that someone else would be prepared to pay £998 later on. And so on… But not 'and so on'. If – if – all possible purchasers are rational and farsighted, lacking desire for eternal torment, it looks as if no one would buy Miss Imp, however large the sum.

As with many philosophical paradoxes, we have a tale that, after a little reflection, traps us. Indeed, if anyone currently owns a Miss Imp – why are you looking at me? – he is already trapped, unless others want to help him out, taking the risk on board themselves.

The tale, you may think, is a crazy tale. Why does it matter? Well, it raises the question of how far ahead it is rational to look. With the Bottle Imp, we casually popped in 'rationality' and 'farsightedness', drawing the conclusion that it would be crazy to buy Miss Imp for even a million pounds. It is crazy because, further down the line, someone would become vividly aware of needing to sell her, impossibly, for one penny or one cent. But is it rational to consider that far ahead?

How much of the future is it rational to take into account?

May it not be rational, in fact, to pay one million pounds for Miss Imp? Remember, you commit to the deal, receive the Imp who then magics the million pounds for you. If it strikes you as rational to buy Miss Imp for one million pounds, presumably someone else may believe it rational to take her off your hands for £999,999. The evidence for that purchaser's belief would be your purchase of Miss Imp for the million pounds: the purchaser would think he could sell her on for £999,998. After all, there is negligible difference between one million pounds and £999,998. Interestingly, what someone considers rational – and what may end up being rational – can be partially determined by what others consider rational. Of course, as we anticipate the trading of Miss Imp for diminishing sums, we become less and less certain whether there would be 'rational' purchasers.

With the Imp, if you are to be a purchaser, you need other people to follow suit. In other cases, you may desire just the opposite. For example, in order to become a priest at the ancient shrine of Nemi, you needed to slay your predecessor. Were you to judge it rational to accede to the priesthood, then, if others sought to follow your example, you would risk meeting with a sticky end.

The Imp makes us wonder how much of the future should influence our actions today. People save up for holidays, and if they saved for another year, they may afford better holidays. Suppose you have a bottle of wine that improves with age: why not wait for another year – and another, and another – before drinking the wine? Of course, we may spot varying degrees of uncertainty, such as risk of bottle breakage; but is such future uncertainty the sole factor that should account for how far we peer?

If you drink the wine after five years, you may regret not waiting until year six, when it would have tasted better. Were the wine to improve indefinitely and were you immortal, you would never drink the wine. Well, you would never drink the wine, if it is irrational to do something that you know you will later regret – and you would regret the wine drinking, if you judge that you should maximize satisfactions. It is, though, that judgement which is mistaken.

Here is a mundane example. People know that faster and cheaper computers become available. If that dominates their thinking, they defer buying a computer – for ever. They are always aware that there will be better deals next year. Searching for the ideal – be it a computer, the best wine, or the finest lover – leads not merely to finding no ideal, but also to lost opportunities of enjoying the pretty good. The tension is, summarily put, between 'good' now and 'better' then. Here is another example: the puzzle of a charitable trust.

Consider a sum of money, say £500, that you could donate to a worthwhile charity right now, saving some people from starvation. That would be good – but maybe deferring the gift would be better. Maybe the returns on the money, if invested within a charitable trust, together with likely reductions in costs for nutrition packages, would lead to that money, if donated in the distant future, saving many more lives. If more lives would be saved in that way, ought you not to let people starve now for the greater future good of others? But that 'future' would never come, for the argument, in principle, could be applied again and again;

the money, though investment returns, could continue to accumulate within the trust.

The examples show that it is often irrational to seek to maximize satisfactions, whatever economists may say. Rationality typically requires us to settle for what is good enough – for 'satisficing'. Regarding ourselves, satisficing may be viewed as manifesting the virtue of moderation over greed. Regarding aid for others, it manifests the virtue of being moved by distressed people *now*, more so than unknown future people.

The distant future weighs heavily for some. Ozone-layer depletion, pollution, nuclear waste: people increasingly worry about future generations. Yet that worry can risk diverting resources and attention – based on changeable projections of benefits to future generations – away from real people suffering right now. Further, the concern for benefiting future generations encourages changes in current social policies. Such changes almost certainly mean that individuals born in the future will differ from those who would otherwise have been born. Paradoxically, future individuals have been helped by producing different future individuals – hardly a benefit for those who, as a result, will not exist. That musing also occurs when facing quandaries of deciding whether and when to become pregnant (please see Chapter 83).

♈

Making sacrifices now for distant future and uncertain benefits, be they for ourselves or for later generations, can be irrational. It is a matter of degree; but as John Maynard Keynes famously quipped, 'In the long run, we're dead.' True, Keynes had no eternal damnation lined up, courtesy of Miss Imp, to build into his calculations. His quip reminds us, though, that we are finite human beings, without perfect foresight, without perfect rationality.

Finite as we are, settling for what comes along that is satisfactory is often more rational than deferring until something better comes along later. And waiting for the best can mean waiting for – well, nothing at all.

76

GOING FOR COVER:
ARMS DEALING TO CASTING COUCHES

'Naturally, we have the highest professional standards,' smiled the woman in glasses so dark.

'Of course,' slurred Dan lazily, 'But why are you wining and dining me? Is there a big TV series you're wanting me to front?'

'Media exposure,' said the woman, 'could be a consequence, so easily a consequence, depending on your decision this evening.'

Dan missed the import of those words: he always became distracted when a little tipsy, with nubile waitresses surrounding him.

'Yes, we're aware of your interest in North Korea – and in "helping" pretty girls into the industry. You're an intriguing man, Dan. Our researchers are fascinated with every aspect of your life.'

Dan felt a chill of sobriety. He now paid attention, his cheeks battling between fear-filled whiteness and embarrassed redness.

'But, but... but... now listen here... '

'Don't worry. You did nothing wrong with those armament contracts – and your private investments and little peccadilloes are no one else's business. Is that what you were going to say? I cannot agree more. That's why I invited you along.'

Dan nodded, but sensed relief would be premature.

'Rest assured, Dan, my company is on your side. But some others are not. Newspapers – scurrilous rags – are already offering our company large sums for guidance concerning your life. Politically, you're an important beast. Now, if you would see your way to making us a donation – it would need to be pretty large – we'd ensure the media researchers turn nothing up. We'll give them different prey to chase.'

'And if I cannot afford to make this, er... er... donation?'

'Well then, the researchers will just have to do what they have to do. They're just doing their job.'

'But this is blackmail,' Dan exploded.

'Now, now, Dan. Watch your language. See this as a staggering opportunity. And we're hoping society will soon become so enlightened that we can incorporate ourselves as Blackmail plc, our motto being: *we cover your uncover*. Whatever we uncover about lives, we keep them covered from the eyes of others – given suitable donations. A valuable service, I'm sure you agree.'

What's wrong with blackmail?

Blackmail is illegal; it is immoral. So it is said. Why? Blackmailers offer clients – 'Not victims' insists the would-be Blackmail plc – opportunities otherwise lacking. If Blackmail plc just spilled the beans, the black-mailed would indeed be victims; but Blackmail plc provides a valuable choice – between publicity and no publicity. True, there are monetary costs involved with the non-publicity route; but individuals are free to take the public exposure route, making no donations. Many, though, would prefer making donations, with no exposure.

Let us concentrate on the morality. The two elements to the black-mailer's offer are individually permissible. There is nothing wrong about exposing the truth. There is nothing wrong in asking for donations for one's own benefit. So, it may be argued, having the choice between two moral options must also be moral.

We can swiftly reject that argument. Driving a car is morally per-missible, but not if the context includes drinking. Kissing can be highly desirable, but not so desirable if one party has eaten garlic. Laughing is surely innocent enough, but not so innocent at a funeral. The drinking, garlic and funeral attendance are themselves acceptable, but not when combined with driving, kissing and laughing. The combinations lack the acceptability of the parts in isolation – and we can easily explain why. Drink driving is dangerous; one-sided garlic kissing challenges the other's senses; and funeral laughs offend the bereaved.

What is it about the permissible elements in blackmail that make blackmail morally impermissible? One answer is that failure to comply to the blackmailer's request means that the blackmailed are harmed by unwanted exposure. Further, compliance with the request means that they are harmed by financial loss. There are, though, numerous – all seemingly morally permissible – instances of combinations with such features. 'If you keep on drinking, I'll divorce you.' 'If we don't get bonus payments, we'll resign and work abroad.' 'If taxes increase, we'll incorporate our business offshore.' True, the latter two examples in recent years have received public distaste with regard to bankers, but the ethos of capitalist society is to encourage efficient economic compe-tition, including minimizing tax liabilities where legal. Recent results, though, certainly in Britain and the US include ever-growing wealth inequalities with little 'trickle down', if any, to the poor.

To sort out the blackmail puzzle, we must resist accepting so readily that the components of blackmail are individually morally permissi-ble. Let us take two extreme cases, relating them to Dan, our black-mailed man.

Here is one extreme. Dan has been involved in some shady arms dealings that merit public exposure. Such exposure would focus the authorities on legal loopholes that need closing. Perhaps Dan's activities have, indeed, been criminal. In such cases, blackmail is wrong because the blackmailer is offering to connive with Dan in a cover-up. The blackmailer ought to be exposing the activities rather than trying to benefit financially by keeping them under wraps. Dan may pay to preserve the cover-up of his activities; but, whether he does so or not, he deserves to be exposed.

Here is a case at the other extreme. Dan has not been engaged in anything that merits public interest. He has been indulging in some private sexual peccadilloes that would embarrass him, if made public – but peccadilloes that harm no one. In this case, the blackmailer is trying to make money out of doing something that is wrong – namely, the public humiliation of Dan. Dan may, of course, pay up to avoid the embarrassment; but, whether he does so or not, he does not deserve exposure.

In these two cases the blackmailer is intent on doing something wrong, either by way of covering up what ought to be uncovered or by threatening to expose what merits no exposure. And that is what is wrong with blackmail in less extreme cases – ones, though, that may be difficult to assess regarding the right thing to do. For example, third parties may discover that some church members use prostitutes and that political leaders who condemn the use of drugs indulge themselves. Sometimes it may be right to expose such matters; sometimes not. The motivation to expose, or not, should not depend on the exposers' potential financial benefit. The motivation should be that of doing the right thing.

♈

Casting couches have, so the tales go, been scenes of wrong motivations. Film directors should cast actresses according to their suitability for roles to be played, not their suitability as sexual partners for directors (unless, arguably, auditioning for that sort of film). Appointment boards should appoint according to candidates' job suitability, not their 'old school tie'.

What of the cases cited earlier that appear similar to blackmail – the investment managers who threaten to resign, if no bonuses are paid; the directors, who apparently will leave the country, unless tax rates fall; and the wife who speaks of divorce, if her husband continues his alcoholic ways? Grey areas arise: sometimes we treat them as blackmail or, at least, effectively blackmail; sometimes as permissible. Certain investment managers may contribute to a nation's wealth, at least to some degree; directors are meant to run companies tax-efficiently; and people can find married life soul-destroying if spouses are drunkards. Of course, other factors come into play: the managers' demands may be exorbitant – akin to blackmail – and directors are failing to show loyalty to their community that has afforded them many benefits. Spouses may be lacking appropriate sympathy during days so dark in marriage.

What is valuable about blackmail, as a puzzle, is that it reminds us that we should do things for right reasons; and those right reasons do not usually involve threats made purely for selfish monetary gain. Of course, that leaves us with the riddle of determining quite what are our real reasons, our true motivations, and what makes them right – or wrong. Once again, we may often find greyness, rather than the clear-cut black or white.

77

'MY BELOVED IS MINE' *or* 'THE TROUBLE WITH FOOTBALL IS THE OTHER TEAM'

Lovers are likened to the mad, the mad with seething brains – and not merely because lovers kiss, bite and whisper intimate childish names. What lovers see in their beloved, the world often sees not at all. And therein lies madness.

Lily finds her man, Lenny, exciting and handsome, everything for which she longed. In Lily's eyes, Lenny lives on the edge, has unusual thoughts – and, as for his ravishing smile, well… The world, though, sees Lenny as no good, a layabout, a little lopsided in the lips department. Ottone gazes at Poppea: she is charming, beautiful, coquettish, yet bountiful. The world spots Poppea as manipulative, scheming and a bit overweight.

Lovers do not see what the world sees. 'Love looks not with the eyes, but with the mind.' Cupid is pictured blind, blind to rules and restraint. Of course, in quick response, we may reflect that love can reveal more than the world first sees: the love of a good woman, or man, may work wonders on those so beloved.

Lovers, of course, often lust for each other. There is the urge to kiss, embrace and much more; and, as the above portrays, lovers possess tendencies to project perfections. They may place each other on pedestals which, as the quip goes, have little scope for manoeuvre and considerable scope for falls. Imperfections may receive positive renderings. Lenny's lopsided smile is distinctively sweet to Lily; and Poppea's slight weight problem is, for Ottone, an abundance to love. When things go well, misperceptions and renderings are mutually for the better.

Why does Ottone not spot Poppea's scheming nature? 'Ah, that's because he's in love.' The love is offered as explanation of Ottone's over – or under – sight; it explains why he finds the weight appealing. Yet, why does Ottone love Poppea? 'Ah, that is because he sees her as such a beautiful, bountiful woman.' This two-way explanation is no true explanation at all, for it loops round: the positive rendering is explained by the love; yet the love is explained by the positive rendering.

Explaining lovers' perceptions forms one puzzle. Maybe the solution needs recognition of the role of time: love develops. A particular feature of Poppea sparks desire in Ottone and, if things go well, other features come to the fore, seen in the light of developing desire. Things spiral and grow – and features become embellished and enhanced, intensifying the flushes and fervour. Desires fan out, turning to a more embracing love. Whatever best explains the spiral and other changes, another puzzle remains: what is it that lovers yearn and lust after, when they speak of wanting each other?

What do lovers desire?

What brings desires to an end may not be what is desired. You may desire a holiday, yet the desire is quelled by an emergency intervening, the holiday forgotten. You yearn for another drink, but the sight of a drunk brings a halt to that yearning: you no longer feel like a drink at all. The emergency and the sight of the drunk brought the desires to an end, but the emergency and the sight were not the objects of those desires.

Consider two lovers lusting after each other. People tend to believe that, because orgasm typically brings an end to immediate lusts, it is the orgasmic end that the lovers really desire. Yet, with the holiday and drink examples in mind, that may be a mistaken belief.

When the lusting is also a loving, what, indeed, is desired? Lovers, metaphorically, devour each other with their eyes, wanting to possess each other – but what is going on?

There may be no simple answer. Certainly, lovers take pleasure in each other, in each other's body, thought and personality; but pleasurable sensations are not the sole end. Were pleasurable sensations all that mattered, a sensation-generating machine would do just as well; but few people love and lust after machines – and machines lust not at all.

Lovers, as with friends, may value simply walking quietly through a glade, hand in hand, eating together and sharing music. They are doing something together, but not merely in that they are each taking part in the same activity. Rather, there is a 'we'; *we* are walking along the seashore. *We* are at a party – even though in different corners of the room. Two people may play chess together, yet not in the loving sense just proffered – for the players may be held together solely by the chess. Two (or more) lovers or friends, though, may play and delight – just as they may dance and sing – as one. And, when it is love and not mere friendship, the 'we' involves, of course, intimacies of body.

Pleasures in love – and friendships – also require reciprocation. Lenny's pleasure in Lily typically heightens Lily's pleasure in Lenny which heightens Lenny's pleasure – and so on. However far we may spiral – presumably the limit falls well below 'the sky's the limit' – its familiarity reminds us that love is between people, people who can delight in the other's delight. That is one reason why the lonely night-time cuddles of the pillow fail to transform that pillow into a substitute lover.

Love typically involves at least *two* people, not one – yet that too creates puzzle. Lovers want more than pillows, yet when lovers speak of 'we', they endanger the individual, the individual being swallowed. We sometimes hear cries, 'Give me space; let me be *me*.' The stronger may devour or overwhelm the weaker, the cries silenced, yet the stronger, the dominant, is now alone, unloved and unloving. How much more so would our human selves be lost, were we to engage in the ecstatic love of a being as dominant as God – for that is an unequal relationship indeed. That relationship would certainly endanger our individuality. Maybe that is why certain religious believers and mystics, when anticipating eternal survival through God, do not look forward to a personal survival at all. They will be lost in the One.

♈

Images of love often display the body as territory. John Donne writes:

Licence my roving hands, and let them go,
Before, behind, between, above, below.
O my America! My new-found-land…

Jean-Paul Sartre – recall the 'self' and our contrary Mary (Chapter 54) – goes pessimistically and metaphysically further. Sexual desire is intrinsically unstable and, in some way, contradictory. In desiring the other, we seek to turn that person into a thing, into flesh, while still wanting that other to be a free agent, loving us.

'I want all of you' we, as lovers, might say; but how can we possess the person, the beloved, with his or her subjective gaze upon the world? Sartre hence quips, 'The trouble with football is the other team.' Yet, with a paradoxical 'of course', the other team is essential to the game and to love.

Plato offers a different picture, a picture of lovers seeking their other halves, perhaps resulting in a mutual unified transformation, the original whole found, with both individuals then lost within that whole.

And so it is that different approaches to love paint love as, in one way or another, endangering individuality – either through conquering the other or losing the self.

Images of love also involve mysterious flights. 'My beloved is mine, and I am his: he feedeth among the lilies,' sings the *Song of Solomon*. 'Behold, thou art fair, my love; behold, thou art fair; thou hast doves' eyes within thy locks: thy hair is as a flock of goats that appear from Mount Gilead.'

Love puzzles – and not only when referenced by a goat-like beauty. With a Sartrean sense, well before Sartre, John Dryden speaks of lovers:

They gripe, they squeeze, their humid tongues they dart,
As each would force their way to t'other's heart,
In vain; they only cruise about the coast,
For bodies cannot pierce, nor be in bodies lost,
As sure they strive to be…

Love puzzles, yet matters to us all. That it matters creates more puzzlement. When in love, love has huge significance, even though we may be able to step back and recognize its absurdity.

Our lives' absurdities, their incongruities, are readily revealed – and not solely because of love – once we detach ourselves from the human immediacy and adopt, so to speak, the viewpoint of the universe. That viewpoint is something that other creatures lack. Pigs, pigeons and partridges, being unable to step outside their lives, are immune from absurdities. (In Chapter 91, we meet Pushkin, McTaggart's cat, displaying that immunity.) By contrast, human beings are aware of conflicting perspectives. From within your life, think of the misery that arises if you develop a cold just before a romantic date or, when dining out, the embarrassment when you notice the stains on your dress. Yet, you can step back: then, you assess such troubles as utterly insignificant 'in the great scheme of things'. There lies absurdity, the conflict between perspectives. Which matters matter?

The absurdity, the incongruity, between what matters to us and what 'really' matters is all the greater where love and sex, jealousy and fidelity, come to the fore. There, our reactions can be tumultuous and so disproportionate. Reflect on the deep engulfing despair, the 'black dog' days, when your loved one is seen with another; reflect on the overwhelming delight when that 'unobtainable' delectable other, the one you have viewed from afar for weeks, yields to your advances. With that latter absurdity in mind, although we are probably unaware of Lord Chesterfield's name, his famous quip may yet spring to the fore.

'In the act of love, the pleasure is momentary, the position ridiculous and the expense damnable.'

78
WILL YOU STILL LOVE ME TOMORROW?

And so the two swore that at every time of their lives,
until death took them, they would assuredly believe,
feel and desire exactly as they had believed, felt and
desired during the preceding weeks. What was as
remarkable as the undertaking itself was the fact that
nobody seemed at all surprised at what they swore.
Thomas Hardy, *Jude the Obscure*, 1895

There is something deeply puzzling about the commitments that we make, into the distant future, when we know that things will change.

Lovers, when in love, soar into sapphire skies, flying on wild and wonderful wholehearted words of sincere commitment and devotion. 'We are meant for each other.' 'I cannot live without you.' 'Our love will never die.' Literally understood, these are false, yet lovers serve them to each other, intent on conveying truths and, when seeking mutual assurances, they also play some startling questions: 'Will you love me, when I'm old and grey?' 'Do you want me just for my money?' 'Just because I'm sexy?' 'Would you love me were I paralysed, my mind gone, my character changed?'

Those questions lead to a desperate plea. 'I want you to love me solely for myself, for being me, not for anything else, just for my true essence.' This is perilous metaphysics; the peril is shown in Chapter 56's Isaac Newton tale. What sense can we make of the *me*, the *self*, *my essence*, if it is meant still to exist, even when all other features of mine have changed?

What is it that we love, when we love someone?

Consider how we relate to items in the world. We want a drink but not just any drink will do. We definitely want a whisky – and whisky of a certain type, say, Talisker. At some stage, specifications cease. It matters not at all whether it is that or this particular glass of whisky – so long as the glass contains Talisker. This particular drink could be replaced by another; so long as it is of the same desired type, that is fine. Things are typically different with people with whom we have a special relationship. You want to see your child, not just any child who resembles yours. Your child, in this sense, is irreplaceable and cannot be duplicated – unlike the whisky.

The replaceable–irreplaceable distinction does not coincide with the object–person distinction. On the one hand, some objects are irreplaceable. You are searching for your father's particular watch, not just any resembling watch. You want to own the original score or painting, not a forgery, even if you cannot tell the difference. On the other hand, some people are replaceable. You just need a milkman to deliver the milk, not any milkman in particular – unless the milkman is your lover. Lovers usually fit on the irreplaceable side of the divide. It is Winthrop that you love. If he has an identical twin, it is still for Winthrop that you yearn. When Winthrop is absent, you do not usually make do with the twin. Mind you, you may just want a man – or a woman. Then anyone, of the right looks, charm, stamina or whatever, will do.

	REPLACEABLE	NON-REPLACEABLE
Physical objects	A whisky A lemon	The original score The watch he gave
Persons	A milkman A man? A woman?	Winthrop Melissa

Irreplaceability highlights the importance of how certain relation-ships develop. The lovers first met under the drinks' table at the birthday party and, from then on, their lives intertwined. The particular causal history of their relationship cannot be duplicated.

None of this gives any sense to there being a 'self' or 'essence' that lovers love, independently of the beloved's characteristics. At best, it suggests a wild optimism that the intertwining of the lovers' lives ensures that the changes in the lovers' characteristics will match, going hand in happy hand. Perhaps there is a suspension of belief about the contingencies and flux of the world, about the reductions in sexual desire for the familiar and about the differences between the sexes' emo-tional developments. We seek to live within a fictional world in which, to use a picture offered by Plato (mentioned in the previous chapter), lovers are those who have been reunited after an earlier division. It is when things go wrong that we may warm to a quip such as 'Marriage is not a word but a sentence.'

♈

When we attend a play, we can lose ourselves within the action. Despite awareness of the theatrical surroundings, we cannot help being moved by the characters on stage. 'Fictional Feelings' (Chapter 86) explores the philosophical perplexities that arise as a consequence. My suggestion is that such fictionalism spills over those in love, generating an erotic fictionalism. When in love, we often cannot help feeling, and believing in, the eternity of that love, despite knowing that, transient and fickle creatures that we are, things may be so very, very different later on; even as early on as the following morning.

Mind you, I am but a male – and where human emotions are involved that can be to the point. That an argument is valid, that the Earth orbits the Sun, that it is morally wrong to torture a child – those do not rest on whether women or men are involved and judging. By contrast, our under-standing of love, of sexual desire, of ways to flourish, cannot sensibly be assumed to be the same for men and women. Women and men differ, obviously differ, in many ways; and, as has been said, *Vive la différence*.

79

A WHOLE CLOUD OF PHILOSOPHY –
FROM *COGITO ERGO SUM* TO A DROP OF GRAMMAR

Philosophers have been known to say crazy things; and the following remark, at least in part, if not in whole, strikes many – philosophers and non-philosophers alike – as crazy.

> I can know what someone else is thinking, not what I am thinking. It is correct to say 'I know what you are thinking,' and wrong to say 'I know what I am thinking.'

Our Prologue gave a little background to the philosophical genius behind the remark, the genius being Ludwig Wittgenstein. Why would he say something that appears so manifestly false? Surely, one thing that I can know is what I am thinking and that I am thinking; and while we often act as if we know what others are thinking, can we ever really and truly know? Can we even know that others are thinking? Let 'thinking' be taken here to guide us to all conscious experiences: sensations, hopes and fears, as well as thoughts. After all, we cannot step into another's mind. 'Other minds', for all I know with certainty, may not exist.

Descartes, as we saw in Chapter 47 with the dreaming puzzle, gave voice to the sceptical position, of doubting whether he knew anything other than his own existence and experiences – until he proved (or so he thought) God's existence, from which he argued that the external world and other people do exist: God would not deceive him into thinking such, if there were no possibility of correction. Until he is satisfied of the divine existence, he is a 'solipsist' – thinking that only he and his experiences exist.

Even today in common sense moods, when we are certain of physical objects, of butter and brains, of mountains and monsoons, we may yet wonder about the existence of other conscious beings. We only ever witness the behaviour of others, never others' experiences. In writing this, I am, of course, assuming that I address other conscious beings: well, maybe – just possibly – a few people are reading these words.

Bertrand Russell's works once suggested to readers that he believed solipsism was true. An American lady wrote to him, saying how pleased she was to learn that he was a solipsist, and how 'I am one too.' If that causes a teeny smile, then we know what solipsism is. Of course, whether the American lady was foolish or satirical – well, that we do not know.

We confront a puzzling conflict, then, between a Cartesian inspired position and Wittgenstein's.

Can I know what I am thinking?
Can I know what someone else is thinking?

Let us approach the first question, thinking in terms of any conscious experiences. Descartes' line is thus: I may be mistaken whether my leg is injured, whether figs, farms and fishes exist – they could be figments of my imagination – but none the less I know that it at least seems to me *as if* my leg is injured, as if there are figs, farms and fishes. Over that, I cannot be mistaken.

Wittgenstein's response is that we can have knowledge only where doubt is a possibility. When I am in pain, I cannot start wondering whether I am making a mistake. So, argues Wittgenstein, I cannot know that I am in pain – though I may utter the words as a joke (so much, you may surmise, for philosophers' humour) or as emphasis that I am in pain when others doubt me. Nothing more is being said about my relationship to the pain, when 'I know' has been added to 'I am in pain.' Both claims, that I know I am in pain and that I do not know I am in pain – if 'I know' is used in its normal sense – are nonsense. Analogously, it is nonsense to claim that virtue is yellow; it is nonsense to claim that virtue is not yellow – unless the latter makes the point that virtue is not the sort of entity that can be coloured.

When we rightfully talk of people knowing or not knowing things, in the normal sense of 'knowing', it makes sense to talk about their evidence, about what they have seen or heard – and whether they are certain or guessing or pretending. But I do not have evidence for my being in pain – or evidence for my *thinking* about the weather. I may well guess about the weather, but not about what I am now thinking. I may wonder whether my leg is broken, but not whether it is painful.

Of course, 'know' can be used in other senses; but then we need to make those senses clear. When people say with a sigh, 'War is war', they are not making the logical point that war is identical with war. They are expressing a certain feeling of inevitability or hopelessness about war's nastiness.

Perhaps use of 'I know', when in expressions such as 'I know what I am thinking' or 'I know that it hurts', emphasizes my special authority concerning certain of my psychological states. Let us call that the 'privileged' use, contrasting with the normal or 'evidential' use. Wittgenstein and Descartes can now agree that we know, in the privileged use, that we are thinking, that we are in pain – and so forth. The dispute over that question has evaporated. Descartes may, though, have mistakenly thought that he knew, in the evidential sense, about his current pain.

~~~

What, though, of the other question? Can I know what someone else is thinking? The sceptical line is that I cannot – but, once again, we need clarity about the use of 'know'. The evidential use of 'know' requires the possibility of doubt, so my knowledge of other people's thinking and of what they are thinking is at least on the cards. Paradoxically, this is so simply because we *can* be mistaken over such matters. That, of course, does not establish that we ever do know evidentially what someone else is thinking, what they are imagining and whether they are in pain.

Certainly we cannot know, in the privileged sense, what others are thinking: that is a point of logic. It comes down to the fact that I, of course, am not in pain in virtue of your being in pain. Your thinking about Wittgenstein does not thereby mean that I am thinking about Wittgenstein, with the numerically same thought. But that ought not to lead us to conclude that I cannot know, evidentially, what you are thinking, or that I cannot know, evidentially, whether you are in pain. A person may open her heart to you – so to speak – and you know only too well what she is thinking, what distress she is undergoing and what her pleasures are. Obviously her thinking is not literally your thinking; her distress is not yours; her pleasures are not yours – though you may be having similar thoughts and, in a sense, be feeling her distress and pleasures.

'Yet my knowledge of her thoughts and feelings are indirect' may come the response. But what would it be to have 'direct' knowledge of her thoughts and feelings? In the evidential sense of 'know', there is no sense in my even having direct knowledge of my own thoughts and feelings. In the privileged sense of 'know', well, that would be for me to be her, expressing her thoughts and feelings – which is impossible.

♈

These points of Wittgenstein were summarized by him, condensed indeed, as 'a whole cloud of philosophy condensed into a drop of grammar', and by 'grammar' here is meant 'logic'. Yet this may leave us dissatisfied. Even though it is logically impossible for me to be experiencing your thoughts and feelings – the one and same identical thoughts and feelings – I may suffer that impossibility as something missing: 'if only I could get into your mind.'

To feel distress – at a loss – because I cannot be in the privileged position over your thoughts and feelings as I am over mine is to want something as nonsensical as wanting a triangle to have four sides – or as impossible as my experiencing a tingle of delight while being unsure if it is I who tingles. 'If only we could quell our yearnings for what is impossible.' Yet perhaps that expresses just such a yearning.

80
WOLVES, WHISTLES AND WOMEN

Butchers, bakers and candlestick makers – or, for that matter, dealers, directors and taxi-cab drivers – do not, typically, rail at being used as (if I may introduce the term) 'job objects'. Yet some women, especially those bedecked in feminist clothing, rail and rage against being treated as *sex* objects. They argue that men frequently (if not always) regard them thus, at work, in the street and even in bed. Men are wolves, ever ready to pounce on women as meat to be violated and devoured. Indeed, where sexual relations are concerned it seems that woman is but:

> An object of appetite; as soon as that appetite has been stilled, she is cast aside as one casts away a lemon which has been sucked dry... all motives of moral relationship cease to function, because as an object of appetite she becomes a thing and can be treated as such by everyone.

Curiously, this quotation derives – admittedly with some modifications – not from an obvious extreme feminist but from the great Immanuel Kant, whom we first encountered as far back as Chapter 1, he who insisted that we ought not to use people just for our own ends. I have modified his comment as if it were directed only towards the sexual treatment of women, but Kant did not discriminate: to him, both men and women are treated as objects in the sexual relation. We use each other solely as means to our ends; when the ends are just sexual pleasures, we degrade each other into mere instruments.

Human love – goodwill, affection and concern for the other's happiness – comes to the rescue. When sexual love is combined with human love, within heterosexual marriage, things are better. The marriage contract gives the contracting partners equal rights to the life-long reciprocal use of the other's sexual organs and capacities. Yes, it has, unfortunately, to be admitted that the sexually abstemious Kant writes in unromantic terms, as if sexual desire is solely for the use of our and the other's genitals – contrast Sartre's subtle line (page 363).

It is not just bedtime that troubles some women (and, of course, men). In the street, at work or at play, some women feel they are assessed primarily as sex objects rather than people. It has been said that women live in sexual objectification the way in which fish live in water. Yet, even if sexual objectification is not so pervasive, some women are still distressed when it is present. The distress is rather puzzling: we frequently use people, yet they do not thereby see themselves as misused or taken as objects; they may welcome the use. Further, where sex is concerned, many women and men value accolades based on their sexual attractiveness.

What *is* all the fuss about being treated as sex objects?

Being a sex object is usually written about in terms of women as the objects of men's desires. Mistreatment is likely also to arise in homosexual and other relationships but – for simplicity – let us stay with heterosexuals. There is the basic, empirical, question of whether women typically are treated as sex objects. Various features cluster round 'sex object'. It sometimes involves being treated merely as a tool for others' use or pleasure. Sometimes there is the idea that the woman's experiences and free choices matter not at all; sometimes that she is treated as if lacking free will, rationality and interests; sometimes that it is acceptable for her to be violated. Sometimes there is stress on her being replaceable – that anyone with her sexual characteristics would do. This clustering makes it difficult to give simple answers to the question above. Let us consider some comparisons.

Male builders wolf-whistle at an attractive woman walking by, purely on the basis of her sexual allure. She is not treated as a person but as sexual flesh on legs, replaceable by any other piece of like or better quality. This example (frequently given) may also be taken as insensitively identifying some people as job objects; builders are, in part, employed on the basis of their physical characteristics – they are replaceable and often replaced. Taxi-drivers are whistled at for their taxi-driving and, if the first cab is taken, the second will do. These are, however, poor analogies: being a woman is not an occupation and walking by is not usually indicative of an occupational role. Further, builders and taxi-drivers are not being regarded merely as means, but also as ends. They are seen as people who have voluntarily taken up their occupation (how voluntarily is a matter for another discussion); in using them we are promoting their own perceived interests.

Caveats and responses are required. Typically we do – and should – treat taxi-drivers as people and not as added pieces of taxi-machinery, but we initially select them on their physical proximity (charges or driving skills). We choose builders because of their muscles and abilities as builders, but do not thereby treat them as objects. When a woman is whistled at because of her curves, it does not follow that, in any resulting relationship, she would be treated purely as a thing curved. Even women have been known to fall in love at first sight; yet we should not conclude that they would treat the men sighted as nothing but objects that manifest whichever features proved so visually desirable. Identifying people by their bodies, being attracted by their physical features, employing them for their muscular prowess or consulting them for their reasoning powers, should not lead us to think that therefore we are bound to deal with them as nothing more than bodies, sets of physical characteristics, brawny muscles or reasoners.

The 'sex object' complaint is *sometimes* well justified. Consider cases when a woman's sexual desirability forms the basis for job promotion judgements that should be made on other grounds. Consider cases when women, hurrying to work, are badgered because of their sexual desirability. Consider cases when oppressive male gazes make women feel vulnerable.

Even here, caveats need to be entered. No one seriously thinks that the way many men and women dress has nothing to do with displaying sexual attractiveness or improving the prospects of promotion. No one seriously thinks that, in social situations – be they work, be they play – many women and men do not enjoy being found desirable. It can be fun (so I hear). The problem is assessing when flirtations, invitations and innuendoes are appropriate. Some women are pleased to receive whistles – as are some men.

♈

What should we make of the 'sex object' complaint, related to the throes of sexual passion?

Sexual relations are often mundane, yet often they involve a medley of activities. Typically, neither men nor women seek inactive *objects* as sexual partners. During sex, if things go well, we are made highly aware of our embodied state, through our and our partner's arousal, which may then heighten further mutual arousals: a kaleidoscope of experiences. That leads some to stress a mysterious interplay between being aware of ourselves and our partners as conscious experiencing subjects, while trying to make each other nothing but flesh. Some feminist writers, though, see an essential asymmetry: men are bound to dominate; penetration is akin to a violence, a brutality, an occupation to which women surrender. Indeed, it can be; but we could equally use metaphors of men being enveloped, smothered, devoured, losing themselves and succumbing. Certain feminist writers seem unaware of the consent that usually occurs between sexual partners, including consent to sado-masochistic activity. They also sometimes appear oblivious to the distinction that usually exists between the sexual activities of female prostitutes and their male clients and those of couples engaged in mutual arousal, without coercion and without any hidden agenda.

With increasing interest in the fetish scene and sado-masochistic sex, perhaps we should resist the generalized, woolly and misleading talk of sex objects – talk which perpetuates notions of woman as victim. Perhaps we should pay more attention to the good old Liberty Principle of John Stuart Mill (presented in Chapter 9), in which whatever people get up to among themselves, including sex, should be permitted so long as it is consensual and directly harms no one else without his or her consent.

Having said that, there are legitimate and far more general worries of the extent to which our values, desires and choices – our lives – are determined by the surrounding ethos. Just as there have been times when men and woman have fallen into unquestioned acceptance of, for example, the Bible and the Victorian idea of 'knowing one's place and its duties', so, there have been times when women have thought themselves as 'freely' accepting the sexual requests of their husbands or 'freely' dressing in the burqa (or fashion's latest scanty clothing) – yet, in retrospect, have felt that they were manipulated and not acting freely at all. Similar questions arise with feminist movements, as seen in Chapter 18: some women may look back and wonder why they bought into the denigration of, for example, being content to bring up children and not worrying about the effects on career and independence.

It is impossible to step completely outside of all values and then judge which ones to embrace; on what basis would we judge? We need to assess matters case by case, accepting that we must hold firm to some values in order to assess others. In the context of rejecting Descartes' quest for truth via systematic doubt, Otto Neurath, a leading figure of the Vienna Circle, the early twentieth-century 'logical positivist' move-ment, observed that we cannot attempt to jettison all former beliefs and start afresh; rather, it is as if we are on a leaking ship in the ocean. In that oceanic plight, it would be crazy to dismantle the ship in the hope of rebuilding from scratch; we have to do what we can to stop the leak with the resources available, still relying on the ship to keep us afloat. Later, we may turn to other parts of the ship to improve.

Returning, in particular, to sexual relations, women and men, in var-ious numbers and packages, consent, it seems, to all manner of things. Yes, we may question whether the consent is genuinely free or more a product of an oppressive ethos; but we need to be sensitive to how our own valuations may affect what we see. And before feminists challenge the authenticity of certain women's consent and endeavour to change and 'repair' those women's lives, it is worth commenting that it is no more likely to be right that, when women say 'yes', they do not mean yes than it is that, when women say 'no', they do not really mean no.

81
ADDICTED TO LOVE

Allow me to introduce you to two friends, Leilah and Luis.

> Leilah and Luis are like two lovebirds; they are inseparable. Where one goes, the other follows. We knew it would develop that way, for when Leilah first saw Luis – he had flown in from Peru – she could not keep her eyes off him, understandably as he stood tall, proud and handsome. Luis reciprocated her gaze, also understandably, for Leilah is a beauty, with graceful neck, large sparkling eyes and cute curves to the ears. It was love at first sight; and the love persists. Even all these years later, Luis still nibbles at those curvaceous ears; and Leilah walks alongside Luis, seemingly admiring his proud gait, doe-eyed with love. Luis' male friends go cavorting with any Pam, Lynne or Harriet, but Luis remains happily faithful to his Leilah.

Love can have that effect, for better or worse, and, allowing for some literary embellishment, our sketch could apply, in principle, to couples we know. People fall in love – both at first and later sights – and remain in love, though the love may develop in various directions. The puzzle being raised here is whether the sketch above could be truly descriptive of Leilah and Luis, when Leilah and Luis are llamas – or, for that matter, any similar creatures, be they alpacas, leopards, zebras – or voles.

'Voles?' you ask. Voles enter the picture because prairie voles are highly monogamous in the sense of bonding together though not, apparently, sexually monogamous. Once two prairie voles have bonded, they huddle as one, protect each other and stay together, in contrast to the rampant promiscuity amongst meadow voles who lack any pair-bonding. Discovery of voles' lifestyles generated press reports of the eternal love

of prairie voles, so dissimilar from the meadow vole's drive for instant sex and 'I want space'.

In contrast to popularist reports, we need not bind 'falling in love' with everlasting bonding. Let us focus on what it is to be in love – and hence whether only human beings can be lovers. We restrict ourselves to romantic or erotic love; we are not engaging questions of parents' love for their children and campaigners' love for humanity.

Do llamas fall in love?

Now, it is possible for llamas, and other animals, to behave in ways that humans do when falling in love and staying in love. The 'possible' is a logical possibility: there certainly is nothing impossible in two llamas living together as described above, except for the question of whether it really is 'love'.

Looking at love biochemically, we may be tempted to see humans in love as merely more complicated instances of animals' pair-bonding. Scientists speak of vasopressin receptors and their neural location. Prairie voles, unlike meadow voles, have sufficient receptors relevantly located; so, a particular prairie partner is associated with reward, thus explaining the bonding with that partner. Prairie voles become addicted to – 'fall in love with' – their partners, and stay committed. If jack-the-lad meadow voles have their low-level vasopressin receptors increased, they too will pair-bond.

Romantic love has, indeed, been likened to addiction, an addiction grounded in biochemistry. You meet someone, like them enough to see them again; and, if things go well, you are soon craving their company. As with cocaine, take a little and you crave more. If the lover goes off with someone else, you suffer withdrawal symptoms.

If love is understood solely as such addictive behaviour – and if addictions are explained by biochemistry – then llamas can fall in love and remain in love. But to see love in biochemical terms may blind us to what love means for individuals. The brain's biochemical traits may help to explain how individuals come to love – as, in myth, do elixirs of love – but they do not thereby show what love is. Knowing that water is composed of hydrogen and oxygen fails to display the wetness of water, its thirst-quenching properties and how we may swim in oceans and be awed by thunderstorms.

Whether or not Luis loves Leilah, he certainly is intensely attached to her – and that can be true whether Luis and Leilah are llamas, human beings or prairie voles. Attachment, though, is insufficient to establish love. You may be highly attached to your car, your job and the whisky bottle – but usually it is, at best, only metaphorical to describe you as being in love with them. The attachment of love is intermingled with appraisals that the loved ones are highly valuable and merit concern for their sakes. You may value your car; but you cannot seriously do things to further the interests of the car from its point of view, for it has no point of view. You cannot act for its sake.

Now, a llama does possess a point of view. And we humans can value llamas and deliberately do things for their sake, furthering their interests. Luis Llama may behave in such a way that he furthers Leilah's interests. Perhaps he moves aside so that she has access to the better grass; perhaps he stands between her and an attacker. Do such actions, though, show that he values her and is acting 'for her sake'?

Llamas lack the language of evaluation; indeed, they seem to lack language altogether. Some, though, may argue that the relevant valuation and concern is sufficiently demonstrated by what the llamas do. If Luis acts as just described, that shows that he values Leilah. Yet even if that is so, we may feel his behaviour is insufficient to establish love. The behaviour does not show that Luis must therefore be acting *for* Leilah's sake – deliberately acting to benefit her.

Let us also reflect on some additional and associated features of love, features that may cast doubt on the status of the love between our two llamas.

Many lovers, for example, believe that the love enhances their lives. Of course, they may be mistaken: there are tragic loves. Typically, though, love blossoms when lovers see each other as valuing each other and their loving relationship, and act in the interests of each other. If genuinely in love, Luis values Leilah for her sake; and Luis' attachment is deepened if he then becomes aware that he is valued by Leilah. Luis' deepening love, when sensed by Leilah, deepens the mutual attachment further. Can our two llamas, though, value each other in those ways of mutual reflection?

The desire to be with the loved one, furthermore, is not without reason. Reasons can be given by lovers for why they love being with the beloved. They may be mistaken reasons; they may be very sketchy – but it is unlikely that lovers would hold fast to the claim that they love each other truly for no reason at all. Can our two llamas provide such reasons?

The puzzle about whether llamas and other non-human animals can fall and be in love, as has been seen, comes down to whether we can rightly ascribe to non-human animals a range of psychological features. The features include being aware of reasons for the attachment, valuing the beloved for their sake, possibly judging that life is enhanced by the love. It is far from plausible to believe that non-human animals possess the capacity, at an appropriate level, to evaluate, to act on reasons and to decide to act in the interests of others, or, indeed, to deceive the others. So, there is no good reason to think that llamas – or dolphins or voles – can fall in love, be in love and be lovers, once love is seen as requiring more psychological depth than mere attachment.

♈

We often project our psychology onto non-human animals – even onto the inanimate. We may imagine ourselves in the animal's place, describing the animal's psychology in terms that would correctly apply to us. Why we may think of this as mere projection or metaphor – the animals are not really in such states – is because the psychological states essentially involve beliefs. Now, beliefs require possession of concepts and concepts point to language possession; and, many argue, non-human animals lack appropriate language structures. Hence, they lack many complex psychological states including those necessary for love.

Llamas have pleasures, respond to scents and snuggle up against scent providers, but does this show that they possess beliefs about such matters? Well, perhaps many non-human animals can possess states akin to primitive belief, but it is difficult to see how, without language, non-human animals can possess concepts of reason, explanation and doing things for the sake of another. And without such concepts, Luis cannot be in love with Leilah. Love may be blind; but not that blind.

82
'HE WOULD SAY THAT... WOULDN'T HE?'

A politician, a government minister indeed, has been caught, literally and metaphorically, with his trousers down. Let's call him 'Sir Cedric'. Sir Cedric is fighting for his political career. Through the media, he abjectly apologizes:

> True, I've been unfaithful to my wife. I've lied and cheated to go off with a floosie or two – or three or more. All that, I now deeply, deeply regret. But, trust me, although I have deceived in matters of love, of romance and sex, I am utterly and completely honest in my political ways, in my sincerity in doing what is best for the country and, for that matter, in everything else. True, I cannot be trusted over affairs of the heart but I am a man of integrity when it comes to affairs of the state.

The matter is of public concern: if public representatives lie to their spouses, are they likely to lie to the electorate? Is it rational to believe Sir Cedric? He has owned up to lying sometimes, so he may be lying now. Perhaps he deceives people not only about affairs of the heart but also about affairs of state. Of course, he may be telling the truth: perhaps he is, as he says, a man of honour in his public service. He succumbs to deceit only when driven by passions of the flesh. Well, now we know that at least one thing has a higher priority for him than telling the truth (one that can interrupt his truth telling), so, maybe, there are other things. Sir Cedric's declaration is an instance of the announcement: 'I am prepared to mislead you over matters concerning such-and-such, but *only* over such matters, not over anything else.'

Although such a speaker may well be speaking the truth, do we have any good reason to believe him, now we know truth telling is not his highest priority in some announcements? If he is telling the truth about his deceit, clearly he lies on some occasions. If he is not speaking the truth, then he is lying right now. Either way, he undermines his commitment to truth telling. A politician intent on, for example, financial fraud as well as romantic fraud, but exposed only in the romantic, may well make the same claim as Sir Cedric makes.

In the 1963 trial of Stephen Ward concerning the Profumo sex scandal, Lord Astor denied that he had slept with Miss Mandy Rice-Davies. She was much reported as observing, 'He would say that, wouldn't he?' Paradoxically, when speakers (unlike Lord Astor) are open and tell the truth in specifying limitations on their truth telling, they also expose themselves to the Rice-Davies riposte.

Is it rational to trust people at all, if they tell us that in some matters they deceive?

I derive this little puzzle from Machiavelli. Machiavelli, in early sixteenth-century Florence, recommends that politicians should deceive the public when it helps to promote the common welfare – but only then. If we think of Machiavelli as a politician, what are we to make of what he tells politicians to do? Maybe he is deceiving them in what he says? Maybe he seeks to deceive far more extensively but does not want to own up?

We often do compartmentalize our lives; we often do know that people are more likely to mislead over some matters than others – perhaps in affairs of the heart but not affairs of state. People who are completely honest in their dealings with friends sometimes lie in wage negotiations about the final offers they would accept. People who would not dream of cheating their newsagent may delight in financial windfalls that arrive courtesy of accounting mistakes by banks and large department stores. This knowledge of how people deceive in one area and not another cannot derive solely from what they tell us. Rather, experience shows us that some people can be trusted in some spheres but not others. Indeed, we may well use our own predilections as a guide to those of others.

♈

Utilitarianism tells us to maximize happiness. That aim, some would argue, takes priority over telling the truth: it trumps truth telling. We should tell the truth only if it is likely to secure more happiness than would deception. Sometimes deception needs to be deployed because sometimes that will maximize happiness; think of little white lies. We know, then, that individuals who wittingly announce that they are utilitarians of this ilk are prepared to deceive. If their announcement is true, they explicitly own up to being prepared to deceive; if their announcement is false, clearly they sometimes deceive. Given their deceptive propensities, if we rely solely on their statements, then, paradoxically, we are at sea over whether, in telling us they are utilitarian, they are even telling us the truth that they are utilitarian. And when they tell us that utilitarianism is the correct morality to adopt, again, we flounder.

The default position is to believe what people tell us – yet if people truthfully tell us of the limits of their truth telling, we cannot rationally rest our belief in what they say on what they say. What they say is akin to saying 'I may be misleading you in what I am saying.' This does not possess the contradiction of the liar who says 'I am lying' (as in Chapter 25), but it should undermine its hearers' beliefs in what is being said. Paradoxically, people's truthful comments about their limits on truth telling are 'doubt generators', as we may term them.

Reassuring hearers that we are speaking the truth creates its own absurdity. If our hearers already distrust us, why should they believe us when we say we are telling the truth? If they already believe us truthful, we fail to *inform* them in telling them of our veracity. If anything, our attempt to tell people of our truth-telling ways may itself be a doubt generator, raising suspicions about our commitment to truth.

Trust me, I am telling you the truth.

83
WHAT SORT OF CHILDREN SHOULD THERE BE?

People typically desire the best for their children; and, when they have that desire, the children are usually already existing – but only usually. We sometimes wonder about the best for children, prior to their existence. These days, concerned would-be parents, even before conceiving, may eat appropriately, resist smoking and alcohol, and undergo medical tests to check all will be well. Concern for healthy offspring means that women, once pregnant, are advised over a whole range of factors – from scans to vitamins to, for all I know, eye-liner choice.

Now, there are some tragic cases – painful dilemmas – when a foetus is so badly deformed that most doctors would recommend abortion: 'better to try again later'. There are also more controversial cases, also tragic, when some would recommend abortion, others not, depending upon likely disablement. Let us, though, avoid the emotional turmoil of possible abortions. Let us, at this stage at least, solely consider pre-conception cases.

A woman is wanting a child, but she has a serious medical problem, a chemical imbalance, such that were she to conceive now, the child born would be disabled. Doctors point out that if she delays conception for a few months, by which time her health would be fine, then all would go well for the forthcoming child.

'It would be better for your child and for you, if you delay conception.'

That paradoxical claim is, well, paradoxical. How can it be better for the child? If the delay happens, then the child who would otherwise have been born fails to be born. Someone else would be born, because the particular egg and spermatozoon would then be different from those now. A question that raises the perplexities here is:

Can there be a wrongful birth?

Most people, in the circumstances cited, would delay conception. Surely, that is the right thing to do. If that is the right thing to do, then there must be something wrong, it seems, about the choice of a woman who goes ahead now with the conception. Yet suppose that she does just that – and the resultant child, disabled, grows up. What harm, if any, has been done?

Has the child been harmed? Had the conception not occurred, the child would not have existed; so the harm, if at all, must hang on whether the child's life is, in some way, a harm overall for him, through too much suffering, inability to look after himself when grown up – or whatever. There are two cases: one in which he is overall harmed; and one in which he is not.

If he suffers so much that he sincerely and consistently believes he would rather not have been born, then he has been harmed: he has been harmed by being brought into existence. So, if such suffering and result-ant attitude is pretty likely to occur, that is a good reason for delaying conception rather than conceiving such a child now. However severely disabled he is, though, he may genuinely value being alive, and so no net harm has been done to him by conceiving him. Had conception been delayed, he would have lost that valuable life.

The considerations above all hang on the likelihood of the child valuing his life; but that is far from the whole story. Remember, we have been considering the position before the child is even conceived. If – and this is a big 'if' – we can make sense of the interests of people even before they are conceived, then we should take into account the interests of others who could have been conceived, but because the woman went ahead with the conception now, they were not conceived.

Once we reflect on how different children could have been cre-ated, had conceptions been delayed, be they delayed by hours, days or months, we should recognize that we are inevitably choosing between different possible individuals. If the woman delays conception, the disabled child is not created, but a healthy child is created later on. If the woman does not delay, then the disabled child is created, but not the healthy one. Whatever the choices, many possible children are being selected against. Although many people find it obnoxious to be choosing between children, that, in a way, is what happens, though usually in ignorance.

Selection between would-be children may be made, of course, not with the interests of the different possible children at heart, but with other interests, such as economic factors. Such factors account for the preference in some societies to have boys rather than girls. Sometimes parents may deliberately conceive an additional child – a 'saviour child' – in order to provide matching bone marrow to help save an existing child. The creation of children can result from a mishmash of motives – and often, of course, the motive of child creation is completely absent, yet sexual intoxication very much present.

Given choices have to be made, it is better to choose the outcome which is likely to be the happiest child. Naturally, this is where disputes can arise. Many of us would be appalled at deaf parents deliberately preferring their child to be deaf rather than permitting medical interventions, be it on themselves or the embryo or the baby, to prevent or cure the deafness. Yet such parents sometimes argue that their family life would be better with the child deaf – and better for the child. We should, though, resist their argument for it appears to justify such deaf parents deliberately causing deafness in their offspring, if born with good hearing.

Perhaps the picture of choosing between possible children is misleading – as if there are numerous possible children, lingering in shadowy waiting rooms, awaiting conception. Choosing between them seems personal: we are discriminating against one in favour of another. Now, of course, we frequently do choose between people – we may prefer the raven-haired to the blonde – even though in many walks of life such discrimination is condemned. With regard to the conception question, though, we are not directly discriminating between individuals – they do not yet exist – but assessing which features anyone would prefer to have, if existing. We cannot harm or benefit someone who does not exist. Harms and benefits need existent individuals.

$$\gamma$$

Assessing which features anyone would prefer to possess does not imply disrespect for existent people who lack the preferred features. To note that anyone, for example, would prefer not to be paralysed does not remotely imply that we lack respect for people who are paralysed. Consider an analogy: valuing contraceptive use does not suggest a disrespect for existent people.

In choosing when to conceive, to avoid creation of individuals with unfortunate features, we inevitably are led into considering which treatments and enhancements we should, or should not, be prepared to permit for foetuses, embryos or women yet to conceive. After all, for existing children, we accept vaccinations – and we correct speech impediments, irregular teeth, even flat feet. Many parents, financially fortunate, arrange additional tuition for their children in the hope of intellectual, linguistic or mathematical improvements.

Now, suppose foetuses or mothers prior to conception could be 'treated' to enhance the future children's intelligence, moral awareness, even feelings of well-being – and perhaps eradicate tendencies towards jealousy and deceit. What objections could there be to such treatment?

Somewhere along the line we feel uneasy at certain genetic interferences even if seemingly for the best; maybe we are uneasy at the underlying promotion of competitiveness. Perhaps we are aware of the dangers of a super-class being created, based on wealth and privilege; perhaps we reflect on how many Victorians would have genetically designed for piety and patriotism – and how Islamic State would certainly seek to blot out liberalism, religious diversity and sexual equality.

The above dangers and caveats to one side, we return to the following simple question. We are keen to make existing people better; so, in addition, why not, from the very start, make better people?

PART IX: AESTHETICS
What's so good about the arts?

Either be a work of art or wear a work of art.

Oscar Wilde

'That can't be art!' The exclamation readily occurs on viewing some art, be it Tracey Emin's *My Bed* or, decades earlier, Malevich's *Black Square* (just a black square) and Duchamp's *Fountain* (a pristine urinal, albeit signed 'R Mutt 1917'). So, what is art? Socrates applied 'What is…?' to beauty, courage and a lot more. Often, though, it is mistaken to expect definitions: look out for Ant and Grasshopper in the next part, Part X.

The arts – paintings, music, literature – typically are said to represent and express: they bring forth tears, sadness, joy and other emotions. Why, though, do we watch tragedies and horror, knowing that they cause distress? Further, the arts sometimes upset social and religious norms: the 'male gaze' at female nudes upsets some feminists; representations of Muhammad offend some Muslims. Does art merit special ring-fencing and protection by society from those offended?

'In life, democracy; in art, aristocracy,' wrote Toscanini. That stance, favouring the 'high arts' – Renaissance paintings, opera, string quartets – is frequently denounced as elitist, rather than encouraged with recognition that some representations are more valuable than others. That value may be understood as a distinctive aesthetic value: a fine painting, poem or song cycle, even Blue Note jazz, in different ways, captures our attention, a disinterested attention.

When purely motivated by the aesthetics, we attend without giving thought to the commercial value of the painting, the poetry book being a first edition or the composer's score and handwritten letter outlining struggles of composition. The devaluing of art occurs when it is seen solely or primarily as an investment opportunity, a hedge against inflation or compensation for low interest rates. The value of art also has to contend with the puzzling facts that originals are usually preferred to copies and that an artist's own work is more highly prized than forgeries, even when the forgeries, for years, were treated as authentic and fine works.

Aesthetic appreciation of the arts, be they high or low, can bring value to human life, helping to make sense of things, even what to wear, if we follow Oscar Wilde. They are distinctively human. Contrast with the feline life of Pushkin, the cat: his contentment is secured, simply by paws before a roaring fire. Pushkin, though, must bide his time, until the end of this Part IX; first, we meet a window cleaner – or do we?

84

THE LIFE MODEL:
BEAUTY, BURGLARS AND BEHOLDERS

A burglar is set on robbing an apartment. He could knock at the door and announce his intentions, but that makes the burglary unlikely to succeed. He needs first to case the joint; so he pretends to be a window cleaner. Of course, just turning up, saying he is a window cleaner, would be suspicious. He needs a story — at least, a bucket, ladder and some more. With the required equipment in place, he climbs the ladder and peers through the windows, to establish the jewellery's location. People are wandering in and out of the rooms; so, again to avoid suspicion, he makes as if he is washing the windows, yet he senses the occupants may be un-fooled. Playing safe, he starts washing the windows properly, and then proceeds to give them a fine shine. Of course, he is only pretending to clean the windows — and yet he is cleaning the windows.

This little puzzle is readily solved: he is pretending to be a window cleaner while really cleaning the windows. Complexities arise if he really is a window cleaner as well as burglar. The tale reminds us that what happens, where people are involved, depends not solely on physical movements, but also on intentions and context. Let us keep that reminder in mind, as we move to a puzzle.

'A group of clothed men are staring intensely at an attractive naked young woman, stretched out before them.' Someone, not in the know, describes the scene thus. Yet the men and woman would reject that description. We are at a life class; painting is about to take place.

Of course, models are sometimes men and artists women; but, to avoid repeated caveats, here we have a female model and heterosexual male artists. The woman may, indeed, be modest, someone who normally dresses very conservatively, who would not dream of flaunting herself. She may, indeed, be suspicious of window cleaners. In a painter's studio, though, things are different: the artists seek the aesthetic. The artists would probably be indignant, were they perceived as delighting in her nakedness, as if in a strip club. To suggest a sexual element displays an uncouth character, it is declared, and a failure to grasp the difference between the nude as ideal and the naked or bare. After all, naked truth and bare-faced lies are neither nude truth nor nude-faced lies. The nude is distinctive, a beautiful art form; the gaze an aesthetic gaze. Yet:

How divorced is the artistic gaze from the real world of desire?

Sometimes the aesthetic realm is seen as ethereal, separate from desire, at least of an earthly ilk. Of course, nudes were sometimes painted expressly for bedchambers, calculated to excite lustful feelings; but, focusing on the aesthetics of the nude, a detached attitude, it is said, is required by viewers, as by artists when creating the paintings. The model and the nude in the painting are to be viewed for their form. Then, there is no shame in our prying, no lascivious thoughts. The aesthetic experience may even ennoble.

Ignoring whether art needs to be of the beautiful, let us focus on those many cases where 'beautiful' would be a natural expression for what is seen, where there is talk of curves and contours, balance and harmony, shadings and textures. The beautiful here need not amount to the good-looking. Rembrandt's paintings are often beautiful, even if the subjects are some distance from looking at all good.

One traditional approach is that beauty is indeed not in beholders' eyes, but resides in certain mathematical proportions, objectively present. Musical harmonies are simple arithmetical ratios between lengths of vibrating strings. Analogously, there are, it has been said, underlying harmonies in beautiful paintings – and this applies to the nudes. Even recently it has been suggested that such beauty, with its harmony, promotes a sense of justice. Of course, it cannot simply be a matter of harmony; harmony is sometimes merely boring. Also, the simple may be beautiful, yet be so simple that it lacks parts to be in harmony.

Whatever the details, there results, it is claimed, a distinctive aesthetic appreciation of the nude, far removed from sexual desire. And so, both sexes can appreciate the beauty of proportion in human bodies and their representation. The desire to experience the beauty of the nude is a disinterested desire. A clear difference exists between, for example, the enjoyment aroused by pornography or photographs of glamour models and that by paintings of nudes, even though the scenes portrayed may be similar. A clear difference exists between a burglar pretending to be a window cleaner and a real window cleaner, even when in both cases the windows get cleaned.

Aesthetic appreciation involves pleasure. When we find nudes beautiful, we experience certain pleasurable sensations, even sensual; and presumably those sensations depend on our biology. Were we disembodied, spiritual, in some non-earthly realm, yet viewing the paintings, could we experience the beauty? Perhaps we could be intellectually aware of the harmonies – but would not appreciation require bodily sensations? Could we sense a sunset's beauty, yet without pleasurable feelings? Simply measuring lines and recognizing proportions do not thereby generate aesthetic appreciation. The body, the feelings, the emotions, are essential to our awareness of the beautiful – bringing us back down to earth. In particular, our sexual constitution would seem to have something to do with which curves and flesh tones are thought beautiful – be it because we identify with them or seek them. If so, the aesthetic delights that men take in female nudes may not be so utterly divorced from other feelings, feelings not directly associated with the eye. This fact – if it is a fact – can lead people to draw mistaken conclusions.

One mistaken conclusion concerns beauty. People often conclude that the beautiful is relative to our biological make-up. Whether gin is nice depends on 'nice *for whom*'; whether something is beautiful – well, that depends on 'beautiful *for whom*'. Indeed, evolutionary psychologists, ever fond of the 'just', sometimes say that beautiful features are *just* those indicative of health; being drawn to the beautiful is *nothing but* being drawn to the healthy, to hand down our genes. I urge, once again, resistance to the relativity claim, to the 'just' and 'nothing but'. Compare with the following.

Probably there is a good evolutionary explanation of why we, evolutionary survivors, can distinguish shapes from colours, land from sea – yet the differences between shapes and colours, land and sea, are not *just* their evolutionary utility. Our biology is required for our awareness of the world and its features; it does not follow that the world and its features depend on our biology. So, too, with beauty: just because we need a certain biology to recognize beauty it does not follow that beauty depends on that biology.

♈

As biology has some role in aesthetic appreciation, people sometimes also mistakenly conclude, not just that beauty is relative, but that the aesthetic gaze by males is *really* or *nothing but* a sexual yearning. It is as if there is no real difference between lusting after someone and appreciating the beauty. The analogous mistake would be to think that there is no real difference between a burglar and window cleaner, when both are cleaning the windows. We encountered errors of 'nothing buttery' when reflecting on, for example, altruism as self-interest.

Differences exist between lusting and appreciating, though differences are sometimes a matter of degree and sometimes intermingled. Artists, for example, have often seduced their models, even claiming aesthetic impulse. Yet models who sit for genuine life classes should not be sitting as objects of lust. If an artist's primary concern is lust – he pretends to draw, or even draws, as a burglar pretends to clean windows and cleans windows – then he is engaged in deception as is the burglar. He is mistreating the model, even if she reclines, unaware of his intentions and desires. He is using her as a means for lustful ends rather than a consenting means towards a successful life drawing or painting. Of course, things may not be like that: model and artist may mutually consent to both the lusting and the artistic endeavour; the two aims need not be incompatible.

None of this is to deny that muddles occur over what is really happening and what matters, when perceptions enter the fray. 'What is that man at the window, or in the artist's studio, really doing?' Think of actors: when acting their parts, they rarely pretend to walk; they walk. They are pretending, say, to cross hills, when really they cross the stage. They do not pretend to kiss and caress, for they do kiss and caress; and yet, because of the context, the kiss and caress lack the significance of kisses and caresses in reality – or often do.

Suppose an actor plays against an actress who happens to be his real-life wife with whom he is angry in real life. And, in the play, the actress plays the part of a wife and he plays that of the angry husband – then where do acting and reality separate? What is really going on depends on intentions, on context, on the bigger picture – and yet are we not also pulled towards thinking that we can tell part of what is really going on without the bigger picture?

After all, the windows do get cleaned.

85

PAINTINGS, WITHIN AND WITHOUT

Paint some doors – and for a while we are painters, but not thereby painters of pictures. The difference between painters and painters, as we may bewilderingly say, is that, in paint application, house painters typically are not aiming to represent things in their brush-strokes, colours and textures, in contrast to painters, artists, who create paintings, destined to be hung or hidden. Let us steer towards the paintings found hanging.

Gaze at clouds, stare at winter's frosty window panes, or peer at foliage – even at the dust around us, or rather, around me. A remarkable fact – a fact worthy of remark – is that what we see is more, far more, than first meets the eye. In the clouds, the frost, the leaves – the dust – we may see a beautiful face, a grotesque beast or the smile of a friend. And when we catch that glimpse, what we see looks different from what we saw before.

The drawing here is seen by many immediately as a duck; many others see a rabbit. Most observers flick between the two, seeing the long protuberances, stretching to the right, first as a duck's beak, then as a rabbit's ears. Although the drawing may be seen as a duck – or a rabbit – we cannot see the lines simultaneously appearing as a duck and also appearing as a rabbit. That is puzzling. A duck cannot also be a rabbit, so perhaps it is impossible for something to appear as a curious creature, a duck-rabbit. But there is no obvious contradiction in a drawing appearing to someone as a duck and also appearing as a rabbit at the same time. Yet this does not happen – apparently.

Paintings often represent – picture or depict – scenes, items and events: people, landscapes, bowls of fruit, be they real or fictional, particular or no. The *Mona Lisa* is of a particular woman. Other paintings

Illustration by David Berger

may represent women, but none in particular. Yet others represent what do not exist: mermaids, satyrs and fauns. One puzzle is – and let us use 'paintings' to include drawings, when speaking generally –

How do paintings picture things?

An immediate answer is 'resemblance'; but that, almost as immediately, puzzles us. Resemblance in which respects and between what? Paintings, hanging in art galleries, usually resemble each other far more than anything they represent. After all, they are mainly rectangular in shape, on canvases, their surfaces brushed with watercolours, charcoal or paint. The pictured horse, the landscape, the face, are nothing like blobs of paint rectangularly surrounded. Does the duck/rabbit drawing really resemble a flesh-and-blood creature rather than, say, just some other drawn lines?

Perhaps this quick criticism of the 'resemblance' approach involves a gross mistake. The painting – the canvas hanging on the wall – does not resemble the horse, the landscape, the woman's face. Perhaps, though, the content of our experience, when viewing the canvas, is similar to that of our experience when looking at a real horse, the landscape, the woman. That, however, fails to explain the experience striking us so differently, depending whether we see the lines as of a duck or as of a rabbit.

Working on the resemblance approach, some suggest that paintings simply aim to deceive; they generate the illusion of our seeing, say, a real horse, when horses are otherwise visually absent. Now, a painting – a *trompe l'œil* – can deceive us: we may be misled into thinking that peaches are present, when in fact there is only a painting carefully placed. But most paintings certainly do not deceive, even though they represent. This chapter's drawing does not mislead spectators into thinking a duck is squashed within this book. Muse upon other representations. Photographs may be black and white, yet the photographed are vibrantly coloured. Cartoons and caricatures paradoxically *mis*represent what they represent.

These implausibilities, concerning representation as mere resemblance, lead some to flip to the other extreme, understanding representation as conventional, cultural and not objectively resembling at all. We may agree, of course, that words, typically at least, represent by conventions. The word 'duck', 'd' followed by 'u' etc., does not resemble a duck. Paintings too, it is suggested, represent because of conventions and upbringings: witness how radically different are the styles of Impressionist, ancient Egyptian and primitive cave paintings. As children grow up, depending upon surrounding conventions, they see some painting styles as the 'right' way of representing things rather than others. That 'right way' depends on us, not on objective resemblances out there in the world. We have encountered that approach far more radically (in Chapter 41) when wondering how the world becomes carved as objects, as stars, as clusters.

This conventional take on representation has major problems. Conventions exist whereby graphs represent temperature changes, yet graphs are not pictures. And is it really just a matter of convention that the *Mona Lisa* represents a woman? If this were so, then, given the right circumstances, the *Mona Lisa* could have represented a horse or hamster, fawn or faun. There is surely at least something about a painting's look, independently of conventions and culture, which sets some boundaries.

Paintings are curious objects. On the outside, so to speak, a painting is a canvas with paint. Yet we are aware of an inside: we see the horse in the painting – as we see figures in the clouds, and a duck or rabbit in this book. We are aware both of paintings as material objects and of what they represent; paintings possess both aspects, a without and a within. We are able to 'see in'. We cannot see, for example, this chapter's drawing *as* a rabbit and duck simultaneously; but, when seeing it as one of those creatures, say, as a duck, we do simultaneously see the material object, the drawn lines, and see in those lines a duck. Awareness of this twofoldness prevents us from mistaking paintings for what it is that they represent. In seeing what is present, the configured surface, we also *see in* what is absent – a duck, landscape or face.

Artists usually paint so that viewers do see things in their paintings. Viewers may, of course, need information, sensitivity, some prompting, in order to see what artists have intended. Once they see, the visual experience differs from what it was before – just as promptings by means of a 'quack' may enable a viewer suddenly to see the duck in the duck/rabbit. We may need to look more closely or carefully to see into some paintings – to see faces and limbs, or crags and valleys. The visual experiences of 'seeing in' differ from those when seeing items in reality or the mind's eye. Paintings, just like words, may stimulate our imagination, but imagining scenes is not, of course, the same as seeing those scenes in paintings.

On the approach outlined, paintings represent in that they offer viewers the opportunity to *see in*. True, when we look at any written sentence, in our own language, we cannot help but see beyond the shapes to the meaning, but this is not because the shapes provide visual experiences of what is meant. We could draw the word 'duck' in such a way that we see a duck in the lines drawn – showing that there certainly is some difference between visual representation and the conventional.

We still lack an account of why it is that we see one thing rather than another *in* a painting. Appeal to resemblance may return: the shapes on the canvas, as we experience them, are taken to resemble physical figures as if seen from a viewpoint in reality. Yet this is unsatisfactory, for those visual experiences depend on what we 'see in' the paintings. We risk circularity, if we explain 'seeing in' in terms of perceived resemblance in experiences, yet explain what we experience in terms of 'seeing in'. After all, the duck/rabbit drawing does look different, depending whether we see a duck or a rabbit. Why we see what we see, when we 'see in' a painting, remains puzzling. Indeed it is puzzling that in an unmoving painting we may yet see movement. 'Is it superstition to think I see the horse galloping in a picture?' asks Wittgenstein.

$$\gamma$$

Many people may, without reflection, assume that the puzzles of representation, of 'seeing in', do not apply to abstract paintings. When we first gaze at the abstract work of, say, Mondrian, Rothko and Pollock, we may feel that they are far, far away from the representational. Yet, even here, we see things in the paintings. With Rothko, we may see colours hovering over or behind others, whether or not the paint was applied in that order. We may see lights shining through, moods and emotions. As we learn to *see in*, what we see before us is, in a way, no longer what we formerly saw.

And if the house painter stops us and says, 'No, that wall I've just painted is not "just painted", but is my painting – can't you see what I've painted?' we may gaze into the colour and see something in the paint, and not just a wall painted.

86
FICTIONAL FEELINGS?

It was astonishing. A large number of people looked on intently as a woman was manhandled by a group of ruffians, beaten, raped and left for dead. The gang had already killed her husband. No one intervened, though the crowd was well aware of everything that was happening, happening before their very eyes. It was macabre. And they ended up hooting and clapping. Not one of them called the police.

Is this the opening statement by the prosecution at a murder trial? Were the onlookers accomplices or just scared of the attackers? In the cold light of subsequent days, were they ashamed of their behaviour, of their cowardice, of doing nothing to help the victims?

The answer to all these questions is the same: 'Not at all.' The onlookers were in a theatre, watching a play. They knew it to be a work of fiction, yet – paradoxically – most were highly involved with the characters. They worried about what would happen to the woman; some felt shivers when the gang leader made his threats, his knife's blade gleaming. They pitied some characters, felt proud of others and hoped justice would eventually be done. Some were on the verge of weeping. As they left the theatre, they discussed how much they felt for the woman. A few awoke in the night, wondering how the characters' lives would develop; a few wondered how things might have gone differently.

We are moved by fictional characters, whether they appear in television soap operas, detective stories or popular films, or are famous individuals from the classics – Romeo and Juliet, Lolita or Lady Macbeth – in productions by the Royal Shakespeare Company, the National Theatre or the Royal Opera House. Typically, viewers and readers are fully aware that the characters are but fictions, yet the fictions may appear as alive as real people – and not just at the times of performance. Some viewers of soap sagas wonder what the fictional characters are doing between episodes. Is not this very odd, contrasting with, for example, wondering what is happening to celebrities answering to weird demands in reality television programmes?

Why do we feel emotions – love, hate, fear, regret, admiration – towards fictional individuals?

When we feel emotions – being scared by Dracula, pitying the young Jane Eyre or feeling angry at Bill Sykes' treatment of Nancy in *Oliver Twist* – we must surely believe, or at least half believe, that the individuals exist and possess features that justify our fear, pity or anger. We know that fictional entities are indeed fictional and lack existence; yet, paradoxically, we experience emotions towards them – or so it seems.

If we stress the sincerity of the audience's belief in, and feeling of emotion towards, what is being represented on stage or in writing, we should expect the audience to be up there, entering into the action in some way. Stress the audience's knowledge that it is just a play, a book, an opera and we are baffled by the audience's being moved – indeed, moved sometimes even to tears.

Irrationality is one answer. Certainly, we can believe and engage in many irrational things. Our emotions too can result from irrationality or mistaken beliefs, but the emotions usually fade when we realize our mistakes. Members of mobs that shout death threats outside paediatricians' homes undergo (one hopes) emotional change when they discover paediatricians differ from paedophiles. Even if paedophiles have correctly been spotted, the anger and hatred may (again one hopes) be reduced by reflection on better ways to help. When we are scared of spiders we think poisonous, our fears should be quelled once we are convinced that the spiders are harmlessly living non-poisonous lives. In some cases, however, although we know such truths, our fears irrationally persist. And so, too, our emotions may persist, even when we know the objects of those emotions to be but fictions.

Irrationality may yet prove to be too easy an answer or, on reflection, not an easy answer at all, if intended to carry conviction. The most rational of people can be moved by fictions yet, even when moved, know full well that they are seated in a theatre, reading a book or watching television. Or do they? Perhaps, one way or another, they suspend their belief in the stagy surroundings, suspend their memories of the tickets they purchased or block out the sound of the book's rustling pages. Perhaps they fall for what is represented as being real, as being, indeed, all for real. Remember though, they cannot be taken in that much: if they were, they would be warning of danger, calling a doctor or exposing the villain – as children sometimes do when at pantomimes.

If irrationality is no right answer, perhaps the emotions are not directed at the fictional characters at all. It has been suggested that fiction leads the audience to have the fear, the pity, the joy – and so on – at real people (not the fictions) who have the relevant characteristics. The causes of emotions need not be the objects at which the emotions are directed. You feared your neighbour's hound (or so you thought) but what caused that fear might have been no hound but a radio's blaring. It is the radio's sound – sound that you *mistook* as canine threatening howls – that caused your fear. Returning to fictions, the pity that comes from reading Charles Dickens' portrayal of the poor, for example, is not directed at the novel's characters but at those in poverty, in the real, real world. The tale brings those real people to mind.

Although that approach to the fictional puzzle makes sense, it lacks plausibility. Often, do we not feel approval for, pity towards or are angered by the fictional characters? Why think we are mistaken? Furthermore, perhaps the approach requires us to have specific real individuals in mind to account for our emotions, yet we rarely have such real individuals in mind when watching a play.

Other attempted solutions to puzzling fictions have rested on claiming that our emotions towards fictional characters are make-believe emotions. Such 'solutions' also lack conviction. The tears we experience when moved by some fictions are real enough; maybe the pity is too.

ᵧ

The very thought of things can generate emotions, without the need for full belief or disbelief – and perhaps that is enough for handling this puzzle. We do not really *believe* that the woman is being harmed, as we watch the staged action; perhaps the mere *thought* (or some other distinct psychological state) of her being harmed is enough to generate our pity, disgust or whatever. Our thoughts are carried along by the play, book or opera and generate real emotions, though emotions whose links to the appropriate behaviour are broken or weakened. The mere thought of your daughter being attacked can cause worry and fear; but, as you have no good reason to believe that it will happen, you encourage her to attend the dance or even the philosophy seminar. Analogously, a fictional violent attack, performed on stage, may cause your fear and distress, as would imagining it; yet, knowing it to be staged, you do not believe it is really happening and you have no tendency to leap from your seat and call the police.

Whether or not the above line is the right approach, we should not lapse into arguing that we are therefore directing our emotions at mere thoughts or ideas. Romeo and Juliet fall in love and die tragically and their tragic love brings tears to our eyes. An idea or thought of Romeo and Juliet cannot itself fall in love. Our thoughts and ideas are *of* Romeo and Juliet, *of* Lolita, *of* the latest arrivals in a soap saga such as *EastEnders* or comedies such as *Curb* and *Fawlty Towers*. Quite what constitutes the relationship between us and non-existent entities, such as fictions, remains obscure. Obscurities may multiply, if we reflect on the peculiar attraction of opera; we may be moved by a character's plight, while simultaneously and incongruously applauding the soprano's vocal skills.

The paradox of fiction has spin-offs. Curiously, we can experience suspense, even when we know what is coming. Many people have seen Alfred Hitchcock's 1960 film, *Psycho*, more than once. The shower scene, with the throbbing music, can still cause suspense even after repeated viewings. The pulse quickens and tingles run down the back – despite our knowing the unhappy and blood-stained outcome, a bloody outcome paradoxically rendered in black and white.

Suspense is just one example of the unpleasant emotions that, it seems, we go out of our way to encounter in novels, film and music. Tragedies cause pain; horror stories cause fear – but we enjoy them. Why? What is going on?

Aristotle suggested that such experiences of fiction provide us with emotional release – catharsis – that helps us carry on in life. Quite how and why this should work are questions that lack easy answers and which raise the further question of what, if anything, are the arts for?

We leave that latest question for... later, when we attend to Pushkin in the role of McTaggart's cat (Chapter 91) and when, later still, we meet the Barbarians (Chapter 98). For now, let us consider 'in the mind's eye' some characters from fiction that have moved us. May I suggest that you conjure up in your imagination characters, be they from film, theatre or sitcoms, that have caused you to laugh at their lives or cry with them; engendered horror, empathy or admiration. Now, quite why have those emotions or feelings occurred? You know full well that the characters are fictional, lacking all substance. Why, then, do you – why do we – care? Have we yet found an answer? Is the care just a pretend care, a self-deception? Is it itself a fiction?

87
SPEAKING OF WHOM?

We approach this puzzle courtesy of a reduced scene from Lewis Carroll's splendid *Through the Looking Glass*.

'Whom do you see on the road?' asks the White King.
'Nobody,' replies Alice.
'Ah, to be able to see Nobody and from this distance too,' muses the King.

The confusion worsens for, when the Messenger arrives, the King asks,

'Whom did you pass on the road?'
'Nobody,' replies the Messenger.
'Quite right,' says the King. 'This young lady saw him too. So, Nobody walks slower than you.'
'What?' says the Messenger indignantly, 'I'm sure Nobody walks faster than I do.'
'He can't do that,' replies the King, 'Otherwise he would be here before you.'

The White King mistakes 'Nobody' for a name (and hence our upper case 'N'). In order to talk of nobody, there is, though, no need for a Mr or Mrs Nobody to exist.

We talk about non-existent entities – about unicorns, Santa Claus and Sleeping Beauty. Our puzzle here, though, is more fundamental and general. How do we manage to talk about items far away in time or space, or even nearby, yet with which we lack contact? How do we know whom we mean when we speak of Zeno, Shakespeare and Newton? After all, none of us has ever met them.

The quick response is that there is no need to meet items in order to talk about them. That is true. The question remains: how does a proper name, when used, target a particular item? In using the name 'Zeno' we manage to speak of the flesh and blood Zeno, a philosopher of centuries ago, rather than of Plato, Julius Caesar or Schubert.

The next quick response could be that Zeno is whomever we designate by the name 'Zeno'; but that traps us into a circle, for who is that person?

Our puzzle relates, of course, to named towns, sculptures and mountains, but to retain focus, let the question be:

How can we talk about people of the distant past?

An easy answer is that we are talking about whichever person was given the relevant name at the time. That, though, usually will not work. When writing of Zeno in this chapter, Zeno, a philosopher, was being pinpointed, yet there are many other individuals called 'Zeno', including some cats and dogs. True, we may now insist that, given the context, the individual designated is *the philosopher named 'Zeno'*. Not even that, though, is sufficient to pinpoint the particular in mind, for there could have been other philosopher Zenos – and there were. Witness Zeno of Citium, founder of Stoicism, different from Zeno of Elea.

The approach above associates descriptions, for example 'philosopher', with the name in question. Building on that approach, we may argue that proper names, to work, require associated collections of quite a few descriptions. The descriptions need sufficient detail to hit one and only one individual, uniquely identifying one individual. Whichever item satisfies the descriptions is the item about which we speak.

Modifications are needed to the above 'description' or 'satisfaction' theory, for we may hold some mistaken descriptions of the individuals in question. Also, some descriptions carry more weight than others.

In talking about Zeno, we are here talking about the Greek philosopher, who flourished around 460 BC, who came from Elea, who produced paradoxes of motion, and who was tall. But, suppose such an individual existed satisfying all the relevant descriptions except for being tall. We should accept that we were talking about the individual who was a Greek philosopher, came from Elea, and so on – but were mistaken about his height. His being a philosopher of paradoxes weighs far more than his height – or even his weight.

The historic persons, therefore, to whom we refer are those individuals who satisfy a weighted number of a cluster of descriptions with which the name we use is associated. This alleged solution, though, of names requiring identifying descriptions – and those descriptions fixing the item designated – has problems, as seen in Chapter 37.

Here is one problem. Think of the numerous names we use every day to talk of historic characters yet concerning which we lack identifying descriptions. We speak of Byron, Newton, Plato – of Zeno – yet many of us have few descriptions associated with the names. Most people probably know of Plato only that he was an important Greek philosopher – but that, of course, fails uniquely to pick out just one individual. Pupils may gather from teachers' comments the names of Newton and Darwin, yet confuse who did what. Surely, though, when pupils say, 'Ah, yes, Newton proposed evolution', they say something incorrect about Newton, not something correct about Darwin.

The problem just outlined is answered by recognizing that we often defer to experts who have the means for identifying whom we mean. Maybe we know a little about Newton, Plato and Zeno, but when we use those names, we ultimately mean the individuals concerning whom relevant scholars possess identifying information linked to the name in question and some minimal information we have. 'Zeno? I mean whichever one the current philosophical purveyors of paradox usually mean.' We pass the 'meaning buck' to others – and it is those others who hold relevant clusters of descriptions associated with the names in question. American philosopher, Hilary Putnam, termed this 'Division of Linguistic Labour'.

♈

The satisfaction theory above, is not out of the woods yet. Here is another problem. Can we not make sense of experts being wrong?

The expert belief is that Shakespeare wrote *Othello*, *Hamlet*, *King Lear* and so on. That, as is sometimes proposed, could be, or could turn out to be, false. Suppose it is false. When we have been speaking of Shakespeare, have we then been speaking of Bacon or Marlowe or some other writer? We should insist that we have often been speaking of Shakespeare. In discovering the mistaken attribution, we say, 'Ah, so Shakespeare did not write *Othello* and the other plays.' In saying that, we do not mean that the author of *Othello* did not write *Othello*.

On the satisfaction theory, we fix the items about which we talk by clusters of descriptions. But, in most cases, those descriptions just happen to apply to the individual – and hence, they may not apply. Aristotle might not have written any philosophy. He might have been a pig farmer, yet through historians' errors or misrepresentations, he was spoken of as the great philosopher, author of the *Metaphysics*. The very fact that we can make sense of that idea shows that, at the very least, satisfaction theories need to be nuanced and handled with great care.

To return to 'Nobody' who started us off, non-existent individuals, fictional characters, are in a different boat from historical figures. We have to identify Oliver Twist, the fictional character, by descriptions – for there is nothing more to Twist than the descriptions given by Dickens. Where Dickens has nothing to say, there is no truth, no fictional fact, that Twist must yet have either done this or that or have liked fried eggs or not: he is indeterminate. That indeterminacy, suggested Leibniz, makes him fictional, not substantial. Further, there is no sense to the idea that Dickens may have mistaken Twist's characteristics. In contrast, there is sense to the idea that we could be mistaken about Homer.

Maybe Homer, the Greek poet, did not create the Homeric poems, the *Iliad* and *Odyssey*, but someone else did. And we may ice the puzzling cake further, by adding that that someone else was also named 'Homer'.

88
'BUT IT'S ART, DEAR AUNT MATILDA'

It wasn't my fault. It was Aunt Matilda, my aged aunt, who wanted a trip round the art galleries – but I knew it wouldn't go well. She was disgusted by the sexuality expressed in Eric Gill's sculptures of a diminished Christ on the cross next to a naked and voluptuous woman ('How can that be art?') and when she encountered the explicit homosexual activity displayed in Robert Mapplethorpe's much-praised photography, she was on the verge of calling the police. Further on, she came across some graphic work by Gilbert and George, with spelt-out obscenities, racist terms – and worse, once she understood the materials some artists used. She was shocked.

~~~

Aunt Matilda's responses raise the question of whether, for art, anything goes. Art is for art's sake, it has been said: it should be left to its own devices.

The mere mention of some things can be inept and discourteous. However much you thought the deceased disreputable, it would be inappropriate and unkind to raise the matter with his family at his graveside. When Engels' wife died, it was inconsiderate of Marx, in his condolences, to move quickly into requesting a monetary loan. And when talking to families who have recently lost sons in battle, it would be insensitive to question the value of those battles. Some things ought not to be said or done in certain contexts. Of course, there are other contexts where those same things may be said or done – sometimes rightly so. Perhaps the deceased ought to be exposed; the justifications for war may deserve to be challenged.

The puzzle here is whether artists, 'in the name of art', ought to be allowed to get away with anything, however controversial, obscene or

even illegal. Once, in Britain, the Lord Chamberlain would prohibit certain displays and writings, be they in galleries, on stage or in books, and today various dictatorships censor the arts. Even the most tolerant society, of course, requires some censorship – for example, to prevent harm to individuals and oppression of certain groups. There are laws against incitement, and against racist and sexist remarks. Should the arts, though, be exempt from prohibitions, be the prohibitions enshrined in custom, morality or law?

Should the arts be ring-fenced?

The fencing clearly fails in some areas. 'In the name of art' is no justification for real murders, real-life thefts and fraudulent investment activities. Such activities typically remain unjustified, even if performed with artistic intent; even if the knife marks display an aesthetic harmony; the thieves conduct their thievery as a ballet; and the fraud involves some fine writing. Putting such cases to one side, what may we say to Aunt Matilda? Matilda thinks that the artistic expressions – of blasphemies, obscenities, racisms – are being wrongly protected. Is she blinkered, out of touch, reactionary?

One natural reply to Aunt Matilda is that art is concerned with form, with structure, with generating aesthetic awareness: 'art for art's sake' indeed. The content need not be key, but the way the content is expressed. Paintings and literary descriptions of Christ being crucified, of the horrors of war, can yet be beautiful and astonishing works. Onetime censored books, such as Lawrence's *Lady Chatterley's Lover*, are significant works of art because of their form and language. Art, it may be said, does not exist to cause political change; and in practice it is usually confined to a few locations with the hallowed aura of 'art gallery' or 'library'. As for delicate souls who may be offended, well, they need neither enter the gallery nor open the book.

Another natural reply to Aunt Matilda is grounded in opposition to the first reply. Even where art is valued for its form, it is often intended to be provocative – and to effect change. Think of Picasso's *Guernica* which symbolized the Spanish civil war and the horrors of dictatorship. Art may question existing laws and taboos, stimulating social change – often for the better. That is why art, even if racist, obscene or challenging of current beliefs, should be protected.

The second reply rightly recognizes that art sometimes can, does and should stir; but its line of argument is weak. It is weak because, similarly, we could argue that riots are provocative, challenging existing laws sometimes for the better; and that is why riots promoting racism or obscenity merit protection. Perhaps the art and riots analogy, though, can be rebutted. Riots may directly harm others: that is why such disorder is resisted. Art being viewed, opera being listened to, books being read, are more akin to seminars with high-minded discussion. Well, so it may be argued, though not well argued.

Even orderly demonstrations, with marchers chanting racist beliefs, even public sexual orgies, causing no direct harm, are currently illegal in Britain. Yet when similar racism or sexuality occurs in art galleries – well, it may escape prohibition. Perhaps it is valuable to designate certain public spaces for the currently unacceptable to be displayed, even accepted. Perhaps the arts offer cover for this. Lovers of artistic freedom, though, would be unhappy with that freedom's defence being that it allows people to let off steam.

This brings us to the delicate perplexity of 'What is art?' If we are unable to distinguish art from, for example, racist demonstrations, then if 'anything goes' for art, so 'anything goes' would apply to the demonstrations, whether or not the demonstrators wore tutus and danced the demonstration.

People often pass the buck to galleries' curators to decide what is art – but how do curators decide? Suppose some 'galleries' displayed only paintings, sculptures and films that glorified the Holocaust and Hitler. Assuming no artistic irony, we should be tempted to think that some political headquarters now had a new designation over its entrance. Suppose a new 'gallery' promoted paintings that represented women as inferior to men in all respects and eternal heaven to believers who killed non-believers. That could be the means whereby an extreme religious faction sought to promote its ideas. If art is to be allowed a special status, those examples remind us that it is important to determine what counts as art.

Presumably curators ought to exhibit good art. Perhaps the above hypothesized galleries – with works glorifying oppression – would necessarily be exhibiting bad art. Yet even if the art glorifies the morally disreputable, may it not possess aesthetic merit?

When judging a painting, you may be attracted by its tone and colours, yet find the shapes too jarring and jagged for what the painting represents. Indeed the jarring and jaggedness may be so great that you fail properly to appreciate the tonal harmony. So, too, a painting *could* attract you for its tone and colours, yet because of what it represents – the glorification of anti-Semitism; the denigration of women – you are repulsed, unable to attend to the aesthetics. It has failed for you. Yet viewers who share the painting's moral stance may value its form as well as the feelings that it arouses. Mind you, the commitment to what it promotes may be so highly valued and stimulating that such viewers lose sight of the painting's aesthetic value.

414 • THE BIG THINK BOOK

The above considerations have not helped us to identify a line between acceptable and unacceptable art, and that is probably because there is no line to find. We need to muddle through, putting up with a lot of questionable art – in the name of freedom of expression, of John Stuart Mill's Liberty Principle, of 'experiments in living' – calling in the authorities only when some serious incitement to harm is likely to occur. We may, though, ask ourselves how *we* should respond to works of art promoting the obscene or morally disreputable. How do you think you would react? How *ought* you to react?

If your truthful answer, in particular cases, is 'with repulsion', then that may show you are a decent sort of person. It may, though, also show a failure on your part to separate aesthetic value from moral value. It may show a failure to recognize that one may be both attracted to, and repulsed by, one and the same work – attracted, for example, by the form and execution; repulsed by content and purpose. When lacking such failures, you may be keen to own the controversial paintings for their aesthetics.

♈

Suppose you find a painting that clearly glorifies genocide, slavery and anti-Semitism, yet you cannot help but admire the execution of the paint, the colouring and textures used. You choose to hang the picture in your home. Well, however fine the painterly form, however splendid the aesthetics, does that not say something about you that you would not want said?

89
EYE SPY

Abraham Bredius was a twentieth-century Dutch art historian, highly influential in his day. He specialized in paintings by the seventeenth-century artist, Jan Vermeer. In the late 1930s, a painting, *Christ and the Disciples at Emmaus*, came to light. Mindful of forgeries, Bredius and others closely examined the work, before hailing it as a genuine – and magnificent – Vermeer. They described the painting in glowing aesthetic terms, considering it Vermeer's finest achievement. The Boyman's Museum in Rotterdam bought the painting through a certain Han van Meegeren. Van Meegeren was delighted, not so much because of the money, but because he had successfully duped the experts. *The Disciples* was a van Meegeren, painted in the 1930s, not a Vermeer, painted in the 1600s. Such was the painting's quality that some experts of the day refused to believe van Meegeren, taking him to be faking it as a fake. Not withstanding all that, and after further researches, *The Disciples* is now firmly established as a van Meegeren; it is no Vermeer.

Sir A was another, more recent, influential art historian. He too was mindful of fakes. He was a friend of Eric Hebborn, a fine forger. It is unclear to what extent Sir A was taken in by Hebborn's fakes but in 1979 it came out that he – Sir Anthony Blunt, a long-serving and distinguished Director of the Courtauld Institute and Surveyor of the Queen's Pictures – had for many years been a Soviet spy.

When *The Disciples* was spied as fake, not merely the monetary value of the painting radically fell, but so – for many – did its aesthetic value. No longer was it such a good painting. No longer was it displayed in the Boyman's.

When Sir Anthony was spied as fake 'loyal servant' of Britain, his integrity radically diminished; yet no one seriously thought his spying undermined his aesthetic expertise and credentials. The man was seen in a different light; his artistic perception was not. We may wonder whether his aesthetic judgements were as deceptive as his apparent loyalty to Britain, but that would encourage assessment of those judgements on their merits. Their truth or falsity would not rest on their having been made by a Soviet spy.

A fake Vermeer can no longer be prized as by Vermeer. Once alerted to a painting's fake status, we may study it more closely, looking for aesthetic signs of the fakery, but why should merely being a fake detract from its aesthetic value? Aesthetic value rests on a work's colouring, composition, grace and beauty: how could it also rest, even partly, on its source?

Why is how you feel about a painting's quality affected by its being a fake?

Art experts, art lovers and, for that matter, the public in general, tend to feel that a fake is not as artistically valuable as 'the genuine thing'. Why?

There could be relevant aesthetic differences between originals and fakes, differences residing there, 'in the painting'. Now that the differences have been pointed out, we can see them – and we see them as detracting from the painting's quality. We may become aware that the composition is not so orderly or the figures not so gracefully drawn. That is true, but, in many cases of fakery, the defects are imperceptible, except under microscopes or through chemical analyses, so it is difficult to grasp what direct relevance they could have to our aesthetic appreciation. In the famous van Meegeren case, the painting's aesthetic qualities had been highly praised. It is true that experts today identify some compositional defects, but those certainly were not seen at the time of van Meegeren's revelation and the painting's fall from grace.

A forgery often is an inferior work, compared to the master's originals. It may therefore be claimed – though without any good reason – that, somewhere along the line, some perceptible inferiority will, as a matter of fact, be spotted in any forgery. Let us, then, purify our example. Consider a case in which there is nothing in a painting that viewers can see which shows the work to be a fake or poor imitation. Consider a case in which the only differences between genuine Vermeers and the fake are factors to do with its underlying chemical composition, date of being painted and so on; experts with no knowledge of the discovery of the forgery would see the painting as a fine Vermeer. Aesthetically, nothing has changed with regard to the painting, once considered an original Vermeer but now known as a fake Vermeer – or so it would seem.

Moral evaluations are available. People have been deceived by the forger; the painting is key witness to the deception. Maybe some illegal transactions of 'passing off' have taken place. Yet why should such things matter aesthetically? Deception and illegality could be absent. A genuine misattribution of a painting to Vermeer could occur. The mistake is discovered – and the same puzzling consequences for the painting's painterly value flow forth. We need to look beyond the brush strokes for any plausible explanation of the relevance of fakery or misattribution to aesthetic valuations, yet such looking beyond seems immediately to take us away from the aesthetic valuations.

Returning to van Meegeren's pretend Vermeer, the painting lacks many features of authentic Vermeers. It was neither handled by Vermeer, nor seen by his friends nor left in an unfinished state while he gazed upon it, wondering how to continue. We are not seeing a painting that Vermeer saw. It lacks those historical associations, those links to the past – and such associations and links often possess value for us. Witness the importance of wearing not a replica but the very watch given to you by your mother; of holding the original score by Bartok rather than a copy, or of standing in the actual room in King's College, Cambridge where Wittgenstein allegedly brandished the poker (noted in Chapter 34). But why should such associations and links concerning paintings possess *aesthetic* value?

Perhaps, when we look at a painting, valuing its composition, colour, texture and so on, we are also valuing it as manifesting an artist's creativity. Perhaps the artist's creativity can be seen in a painting. Forgeries are often straightforward copies, displaying the forger's skill but lacking originality. If so, how we see the painting changes. Compare how a line drawing, as on page 397, may be seen solely as a duck, until someone points out that it is also a rabbit.

This approach, relying on creativity, fails to solve the problem of van Meegeren's 'Vermeer'. Van Meegeren's was an original composition, though painted in Vermeer's style. That it was painted in Vermeer's style should not itself undermine its originality and aesthetic value, for Vermeer's later paintings themselves manifested work in his style, yet are no less valuable because of that. Perhaps, paradoxically, van Meegeren's *The Disciples* should be seen as much as a Vermeer as Vermeer's own late Vermeers. Van Meegeren, when painting that painting, was showing what could be done with that style of painting as much as Vermeer did. Seeing it *as* a Vermeer should be no different aesthetically from seeing a Vermeer.

♈

Sexton Blakes (rhyming slang for 'fakes') have often been successfully produced by the likes of van Meegeren, Hebborn and Tom Keating. Hebborn claimed that some of his fakes still hang in galleries, undetected. Were their fakery discovered, they would be removed as mere copies. Yet, paradoxically, galleries sometimes cloak copies with the status of original art. An historically famous case is the 1917 Paris exhibition, which contained Duchamp's *Fountain*, mentioned in this Part IX's introduction. This 'work of art' – the original – is just one white urinal among millions, save that it is signed by Duchamp and displayed as an exhibit. This raises the puzzle, as seen earlier, of why one thing is a work of art when something indistinguishable from it, save for location, is not. Placed in the right setting, items such as Duchamp's urinal are works of art – or they are often taken to be such. Even though Duchamp's original was not made by him, that original exhibit is the valuable *Fountain* and a completely indistinguishable copy will not do.

Perhaps what carries the greatest artistic value is the art gallery, for its embrace can turn almost anything into art. Maybe the next exhibit for the British Turner Prize should itself be an art gallery such as Tate Britain, Tate Modern or a Guggenheim. If only it were easy to pop a Tate into a Tate, even a full-blown copy of a Tate into a Tate – and if only I were under forty – I would exhibit it myself for the prize... or exhibit even just myself, that latter proposal showing how, it seems, a work of art, these days, can be without art, may need no work and can even lack artistic design.

90
MUSIC: BEYOND LANGUAGE?

When Annie is happy, she may smile and beam; she may walk with a lightness of limb, talk with a lightness of lilt and cook with a hint of the crazed. That is how Annie expresses her happiness, be the happiness a result of having finished a painting, finding an unexpected £50 note or hearing of her grandson's progress. Annie, being a person and neither pebble nor pineapple, is sentient and experiences happiness and sadness, anger and sympathy, fears and hopes. Annie expresses her feelings – her emotions, passions and moods; her loves, lusts and life.

Music too expresses emotions, yet music is not, of course, a sentient being. Music is a sequence of organized sounds, usually composed with much deliberation, though it may also be the roar of the ocean, the sweep of the gales and the song of, er... birdsong. The music itself does not experience pleasure or pain, happiness or sadness, love or fear, yet many of us, the 'music-blind' excepted, readily and paradoxically speak of music expressing such emotions and moods. As the music unfolds, we may hear sadness and yearning within; we may respond to the sounds as sad. What is going on?

To give us undistorted focus, we steer clear of music with words, despite the possible thought that they must be key to music's significance. Words can mingle so closely with the music that we should be unable to spot what, if anything, the music alone expresses. So, listen to an instrumental work that strikes you as particularly expressive. The music may be classic, jazz or pop. The work's title may be suggestive; but focus attention on the sounds. Let me mention a motley few in case they help: Richard Strauss' *Metamorphosen*; Vaughan Williams' *The Lark Ascending*; George Gershwin's *Rhapsody in Blue*; Santana's *Samba Pa Ti*; Miles Davis' *So What*.

We steer away from musical analysis. That certain musical devices and structures give rise to musical phrases expressive of happiness, sadness or other emotions, does not solve the philosophical puzzle of what it is for such phrases to be expressive in those ways.

One immediate response to our puzzle is to deny that music can be expressive. When you express happiness or sadness, hopes or fears, you usually have some objects in mind that are the source of those states. Your son has now married again for money; that is what makes you happy. The movement at your bedside is that of a snake; the snake is what you fear. Music, though, does not have thoughts; it does not experience objects – so how can it possibly have emotions and feelings to express?

That simple reflection reminds us that music's expression of emotion cannot be understood in the way in which Annie's expression can. That is assuredly true; but instead of concluding that music cannot express emotion, it is wiser to see if we can resolve the puzzle by grasping music's expressiveness differently. Let us remember: it just is true that most people find it appropriate to speak of music as expressing emotions that can move them. It would be paradoxical indeed if we so quickly concluded that they are mistaken – and then went for a drink. That is too easy a way out.

How can music be happy or sad, angry or peaceful?

The same adjectives may be applied to music, also curiously to fictional characters, as to people. 'Happy', 'sad', 'bleak', 'angry' are words we learn to apply to persons, to some other animals, as well as to music. Of course, some may insist that those words have different meanings from the usual, or are metaphorical, when applied to music – but why, then, do such words sound appropriate? Applying 'sad' to a musical phrase is not arbitrary. There exists, it seems, a similarity between the sadness expressed by human gestures and those musical phrases expressive of sadness.

'Similarity' is the key. We need, though, to distinguish similarity from just any connection. We need also to ask: similarity regarding which features? A handkerchief's knot reminds you of the shopping, but the knot neither expresses nor resembles your intended purchases. In contrast, when music causes us to feel sadness – when it arouses feelings of sadness – we may attribute sadness to the music. Music perhaps 'expresses' the emotions which it arouses in us.

The 'arousal' answer is surely mistaken. We may recognize that some music is expressing sadness, yet not experience sadness aroused within us. A sad clown may make us laugh rather than arousing sadness. Looking at things the other way round, a logical puzzle may cause depression, yet not be a depressed puzzle. And when there is a link between the expressive music and the emotion aroused, the 'arousal' explanation goes the wrong way round. It is not because the music arouses sadness that we consider the music sad. It is because the music is sad that it may arouse sadness. By analogy, it would usually be mistaken to claim that your being scared explains why the lion is looking at you hungrily. Rather, it is the lion's salivation and napkin preparations that explain your being scared.

We have been searching for a connection between music and emotion. The arousal theory connects the music to the hearers' emotions – but, as said, hearers can hear music as expressive of sadness without themselves becoming sad.

Some have argued that music's expressiveness results from the composer's emotions when composing; but who knows what composers may be feeling when hurrying to finish their compositions? Composers may write cheerful music for the fee without being cheerful at all.

For music to be happy or sad, angry or solemn, there must be some similarity connections – let us reiterate – with items linked to such emotions. Let us try again to find the connections.

Consider the classic example of the drooping face of a basset hound. It looks sad; it is expressive of sadness. Look into the clouds and you may see menacing faces. Obviously the clouds are not experiencing menace; and the hound may be far from sad. Yet we are not describing them thus on a whim; we are not projecting emotions onto them willy-nilly. The features of the hound's face resemble the features of a person's sadness, when displayed. Similarly – and arguably – sad music is sad because it possesses features that put us in mind of the sadness of people. Obviously, the music does not 'look' sad; but the way in which it moves, its sound contours, may resemble the pace and contours of the movements of sad people. Well, that is the suggestion.

♈

Music is a special case, an intense case, of two features of human life that are mysterious.

First, we use the same words to describe very, very different things. As a result, we often feel that there must be similarities between those things. The words are not ambiguous terms such as 'bank' (river) and 'bank' (financial) or 'entrance' (way in) and 'entrance' (enchant). Yet often the sole similarity appears to be that we use the same words for the items in question. We describe a sound as 'low', yet is it akin to a bridge that is low? With Vaughan Williams' *The Lark Ascending*, we picture a skylark high in the sky; yet what similarity exists between the violin's 'high' notes and the skylark's height and flight?

Secondly, even though well aware that sad music is not itself sad, we may yet experience emotional reactions to the music as to a sad friend. And think how we do this in other areas of life. We can feel sorry for the basset hound solely based on the drooping face, despite knowing how silly that is. We are moved by fictional characters, despite their being fictional. We may be upset by imaginary disasters happening to loved ones, even though we know that they are only imagined and will not happen.

Our human capacity to find similarities and to be moved by appearances is indeed mysterious – or perhaps just the way we are. Our experience of the expressiveness of music is mysterious – or just the way it is.

Some music is deep – but as deep as the oceans are deep? Some music is light – but as light as a feather or the light of day? And some music is sad – but as sad as a person is sad? Whatever the degree of expressiveness in music, the meaning that we find in music is surely something beyond expression – save by music.

The film *Casablanca* is probably most famous for the misquotation of 'Play it, Sam' as 'Play it again, Sam'; but allow me to use the spirit of the misquotation to respond to the questions about what music says.

If asked what a piece of music means, what it expresses, what it says, what it evokes and so forth, the best response is just to play it again. Yes, play it again, Sam.

91

FRAGILE CREATURES THAT WE ARE...

McTaggart – John McTaggart Ellis McTaggart no less, though also no more, a philosopher at the turn of the twentieth century – kept a cat, a cat named 'Pushkin'. In winter, people who visited McTaggart in his Cambridge rooms were astonished to see Pushkin enjoying pride of position fireside front, while McTaggart shivered at his corner desk. 'Why ever do you give Pushkin the warmest slot?' 'Because,' replied McTaggart, 'that's the best it gets for a cat.'

Human beings often reflect on their lives – unlike our feline friends. We reflect not only when in philosophy classes and on therapists' couches, but in pubs and clubs, while trapped in airports, or lazing on seashores, alone or with friends – and also in the night's stillness when sleep is elusive and only breathings and heartbeats sound. And while it is not uncommon, when the going gets tough, to wish to be feline – my mother's wish when ensnared by shrinking, twilight years – most of us value being a person much more than being a cat. Only we humans can chart the heavens, be compassionate and just, and laugh when the barmaid, having asked which drink – 'Bitter?' she says – receives the reply, 'No, just tired.'

There is far more to human life than to the feline; and we value the more. Yet, once reflecting, we meet trouble, for we may trouble ourselves about what gives meaning or sense.

How can we make sense of our lives?

Some think that lives can only make sense if they exist for purposes beyond themselves; then, looking for purpose beyond all human lives, they are either overwhelmed with despair at its absence or embrace the

mystery of purpose divine, the divine apparently requiring no purpose outside. Puzzling about purposes and ends, about lives mortal and immortal, occurs in the forthcoming Part X on values; here we focus on sense within our lives.

Making sense of our lives may occur when we cast light on moments, relationships and activities, seeing them as holding together in recognizable patterns, with values, histories and developments. The arts – especially the narratives of drama, novels and opera – can help us to see sense by casting light on fictional lives, that is, by telling stories.

Stories open our eyes, proposing perspectives, revealing connections and pinpointing clashes. We may come to understand the characters' lives and meaning, through seeing how the characters connect, how their pasts stand with their futures, and which values they grow to espouse. Stories appear as myths and sagas, tales and drama, poems and opera – and today's ever-playing operas of soap. Instead of ancient gossip, Grecian in mode, about Zeus, Apollo and Dionysus, today's audience speculations may relate to the developments in *EastEnders*, *Californication*, *Episodes* – or whatever is the latest promoted series.

Although the arts do not exist with the purpose of helping us through life, in appreciating them we may relate them to ourselves.

We see how lives hang on contingencies of birth, on flicks of the hair, on chance encounters. We meet with fragilities and tragedies, yet also resolutions and magical ways of seeing. Think how, centuries on, we still live lives through Greek myths, our understanding of ourselves being shaped by updated tales and psychological theories, invoking Oedipus, Narcissus and Helen of Troy.

A life may lack sense because experiences are fragmentary, no pattern discerned, emotions in turmoil. And, as sketched via 'A pill for everything' (Chapter 62), we may then anguish over what we truly are and want, rocked by seen and unseen conflicts. By way of example, here is a conflict, captured in Greek myth: the Apollonian versus Dionysian.

On the one hand, the image of Apollo signifies a rational world of limits, of distinct objects, of rules: a clenched fist in control. The image gives rise to aesthetic ideas of the simple, beautiful and precise. We humans often aspire to such ideals. On the other hand, the Dionysian is intoxication, drunkenness, where boundaries become blurred, through ecstasy and frenzy: palms are open, welcoming, yielding; we melt and meld with others. Few of us think in terms of such explicit categories, itself an Apollonian enterprise; yet many of us recognize the conflict between control and succumbing – between straight lines and tangles. We need, though, the particularities of characters, details that novelists offer, that philosophy alone too easily lacks, to enlighten our struggles.

Thomas Mann's *Death in Venice*, for example, brings to life a conflict – be it through the novella, Visconti film or Britten opera. Gustav von Aschenbach, the Apollonian personification, the disciplined writer, admirer of aesthetics, is struck by the beauty of a mysterious youth. Aschenbach's Apollonian, aesthetic appreciation transforms into a Dionysian, obsessive, sensual desire – all from afar. Aschenbach becomes desperate and degraded, degraded by an elderly man's erotic love, a yearning for youth. Yet ambiguities persist. His death on the shore, his dying gaze towards the ocean – they may generate new ways of giving sense to his life, of feeling at one.

The brief description does not captivate – but the novel, the film, the opera captivate many. We may lose ourselves in the work's beauty, while also relating to conflicts within ourselves and others. The arts, at their best, paradoxically both free us from self-absorption and shape how we see our lives and others, bringing new perspectives to bear. Great art also carries new relevances, being re-interpreted, mirroring contemporary worries and ways of thinking. Religions do that too. Religious believers live lives in the light of stories, rituals and music, derived from scriptures and tradition, often seen afresh: reflect on how differently the Bible has been interpreted over the centuries regarding slavery, homosexuality and the treatment of animals.

Let us not, by the way, foolishly and optimistically, think that good art leads to good deeds. Some tormenters – those responsible for the Shoah, the Holocaust – have marvelled at the splendour of, for example, Beethoven and Schubert. The arts do not make our choices for us.

<center>~~~</center>

'Life can only be understood backwards; but it must be lived forwards.' Kierkegaard's words formed the apt aphorism for Part VI on the self; and to make some sense of our life, we need a sense of self unfolding. Our life, though, can never be grasped properly because we are never at rest to adopt the backwards-looking position. Even were we to rest, we should receive distorted pictures: how we should read the past depends in part on the future. Imagine a football game frozen ten minutes before the end: how the game is assessed up to then could differ radically from how that period is assessed, once at end of play. What was viewed as dreadful formations, by the end is praised as inspired.

'In retrospect' has value, as does what is in prospect. Narrative art displays both: lives in prospect and retrospect. Jean-Paul Sartre saw that, prior to death, we are free to create our lives, to take them in new directions, leading to fresh 'in retrospect' views. The sting in death, according to Sartre (as noted in Part VIII's Introduction), is awareness that, once dead, we are prey to the Other: we are impotent, as others try to interpret, fix and classify us. Narrative art, though, should remind us that such attempts may receive continual revision.

♈

Earthly life, as also paradoxes, offers both too much and too little. There lies tragedy. Perhaps we should like all our life to be that of an itinerant global traveller, yet we may also long for a life growing within one small, stable community. We may crave the life of the unworldly, yet also the worldly; of the loyal family man, yet also the Casanova – of the woman about town, a poetess, a courtesan, yet also someone down to earth. Lifestyles rule out others. We cannot try them all. Storms rule out calm. Greyness rules out rainbows.

Many of us give wry smiles at life's clashes, incongruities and absurdities. Pity Pushkin the cat; he knows of no absurdities, of no smiles. Yet pity us too – for we cannot know for certain how our lives finally work out. 'Pity us', did I say?

Knowledge of our lives as ultimately viewed, if viewed at all, may be knowledge best not to have; but what is worth having is the mishmash, the muddles, the mêlée of life as we live it. There is a richness to the human life that eludes Pushkin's. We humans can revel in reflections, ambiguities and humour, flying close to the sun with loves and aspirations. We can also, though, lose ourselves in art, in music, in wonder – in wonder at the land, the sea, the stars, at the vibrant jazz of city life, and the lingering look on a face.

With philosophy an analytical and reflective art, this book's perplexities engage reflection – reflection upon reflection, as does this sentence. It is fitting, though, to emphasize that *not* reflecting also brings sense to our lives. Paradoxically, there can be delight in losing the self, in simply surrendering, as perhaps Pushkin does, to dawn, to dusk, to desires – to mosaics of colours and sounds, from scuffling leaves and storms of snow to a skylark ascending over a heath. As well as charms of reflection, of musings and mullings, there can be charm in saying nothing, in saying nothing at all. There can be charm purely in – experiencing.

> *When the mountain flowers are blooming,*
> *Their scent carries their meaning.*

PART X: VALUES

Is there more to life than…?

'Tis better to be a dissatisfied Socrates than a satisfied pig.
John Stuart Mill

Human that we are, we cannot help but reflect on values, on our dealings with others – and ultimately on the question: what does it all mean? Some insist that there are no values, yet curiously conclude that they must therefore try to get whatever they want. They hence make their own satisfactions – accumulating wealth, for example – of final value. So, wittingly or no, they do believe in values. They value, it seems, whatever it is that they want; but if the sole value of what they want is that they want it, why want it?

Perplexities certainly arise when seeking to grasp how there are values within and beyond humanity – look out for the jerboa – and, indeed, how anything about life can be valuable, bearing in mind that life comes to a sticky end or simply that it comes to an end, sticky or no. Despair at life having an end naturally gives rise to questions of whether immortality, life eternal, could be preferable – the questions of Chapter 95.

Once we recognize values, we cannot help but hit dilemmas that seem impossible to resolve. Values compete. Optimists may think that, regarding every dilemma, there must be a right answer declaring what must be done; if only we could see clearly and fully, we should see that answer. Realists – the author is one – accept that there just are some genuine moral dilemmas: how can one weigh up, in all cases, the moral significance of loyalty to a friend against that of exposing the truth – or the moral acceptability or otherwise of paying for a child's expensive piano lessons against using the money to help those children lacking clean water in Malawi? This realistic stance does not imply that there are no clear-cut cases, where there is no doubt concerning what is right and what is wrong. There are many such cases.

On our tour through these puzzles, we find regard for humanity, paradoxically through *schadenfreude*; we also witness an argument between Ant and Grasshopper on the conduct of life, and a fundamental moral drawn from, and about, logical reasoning, courtesy of Mr T our tortoise. Yes, that Mr T who, much earlier, entangled us in space and time. This time he comes to our rescue; well, he comes to our rescue, if we draw the right moral from his tale.

And we end – at least Part X ends – with worries about Barbarians and then the haunting question that can cause so much trouble: what *is* the point?

92

MISFORTUNE, MISS FORTUNA –
AND MALICIOUS DELIGHT

'Happy is the man whose best friend falls off a roof,' said Confucius. That comment is at the heart of the puzzle. To give it meat, conjure up a fictional figure.

> Lady Assured was until yesterday a high-ranking government minister. Civil servants agreed that she did her job exceptionally well, though she was somewhat arrogant. Today her world crashed. She had been overheard, in private conversation, making some tactless remarks about the Prime Minister; she also spoke of her support for fox-hunting, despite having voted against it; and, on top of that, her department had managed to lose confidential data. Today's newspaper headlines scream against Lady Assured. She resigns.

How should we react to such news? Of course, we may have no view; but some people would feel sorry for her. People often make tactless remarks privately with the remarks remaining private. Government ministers have to toe party lines, for example concerning fox-hunting, even if the lines conflict with personal beliefs. Further, Lady Assured was unlucky with the data loss: misfortune struck. Lady Assured did the decent thing, taking responsibility: 'the buck stops here.'

The puzzle here, though, concerns *schadenfreude*. That is, it concerns those people who take some pleasure in Lady Assured's misfortune. They cannot help but smile. Many of us, at certain times, experience *schadenfreude* – despite quips about how only the Germans have a special word for the feeling. In Britain at the 1997 election, millions took pleasure in seeing the then young and conceited government minister Michael Portillo lose; and many have been and will be pleased by the political demise of various individuals, across both European and US more recent elections.

Schadenfreude is understood as malicious. The odds are already stacked against it, if we are wondering whether it is wrong. People usually feel it unworthy of a good person; but why? May there not be something good about the existence of *schadenfreude*?

Can *schadenfreude* be a good thing?

Suppose you take delight in someone else suffering, in cases such as a burglar having been caught and beaten, or a drunk driver fined. Your delight may be because the individuals deserved what they suffered. That it is a matter of desert may indicate that the delight is not malicious. Some people may be pleased about Lady Assured's downfall simply because they judge that hypocrisy merits a fall from grace.

Some high-minded individuals would argue that any delight through people's suffering can only be justified if the suffering is a necessary albeit unfortunate result of justice being done. The delight should be in the maintenance of justice rather than in the suffering. Indeed, we can – perhaps we should – pity the person who justly suffers. 'It hurts me more than it hurts you' is the quip of old-fashioned headmasters caning bright pupils. They may feel sorry for the boys caught stealing apples, yet pleased that they were caught and are taking their punishment.

Even when desert is not at issue, we sometimes experience feelings of delight about a misfortune – feelings justified on consequential grounds. Supporters of fox-hunting may be pleased about Lady Assured's downfall because the downfall could lead to the anti-hunting law being repealed. They may also feel sorry for Lady Assured having to suffer. They may argue that their delight is in the likely consequences rather than in the Lady's misfortune.

Desert and consequences for particular projects drift us away from *schadenfreude* pure and unsullied. The pleasures of revenge also drift us away – for the subjects of our *schadenfreude* may have done us no harm. Sometimes we may simply experience pleasure in the misfortunes of another. We can experience such pleasure about Lady Assured's fall from grace, but not because we are especially worried about the 'tally ho' or because we believe that ministers ought to have departments in perfect working order. The pleasure in the downfall may be *schadenfreude*, pure and simple. Now, ought that to be condemned, given its element of malice?

Taking pleasure in others' sufferings could suggest that we hope for such sufferings to occur. To hope for others to suffer is surely malicious. Yet it is far from clear that people who experience *schadenfreude* must hope to have the experience. Rather, some misfortunes occur that provide them with the experience. Now, delight in certain types of misfortune clearly manifests a vicious character. People would be amazingly nasty if they delighted in those who were already having a rotten time suffering even more. Consider victims of earthquakes who then undergo yet more harms from aftershocks. Consider the poor whose lives are made worse through war. Nothing can justify taking pleasure in such pains.

If *schadenfreude* is to be justified at all, it needs to be directed at those doing relatively well in the relevant society. Further, it needs, arguably, to be directed to those who are self-satisfied and smug. Perhaps Lady Assured's arrogance stimulated some people's *schadenfreude*. This, though, runs the danger of returning us to desert. The proud deserve to suffer a fall; the arrogant deserve to be humbled. Once again, we meet the high-minded stance. The stance is that the pleasure ought to be in people getting what they deserve, not in the suffering. If so, then justifying *schadenfreude* directly, without reference to desert, has once again failed.

Let us see if justified *schadenfreude* can be prevented from collapsing into pleasure at people getting what they deserve.

You watch a confident man in a fine suit – perhaps a four-piece suit, as Virginia Woolf quipped of T. S. Eliot's attire – walking out, swivelling his silver-topped cane; but... A moment later, he is victim of a well-aiming pigeon or heavy storm. That can cause us delight, not merely at the incongruity, with the resultant laughter. The man does not deserve the little mishap. The pigeon and storm were unexpected and outside his control: he was suddenly at their mercy. He was unlucky. Lady Assured hit unlucky about the loss of confidential data. Her downfall, the object of our *schadenfreude*, could have resulted solely from that misfortune. What do such examples show?

The man and Lady Assured are shown to be equal to us all in being exposed to Miss Fortuna, being at the mercy of misfortune, of chance. Machiavelli spoke of Fortuna as a woman whom we may try to discipline, yet to whom, in the end, we are all vulnerable.

The man's fine suit, the silver-topped cane, the confident gaze, parade someone safe, utterly safe from life's vicissitudes; yet the pigeon's digestion, the storm, prove otherwise. Lady Assured's high position suggested security; yet, through bad luck, the security crumbled. These misfortunes highlight our common frailty. They restore the equality of human beings in the face of Miss Fortuna – well, at least a little. *Schadenfreude* celebrates the restoration.

Is *schadenfreude*'s celebration thereby malicious and unworthy? Some would claim that such examples merely show that we are envious of others' success. No doubt that is sometimes true, but not always. Indeed, if things are going too well for us, we may delight in a touch of *schadenfreude* about ourselves – when we fall. *Schadenfreude* relies on a sense of humanity, of how we all sail on life's oceans of uncertainty.

♈

Harold Macmillan, a former British Prime Minister, when asked about what determined his policies, spoke of, 'Events, dear boy, events.' *Schadenfreude* is delight in recognizing that 'Events, dear boy, events', otherwise known as Miss Fortuna – be she in the form of lost data, an unexpected storm or a careless pigeon – bind us, bind us all in a common humanity.

93

SHOULD WE SAVE THE JERBOA?

The long-eared jerboa has – er – long ears. It lives in the deserts of Mongolia and China – with its ears. A tiny nocturnal mammal, it is dwarfed by enormous ears. It hops like a kangaroo; and, for mammals, it possesses one of the biggest ear-to-body ratios. That is, it has very big ears for its size. There are little hairs on its feet, almost like snow shoes, which allow the jerboa to jump along the sand. It is said to be cute and comic. It is classified as endangered. Oh, and did I mention the ears?

Why should we care about the jerboa? Our question is about the species, as a kind, or a class of creatures. A species is easily confused in speech with the individual members of the species, not least because our language so easily flips around: 'the jerboa' could designate a particular jerboa, or the species taken to be a group of jerboas, or the species taken to be the type of creature it is. Individual jerboas have two long ears each, but the species, as a collection, does not really have long ears and certainly not merely two, though the species as a type of creature is that type that normally has two long ears. When people are concerned about a species' survival, they usually want to promote the existence of a collection of creatures of a certain type, but not any individuals in particular. Particular individuals die, but the species, the collection with members of a certain type, may persist.

Naturally, we may also care about individual jerboas: probably we do not want any individual jerboa to suffer. We recognize that there is something that counts as going well for an individual jerboa. But the species, as a species, is not the sort of thing that suffers pain. Preserving a species may, in fact, involve culling, killing some members. So our general question is – and a couple of examples are –

Why save a species from extinction?
Why save the jerboa?
Why regret the loss of the dodo?

Some simple quick answers in favour of preservation concern the benefits or possible benefits to humans. Preservation is justified on the grounds of the species' value as an instrument to aid us. Perhaps the different species help maintain Earth's ecological balance. Maybe their genetic information, one day, could aid development of pharmaceuticals. In addition, people gain pleasure from seeing members of different species. For similar reasons, we may regret the loss of the dodo.

Suppose the jerboa lacks such instrumental value with regard to ecology and future genetic researches. Suppose too that the jerboa is so furtive, living in such inhospitable conditions, that people typically will not see a jerboa and so will not gain pleasure from sighting experiences. May the species yet possess value?

Yes. People may value simply knowing that the jerboa exists, know-ing that there is such a species and such variety around them. We are identifying a curious instrumental value, curious in that it fails to involve our direct experiences of the jerboa. Once again, though, we are finding value in the jerboa's existence because of its effects on humans, albeit not directly experienced effects. May the jerboa, though, or any spe-cies, have an intrinsic value, a value that does not depend for its being a value on something else – that does not depend, for example, on what humans want?

The question does not presuppose that a species cannot have both instrumental value and intrinsic value. This is not an either–or matter. Some items have both. Philosophizing, arguably, is intrinsically valuable, yet may also possess instrumental value in bringing peace and harmony to the universe. Well, true – maybe that last point is a little fanciful. What is not fanciful is the thought that some things have intrinsic value. Somewhere along the line we stop ourselves from saying 'this is only valuable because it is a means to that…' For example, the stop-ping point is often happiness, usually human happiness: happiness has intrinsic value. Certainly, many people, after a little reflection, would readily embrace that thought – though further reflection should lead to worries of quite what constitutes happiness and how happiness relates to pleasures, satisfactions and contentment.

Returning to the jerboa, by pretending that it lacks all instrumental value, we focus on whether there is any other value, an intrinsic value, that applies to the species. Perhaps there is value in the jerboa's exist-ence simply because it is a species of living individuals. Well, it is not obviously the case that 'living' thereby makes something valuable. The smallpox virus, HIV and malarial mosquitoes are living, yet we question whether they are thereby intrinsically valuable. Our negative attitude, though, may result from their harming us: they could still be intrinsi-cally valuable.

Possibly there is something valuable about nature being left, undis-turbed by human beings; however, that certainly does not point to species' conservation. Nature ensures the extinction of vast numbers of species – and it may be in our human nature, quite whatever that means, to destroy species, just as it is to tame parts of nature. The rural landscapes of fields, crops and national parks would be non-existent, but for human interferences – as would be spectacular bridges, sculptures and architecturally stunning galleries.

♈

Perhaps we should simply recognize that we value the presence of a variety of species. We value that presence independently of our purposes and independently of any value for us. We value the jerboa for its own sake. Note, though, that even here its value may be resting solely on the fact that we humans value it 'for its own sake'. There is, though, a stronger suggestion: that the jerboa – or any species – possesses value independently even of our valuing it. After all, if the species in question did not possess such value, why should we value it for its own sake? Why value something unless it is worthy of being valued?

It is difficult, it seems, to get a grip on 'for its own sake' when applied to a species. If we do something for an individual jerboa's sake, we have some idea of how we are acting in its best interests, how its life may go well. We know that it needs food and shelter; but it is far from clear that a species, as opposed to particular individuals, has an interest. It is far from clear how things go well for the species, from the species' viewpoint. After all, a species lacks a viewpoint.

Human beings promote the existence of some things and not of others. We value. We are *valuers*. Perhaps – and perhaps conveniently for human beings – possessors of intrinsic value include at least those individuals that are themselves valuers, such as we are. We may, though, wonder why that should be believed. Without valuers, nothing would be valued; but it neither follows that valuers are valuable nor that items are only valuable if they happen to be valued.

In our valuing, having preferences, recognizing things as worthy of desire, perhaps we become aware that there are items that are intrinsically valuable, whose value is other than being experienced by us or even being experiences. Maybe that is why so many of us, even when godless, stand in wonder at the different species, seeking to preserve them against the ravages of both man and impersonal nature. Maybe that is why some of us see beauty in sunsets, in landscapes, in seascapes, a beauty that is valuable and would still exist even without humans around to appreciate that beauty.

In some cases, it may be better not to have human beings around at all. Just think of those seashores splattered with empty beer cans, cigarette ends and worse. They offend the eye and detract from beauty; yet, without the humans around, could there be any offence, any loss or gain in beauty at all?

Suppose the shores by the oceans, the coral reefs, the lakes, lagoons and mountain heights – the forests of rain, windswept moors, the Arctic and Antarctica – all have their beauty much tarnished by human beings, with ever more rubbish, oil explorations, pollution and concrete blocks. Suppose human beings do their worse, so to speak, yet then the human species falls into extinction; perhaps all life eventually expires as a result. With no human beings, with no human valuations, with no human disgust at what has been done, no sadness, no regrets, no remorse, could there be any disvalue – any disvalue at all – in what remains? Would it then matter that the environment had suffered so badly, if badly it be?

Or would the eye of the universe still shed a tear?

94
IF THIS BE JUDGING...

Lawyers and lovers, doctors and dealers, politicians and priests – all of us, in fact – face difficult and dicey dilemmas. We want to do the right thing, yet sometimes, it seems, whatever we do involves doing the wrong.

'I should be kind to people; but if I am kind to Arnold, then Zoe will be upset; and if I am kind to Zoe, then Arnold gets upset. And if I ignore both of them, they both get upset – and so do I. What am I to do?' Here, there is just one value involved – not upsetting people. Another 'one value' puzzle arises with fairness. We should be fair, so parking fines should be the same for all offenders, say £200. 'But that is so unfair. £200 is a week's wages for some, an hour's salary for others. Fairness requires a percentage figure of income or capital or vehicle value.' How do we judge such matters?

Dilemmas also arise because different values, different 'right things', pull us in opposing directions. You signed a confidentiality clause about your consultancy work for a bank, yet you are now aware of some dubious dealings. Should you break your contract?

Terrorism: If we torture these suspects, we may learn where the next bombings will occur; yet if we engage in torture, we're acting abominably, against our principle, our integrity. The suspects may even be innocent.

Love: My future life and the life of the man whom I love would be so fulfilled if we ran away together, yet my elderly parents think it dishonourable – and I'd be letting down my husband, my commitment.

Values conflict. Absolute principles may appear fine in heavenly abstract, but, here on Earth, they engender clashes. You should never torture, yet if it is the only means of possibly saving many lives... ? How many? How strong the possibility? You should keep your marriage vows – even if your resultant years would be inauthentic? You should respect a woman's right to choose – even if you sincerely believe abortion is murder? Should governments improve the quality of lives already fortunate, through arts subsidies, rather than directing the money to ameliorate conditions for the starving?

Morality, both private and public, embraces a medley of values – freedom, happiness, promise-keeping, respect, rights, fairness, welfare – and virtues, such as courage, generosity, justice. There are also finer values: courtesy, decency, dignity, discretion, poise, beauty and grace. Quantities are relevant; so are qualities. What should we do when concerns conflict – as, unnoticed, they often do; and, noticed, they sometimes do?

'It is a matter of judgement.' But while we may know what the matter is, and what the judgement eventually is, how should the judgement be reached?

How do we judge what is the right thing to do?

Sometimes judgement is easy, at least in principle. There may be a common measure between the different values, our principle being to maximize or minimize whatever is measured. We should, perhaps, maximize number of lives saved, or minimize overall suffering. Difficulties may persist. How do we assess probabilities? What is to be done, if two possible actions have equal value, with fine tuning in calculation impractical? Factual disagreements may also arise: for example, whether capital punishment deters, whether torture is effective. They are practical problems, though not solely so: do we really want the authorities to keep torture equipment in working order – just in case needed?

We focus, though, on – to my mind – a deep philosophical puzzle. What is to be done when there seems no common measure, when values turn out to be incommensurable? How can we judge between quantities and qualities concerning freedoms, rights, virtues, fairness, welfare? An action may be both manifesting someone's right to free speech, yet offending the religious. An action may be both keeping a promise, yet thereby allowing a crime to go undetected. It is not that the factors on each side of the scales are exactly balanced, but, rather – at least, it seems – we lack the scales.

This point about lacking scales requires a caveat. If the choice is between lying to a terrorist, thereby saving many lives, and telling the truth, leading to the loss of many lives, then we should lie. But when we are not at such extremes, have we any idea how to judge the right path?

Some may argue that, because we do judge in extreme cases, the scales must exist, measuring 'moral worth' or something similar, the problem being, so to speak, poor eyesight or poor calibrations, in the difficult cases. But just because, when confronted with extremes, we often know what ought to be done, there may yet be no common measure available in the large range of less extreme cases. It is not clear how talk of 'moral worth' helps us to judge. Further, some conflicts are between, for example, items of moral worth and those of the aesthetic. Do we know how to compare the value of extending lifespans for many with saving some Venetian architectural wonders?

When facing these difficult dilemmas, we want to make wise judgements, yet the judgements may appear arbitrary or motivated by factors such as 'just how I happen to feel'. Of course, we want to distinguish our deliberations from flicks of the wrist or throws of some dice. We recognize that serious matters are involved, yet we lack, it seems, appropriate procedures for resolution.

When expert judges, in the American Supreme Court or Britain's, speak of weighing the evidence, balancing factors, yet reach opposite conclusions – with, to take a landmark, but controversial, ruling, five judges concluding that same-sex marriage is a nationwide right, albeit with four judges concluding that it is not (an example of the American Supreme Court in action in 2015) – is accepting the majority view as determining the right answer much better than spinning a coin? The allusion to the coin spin may appear all the more apt, when we remember that, had certain other expert judges been sitting or been appointed, then the overall decision could well have been different.

Reflect on capital punishment, the death penalty, that ultimate of punishments. A majority of US states still maintain the penalty, despite the erratic sentencing, the grisly process of infliction and the numerous mistakes that come to light 'too late'. Here, the metaphor of the 'coin spin' is not completely apt, but rather the reality of injustice is more to the point. The evidence seems to be that, for the same type of crime, a black man is more likely to receive the death sentence than a white. We have, though, strayed into the particular immorality of certain laws and their implementation; this chapter's focus, though, is that of genuine moral dilemmas, to which we return.

♈

Moral dilemmas often irritate. People often want *the* answer, determining which one of various alternatives should be chosen, given the circumstances. Maybe, though, there is no right answer, in that sense. Maybe the right answer is that, whichever option is chosen, the choice will have good and bad features which are incommensurable. It is not as if – well, not obviously as if – there is some path that is the one right path, known by God, but undiscoverable by humans.

Sometimes we look back at decisions; sometimes we reflect: 'Now I see – that is what I just had to do.' This is where, upon reflection on choices previously available to us, we may feel that we could have done no other. That does not mean that physically or psychologically we could not have done otherwise, but that, to be the sort of people we are or have become, we could not have acted otherwise.

Consider: two pregnant young women, students, serious, same circumstances – each are deciding whether to have an abortion. They reach different decisions, despite being concerned by the same troubling factors concerning relationships, the significance of life, of becoming a mother, and the effect on their families, finances and careers. In reaching their decisions, mysteriously they may have contributed to making their moral selves, to making themselves into the sort of people they are. One now sees her decision to have the child as courageous, valuing the creation of life, of nurturing the life within her. The other reflects upon her courage in having the abortion, committing, maybe, to developing a career, possibly a family much later on, and deeply feeling that having a child was not the right thing for her to do at her stage of life.

What are we to say?

Some may insist that one is right, the other is wrong; but perhaps that is a mistake. Perhaps they could both be right, even if, at the time, they were equally concerned about life, career and future relationships – and so forth. Of course, some will then insist that there must have been a difference all along in what weight they gave to the different factors; but why insist on that? Perhaps the so-called difference that exists in their weightings is nothing more than their reaching different decisions.

I have provided an optimistic example: both women look back, feeling that they did the right thing – and did. There are, naturally, bleak scenarios, where pessimism would have been in order: we sometimes look back, reflecting on how wrong our decisions were, even on how difficult we find it to live with what we have done.

We often have to judge what appears impossible to judge. What justifies the judgements that we make remains a mystery. As we have seen in this book, via various examples and thought experiments, with bears on the run, with equality between the sexes, with beats and peeping Toms, with being attached to a violinist – and many more scenarios – all we can do is often just muddle through. 'Muddling through' lacks a certain gravitas, lacks academic respectability; hence, I deem the line that I promote 'eclectic ethics', recognizing that ethics possesses a vast medley of moral concerns, from welfare to respect, from quality to quantity, from impartiality and fairness to loyalty and putting family first – and from much more to many more. With such a mishmash, well, we have no option but to muddle through.

Morality and human beings – and being human – make for an extremely strange brew.

95

LIFE WITHOUT END:
TOO MUCH OF A GOOD THING?

You can have too much of a good thing, or so it is said; but, when the good thing is life, many would cherish the much – and much, much more than even the much. Many would seek immortality. More accurately, many wish for the *possibility* of immortality, of living forever, of eternal life.

The desire for immortality need be no religious yen for a timeless disembodied existence, but rather a focus on the forever as a well-embodied immortal life, down here on Earth or planetary successors. Of course, things could go so disastrously badly that even those most intoxicated with living may wish for no more; but, assuming disasters unrealized, many yearn for more life, not less, and many would see no reason why that more should not be infinitely more. An infinite life is a life without end, and that is what many desire.

〰〰

'I wish I could live forever.'

Fliss is enjoying her life; she has no good reason to think things will go badly. She is intelligent, attractive, emotionally composed, with high earnings. All is well. 'If only my life didn't have to come to an end. If only I didn't have to cease to be,' sighs she.

'Drink, then, of my life-sustaining elixir,' mumbles the craggy-faced old man, sitting in the dusts of a Mongolian market, possessor of few teeth and to whom soap seems unknown. He points to a potion, as he eyes Fliss, clearly a tourist now off the well-beaten track.

Being a woman of sense, Fliss would right now be dismissing the old man as a crank, a salesman of snake oil, with a potion worthless or worse – but this is a tale of mine and, in this tale, the craggy-faced ancient is no crank and Fliss knows that the offer is genuine. It is, after all, possible that one day, through genetic engineering and medication, humans could be made immortal. Well, it is no obvious contradiction.

'A great idea,' beams Fliss, 'but why haven't you taken it yourself?'

'How do you know that I haven't?' comes the reply.

'But I don't want immortality if I'm going to become exceedingly old and infirm – and with few teeth and no soap.'

'Rest assured, the potion gives you eternal life guaranteed always at your age when drinking. You'll continue at age twenty-seven forever, if that is what you want.'

Fliss, flattered by the 'twenty-seven', quickly establishes that she would not be trapped with the immortality if she changed her mind centuries ahead. With the elixir, she would be receiving antidote pills which cancel the elixir's effects. And so, enthusiastically, having handed over payment, she drinks. Now, the question is, will Fliss at some stage take the antidote? Must not a time come when, if rational, anyone would have had enough of life?

Could immortality ever be good for us?

People often have strong immediate responses to the value of such earthly immortality. For many, it is obvious that a never-ending life at least *could* be good for the subject, the one who lives on; for others, the opposite is obvious. To evaluate such responses, some ground needs clearing with regard to both the immortality and the surviving subject.

A never-ending life could be one in which we are unconscious, in deep dreamless sleep without end. That would give people neither what they want, if they seek immortality, nor what they fear, if they seek avoidance. The life sought, or to be avoided, is a life which contains consciousness, presumably, with some psychological continuity running within. That does not mean that immortal beings, to have valuable immortality, need remember everything; but minimally they require some self-awareness as continuing persistent selves, with memories and projects. Anything less would not be in the spirit of what Fliss, our immortalist, craves.

A never-ending life could be conscious enough, but with its endlessness resulting from an endless recurrence of the same events: you live your life again and again, from zero to age eighty, unaware of the repetition. Recall the Prologue, where Nietzsche's 'eternal recurrence', that horror of horrors, is described. Such an infinite life is not what is typically sought, when people desire immortality.

The immortality desired is one in which we are conscious of ourselves as continuing to live on and on, undergoing different experiences – presumably, we know we are immortal – yet still being ourselves, our mysterious selves. Now, which questions arise?

One question is whether the elixir protects us from death by accidents and illness – and whether it saves us from significant harms. If it does, then an immortal life would be very different from the mortal. We should lack many worries about dangerous roads, nuclear war and dying from starvation. Deployment of concepts such as 'courage' and 'safety', and our concern for others, would be very different. For that matter, our blood, bones and organs would need to respond very differently to radiation, high-level impacts and excess alcohol. Our life would scarcely be recognizable as human.

Another question concerns the numbers involved. If I am the sole immortal, then I shall see friends come and go in life; I shall go through the gamut of relationships with different people – and maybe eventually with no people at all, just fading memories of them. If, though, I and a few others are immortal – maybe those wealthy enough to afford the elixirs – would we not be akin to a species different from regular humans? And if numerous people are made immortal, then the eventual 'lack of space' for newly created people suggests relationships between man and woman would eventually be altered: desires for children would need radical revision.

Lack of space prevents detailed review of possible immortalities and their human impact; but key reflections touch tedium and motivation.

If I retain sufficient memory to make sense of myself as continuing, then, after millions of years, would I not be bored by having yet again to start up relationships with new people, if in the world where I am the sole immortal? And if I am in the world where we all are immortal, would I not be bored by meeting the same people eternally?

In response, maybe there are some worthwhile pleasures that could be repeated infinitely, or maybe we would possess the capacity to devise endlessly new projects. If, for example, I am fascinated by numbers, my infinite time could be filled with further reflections on yet higher numbers and their properties: there is no end to numbers. Or maybe, as in a drugged haze, I could value the same heightened sensations returning eternally, or listen to the same music – the same Bartok string quartets – literally endlessly. Or could I?

Even if the boredom and horror can be avoided, there remains a problem for motivation. If something can be put off until tomorrow, why not put it off? There would be an infinite number of 'tomorrow's – so there would be little urgency to engage in anything today. Indeed, with no end in view, unless we repeatedly deceive ourselves into thinking otherwise, we may rightly wonder what structure could be given to our lives. Paradoxically, although many people view life as meaningless if ending in the finality of death, it may be eternal life that endangers meaning and engenders meaninglessness.

♈

For life to have meaning, arguably it needs an end: it needs death to provide a framework within which to pattern our lives. That does not imply that current lifespans are ideal. Perhaps lives of a thousand years would or could be good. Our wave at puzzles is merely to challenge the casual assumption that an eternal life could be a valuable life. We may question how a life can be judged as desirable or not, if we lack conception of its end. We may wonder what sense there is in its being 'me' living immortally, given the radical difference between a life mortal and one immortal. We may despair at the apparent need for an immortal life to contain an infinite variety of experiences, aims and commitments, if monotony is to be avoided. As seen in Part VI, there is trouble enough in making sense of personal identity, of what it is to be me, in a mortal life; that trouble is greatly aggravated, if immortality must be fitted into the picture.

Our wave above at some puzzles also provides excuse for display of a logical point. The point relates to the difference between, on the one hand, my declaring every day that I shall resist the wine on that day and, on the other hand, my declaring that I shall on every day resist the wine.

There is a difference between always wanting something to be so and wanting that something always to be so. Suppose that every day I have a choice between immediate death or an extra day's life. Every day I choose to live for the extra day – hence, I would live forever – yet I may well not choose to live forever. Perhaps we always yearn for the possibility of the extra day; yet maybe most of us know that what we do not want – if sense can be made of it – is the possibility of our life continuing for all days, without end.

Bad things, of course, we want to end; and, odd as it may seem, good things really do need to come to an end.

96

... AND THE LIVING IS EASY

Summertime — and, yes, the living is easy, well, easy for some. Our roving reporter is experiencing rural life, interviewing the locals — but what's this? It's bizarre… She's interviewing a grasshopper and ant.

∿

What do you do all day, Miss Grasshopper?

'I sing and dance, and dance and sing, across meadows of green, under skies of blue, the sun a-light, a-blazing upon my wing.'

You smile blissfully, Grasshopper, but Ant, I hear you dispute Grasshopper's lifestyle.

'That's right. You should reject it too. The living is easy for this young lady and other grasshoppers — but we workers don't have time for such trivial leisure stuff. We work our socks off day and night — well, we would, if we had socks. Not for us all the flimsy and fluttering finery of lazy Grasshopper here with her game-playing. We trek out, day after day, food to be gathered, then painstakingly stored for those cold, cold winter days ahead.'

'Hey, no need to rant, dear, dear Ant. Join in with us. Sing and dance, and dance and sing; all your utility is futility, futility. What's the point to your labours, your work, your toils of woe? They're all so, so without point, you know.'

'I'll tell you the point, young lady. You'll come a cropper, believe me. Work is what you have to do to survive. And you listen here: don't you come knocking at my door when you're cold and hungry, freezing in winter's frost — then you'll be sorry. Mark my words!'

'But that's all tomorrow, tomorrow, tomorrow. Think of today — come here, come hither, come play.'

'Frivolity – time wasting. Why am I wasting my time even talking to you? I must get on – must get on.'

Here, I'd better return us to the studio for a time check and traffic news. We mustn't let listeners lapse into grasshopping mode. They have their work to get to, money to earn, bills to pay; but...

Is it better to be the grasshopper?

The Aesop fable alluded to here encourages prudence. If you waste time today, what becomes of you tomorrow? And would Ant be morally obliged to help Grasshopper if she knocks at his door in winter, desperate for food? She would have wittingly allowed herself to slide into winter starvation. Her starvation would have been her own fault. She could have toiled under the summer's sun as Ant did so toil. She brought any winter misfortune upon herself. The fable may, though, generate a puzzle different from that of our moral responsibility for feckless others. This different puzzle asks: what is most valuable in life?

The contrast between Grasshopper and Ant is presented as that between leisure and work, between doing nothing and doing something.

Most people, though, readily accept that doing nothing possesses little value. In fact, what exactly is 'doing nothing'? Maybe just lying on a seashore, looking into the blue sky, feeling the warmth of the sun; but would that count as the most valuable life? It may be part of a valuable life, but do we not value more, much more?

Grasshopper may be understood as representing those who do things, but who – in contrast to Ant – do not do things that have to be done. Grasshopper plays. Ant toils. Ant toils not because toiling in itself is valuable, but as a necessary means to an end, an end that is valued – namely, being well-fed in winter. Grasshopper plays. In playing, she does something, but the ends of play are neither necessary to achieve nor do they need to be desirable for their own sake. It is the playing that is valuable. Play is typically associated with games; and games, some suggest, are voluntary attempts to overcome unnecessary obstacles.

In work and games we accomplish things, but with games, the goals typically lack value other than being parts of the games. Ant would be much worse off, he thinks, if not well-fed in winter. Pure game-players are not much worse off, if golf balls fail to get holed, footballs never land in goal, and crosswords remain uncompleted. A charm of games can be the utter pointlessness in the ends that are sought. Of course, further ends may be added, such as winning prizes.

The pointlessness of games' ends is matched by the perverse means required to achieve those ends. Players are not allowed to drop golf balls in the holes, carry the football into the net, or look up answers in order to solve the crosswords. Rules constrain how the goals may be achieved. Games can be good – they can be bad – as games. Good games must be neither very easy, nor yet impossible to complete.

Why value Grasshopper's lifestyle over Ant's toil? Well, Ant's activities are undertaken because of the necessity of the ends. They are undertaken not for their own sake, but for something else. Maybe this detracts from the value of Ant's activities. Play and games lack that external pressure. Of course, Ant triumphs in the end because those hard frosts and snows do come along. But at what cost has he triumphed? What is the value of a life of toil, if one toils only to be well-fed – in order to toil yet again and again? Grasshopper's life, albeit short, has been freed of toiling necessities.

We should, in passing, question whether 'play' captures all that can be valuable, without needing external ends. Paintings and music – creating and appreciating – can be valued in themselves, as suggested earlier in Part IX, without any further ends in view.

♈

People – even philosophers – often favour black or white answers and sharp distinctions. 'Are you journeying to get from A to B? If so, then it would be better to be at B, without the journeying.' Now, on occasions that may be true; but often, when we journey to B, the journeying is also valuable. We should not forget that activities undertaken for a required end may yet also be valued in themselves; and activities valued in themselves may possess the additional value of being the means to something else that is also valuable. How much better, we may imagine, if Grasshopper's game-playing also helped to store food for the winter. How much better if those who – perversely? – delight in peddling gymnasium exercise machines, at the same time generated electricity.

The discussion above raises two further matters, one that is general, about the nature of the meaning of words, and one concerning the ever baffling self.

The first matter is this. Wittgenstein famously pointed to the term 'game' as an example of how we can successfully understand words, even though they lack a certain type of definition. Some think Wittgenstein mistaken; hence the definition of 'game', summarized above, as a voluntary attempt to overcome unnecessary obstacles. That definition merits challenge: mountaineering and writing haiku seem to be voluntary attempts to overcome unnecessary obstacles, yet are not usually games; and some necessary work could be nothing but a game for some.

Whether or not Wittgenstein is right about 'game', he is surely right that not all words can be informatively defined by setting out necessary and sufficient conditions for their use. Recall the futile quest for a definition of 'harm' (Chapter 9). We often need to see how words are used in everyday circumstances rather than seeking formal definitions; we need to accept grey areas. 'Game' is certainly an example of that: an activity may have some features of a typical game, while lacking others that are also gamely typical. We need, on occasions, to resist the 'black or white', the 'yes or no'.

The second 'further matter' is that of identity. Why does Ant in the summer concern himself with how he will be in the winter? Why slave away now, when the future is uncertain – and future fun less likely? After all, age slows us all down. More deeply, we have puzzles of personal identity, as seen in Part VI. Why do I, Peter Cave, identify with Peter Cave a year ago or twenty years ago, and Peter Cave a year into the future, when my desires and beliefs and character may have radically altered?

Returning to Ant, there is a future winter ant, one who has a hold over our Ant, toiling away here in the summer. Why should our Ant now have any regard for that future Ant? 'Because it will still be *me*,' replies our Ant of today. But will it? Is that again too much 'black or white'?

97
WITHOUT END?

Tortoises need to be taught a lesson and the lesson we have in mind for Mr T, our tortoise, is a simple piece of logic, a piece so simple that none should dispute. Here, Mr T, say we, is a valid argument, a piece of deduction upon which not even you can trip us.

'I am but a humble servant, sir, eager to learn, a devotee of that stern yet fair mistress, Miss Logic.'

'Excellent, Mr T. Let me show you the power of deduction. Suppose it true that all tortoises glory in champagne.'

'Appealing as that sounds, I fear that it is untrue, being such a humble tortoise with no pretensions to champagne and...'

'That is why we said "suppose", Mr T, to stop you from speeding off into tales about your sorrowful upbringing with only a second-hand shell despite your wealth. This bit of logic is not concerned with the truth of its starting point, with its premisses, but with what can be deduced from the premisses.'

'Fair enough, sir, but please be not angry with me. I am but a humble tortoise.'

'Oh, cut that out, Mr T.'

'Right, sir, I am paying attention. I am entertaining the thought that all tortoises glory in champagne. And I bet you want me to entertain the further thought that Mr T is a tortoise.'

'That's right.'

'And you're going to tell me that, therefore, I should conclude from those two premisses that Mr T glories in champagne, even though, of course, I do not.'

'Yes. Let me set it out.

Premiss 1:   All tortoises glory in champagne.
Premiss 2:   Mr T is a tortoise.
Conclusion C: Mr T glories in champagne.

We know that the conclusion is false, but logic is making the point that the conclusion *follows* from the premisses; that is, were those premisses to be true, then the conclusion would be true too.'

'That Miss Logic is very rigorous and disciplined indeed, sir. And, of course, I bow to her wisdom; but may I just check things out? For the sake of the argument – isn't that what you say, sir? – I'll accept that all tortoises glory in champagne and that Mr T is a tortoise, but – and here I must scratch both my shell and my head – I am not all that sure. Do I have to accept the conclusion that therefore Mr T glories in champagne? You see, sir, I am not sure if I quite follow – despite the sternness of Miss Logic's gaze.'

Can we help Mr T to see that the conclusion must follow?

We may be tempted to reply, with the dialogue continuing:

'Look, Mr T, can you not see, through that thick shell of yours, that…'

'I am sorry, sir, but I have never seen through my shell.'

'It was just a manner of speech, Mr T.'

'It may be "just" to you, but not to me, brought up as I was with only a second-hand cracked shell and…'

'Let's get on, Mr T. Can you not see that, if all tortoises glory in champagne and Mr T is a tortoise, then it must follow that he glories in champagne?'

'Ah, you mean, if Premisses 1 and 2 are true, then the Conclusion C must be true… ?'

'Exactly.'

'So, that is an important step in my grasping the argument?'

'Er, yes, I guess so.'

'We had better write it down, in case I forget it. It is another premiss that seems essential to the argument.'

'Well, yes – er, yes, yes, so the full argument is:

Premiss 1:   All tortoises glory in champagne.
Premiss 2:   Mr T is a tortoise.
Premiss 3:   If 1 and 2 are true, then Mr T glories in champagne.
Conclusion C: Mr T glories in champagne.'

'Ah, I see.'

'I hope very much that you do see, Mr T, for if you do not, Miss Logic will grab you by your throat, dance on your shell and…'

'Now, don't get carried away, sir. Let me check it through, to make sure I understand. I accept Premiss 1 and I accept Premiss 2 and I accept Premiss 3, but, I still wonder about the conclusion.'

'Oh dear, Mr T, you are a dunce. Do you really not see that if Premisses 1 and 2 and 3 are true, then the Conclusion C *must* follow?'

'I feel another premiss coming along, sir. You have just explained why the conclusion follows by giving me a further premiss,

Premiss 4: If 1, 2 and 3 are true, then Mr T glories in champagne.

You must pop that premiss into the argument too.'

≈

At this, we all sigh, for, of course, now that Mr T has got us going, into offering additional premisses, there will be no end, well, no logical end, though there may be a weary end to the conversation. And Mr Lewis Carroll who first wrote, so splendidly, of a tortoise setting these challenges, had his Achilles writing down more and more premisses in his notebook, in his attempt to justify deduction. He would indeed need a notebook with an infinite number of spaces for writing – which, of course, all notebooks have, but that is another story about the endless division of space, as seen via the race in Chapter 33.

It is readily accepted that deduction cannot be justified by offering more premises. As a result, some say that what justifies particular deductions is their conforming to certain rules or schemes of logic, for example: All S are P; a is an S; therefore a is a P. I doubt if this would silence our Mr T, for, once such a rule is offered, he can set off again, asking for a further rule concerning the application of the offered rule – and so on. Further, in explaining all this, we are already making use of such deductive arguments: if you accept this Mr T, then you should accept that. You do accept this; therefore you should accept that.

♈

'Er… er…'

'What is it, Mr T? About to cause more trouble for Miss Logic?'

'Certainly not. I wonder if I may help you all out.'

'Go on, Mr T.'

'Your mistake, if I may be so bold, sir, was to attempt to justify deductive practices. It was understandably kind of you to try to explain matters. Maybe making some of those comments that I forced you to write down as premisses could help in some cases. Drawing little diagrams also can help. These, although valuable tricks to open eyes to validity, do not make the arguments valid. That an argument is valid, if it is, is simply manifested in, for example: Premisses 1; 2; therefore Conclusion C. Rules and schema and additional premisses do not justify C's following from the premisses. Conclusion C just does follow. Indeed, sir, the rules and schema are derived from the particular cases – such as the champagne case just cited.

'This too should remind some that from the premiss that a figure is a square, it validly follows that the figure has four sides. There is no need painstakingly and wrongly to insist that it only validly follows if we have another premiss such as "All squares have four sides."'

And with that, Mr T set off, his head held high – well, not that high, given his tortoise's height – muttering something about the muddles that Humpty Dumpty and Ms Turkey were getting into, thinking that inductive reasoning too needed justification, muttering, too, how even in life, we need to learn when to stop asking for more. Of course, in view of his race with Achilles, how Mr T managed to move through space and time, reaching a desired end at all, remained something of a mystery for him – if not also for us.

98

MINDFUL OF BARBARIANS – WITHIN AND WITHOUT

'Baa, baa,' bleat the sheep; and those 'baa, baa's resemble burbling babbles in unknown foreign languages and perhaps also in English when rambling, technical or even philosophical in mode. So, we may dismiss what is said as so much 'blah, blah', as did the ancient Greeks who heard things that way when meeting with foreigners, those 'others' who lived outside civilization, outside civilized language – that is, outside ancient Greece. Thus, so it said, derived the word and concept: 'barbarian', blah-barian.

Barbarians, as the ancient Greeks recognized, could be powerful, prosperous, successful in battle; but they lacked something. They lacked civilization, Greek culture, at its finest.

Barbarians are often outside city walls. They are without. Today, as maybe always, they are also within – within the city, even within ourselves. The barbarous character can be promoted by society: by its laws, structures and those in power. It can be manifested in the *Zeitgeist*, the attitudes, the spirit of the times.

What do you sense as barbarous – deep down – within today's society? Allow us to put mainly to one side easy answers such as extreme religious intolerance and those fundamentalisms that lead to well-known horrors. Let us reflect on what is needed for a good life, a civilized life, given Western societies as lived today. What corrupts the good life? To voice the puzzle in our barbarous terms:

Who are the Barbarians now?

The good life, the civilized life, let us quickly acknowledge, is enhanced by certain competitive and technological advances. Although we may dream of simple lives unencumbered by scientific success, for many of us our water on tap, light at night, anaesthetics and welfare provision are bounteous boons. They permit time for reflection, for literature, for the arts. Yet we know full well that the advances also promote the barbarous, the vulgar, the lowest desires. Audiences are targeted; artists are big business – and educational institutions seek economic impact. We also know that societies and people materially poor can possess refinements and sensibilities that we often lack. They may be sensitive to subtle changes in the sky, the habitat of birds, or the weave in the mat; they may gain insight from myths and traditions; they may have a nuanced grasp of life's significance, untainted by personal ambition and greed. The materially poor certainly are not thereby the barbarous.

Some barbarities in our society immediately strike home: unprovoked aggression, selfishness and expectations fuelled by commercialism. Today's ethos, certainly of the US and Britain, praises economic growth and celebrity lifestyles, with urgings to acquire more, to consume more – and throw away more. Think of governmental delight when car sales soar; note the night queuing to buy the latest mobile phones; be amazed at the city-executive remunerations and payments to celebrity footballers, so vast compared with those of other employees who may work just as hard, if not harder, in radically less glamorous jobs. Time, then, to reflect further on these barbarisms.

Barbarians are materialists, in the popular sense of the term. Materialism, thus understood, involves increasing self-centred consumption, with ever more expectations. As resources permit, even fail to permit, Barbarians flaunt gold watches, designer clothes and bigger cars. They seek to acquire more – maybe to drink more, to engage in sex more – as competitive activities lacking imagination, lacking refinement. Quantity and immediacy – 'I must have it now' – swamp quality and taste, reflection and deferment. Contemplation of the sky's colours, the Venetian basilicas or the Louvre's art, gives way to snapping more photographs, another sight to squeeze in, posting another selfie, while ticking off shopping lists *en route*.

To correct for materialism, some embrace religion. Scripture usually discourages self-centred excess; scripture can lift eyes to the spiritual.

Yet certain religious believers, even ignoring the roguishly religious, sleep too easily with another barbarism – the imposition of belief – forcing their 'good life' on others, through, for example, en-veiling women or criminalizing extra-marital sexual relations.

Unquestioning conformity is a barbarism, be it derived from religious stances or political ideologies. Fortunately, we need not be religious to resist conforming to materialism's vulgar excess. Belief in God is not necessary for us to appreciate the flutter of autumn leaves, the glide of musical phrases, the graceful curve of a neck or to sense the needs of others – or even, paradoxically, to value certain scriptural reflections. Note, only 'certain': some scriptural readings merit strong rejection.

≋

Barbarians may be nourished by the *nothing but* – a danger we have already encountered in various contexts. Physical reductionism, scientism – a 'materialism' different from the above – understands love, aesthetic appreciation, our sense of awe before crashing oceans and darkening skies, as 'nothing but' neurological states to be explained by chemical changes and evolutionary psychology. Scientism can mistakenly lead to barbarous devaluations of love, beauty – even, paradoxically, the quest for truth – with conclusions drawn that all we can and ought to do is satisfy our desires. Of course, if scientism really does undermine values, it thereby undermines Barbarians' valuations that favour self-interest.

We should challenge the reductionist claim, the scientism. There are no scientific laws that speak of awe, beauty and the quest for truth. There are no laws of prettiness, portmanteaux and petticoats. True, explanations may be given of the origins of sensitivity, awe and refinement, but their present existences are not thereby other than they seem. Today's ice remains cold and hard, although, as we now know, it is constituted by hydrogen and oxygen atoms formed in earlier times.

'Tis better to be a dissatisfied Socrates than a satisfied pig.

Thus wrote our favourite Victorian already encountered, John Stuart Mill. Barbarians who embrace materialism in the popular understanding, or who misunderstand scientism's consequences, follow ways of the metaphorical pig. Mill, in swinish rejection, lifts eyes to higher pleasures and improved characters: pleasures of poetry, music, nature; characters of nobility, compassion and honesty. Once educated in the higher pleasures, we recognize their superiority – well, so Mill reasoned. Of course, Mill may be wrong. There is room for argument, reason and reflection about life's values. Such argument, reasoning and reflection, though, already distinguishes those who do so from Barbarians.

Picture some friends having a drink, deep in discussion, be it about politics, the latest soap-opera adventure or using coriander in cooking. Contrast with those friends having a drink, not speaking, but just texting or tweeting that they are having a drink, feel tired or are about to eat. Picture someone looking after his guinea pigs or feeding the pigeons or appreciating the aesthetics of Art Nouveau compared with those of Art Deco or struggling to learn a foreign language, play the piano or understand Kant; contrast with someone who makes no attempt at achieving worthwhile things. Recognition that some ways of living are better, more fulfilling, than others is no commitment to elitism; at least, it is no more elitist than the recognition that someone's singing is more tuneful than another's, that a footballer's play has greater elegance than an opposer's and that some novels engender deeper thought than typical flavour-of-the-month best-sellers.

It is best to resist 'pleasure' as our ultimate aim. Pleasure is not the measure: well, it ought not to be. A better expression, from the ancient Greek *eudaimonia*, is *flourishing*. Mill – and many others – at heart promote the good life, the happy life, as the flourishing life. Satisfactions of lust and sex, of food and drink, even of sloth and *schadenfreude*, are valuable especially when nuanced with sensitivities and excellences – a point downplayed, it seems, by Mill. Such satisfactions may feature in flourishing lives just as, more significantly, may investigations of, and experiences through, travel, gardening, cosmology, poetry, crafting in wood – and the sublime art of opera.

Flourishing lives need to be embraced reflectively, and authentically, as truly 'ours', with imagination and perceptivity – and typically with arms outstretched to others. Of course, such lives run risks: things go wrong. Trying, as has been quipped, is the first step to failure. Here we meet another barbarism: the expectation that things should always go well, the conceit that we deserve comfortable lives, and the demand for compensation when upsets happen.

♈

In C. P. Cavafy's 'Waiting for the Barbarians', those who waited eventually came to realize that there were no Barbarians without. As a result, they fell into confusion.

> *And now, whatever would happen to us without the Barbarians?*
> *Those people – they are a solution of sorts.*

Paradoxically, we need the Barbarians to keep us on guard, to save us from collapse into self-barbarity. Puzzlingly – unhappily so – we should perhaps parade gratitude to the uncouth, to 'artists' who display nothing but flashing lights or dishevelled beds as great aesthetic achievements, to those celebrities who value solely riches and their status on display, and to the city traders and executives who grab at greater wealth, forever demanding lower taxes. Of course, we need also to keep them in their place. The splendid Keynes, for example, argued that it is better to let tyrants tyrannize over their bank balances than over fellow citizens; it is better that the selfish self-centred roam the city rather than the corridors of power. That was once true, but with corridors of power now within the city headquarters of global corporations, keeping those barbarous in check is far from easy.

Barbarians, in their various manifestations, can help us to see that there is more to life than the barbarous love of consumption, of the flaunting of wealth, of disparaging the poor as 'losers'.

Barbarians serve as reminders of how *not* to be.

99
IS THIS ALL THERE IS?

You awake one morning, alone. Your family and friends are lost, forgotten or are no more. No longer do they matter: no longer does anything matter, save one thing: the itch. The itch nags away, just below your shoulder-blades, right in the middle of your back. It distracts you from all else. It irritates; it puts you on edge. Devilish, but subtle, torturers would create such itchy sensations, just to see you wriggle, while they prevent you from scratching. You twist your arm, stretching and straining – and just about, yes, just about – you manage to scratch. What a delicious sensation, that scratch. And what relief from the itch. What amazing relief!

Now, let us consider two continuations of this tale, to see where they take us. We call them: *Discontented* and *Contented*.

Discontented: What amazing relief! – yet 'tis short-lived. Another itch is felt. Once again, you twist and turn, scratch and dig at your skin. Once again, peace returns; but only momentarily, for, yet again, an itch starts up. And, as soon as that itch is quelled, yet more arise, criss-crossing, of differing degree, tingle and tickle, of different shadings of irritation and location. As they arise, you writhe and wriggle, squirm and scratch. And so life goes on... and on... and on... Itch and scratch, itch and scratch, itch...

Contented: What amazing relief! Contentment warms your body, the distressful itch having vanished. You bask in the feeling of bliss. Yet it quickly subsides, leaving you satisfied by absence of itch; but that is all. Nothing else stirs within you: no hopes, no desires and no curiosity. And the sun rises, crosses the sky and sets. Nothing is left to thwart you... Nothing to entice you; nothing to distress you... You just are; you be... That is all. You be...

What more is there to life than either the *Discontented* or the *Contented*?

Life is a kaleidoscope of pains and pleasures, despairs and hopes, family and friends, careers and games, loves and luck, learning and failures, and health and illness; not mere itches and scratches. But do not all these things come down to itching and scratching? Are not itching and scratching representative of what goes on in life? All the things mentioned in our list are, ultimately, matters involving having some discontent (itches) to overcome and (if we are lucky?) the overcoming (scratching) which provides relief. What is the value in that?

If contentment only arises through overcoming discontent, would not states without the initial discontent be preferable? Yet such states seem to be totally without point — as pointless as being a pebble is to a pebble. Human that we are, though, even contentments usually (and pretty quickly) become transformed into discontentments of boredom: moans of monotony, tears against the tedium, sighs of emptiness. We may even rage and rail, 'What's the point? What *is* the point?' Maybe, after all, a pebble is better off, having none of those states.

Why is human existence preferable to a pebble's?

In the nineteenth century, Schopenhauer, known as the 'philosopher of pessimism', stressed the suffering of human life: either we want something that we lack or we have got what we wanted. Either way, we suffer — through the lack of what we want or through boredom from the lack of want, now having what we wanted. True, a multitude of different wants may criss-cross; we may be satisfied (or not) at different times, but a mishmash of sufferings and boredoms does not detract from the suffering and boredom. If Schopenhauer is right, would it not be better to be a pebble, lacking all experiences? Were we just pebbles on a beach and in the shade, all life's waves and turmoils would (dare I quip?) wash over us.

Schopenhauer is wrong, at least in the specifics. With many things, we simply enjoy or value the activity of overcoming or, at least, trying to overcome the dissatisfactions. As is often said, 'tis better to travel hopefully than to arrive.

It is a mistake to think that if we deploy means to an end, the means are irrelevant, lacking all value in themselves, and it is the end alone that matters. Our goal may be to reach the top of Mount Everest, but we do not want to reach it by just any means. We want to climb the mountain, do battle with blizzards, struggle on, up and up. When (in my case, better to say 'if') we reach the top, we have achieved our goal and by the right means. Achievements are measured not solely by the outcomes, but by how those outcomes were achieved. To find ourselves transported to Everest's summit by helicopter or at the press of a button would lose the appeal of achievement, unless the sought achievement was that of managing successfully to fly the helicopter or to build a machine that could whisk people from A to B at a button's press.

Schopenhauer may be right in his pessimism, in as far as most lives involve more sufferings than satisfactions. Many sufferings seem more or less inevitable – even for those who are life's winners. There are losses of family, friends and lovers; awareness of the increasing disabilities likely in old age; and, in all likelihood, direct experience of those disabilities ourselves one day and for some years – and then the pains of dying. There is awareness of the sufferings of millions of others, past, present and future, and the sufferings of animals. Further, some of us grow deeply attached even to objects – a book, a gown, a much loved car – sometimes even ascribing them a life of their own, with resultant distress when they too collapse, worn with old age. With such reflections, we may well agree that the happiest are, so to speak, those never to have been born.

〰〰

What is the point of it all? Many cannot resist asking that question. Before we assess the point of all life, what can we make of the points and purposes of an individual life? How do people typically answer about the purposes and points of their lives?

Some answer by explaining how their lives gain point through help-ing their children, working to improve lives of the poor or advancing some political cause. But that is to pass the purpose buck, the point buck: what is the point of the children's lives or the political cause?

Whatever answer is given, we may ask a similar question. Some turn to the hope of an eternal afterlife, but that too has no more ultimate point than a finite life. If there is a genuine question to be asked about the point of a finite life, there is also a question about the point of an infinitely long life. Before we pop in the answer 'serving God' or similar, we should be aware that we may then ask: what is the point of such service and of God's existence?

We should come to realize, we need to realize, that, for something to have value, there need be no point to it. That is one way of answering earlier worries about the point of certain plays, music and literature. Mind you, the point of saying that valuable things need have no point may be to pre-empt those, despite nearing this book's close, still asking about the point of philosophy. To that question, some answers can be given. For one thing, philosophy enables us to appreciate that various activities may possess value even though without point. Philosophy also shows itself to be an activity, an intrinsically valuable activity: that is, many of us value it for its own sake, valuing reflection and attempts at understanding, at seeing matters more clearly in this or that light.

Lives may be valuable, not least because they are lives of valuers who value features of the universe, life and living. True, lives end; but, as raised earlier about immortality (Chapter 95), could we even face eternal living? Awareness of dying, though, enfolds many with the recurrent bleak and haunting melancholies of 'What's the point?' yet again, as they adopt a horizontal position of hopelessness and despondency. Let us remember, though, a logical point about points: there can be no point beyond all points.

Let us also reflect, as we did earlier (page 364), that absurdity shines over human lives: the importance that we give to our lives, our despair at the human condition, stands incongruously against the utter unimportance of our lives from a more distant viewpoint, from the perspective of the universe; our wanting to live on for another year clashes with an awareness, at least for many, of the horror of living our lives eternally. Those absurdities, those incongruities, merit a smile, even if ironic. If only briefly, we may stand back – aware of both our attachments and of our standing back – and laugh at ourselves, laugh loudly at ourselves. And then get on with living. After all, if, from the standpoint of the universe, we do not matter, then it matters not at all that we do not matter. Back to living.

Back to living, yes, yes, indeed… Yet, still we may worry and wonder and feel disquiet…

♈

When days, weeks and years come round and round – when we seem forever to be running, yet getting nowhere or even getting somewhere – we may feel for Sisyphus, condemned by the gods to roll a boulder up a mountain to the top, eternally so, for the boulder always rolls back down. Another ancient Greek myth, the Ixion myth, affords a similar image, Ixion being chained to a fiery wheel, spinning to eternity. Schopenhauer, who mused upon such images, offered an escape. As noted when as 'fragile creatures' (Chapter 91), we can lose ourselves in art and, especially so, in music.

Normally we cannot help but to strive; we struggle to achieve. That is part of a meaningful human life. We do, though, possess the capacity to do otherwise than striving. That otherwise can be the emptiness, the waste, of wallowing in nothing of value, of sighing with boredom; that otherwise can yet be of value, for we may lose ourselves in what is valuable, in – for want of better words – transcendent mysteries of the arts. Whether atheist, agnostic or believer, few can resist the inspiring sounds of, for example, Allegri's *Miserere* and Tallis' *Spem in Alium*.

To quote our pessimistic philosopher, suddenly with a touch of optimism, aesthetic experiences provide us with 'the Sabbeth of the penal servitude of willing'.

When lost in aesthetic experiences of music – when, Zen-like, lost in the colours of a flower – we cease to strive; our quest for a point to all things is quelled and forgotten.

Paradoxically, we can be at the best for ourselves, when lost to ourselves.

EPILOGUE
Ending Without Ending

How small a thought it takes to fill a whole life.
Wittgenstein

An epilogue – an 'in conclusion' – may urge no conclusion at all. Philosophical plunderings need revisiting, mulling anew, revising and enhancing. Perplexing problems, informed by prior philosophical insights, can yet be viewed in fresh lights, seen through new eyes. One generation uncovers meanings to which earlier generations were blind. Art too may receive fresh castings of light; witness the tale of Gertrude Stein, who posed for Picasso. When she saw the painterly outcome, she announced that it looked not at all like her; Picasso's reply was, 'No matter; it will.' Compared with centuries, even just a few decades, ago, muse upon how different today's ethos is, at least in many countries, regarding animal welfare, sexual orientation, slavery – and our place in the universe. That is not remotely to suggest that the latest ways of seeing are always or necessarily superior.

'All things conspire' appeared in our Prologue. The West often conveniently overlooks that truth. Our lives are intermeshed with, conspire with, others across the seas and continents; our well-being depends in part on the radically poor existence of those unknown to us, be they children working in appalling factories or elderly labourers on plantations. Reading a book of philosophy and, yes, writing a book of philosophy, are valuable activities – yet they are unavailable to the vast majority of people, people who are swamped by the need simply to survive. We should not forget. And in saying that, we display a privileged position; that position itself may offend.

Explanations must come to an end

Philosophizing is a continuing activity. Having said that – 'having said that' runs the danger of presenting a contradictory stance – we can draw some morals that hold firm. One, as just noted, is that we should not close our eyes to our common humanity; we should not ignore the plight of others. Here are some more.

Be it courtesy of Mr T, our logical tortoise – or our reflections on dreaming and knowledge or quest for morality's foundations – we need to recognize that explanations must come to an end. Somewhere along the line we must stop.

Mr T showed how 'in the end' we have to accept some simple ways of arguing. If, 'in the end', someone cannot see that, when all men are mortal and Socrates is a man, then it must follow that Socrates is mortal – well, there is nothing more that we can say or do. So, too, with certain basic examples of moral wrongs: recall the puzzle of Thug (Chapter 11). Torturing an innocent girl, against her consent, for the sheer fun of it, is wrong. We may appeal to 'what if it were you', 'imagine the terror and pain', or 'suppose your daughter to be the victim' – we may reason to and from certain principles – yet, if someone still cannot see it is wrong, well, nothing more can be said. Of course, maybe something should be done, if only by way of keeping at least a sharp and nimble eye on that person.

That explanations must come to an end also relates to life's meaning, purpose or point. True, however long we live, we may always ponder 'why?' seeking for more explanations, more meaning, more reasons; yet, always to expect further answers is the road to despair. To be satisfied that ultimate answers exist in a transcendent, supersensible being is to settle for divine mystery; mystery, though, is no explanation, no explanation at all. This book's last puzzle, the ninety-ninth, showed how the question 'What's the point?' may haunt, even oppress. The answer is to try hard to accept that there can be no point beyond all points. What is logically impossible should be no source of regret. Points must come to an end, as must explanations.

Returning to morality, that some things are clearly wrong should not mislead us into thinking that there are no genuine dilemmas. There are numerous. Plato noted that if people differ about the larger and smaller – about calculations, about distances to Athens and so forth – measurements can settle matters; but, continued Plato, differences over the just and unjust, the beautiful and ugly, the good and bad, can make people angry and hostile. There often are well-grounded disagreements involving values that cannot be measured against each other: recall 'If this be judging...' (Chapter 94). Sharp dividing lines between right and wrong are not always available. Grey areas are common.

For what shall it profit a man...

'Tis not contrary to reason to prefer the destruction of the whole world to the scratching of my finger – so observed David Hume. Good reasoning, he thought, can show us how best to secure an end: the quickest way to Zurich, how to evade some taxes or store the champagne. Good reasoning cannot tell us which ends to pursue. Luckily, we find ourselves with basic desires, preferences and sentiments most of which are in common with others. We can sympathize and empathize.

Hume needs, though, to be reminded that preferences can be distorted – for the worse. Children born into slavery, or sent up Victorian chimneys, may be satisfied with their lives because they know no better. Were improved opportunities to be presented, victims could even be too damaged to grasp them. Some prisoners develop reliance on authority so great that, on release, they re-offend in the hope of prison return. In words from Rabindranath Tagore, 'To those with low self-regard, neglect does not seem unjust, and so it does not cause them pain.' Yet, even if without pain, they have suffered mistreatment; they deserve better days.

The *Zeitgeist* – the spirit of the times – preys on us; it affects our preferences. For example, governments, media and corporate leaders proclaim and repeat the mantra that entrepreneurs, financiers and corporate leaders (!) will not enterprise, finance and lead, unless paid more and more, with golden handshakes, bonuses, lower taxes and (paradoxically) golden goodbyes; hence, it is said, radical inequalities in wealth, in capital and income, are properly justified. So it is that today's central *Zeitgeist*, at least that of Britain and the US, has been created – and is self-fulfilling, self-perpetuating and little challenged. The enterpreneurs, financiers and corporate leaders typically buy into the myth, believing that they merit their riches; only riches can validate their work. The myth spreads, contaminating the leadership of universities, health services, even some charities. To aspire is understood as to aspire for greater wealth, more possessions, more ownership – and, especially, more than others.

Philosophical reflection may help towards some detachment, enabling us to dissent from that *Zeitgeist* and its accompanying elements. The reflection may help us to challenge obsessions with gross national product, business models and corporate profits – obsessions that turn all days into shopping days and risk transforming education, health and the arts into commodities valued solely by market price. Recall the Barbarians. Of course, business, manufacturing, technology, services all have their place; but that place should not be one for persuading people ever to consume more and more, regardless of worth. Should we not look with despair at built-in obsolescence, campaigns to sell more junk food and the transforming of children into market consumers – solely to expand profits and power?

Focusing on material accumulation, many are blind to the resultant devaluation of values – to the inequalities that can generate arrogance and disdain by the rich for the poor and, often, low esteem in the poor, at times accompanied by envy of the rich.

Keynes, the eminent economist whom we have already encountered a few times within the course of this book, was appalled at money being the measure of success and status: 'the moral problem of the age' is love of money. That was in 1925. He would, no doubt, be appalled many times over by today's ethos manifested, for example, by corruption at the highest levels of developing countries that prevents aid from reaching the destitute and, closer to home (as already implied), by the financial demands of celebrity footballers, corporate directors and celebrities famous only for being celebrities – and by accountants and bankers encouraging aggressive tax avoidance, even evasion. It is small wonder, then, that those closer to home without money may be ever sensitive to anything that may be seen as an attack on their dignity. It is easy for the well-off, well-heeled and confident, or those with a wealthy family behind them, to handle slights by shop assistants, errors in payments and telephone calls unreturned; it is far from easy for those already suffering unjust devaluation because of society's admiration for wealth, for Mammon.

Wealth and inequalities ground many devaluations, some blatant, some subtle, and many in between. The pleasures of football prove elusive to this author; but the football 'business' provides a simple example – well, so it seems – of a monetary inspired devaluation. Ignoring the international corruption, consider how major football clubs in Britain are mixtures of profitable business and status symbols for wealthy owners. Consider the astonishing transfer fees and salaries paid, with the resultant high ticket prices, sales of 'bling' merchandise and players' loss of commitment to their teams. Have things really improved, compared to fifty years ago, when normally owners and players genuinely represented their towns and cities, when supporters could feel an affinity with their teams and when, indeed, those support-ers could more easily afford to go along to the matches?

A devaluation is also on display when the wealthy purchase great works of art for vast sums – a Raphael, Rembrandt, Picasso – yet leave them hidden away, far from being on display. The aim is for the paint-ings to appreciate in financial value; they are otherwise unappreciated. The paintings are effectively lost to the world. Of course, a few of the wealthy have been, and are, splendid philanthropists, founding wonder-ful art galleries, encouraging musical awareness or supporting medical research and projects to combat poverty. They are the exception and while splendid in deed, not merely in word, and meriting praise, let us reflect that their donations typically do not significantly impinge on their luxurious living; contrast with the small charitable donations from the radically less well-off who really can ill afford to give what they give.

Reflection may open eyes. Many people – including some eminent economists, politicians and media pundits – see taxation as devilish punishment; 'punishment' is the term used. Greater awareness of the value of community, of fellow feeling, of the benefits of stable society – of, indeed, the corporate world's reliance on infrastructures, schooling, police and health services, without which that world would crash – should counteract that unjustified demonization. A proper grasp of values such as fairness and compassion should enable us to see that there can be no moral justification for the *Zeitgeist*, mentioned earlier, that promotes vast inequalities of wealth and supports the wealthy's (and even the just 'well off's) typical reluctance to pay increased taxes, threatening departure to tax havens if such increases come about (recall Chapter 76's blackmail). Successful women and men, eager to claim that they deserve their success because of hard work, should reflect on how lucky they are not to have been born in poverty, desperately fleeing a war-torn country or, as refugees, drowning in the Mediterranean. They should reflect how lucky they are to have been born with talents and dispositions to strive, in circumstances conducive to their development. Citing the odd exceptional case of 'rags to riches' in no way undermines those general points.

Reflection may also expose myths that aid only oppressive and unjustified inequalities. 'We are all equal before the law,' it is said; yet that mantra is surely tarnished, once we reflect that many people cannot afford to go to law and, of those who can, wealth often determines how well the cases are presented – and outcomes, as mentioned in Chapter 94, can depend on luck regarding juries and which judges are sitting. 'To no one will we sell, to no one deny or delay right or justice,' declares the Magna Carta. So much, we may sigh, for the much vaunted claim that such clauses remain the bedrock of rights in Britain and elsewhere.

Many non-religious, as we have seen, fall into an unquestioned 'scientism', as if all things – the sunset's beauty; the importance of promise-keeping; the ravages of love – are best understood as 'nothing but' physical particles in spin. Some non-religious treat nature as just another commodity to be priced; some take literally the 'selfish gene', mistakenly using it to justify universal self-interest. In response, religious metaphors may appear welcoming: nature is a gift from God, a gift to be respected. Jesus' words are quoted (King James Version): 'For what shall it profit a man, if he shall gaine the whole world yet lose his owne soule?'

Philosophically, we need to think further on the deliverances of religions: religious belief leads some to view the animal kingdom as at the disposal of human beings; some see saving the soul as necessitating the killing of apostates; even Jesus, according to St Luke's Gospel (19,27), wanted slain those who did not recognize him as king. Less importantly, though still of importance, the religiously inspired, Christian, Muslim and others, have often destroyed antiquities and historical sites of value, when in conflict with their godly beliefs; and that destruction continues, even today. Religious belief is clearly no secure source of moral truths.

At a slight angle to the universe

When discussing Barbarians, we met the modern Greek poet Cavafy. Forster described him as 'a Greek gentleman in a straw hat, standing absolutely motionless – at a slight angle to the universe'. Philosophizing may remind us of what we knew all along: that we too stand, or can stand, at a slight angle to the universe, with our own perspective, our own take, on the surrounding landscape of nature and humanity, of ideas and the arts – on the friend to whom we wave, the unknown woman who smiles, the memories, music and humours that convey intimacies once shared.

Thus it is that we gain a perspective on our life and the lives of others. That perspective may be inspirational and aspiring; it may be resigned and melancholic, serious or whimsical, rational or sensual, stable or changing. It may paint the heavens – or dwell on Earth, aware of limits and inevitable losses. Whichever mixture – it is our own, our own genuine grasp of life. That is what it can be – what it is to be – human, to be at a slight angle to the universe.

ϒ

'The meaning of life is that it ends,' wrote Kafka. What it is to be human, standing at a slight angle, is also to be aware, through others and ultimately through ourselves, of lives and life ending. When that awareness fills our being, then – despite all our philosophizing – we may yearn yet again for a deeper meaning. Despite world weariness, we may be unable to stop ourselves from longing for an ultimate point or an everlasting future when there is none. Then – and now – it is well to remember, to welcome, to embrace, what is valuable, however transient – for even the transient shines with a gleam of eternity. It is well to reflect:

All the things we value, however rare, however small, that give point or meaning within our lives – the friendships, loves, humours and absurdities; those soundscaped memories entwined with shared passions and glances that magically ensnare and enfold; the intoxications of wines and words, of music and wonder and wayward musings, with which we wrestle into misty slumbering nights, our senses revived by sparkling waters, much needed at dawn; the seascapes of wild waves, mysterious moonlights and images and widening skies that stretch the eyes – do indeed all cease to exist; and curiously the most enchanting are oft those within which we lose ourselves and also cease to be – yet that they, and we, existed at some time remains timelessly true, outside of all time.

For lovers of eternity, that is as good as it gets.

> *Blow, bugle, blow,*
> *set the wild echoes flying;*
> *And answer, echoes,*
> *answer, dying,*
> *dying, dying.*

TENNYSON

NOTES
and further reading

References and quotations are easily found these days through online searches, be they in bookshop, library or at home; hence, the notes are uncluttered with details of publication. Quotations and aphorisms have been abbreviated where necessary, without, it is hoped, losing their sense.

Prologue: let's do it

Let us first deal with the Prologue's straightforward puzzles. The answer to the logical one is 'Yes'. Penelope is either a philosopher or not. If she is, then she, a philosopher, is in love with a non-philosopher. If she is a non-philosopher, then Osbert, a philosopher, is in love with a non-philosopher.

Regarding Monty Hall, contestants should always switch, improving their winning chances from one-third to two-thirds. Here is the reasoning. You initially chose A, with one-third winning chance. Had you been able to select both B and C, you would, of course, have secured a two-thirds' winning chance. The presenter, though, has shown that door B should not be chosen. Hence, if you take the opportunity to switch, in this example, from A to C, it is as if you have been given the combined B and C chance of two-thirds. If you play the game many times without switching, you would expect to lose in two-thirds; by always switching, all those losing games, two out of three, become winning games.

For sceptical readers, a computer simulation has been run thousands of times, I believe, making the point empirically.

For exposure of some 'postmodernist' muddle, dubiety and pseudo-profundity, see Sokal and Bricmont, *Intellectual Impostures*.

The Wittgenstein/Johnson tale and other Cambridge reflections appear in my 'Weavings' in Karl Sabbagh, ed., *A Book of King's*. For W. E. Johnson, undeservedly little known, see Stuart Brown, ed., *Dictionary of Twentieth-Century British Philosophers*. Cole Porter, of course, is the source of the educated fleas with the birds and the bees.

Turning to recommended readings, an excellent collection of classic and modern texts, 800 pages' worth, relevant to all parts of this book, is John Cottingham's *Western Philosophy: An Anthology*. For readers unenthusiastic about weighty volumes, try the slender modern classic: Bertrand Russell, *The Problems of Philosophy* (first published in 1912). For accessible works of considerable influence, turn to Plato's dialogues; some introductory early ones are published as *The Last Days of Socrates*. Note also Bernard Williams' small introduction, *Plato*.

Modesty does not prevent me from suggesting my recent *Philosophy: A Beginner's Guide*. For entertainment and philosophical puzzles, remember Lewis Carroll's wonderful Alice: see *The Annotated Alice*, notes by Martin Gardner; and for papers on philosophy and humour, please see *The Monist* January 2005's volume, Laurence Goldstein, ed., *Humor* (yes, American spelling).

For lovers of screen reading, I suggest use of the freely available online *Stanford Encyclopaedia of Philosophy* and, for greater accessibility, the Royal Institute of Philosophy website, as well as the more introductory philosophy website of Rick and Anja's *Philosophy Now*. Note also the websites of, for example, Simon Blackburn and Jonathan Glover, and the interviews and papers available on university websites and YouTube. For example, Bertrand Russell, in his eighties, with a glint in his eye, his white hair flowing, can be seen, interviewed by John Freeman in 1959 on BBC's *Face to Face*. For intriguing photographs of some recent key philosophers, try Steve Pyke's webpage, 'pyke-eye'.

The human face of philosophers is often found via autobiographies and biographies. Try Plato's *Apology* for Socrates' defence of his life; David Hume's modest and short *My Own Life*; and John Stuart Mill's *Autobiography*. For flavour of a particularly fascinating period in philosophy, with Wittgenstein as centre, Ray Monk's *Ludwig Wittgenstein: The Duty Of Genius* is rightly praised. For wider connections, it is worth pursuing John Maynard Keynes, famous for his economics, yet also a highly significant figure in many fields, from the Bloomsbury Group to arts funding to sexual diversity to Wittgenstein; see, for example, Richard Davenport-Hines' 2015 work, *Universal Man: The Seven Lives of John Maynard Keynes*.

I. Ethics: what ought we to do?

A starting point is Bernard Williams' *Morality: An Introduction to Ethics*. Short extracts from key thinkers are in Peter Singer, ed., *Ethics*. Longer extracts with commentary are provided by Fricker and Guttenplan, eds, *Reading Ethics*. My own take is in my 2015 *Ethics: A Beginner's Guide*, covering theories, application and life's meaning. For a few of my burbles on ethics, together with some animations of ethical dilemmas, using the monkeys that 'see, hear, and speak no evil', please see my YouTube video, found via: Peter Cave Ethics.

Morality grounded in consequences is famously associated with utilitarians: Jeremy Bentham and John Stuart Mill. Bentham still sits in University College London – on public view. The Liberty (Harm) Principle derives from Mill's *On Liberty*. Judith Jarvis Thomson first told of the violinist, relating to abortion, reprinted in Peter Singer, ed., *Applied Ethics*.

Regarding self-interest, Hobbes' exact position is debated. For genetic explanations, see Richard Dawkins, *The Selfish Gene*; his use is challenged by Mary Midgley. Moral luck was mischievously labelled thus by Bernard Williams with reply by Thomas Nagel: see Statman's collection, *Moral Luck*. For people down on their luck and our 'by-walking' my comments and examples owe much to Christine Sypnowich's 'Begging' in her collection, honouring G. A. Cohen, *The Egalitarian Conscience*.

Ritualized humiliation occurs in Samuel Beckett's *Catastrophe*. A Charity Paradox occurs in Avishai Margalit, *The Decent Society*.

Many of us support toleration, yet also, therefore, courtesy and non-intrusions upon others; Kafka's short piece 'Great Noise' and Proust's letter 'Beat the carpets later' strike chords (both are accessible via the internet). Many of us also support free speech and free press. Newspapers' headlines, though, are often exaggerated, misleading, even downright nasty and false, yet influence hundreds of thousands. Support for free speech surely requires support for 'right of replies' that receive as much coverage as the original disreputable articles; yet when there is conflict between truth and profit, in many instances the latter triumphs.

Turning to animals, testing on chimps still occurs in many countries, but is now banned in the European Union. Testing on other animals continues apace. 'Speciesism', introduced by Richard Ryder, was made famous by Singer: see his *Practical Ethics*. An accessible survey, covering Bentham, Singer, Regan and Midgley's 'family-ism', is Rosalind Hursthouse's *Ethics, Humans and Other Animals*. A little-known early thinker, defending animal rights, is Henry Salt. See Hendrick and Hendrick, eds, *The Savour of Salt*. I encourage Salt savouring.

II. Politics and society: what's all this about democracy and the law?

Many topics here overlap with the readings for Part I Ethics, above. See also Jonathan Wolff, *An Introduction to Political Philosophy*. For justifications of punishment, relevant to Thug (Chapter 11) and to justice, see Duff and Green, eds, *Philosophical Foundations of Punishment*.

Democracy is famously said to be the worst form of government – except for all others. In Britain there is eagerness for the second chamber, the House of Lords, to be democratically elected. Wisdom would recommend a second chamber Plato-style, with experts from different walks of life, checking the 'democratic' deliverances resulting from party machines, wealthy donors and short-term electoral popularities. For a defence of democracy, see Dahl, *Democracy and its Critics*; for classical erudition, try Mara, *The Civic Conversations of Thucydides and Plato*. Regarding democracy in the UK and US, it is worth noting that, for example, in the 2015 UK election which put the Conservative Party in power, the party won 330 seats with 36.9% of the votes, whereas Ukip with 12.9% won only one seat. Of voters registered, the Conservatives won just 24.3%; the percentage would be lower, of course, if of those unregistered and those registered. So much, we should proclaim, for the goverment's talk of having a 'mandate from the people'. Chapter 13's quip, by the way, about restaurant managers deciding what to serve patrons, whatever patrons request, once applied to the splendid Gay Hussar, Hungarian restaurant in London's Soho, haunt of left-wing politicians; as I write, as with left-wing politicians, it too is under threat.

Hobbes' 'nasty, brutish' appears in his *Leviathan*. I first heard 'it could be worse' from Jerry Cohen, passing it on from – who can remember? It is in Hume's essay 'Of the original contract' where Hume parodies free consent as that of a man who, finding himself on a vessel in the middle of the ocean, 'freely' stays aboard. Ronald Dworkin gave the 'hypothetical contract' jibe. See Wolff above for more details and references, taking us from Hobbes, Locke and Hume to the recent John Rawls, Robert Nozick, Dworkin and others.

Regarding when and where actions take place, the reference to Leibniz is but a glance at his fascinating and fertile, carefully reasoned, metaphysics. Leibniz argued that reality consists of soul-like individuals, unities, 'monads'; they are worlds apart, yet each represents in some way everything else. Each is burdened with the past and pregnant with the future of the whole world. See, for example, his *Monadology*. It may sound like a fairy story, but Leibniz is seeking to resolve some puzzling problems about the reality that underlies appearances. Indeed, Leibniz goes so far as to say that he is a defender of common sense, unlike that paradoxical Irishman, Bishop Berkeley (met in Chapter 38).

On exemptions, the non-religious worry about privileges granted to religions. Do consultants who believe abortion is murder chat easily in hospitals to those involved in such 'murder'? For the state and religion, see my *Humanism: A Beginner's Guide*. For lifespan satire and equality myths, see John Kekes, *Against Liberalism* and *The Illusions of Egalitarianism*. G. A. Cohen's *If You're an Egalitarian, How Come You're So Rich?* is an enjoyable read. Jerry – 'Gerald' of the 'G' becomes an alphabetically advanced 'J' – was not merely a distinguished Oxford professor, but also something of a stand-up comic, having briefly trod Canadian boards when a teenager. His impersonations of Isaiah Berlin on YouTube are worth watching.

Turning to relativity, Protagoras was the first celebrity sophist, said by Aristotle to be someone who could make the weaker argument appear stronger – a good rhetorician. Barristers and politicians should applaud. Philosophers see themselves differently – as seekers after truth, rather than argument winners. For rejection of relativism, try Thomas Nagel's *The Last Word*. Protagoras reappears as key witness in Chapter 26.

On *Sharia* law and stoning, the Iranian Penal Code's Article 104 states, concerning adultery, that stones used should 'not be large enough to kill the person by one or two strikes nor should they be so small that they could not be defined as stones'. Should we be dealing with such countries while remaining mute about their horrendous laws and enactments?

III. Logic: so much for reason...?

For more paradoxes and more on these paradoxes, with detailed references, please see my *This Sentence Is False: An Introduction to Philosophical Paradoxes*. Paradoxes, with lightness and historical touch, are in Roy Sorensen's *A Brief History of the Paradox*. A good, more orderly presentation is Michael Clark's *Paradoxes from A to Z*. See also Doris Olin, *Paradox*.

On the money pump, Kenneth Arrow proved that there is no rational and fair social welfare principle for combining individuals' preferences. See Amartya K. Sen, *Collective Choice and Social Welfare*. For rational choice, try Alfred R. Mele and Piers Rawling, eds, *The Oxford Handbook of Rationality*. My 'ice cream choice' derives from Sidney Morgenbesser, he of the 'yeah, yeah' quip (Chapter 31).

On the famous 'Liar', Epimenides (sixth century BC), a Cretan, famously said, 'The Cretans always lie.' If some other Cretan speaks truly, that will be simply false, but if not, then we have a paradox akin to 'I am lying.' The comment about Cretans is in the Epistle of Paul to Titus: 'One of themselves, even a prophet of their own, said, "The Cretans are always liars, evil beasts, slow bellies."' The Liar itself is usually credited to Eubulides, fourth-century (BC) logician from Megara.

Arnold Zuboff, who entices us with Beauty and probability (Chapter 27), is a splendid guy, a one-time lecturer at University College London (UCL) – and so in a sense are we all, according to his one-person view. Crazy theories are sometimes true, yet often not.

Regarding the gazelle, sloth and chicken, what we commit to, when using the indefinite article – 'a' mammal – was discussed by medieval logicians such as Peter Abelard and Duns Scotus. Distinguishing between inference conditions occurs in W. E. Johnson, *Logic*, vol. II.

For handling the infinity puzzles and Russell's paradoxical set, please see Adrian Moore, *The Infinite*. 'The Card-Sharp Camel' – and many other puzzles here – tempt me to quote John Maynard Keynes, from his *A Treatise on Probability*: 'the author must, if he is to put his point of view clearly, pretend sometimes to a little more conviction than he feels.' I sometimes do that, yet the clarity can still remain elusive.

IV. Metaphysics: what is there – really?

Overall, please see Part III's paradox references and Moore's *The Infinite*. 'Achilles and the tortoise' is Zeno's most famous argument against motion. Zeno (of Elea), c.470 BC, was a follower of Parmenides. For the Eleatic philosophers, try Jonathan Barnes, *The Presocratic Philosophers*.

For time, see Robin le Poidevin, *The Images of Time*. Time continues to baffle. St Augustine's bafflement is in his *Confessions*. McTaggart offers his arguments for space and time as illusory, reality being loving souls, in his curious *The Nature of Existence* (no easy read). Wittgenstein and poker have reached book-length investigation: see Edmonds and Eidinow, *Wittgenstein's Poker.*

Dressing up (Chapter 37) shows how we may admire and loathe one and the same item, failing to realize it is one and the same. This 'referential opacity' occurs when psychological attitudes such as beliefs, or modal properties such as necessities, are present. Jennifer Saul, through tales of Clark Kent entering a booth and Superman departing, highlights identity problems elsewhere in what we say. See her *Simple Sentences, Substitution, and Intuitions.* The difference between what is strictly said and what is conveyed was stressed by H. P. Grice via conversational implicatures; he also associated dossiers with proper names.

The classic defence of idealism, where reality depends on ideas, on the mind (discussed in Chapter 38), is given by Berkeley (1685–1773): see his *Three Dialogues between Hylas and Philonous* (lover of matter and lover of mind). For carving up the world (as in Chapter 41), Jorge Luis Borges bamboozles readers with much thought-provoking fun. The Chinese taxonomy is in his brief essay, 'The Analytical Language of John Wilkins'; see also his collection of short stories, *Labyrinths*, especially 'The Library of Babel'. For Nelson Goodman and responses, please see Peter J. McCormick, ed., *Starmaking.* A good recent collection of papers covering all areas of metaphysics is Manson and Barnard, eds, *The Bloomsbury Companion to Metaphysics.*

V. Knowledge: drowning in seas of doubts?

Modern scepticism is famously associated with Descartes (1596–1650) who presented his dreaming and evil genius hypotheses in his *Meditations on First Philosophy*. Descartes used scepticism to overcome scepticism and rebuild knowledge.

Regarding 'Pinter and Isabella', that knowledge needs tethering down derives from Plato's *Meno.* For a very good overall introduction, please see the third edition of Duncan Pritchard's *What is This Thing Called Knowledge?* For earlier papers on luck, reliability and knowledge, see Pappas and Swain, eds, *Essays on Knowledge and Justification*. Turning to indoctrination, whether we can just decide to believe is raised by Pascal's Wager, outlined in Chapter 69; for problems of belief in general, see Bernard Williams, 'Deciding to Believe', in *Problems of the Self*.

Inductive reasoning, using Humpty Dumpty, alludes to Lewis Carroll. Wearing a financial hat, I once wrote to regulators and investment companies, asking why they allowed past performance figures to be published with 'the past is no guide'. Responses were evasive or muted. An accessible and enjoyable denial of any deep inductive problem is D. H. Mellor's 'The Warrant of Induction', in *Matters of Metaphysics*. Hume's first sceptical offering, 1739, is in *A Treatise of Human Nature*. For genuine scepticism about the future, try a day without accepting in any way that the past is a guide to the future.

The hanging of 'Just hanging around' – sometimes a surprise examination – derives from a Second World War Scandinavian broadcast. It is discussed in some detail in my *This Sentence Is False*.

Sloth's Lazy Argument occurs in Cicero's *De Fato*, derived from Chrysippus of Soli, a Stoic philosopher, third century BC. Chrysippus apparently defended cannibalism and incest. For accessible discussion, orientated to Aristotle, see Richard Sorabji, *Necessity, Cause, and Blame*.

Our creamy philosophers are often presented as children with muddy foreheads, apparently from Rabelais' *Gargantua and Pantagruel*. For common knowledge puzzles, see D. K. Lewis, *Convention* and R. Fagin *et al.*, *Reasoning about Knowledge*.

On Hempel's Paradox and Goodman's Grue (Chapters 51 and 52), please see my *This Sentence is False* or Clark's *Paradoxes A to Z*. That science should progress by conjectures and refutations, rather than inductive support, is famously associated with Karl Popper.

VI. The self: what am I?

Starting with cream buns and weak will, please see Plato's *Protagoras*, Aristotle's *Nicomachean Ethics*, and, somewhat more recently, John

Searle's *Rationality in Action*. Moral weakness is summed up by Ovid as 'I see the better course and approve it; I follow the worse.'

For 'Mary, Mary', my approach derives from Gilbert Ryle, much influenced by Wittgenstein. Ryle was philosophy's kingmaker in mid-twentieth-century Oxford, yet, somewhat to his chagrin, he became eclipsed by J. L. Austin. Ryle's writing can sparkle. Try his *The Concept of Mind*, where he coined the 'ghost in the machine', ridiculing Descartes' defence of the mind as an immaterial substance.

Jean-Paul Sartre (1905–1980) promoted the existentialist angst of free choices and our personal responsibility. The most accessible route into Sartre is his *Existentialism and Humanism*, though he later repudiated some parts.

In our cat and mouse tale, shame was highlighted by Richard Moran's *Authority and Estrangement*. Moran used Kingsley Amis' *That Uncertain Feeling*, where a rakehell (rake, dissolute man) feels ashamed.

Moving into personal identity, the Isaac Newton phantasy is essentially Bernard Williams' duplicate Guy Fawkes tale: see his *Problems of the Self* and Derek Parfit's *Reasons and Persons*. John Locke, of the seventeenth century, is a key figure here, with tales of a prince entering a cobbler's body, or was it a frog's? Julian Mayers is to blame for my succumbing to 'Aussie' and the gravity of the tale. Hofstadter and Dennett, eds, *The Mind's I*, offers various scenarios: look out for Zuboff on the brain.

The question 'What is it like to be a bat?' (in 'I am a robot', Chapter 57) indirectly derives from Timothy Sprigge, but achieved fame through Nagel's paper in his *Mortal Questions*. See Keith Frankish's *Consciousness* for explanations of 'zombies' and even 'zimbies' (yes, it gets worse). There is also John Wisdom's *Other Minds*; many consider it quaint and enigmatic – a few of us delight and admire. Wisdom (1904–93), horse owner and keen on horse racing, would, it is said, sometimes deliver his philosophy lectures wearing jodhpurs, ready to leap on a horse parked outside.

The teeth-clenching example (Chapter 60) is from Elizabeth Anscombe, *Intention*. Anscombe, mentioned in Part IV's introduction,

Donald Davidson's 'Swampman', both discussed in A. Barber's *Language and Thought*.

We find Aunt Matilda's worries in Jerrold Levinson, ed., *Aesthetics and Ethics*. Eric Gill, through his art, attempted 'to destroy the morality that is corrupting us all', but some viewed his sculptures as sexually depraved; and they would have been even more shocked by his sexual activities, had they known of them, though others saw his art (if not his way of living) as deeply religious. On what we say about ourselves: well, dog ownership can say something about the owners; and, in the case of vicious dogs, it is something better not to say – better still not to have such ownership. For expression in music, hound exemplifying, see Stephen Davies in Levinson, ed., *The Oxford Handbook of Aesthetics*. How do words apply across the senses: when literal, when metaphorical? How similar is Ariadne's psychological stress to the stress in a girder?

On 'Eye Spy' and fakes, see again the Neill and Ridley collection, and for van Meegeren, see Frank Wynne's *I Was Vermeer: The Legend of the Forger Who Swindled the Nazis*. Note also Alan Bennett's splendid BBC play on DVD, *A Question of Attribution*.

With ourselves as 'fragile creatures', we see the relevance of the arts. For the ancient world, see Goldhill's *Love, Sex & Tragedy*. For Kierkegaard, dip into his *Papers and Journals*, ed. Alastair Hannay. At the political level, note George Orwell's aphorism: he who controls the present controls the past. Winston Churchill quipped that history would be kind to him – because he would be writing the history.

Some claim that fictions are valuable preparations for what we may one day meet. Consider Shakespeare's Hamlet. 'What are the options were I to suspect that my uncle killed my father, took his position, and married my mother?' See Pinker's *How the Mind Works*. My comments are not supporting such speculations; the speculations run the danger of identifying what we 'really' value with what gives evolutionary success. It is far better to reflect on the meaning of art for life; try, for example, Philip Kitcher, *Deaths in Venice*.

The two lines quoted are Zen verse. For Tao, I recommend Smullyan's excellent *The Tao is Silent*. Pushkin may know that one can reflect too much, lining up with Basho's verse: How admirable / To think not 'life is fleeting' / On seeing the lightning flash.

X. Values: is there more to life than...?

Straight into *schadenfreude*, little exists in the literature; but see Portmann, *When Bad Things Happen to Other People* and Nietzsche's *Daybreak*, §224. Machiavelli speaks of Fortuna in *The Prince*. Fortuna, he says, is a fickle woman who deserves to be beaten – and who likes virile young men. Machiavelli would be wary of expressing his views today. Relating to *schadenfreude*, I recently encountered, courtesy of John Foulkes, a streetwise gentleman who hangs out, with ear to the ground, today's 'urban slang' term: FOMO or 'fear of missing out'.

Extending beyond humanity, with the jerboa, I have spoken of 'species' loosely. Details of biological classifications are unnecessary here. Animal defenders and 'green' conservationists may conflict: see Christopher Belshaw, *Environmental Philosophy*. A lighter tone is set by Archy, Don Marquis' cockroach, and one-time poet, mentioned above, and Mehitabel, allegedly Cleopatra reincarnated as a cat. Archy bemoans the haughtiness of Mehitabel and lack of concern for his cockroach species.

For immortality troubles, see Bernard Williams again – this time: 'The Makropulos case' in *Problems of the Self*. The case is Karel Čapek's play, now a Janáček opera, which tells of E. M. eternally aged 42. See A. W. Moore's 'Williams, Nietzsche, and the Meaninglessness of Immortality', *Mind* (2006).

A darker tone returns when we reflect on the reality of capital punishment and its application; for a recent US survey, showing the injustices, please see Evan Mandery, *A Wild Justice: The Death and Resurrection of Capital Punishment in America*.

How far ahead we should plan – recall 'Bottle Imp' (Chapter 75) – is raised by Ant and Grasshopper. Bernard Suits has sought to define 'game', and he also defends Grasshopper; see his *The Grasshopper: Games,*

Life and Utopia. Wittgenstein's 'games' example occurs in his *Philosophical Investigations*.

'Without End?' uses Lewis Carroll's excellent 'What the Tortoise said to Achilles' (*Mind*, 1895). More on this impossible demand, relating it to Zeno's paradoxes, is in my 'With and Without End', in the philosophy journal *Philosophical Investigations* (2007).

Regarding our Barbarians, Michael Sandel questions morality and markets in his *Justice*. For questions about capitalism and myths, in accessible form, see Ha-Joon Chang's *23 Things They Don't Tell You About Capitalism* and G. A. Cohen's, *Why Not Socialism?* Mill's higher pleasures are in his *Utilitarianism*. For many excellent observations, see John Armstrong's *In Search of Civilization*. 'Is This All There Is?' refers to Peggy Lee's Leiber and Stoller song 'Is That All There Is?' The song's tale derives from Thomas Mann's story *Disillusionment*. That affection may animate inanimate objects is manifested in a loss of mine, or transformation, of Silver Streak, a car that did her best for twenty years; she could not go on. That, in the end, one may feel lost to the world is expressed in Mahler's *Ich bin der Welt abhanden gekommen* (I am lost to the world); YouTube has many renderings.

Epilogue: ending without ending

This Epilogue is a review of the topics raised; hence, for references, please see relevant parts above. For a little more Keynes, morality and Bloomsbury, try his short and intriguing 'My Early Beliefs' in his *Two Memoirs*. Despite his disparagement of monetary greed, Keynes was not adverse to investing, taking risks and, indeed, accepting some inequality (his main objection being to the hoarding of money and the unfortunate consequences for society). Unlike many today, he valued the arts for the nation, as opposed to being hidden away; for example, he persuaded the Treasury in straitened times to provide cash for the purchase of Impressionist paintings for the National Gallery. For evidence about wealth equality, see Thomas Piketty, *Capital in the Twenty-First Century* and the already cited Ha-Joon Chang's *23 Things*.

On the international stage, as I complete writing, the wealthy and powerful members of the European Union have been displaying scant regard for values other than those of the financial. They have been humiliating Greece, demanding their 'pound of flesh' – ignoring their connivance in the origins of the crisis, oblivious to notions of compassion, ignorant of respect for a country's traditions and forgetful of how they have themselves benefited, in the past, from debts being written off. Greece, as I write, is now at the mercy of the financial Barbarians, with every day to be a day for trade and with key assets to end up in international corporate hands for private profit. Still, with that declaration of bleakness now aired – who knows how and when things will 'eventually' turn out? – let us take a breath and turn to the arts; the arts may uplift, while also offering some realism about, and different perspectives on, the world.

For reflections on life through novels, as modern classics with philosophical import, try Jean-Paul Sartre, *Nausea*; Hermann Hesse, *Steppenwolf*; Albert Camus, *The Outsider*; Heinrich Böll, *The Clown*. Samuel Beckett's plays, such as *Happy Days* and *Rockaby*, should not be missed. Early advocacy and observations on Cavafy are by E. M. Forster; see his *Pharos and Pharillon*. Tennyson's poem, 'Blow, Bugle, Blow', forms part of Benjamin Britten's beautiful and disturbing *Serenade for tenor, horn and strings*.

Without the then BBC Third Programme, I might well never have encountered Sartre's plays and Mahler's symphonies. Let me recommend BBC Radio 3 for, despite some decline, much can still be discovered there. If you are unfamiliar with a spread of classical music, it is worth giving it a chance, for example, through Radio 3's *Private Passions* (Sunday noon) and *CD Review* (Saturday mornings).

For intriguing pieces, also try, via YouTube, Klaus Nomi singing Purcell's 'The Cold Song'; Gerald Finley singing Donne's 'Batter my heart' from John Adams' *Doctor Atomic*; and Philip Glass' *Satyagraha*. The latter two, together with many others, have been outstanding productions at ENO in London. While preparing this work, ENO, despite its artistic successes, is under threat, with subsidies being withdrawn. Is that fair and justified – or, as with attacks on the BBC, are Barbarians gaining the upper hand? It certainly is not an example of the British government ensuring that more funds are diverted into helping the poor.

For more classical music, as an eclectic mixture, try Charles Ives, *The Unanswered Question*; Messiaen's *Turangalîla* and *Quatuor pour la fin du temps;* Schubert's *Winterreise*; Beethoven's String Quartet 132; Dietrich Buxtehude, 'Quemadmodum desiderat cervus' (BuxWV 92); and, inevitably, as mentioned in Chapter 99, Tallis' highly moving *Spem in Alium*.

♈

Even notes deserve a thoughtful end. Tallis' *Spem*, for example, would be a most thoughtful end, were this book to blossom into musical life. As it lacks musical prowess, allow me to pass on a reflection from my *Ethics* book. To recognize our concern for others, our common humanity, we should warm to the following:

Before you judge a man, you must walk a mile in his shoes.

Reflecting on that reflection (a meta-reflection), we cannot help but add: well, if you end up judging him severely, you are at an advantage – being a mile ahead of him and he has no shoes.

ACKNOWLEDGEMENTS

'There is no new thing under the sun' occurs in Ecclesiastes. Although not under the sun for all times, the underlying problems of the puzzles here have been around for many centuries; the presentations, however, are distinctively mine. I therefore acknowledge numerous philosophers, lectures, conferences, books, articles and discussions, dreams and beautiful nightmares – so numerous, it would be impossible to specify all. Allow me, though, to mention some.

For my own philosophical development, limited as it is, I am indebted, many years ago, to University College London and King's College, Cambridge – and, more recently, to many students and colleagues at City University London, New York University (London) and, especially, The Open University – as well as to lectures at the Royal Institute of Philosophy and the Aristotelian Society in London.

Thinking and drilling's screeches are unhappy companions, at least for me – and for many colleagues and friends. Central London, for years, has been and continues to be a noisy building site. Were the political will to exist, no doubt equipment could be silenced and, indeed, scepticism would be cast over development proposals that usually, once realized, destroy local character, being motivated solely by profit, consumerism and satisfying the appetites of the wealthy. A lot can be said in favour of the shabby.

With escape from noise a high priority, many of the chapters' initial drafts were written in the British Library with its splendid collection and helpful staff. My use of that library, though, has been reduced, sadly so, because of increasing irritants of laptop and mobile sounds.

The bling blongs and similar, courtesy of Microsoft and Apple, are too many and too much. Many readers lack the consideration, awareness or courtesy to have sounds turned off. More recently, I have hidden away in The Athenaeum's library. I thank all the club's staff for their immense courtesy, helpfulness and respect for library silence. I also thank the Algae members, particularly Hazhir Teimourian and Dan Cohn-Sherbok – and other club members – for wide-ranging talks and conversations, usually outside of philosophy, that have often stimulated my philosophical thinking.

Specific help at various times over the puzzles has been given, some-times wittingly, sometimes unwittingly (in no particular order), by Nick Everitt, Adrian Moore, Andrew Harvey, Jonathan Wolff, Jerry Valberg, Martin Holt, Gerard Livingstone, Richard Norman, Julian Mayers, Nick Romero, Alison Fleming, Malcolm Bishop, David Blatherwick, John Shand, Rose Allison, Jonathan Katz, Peter Atkins, Ray Tallis, Sophie Hyphen Grace Chappell, Jeremy Barlow and Stephen Williams. Allow me also to thank, for active encouragement to battle on, David Ferris, Annie Bradford, Charlotte Corne, Martyn Scott, Andrew Cooper, Susanne Mathias, David Morfill, Andrew Reeves, Frank Blackmore, Andrew Copson, Hymer Shortt, Laura Doran, Martin Cooke, Stephanie Kearins, Simon Groom and Paul Bowen. My apologies are extended to those whose names are momentarily, or longly, hiding from my memory. For additional help, practical and motivational, I thank Oneworld's Mike Harpley, Paul Nash and the Oneworld team. And for recent stimulating reflections philosophical, I add Douglas Hedley, Paul Fletcher, Chris Galvin, Nina Daubeny and, yes, the wonderful and fanciful flutterings of Nick Daubeny.

For particular philosophical insights and encouragement, special thanks go to Michael Clark, Arnold Zuboff, Sophie Bolat and Derek Matravers, not least because they have suffered reading through vari-ous chapters in various versions, versions that came and went and then reappeared.

Let me make special mention of Ossie Hanfling and Laurence Goldstein, both now sadly no more. They were fine philosophers and fine people – and, over many years, they improved my thinking considerably (it needed it). Laurence Goldstein rekindled my interest in paradoxes and read through early versions of much of the work here, some time ago – with insight, humour, expletives and friendship. I also thank Angela Joy Harvey for many years of encouragement and philosophical discussion.

My greatest philosophical debt is to Ardon Lyon. I have learned most from this fine philosopher and friend who, even as I write, still foolishly has many books only 'out of print' – true, a euphemism for 'unwritten'. His articles merit careful reading and reflection. Ardon has suffered much, having read all these puzzles at various developmental stages. He has made numerous helpful comments, a few unhelpful, always with good humour, insight, even truth, as well as providing occasional apples and butler services and frequently loud laughs.

Of course, there are bound to be errors in this book – well, contingently so, unless the human condition necessitates error. In recognition of Ardon's being a true friend, philosopher and also philosophical, as he has read all the chapters (true, only in early stages), allow me to make him responsible for remaining errors. After all, life is unfair. His shoulders are as broad as his laugh is loud.

INDEX